BYRON'S *DON JUAN* AND
THE DON JUAN LEGEND

Byron's *Don Juan* and the Don Juan Legend

MOYRA HASLETT

CLARENDON PRESS · OXFORD
1997

Oxford University Press, Great Clarendon Street, Oxford OX2 6DP

Oxford New York

Athens Auckland Bangkok Bogota Bombay
Buenos Aires Calcutta Cape Town Dar es Salaam
Delhi Florence Hong Kong Istanbul Karachi
Kuala Lumpur Madras Madrid Melbourne
Mexico City Nairobi Paris Singapore
Taipei Tokyo Toronto
and associated companies in
Berlin Ibadan

Oxford is a trade mark of Oxford University Press

Published in the United States
by Oxford University Press Inc., New York

© Moyra Haslett 1997

All rights reserved. No part of this publication may be reproduced,
stored in a retrieval system, or transmitted, in any form or by any means,
without the prior permission in writing of Oxford University Press.
Within the UK, exceptions are allowed in respect of any fair dealing for the
purpose of research or private study, or criticism or review, as permitted
under the Copyright, Designs and Patents Act, 1988, or in the case of
reprographic reproduction in accordance with the terms of the licences
issued by the Copyright Licensing Agency. Enquiries concerning
reproduction outside these terms and in other countries should be
sent to the Rights Department, Oxford University Press,
at the address above

British Library Cataloguing in Publication Data
Data available

Library of Congress Cataloging-in-Publication Data
Haslett, Moyra.
Byron's Don Juan and the Don Juan legend/Moyra Haslett.
Originally presented as author's thesis (Ph. D.)—Trinity College,
Dublin.
Includes bibliographical references (p.) and index.
1. Byron, George Gordon Byron, Baron, 1788–1824. Don Juan.
2. Politics and literature—England—History—19th century.
3. Working class—Books and reading—History—19th century.
4. Women-Books and reading—History—19th century. 5. Don Juan
(Legendary character) in literature. 6. Epic poetry, English—
History and criticism. 7. English poetry—European influences.
8. Seduction—Social aspects—Europe. 9. Seduction in literature.
I. Title.
PR4359.H37 1997 821'.7—dc21 97-2023
ISBN 0-19-818432-8

1 3 5 7 9 10 8 6 4 2

Typeset by Best-set Typesetter Ltd., Hong Kong
Printed in Great Britain
on acid-free paper by
Biddles Ltd,
Guildford and King's Lynn

TO MY MOTHER

Acknowledgements

In its original form this book was a Ph.D. thesis at Trinity College, Dublin. Principal thanks for first suggesting that I undertake this work go to Dr Ian Campbell Ross of the School of English. His constructive advice and painstaking reading of successive manuscripts were invaluable in its formation, while his enthusiasms for music and for Spain contributed greatly to its enjoyment. I am grateful to the Modern Language Departments of Trinity College, whose award of the A. J. Levanthal Scholarship permitted research on the Don Juan legend in Madrid. Thanks are also due to the staff at the British Library, Biblioteca Nacional (Madrid), Birmingham Museum and Art Gallery, and the Berkeley and Lecky Libraries at Trinity; to Clionagh Boyle and Kevin O'Connell who read sections of the thesis in manuscript; to David and Mark Haslett who enabled its printing; and to Ruth Robbins and Carlota Larrea of the University of Luton for their careful corrections of translations from French and Spanish. I am grateful too to the readers at Oxford University Press for their advice and suggestions, and to the editors Jason Freeman and Sophie Goldsworthy for their assistance and encouragement. I am most fortunate in having an additional editor in my colleague and partner, John Brannigan, whose support, patience, and love ensured that the thesis became this book. And lastly my thanks go to my mother Maisie who has been unfailingly supportive. This book is dedicated to her, because I was given the opportunities she did not have.

Contents

Introduction

[T]he line between straining at truths that prove to be imbecilically self-evident, on the one hand, and on the other hand tossing off commonplaces that turn out to retain their power to galvanize and divide, is weirdly unpredictable. In dealing with an open-secret structure, it's only by being shameless about risking the obvious that we happen into the vicinity of the transformative.[1]

Eve Kosofsky Sedgwick, in *The Epistemology of the Closet* (1991), wrote thus of the 'open secret' which is gay and lesbian discourse. This book is similarly shameless about risking the obvious in that it considers the importance of the legend of Don Juan to Byron's poem, *Don Juan*. Kosofsky Sedgwick's consideration of the 'position' of homosexuality in literature is in itself of obvious significance to a study of Byron. Indeed, her work reflects that of recent critics who have commented upon Byron's sexuality, its inscription within his poetry, and its relevance to the interpretation of his work. The importance of this 'unspoken' element is exemplified in the debates concerning what awful secret Lady Byron told her attorney, Dr Lushington, to justify her desertion of her husband. While such considerations have raised questions of codes and their interpretations, these critics, like others, have continued to ignore the significance of the Don Juan figure, a figure who, like Poe's purloined letter in the story of that name, is hidden in such a way that it is '*so* plain'.[2] The failure of Poe's policeman to discover the deliberately conspicuous letter is equivalent to Don Alfonso's search of his wife's bedroom in an attempt to discover her hidden lover, since the one place he neglects to inspect is in her bed, rather than under it (I, 144).[3] Such

---

[1] Eve Kosofsky Sedgwick, *The Epistemology of the Closet* (Hemel Hempstead: Harvester Wheatsheaf, 1991), 22.

[2] Edgar Allan Poe, *Selected Writings* (Harmondsworth: Penguin, 1967), 'The Purloined Letter', 330–49, 335.

[3] Lord Byron, *Don Juan*, ed. T. G. Steffan, E. Steffan, and W. W. Pratt (Harmondsworth: Penguin, 1973). All future references to *Don Juan* are taken from this edn. and will be quoted in the text.

failures are paralleled by modern criticism's varied interpretations of *Don Juan*. Bernard Beatty (1988) and Hermione de
Almeida (1981), for example, addressed the issue of 'myth' in
their considerations of Byron's poem, but both reserved their
commentaries to the 'primary' myths of, respectively, the Fall
and Odysseus.[4]

Both literary and myth-criticisms concerning Byron's *Don
Juan* demonstrate that the theme of the Don Juan legend has
been almost unanimously slighted, if not altogether neglected.
Most literary critics have invoked the legend only to argue
that it is irrelevant to a reading of Byron's poem, while myth-
critics have dismissed *Don Juan* as an aberrancy within the histories of the legend which they trace. For example, Leo
Weinstein, in *The Metamorphosis of Don Juan* (1959), wrote: 'By
taking the utmost liberty with hero and subject, Byron opened
the way to what amounts to license. Henceforth Don Juan becomes a name that an author may freely bestow on any hero,
just so long as he has some adventures with women—and even
this will not always be necessary.'[5] Similarly, many literary critics
have acknowledged that the poem's title and eponymous hero
share a name with that of the legendary seducer—but no more.
Robert Torrance (1978) exemplified this consensus when he
wrote: 'This thoroughly contemporary Don Juan owes little
more than his mispronounced name and birthplace to the
blasphemous libertine of the pantomime.'[6] That Don Juan's
'name' is the only exception to the general rule of difference is
itself inaccurate (a point which Torrance does at least acknow-

---

[4] Bernard Beatty, 'Fiction's Limit and Eden's Door', in Bernard Beatty and Vin-
cent Newey (eds.), *Byron and the Limits of Fiction* (Liverpool: Liverpool University
Press, 1988), 1–38. Hermione de Almeida, *Byron and Joyce through Homer* (London:
Macmillan, 1981). The phrase 'primary' myth is from de Almeida (p. 33), where
the myth of Don Juan is referred to as an 'ancillary' myth. In *Byron's Don Juan*
(Beckenham, Kent: Croom Helm, 1985), Beatty did discuss the precedent of the
Don Juan legend in a chapter entitled 'Commandant and Commendatore', although always with the qualification that Don Juan is seduced rather than seducing
(e.g. p. 32).

[5] Leo Weinstein, *The Metamorphoses of Don Juan* (Stanford, Calif.: Stanford University Press, 1959), 81–2. See also *The Theatre of Don Juan: A Collection of Plays and Views,
1630–1963*, ed. Oscar Mandel (Lincoln, Nebr.: University of Nebraska Press, 1963),
447 and 11.

[6] Robert M. Torrance, *The Comic Hero* (Cambridge, Mass.: Harvard University
Press, 1978), 214. See also August Steiger, *Thomas Shadwell's 'Libertine'* (1904; repr.
Hildesheim: Verlag Dr. H. A. Gerstenberg, 1975), 8.

ledge) since one thing which Byron's poem does not share with the original legend is its hero's (phonetical) name. Byron's pronunciation is an Anglicized form which makes of 'Juan' two syllables.

Many critics have argued that the Don Juan legend was merely a 'pretext' for Byron's poem. Elizabeth Boyd, for example, wrote: 'For Byron . . . the legend of Don Juan was merely a framework on which to hang his view of human life and his moralistic philosophizing' (1945).[7] These dismissals have been repeated in Spanish commentaries on the poem. A. Espina in the prologue to his translation of *Don Juan* (1966) also wrote: 'The figure really does not correspond to the general notion of which it partakes. This Don Juan, of Byron, is more a pretext to enable the poet to reflect, always in a satirical tone, upon very diverse themes.'[8] This argument considerably underestimates Byron's initial decision to make Don Juan the subject of his poem and it implies that Byron's was a casual, if not inapt, choice.

Other justifications for the critical neglect of the Don Juan legend have included the argument that the narrative of Byron's poem is altogether different from that of the traditional 'myth'. Anne Barton's *Byron:* Don Juan (1992) is only the most recent of many examples. She described Byron's hero as: 'a Don Juan who is gentle, tender-hearted and, although amorous, forever being seduced by women rather than seducing, with none of the traits of his treacherous archetype'.[9] As Barton's statement demonstrates, many of these judgements are made because the character of his hero is interpreted as entirely dissimilar from, if not antithetical to, the legendary seducer. The editors of the modern Penguin edition of *Don Juan* (1973), after considering versions of the legend which Byron might have known, dismiss their relevancy: 'These earlier conceptions

[7] Elizabeth Boyd, *Byron's* Don Juan: *A Critical Study* (New Brunswick, NJ: Rutgers University Press, 1945), 35.

[8] *Don Juan*, tr. A. Espina (Madrid: Editorial Meditterraneo, 1966), 9–10: 'Realmente el tipo no corresponde a la idea genérica que de él se tiene. Este Don Juan, de Byron, es más bien un pretexto del poeta para discurrir, casí siempre en tono satírico, sobre muy diversos temas.'

[9] Anne Barton, *Byron:* Don Juan (Cambridge: Cambridge University Press, 1992), 3. See also M. K. Joseph, *Byron the Poet* (London: Victor Gollancz, 1964), 177, and Georges Gendarme de Bévotte, *La Légende de Don Juan* (1906; repr. Paris: Hachette, 1929), p. 258.

of a crudely licentious Don Juan had little influence on Byron. His Juan is not a roué, but an affectionate lad, thrust by circumstance, or enticed, into amorous adventure.'[10] Indeed, several critics have claimed a similarity between the legendary Don Juan and the earlier heroes of Byron's tales, a point which only highlights the perceived disparity between the appellation and character of *Don Juan*'s eponymous hero.[11]

These kinds of dismissal date from the mid-nineteenth century—the responses of Swinburne in 1866 and of Symonds in 1880 also invoke the legendary Don Juan only to claim that Byron's hero has little in common with such a figure.[12] However all of these responses may be a reflection—not of any 'true' reading of Byron's poem—but of the status of the Don Juan legend itself. Theatrical Don Juans dominated the London stage between 1817 and 1825, years significantly contemporaneous with the publication of Byron's *Don Juan*. With at least eleven parodies, burlesques, and pantomimes of the legend all competing against and drawing attention to each other, most readers of Byron's poem probably knew several if not many versions. In contrast, comparatively few English versions of the Don Juan legend existed between the parodies of the 1820s which Byron's poem inspired and the beginning of George Bernard Shaw's interest in the legend in the 1880s.[13] Thus while contemporary readings of the poem reveal that the Don Juan legend was always presumed as a standard with which Byron's version would be compared, and only rarely contrasted, subsequent readings, from the mid-nineteenth century to the present day, have cited the legend's importance to the text as, at best, trivial. Since 1825 the context of the Don Juan legend, including the public debate which the many competing versions created, has been lost.

Exceptions to this critical consensus have been relatively

---

[10] *Don Juan* (1973), note to I, 1, l. 7, p. 570. See also W. H. Auden, *The Dyer's Hand* (London: Faber & Faber, 1948), p. 392.

[11] See e.g. Peter L. Thorslev, *The Byronic Hero: Types and Prototypes* (Minneapolis: Minnesota University Press, 1962), 199.

[12] For the responses of Swinburne and Symonds, see Andrew Rutherford (ed.), *Byron: The Critical Heritage* (London: Routledge and Kegan Paul, 1970), 382 and 415.

[13] See Samuel C. Chew, *Byron in England: His Fame and After-Fame* (London: John Murray, 1924), 50–61.

few.[14] Arguments denying the relevancy of the legend to Byron's poem have often agreed tacitly with the precepts of traditional myth-criticism. These precepts have entailed that the interpretation of myth or legend is bound to a literal adherence to detail and absolute conformity with a traditional formula. The legendary Don Juan of myth-criticism has become a kind of synecdoche, a character who represents the whole of a story that has been told and retold in a wildly disparate manner by a number of authors—over 1,700 versions according to one estimate.[15] Yet the aim of myth-criticism has been that of hypothetical unity at all costs. An essential or Platonic form of the Don Juan figure and story has been imposed, against which every manifestation of the character must be measured. However, this reductiveness forgets that it is only through interpretative variety that the legend is enabled to continue. It is no coincidence that Søren Kierkegaard included a consideration of Byron's *Don Juan* in his study of the legend, since he recognized that the exigencies of each succeeding generation will change its narrative details. In *Don Juan* (1814), a version by the Danish writer Heiberg, Kierkegaard applauded the character of Mr Paaske for more practically putting Don Juan into the debtors' prison: 'This would be entirely in the spirit of modern comedy, which does not need such great powers in order to crush, simply because the moving powers themselves are not very grandiose. It would be quite modern to have Don Juan come to know the commonplace bounds of actuality.'[16]

[14] See Frederick L. Beaty, 'Harlequin Don Juan', *Journal of English and Germanic Philology*, 67/3 (1968), 395–405; Peter Conrad, *Shandyism: The Character of Romantic Irony* (Oxford: Basil Blackwell, 1978), ch. 3, 'The Virtuoso and the Libertine'. Peter W. Graham, Don Juan *and Regency England* (Charlottesville: University Press of Virginia, 1990), ch. 3, 'All Things—But a Show?'; Albert Laffay, 'Le Donjuanisme de "Don Juan"', *Romantisme: Revue de la Société des Études romantiques*, 7 (1974), 32–43; Robert E. McDowell, 'Tirso, Byron and the Don Juan Tradition', *The Arlington Quarterly*, 1/1 (Autumn 1967), 57–68; James D. Wilson, 'Tirso, Molière and Byron: The Emergence of Don Juan as Romantic Hero', *The South Central Bulletin*, 32/4 (Winter 1972), 246–8; Sheila J. McDonald, 'The Impact of Libertinism on Byron's *Don Juan*', *Bulletin of Research in the Humanities*, 86/3 (1983–5), 291–317; Caroline Franklin, *Byron's Heroines* (Oxford: Clarendon Press, 1992), 1, 117, and 123–4; James Bennet Mandrell, *Don Juan and the Point of Honour: Seduction, Patriarchal Society, and Literary Tradition* (Philadelphia: Pennsylvania State University Press, 1992).

[15] David G. Winter, *The Power Motive* (New York: The Free Press, 1973), 165.

[16] Søren Kierkegaard, *Either/Or: Part I* (1843), ed. and tr. Howard V. Hong and Edna H. Hong (Princeton: Princeton University Press, 1987), 112.

Kierkegaard here acknowledges the necessary and inevitable historicity of legend which dictates that it will alter, and this fluidity applies not just to versions of the legend, but equally to performances of each version. For example, Mozart's *Don Giovanni* has enjoyed a particularly diverse stage history. In the *singspiel* period (before 1800), the opera was virtually transformed into a play in which arias and ensembles functioned as interpolations. Translated into the vernacular, the *singspiel* became an expression of German nationalism. Don Giovanni was portrayed as, for example, a sentimental sensualist at Mainz, Frankfurt, in 1789 and as an ordinary criminal in Hamburg, again in 1789. The final sextet, in which the other characters sing of their moral victory over the libertine—*Questo è il fin di chi fa mal!*, 'This is the end which befalls evildoers . . .'—was stripped of all potential irony in the unshaded bourgeois moralization of these productions: '. . . And in this life scoundrels | Always receive their just deserts'.[17] The finale of the legend predictably divided opinion, since the punishment of Don Juan alone justified the legend's risky depiction of his pleasurable sins and authenticated its own status as moral didacticism. This precarious imbalance remained a focus for debates concerning the legend's propriety throughout its history, although it was most particularly the case in the earliest centuries of its popularity. Contradictory responses to the opera's denouement are evident in the differing responses of Thomas Love Peacock and Shelley, who attended the first professional performances of Mozart's opera in London together. While Peacock complained that the production excluded the traditional moralizing sextet in favour of a vulgar pantomime finale with a 'dance of devils flashing torches of rosin', Shelley was puzzled that Mozart's opera should be considered as anything other than tragic.[18]

In the Romantic period, Don Giovanni's eternal longing for an ideal became the more popular interpretation. E. T. A. Hoffmann's idealist reading of the legend was explicitly in-

---

[17] Lorenzo da Ponte, *Don Giovanni*, tr. William Murray (1961) in EMI CDS 7 472608 booklet, pp. 202–3.

[18] Thomas Love Peacock, *Memoirs of Shelley and Other Essays and Reviews*, ed. Howard Mills (London: Rupert Hart-Davis, 1970), 190, and *Peacock's Memoirs of Shelley*, ed. H. F. B. Brett-Smith (1858; repr. London: Henry Frowde, 1909), 39–40.

spired by a performance of Mozart's *Don Giovanni*, the overture of which is described by his narrator as imaginatively recreating 'the conflict between man and the mysterious forces that play upon him and entice him into their hideous clutches'.[19] The final sextet was usually omitted in nineteenth-century productions, an omission which allowed the tragic character of the work to remain as the final impression of the exiting audience. Goethe's statement on *Don Giovanni* was, and continues to be, frequently quoted: 'on the surface events go merrily, while in the depths gravity rules'. But it is consistently forgotten that this interpretation is itself a product of the historicity of the legend. Goethe's statement dates from thirty-six years after its première in Prague, that is, when *Don Giovanni* was already being performed as a Romantic work.[20] In the 1834 production of *Don Giovanni* in Paris, Donna Anna committed suicide and the final scene consisted of her funeral procession of virgins and of the damned, with Mozart's rather jaunty sextet replaced with the *Dies Irae* from his requiem. The opera survived the censorious years of the Victorian period, frequently performed as a drama of ideas with almost mythological dimensions, permeated with Christian or Wagnerian imagery. In one Victorian production Donna Anna sang 'Non mi dir' kneeling in prayer while Don Giovanni died with his house collapsing around him like Valhalla.

Many twentieth-century productions began to question and explore political readings of the opera. In the productions of the 1930s and 1940s racial tensions replaced class tensions as fair Nordic womanhood (as sung by Nordic or Slavic sopranos such as Elisabeth Rethberg, Ljuba Welitsch, Jarmila Novotna and, by 1950, Elizabeth Schwarzkopf) was seduced by dark, lustful Latin manhood (often sung by Italian basses such as Cesare Siepi). And, when Leontyne Price adopted the roles of Anna and Elvira in the 1950s, her difference from the otherwise white cast emphasized her isolation and status as

[19] E. T. A. Hoffmann, *Six German Romantic Tales*, tr. Ronald Taylor (London: Angel Books, 1985), 'Don Giovanni: A Strange Episode in the Life of a Music Fanatic' (1813), 104–17, 105.

[20] See Frits Noske, *The Signifier and the Signified: Studies in the Operas of Mozart and Verdi* (The Hague: Martinus Nijhoff, 1977), 80–1. See also James Parakilas, 'The Afterlife of *Don Giovanni*: Turning Production History into Criticism', *The Journal of Musicology*, 8/2 (Spring 1990), 251–65, 251.

8 *Introduction*

victim.[21] In the fringe section of the 1987 Salzburg Festival a Mexican group performed *Donna Giovanna* in which all the parts were played by women, each one taking her turn at portraying the 'hero'.[22] Peter Sellars's televised production (1991) was prefaced with an introduction which quoted rape statistics in contemporary America. The production itself was set in Spanish Harlem, portrayed as a sphere of economic and moral dysfunction, characterized by graffiti and burnt-out cars, a place where Don Giovanni shoots up with heroin.

It is thus a major weakness of myth-criticism that it has overlooked the historical vicissitudes not only of the many versions of the legend but of the changing performances and interpretations of each version. Theatrical performances are materialized in different stage practices; interpretations vary as the text's 'performance' is realized in different readings. Byron himself recognized that legends were mutable, like most other things. In *Sardanapalus* (1821), the King reflects on the irony that Bacchus is celebrated only as the god of wine while the 'landmarks of the seas of gore he shed, | The realms he wasted, and the hearts he broke' are forgotten.[23] In the same way, in Tirso de Molina's *El burlador de Sevilla* (1630), and in many subsequent versions, Don Juan's greatest offence is his presumption that God's mercy can be taken for granted and will be available to him whenever he wishes to repent. And it is for this that he is finally punished. However, although many Don Juans break their promises to God, and to men too, Don Juan's reputation rests exclusively on his ability to 'conquer' women. Such examples illustrate the provisionality of myth, that it is a narrative which can be not only rewritten but also reinterpreted. They also expose the over-reliance on plot by myth-criticism as misplaced because the real influence of the myth or legend may be elsewhere.

Claude Lévi-Strauss's structuralist approach to myth is important to this study in that he countered the rigidity of semantic interpretation by accepting a more generous understanding of what constitutes a 'myth'. Lévi-Strauss opposed the Jungian

[21] See Parakilas, 'Afterlife of *Don Giovanni*', 264.
[22] This production is referred to in Smeed, *Don Juan*, 173.
[23] *The Complete Poetical Works of Lord Byron*, ed. Jerome J. McGann, vi (1991), 27: *Sardanapalus*, I, 2, ll. 168–79; 239–40.

attempt to establish direct connections between the content and meaning of myths, that is, between isolated mythological 'archetypes' and specific unconscious messages. Applying the semiological approach of Saussure, Lévi-Strauss proposed that any 'meaning' to be found in mythology was not to be found in isolated elements, but only in the way these elements are combined. Every version as it emerges diachronically in history is a sort of mythic *parole* which unfolds within the synchronic system of the mythic *langue*. In this way Lévi-Strauss was able to combine a historicist approach (which recognizes particular versions) with the more essentialist versions of mythology (which consider all versions). The generalizations of the synchronic approach cannot do justice to each particular version and are, to that extent, often unduly normative. Yet, however invalid they may appear, they have nevertheless often conditioned reception, an audience's perception of the myth.

Lévi-Strauss argued that traditional myth-criticism was flawed because preferred versions were selected. In his approach, the quest for a 'true' or earlier version was unnecessary because every individual manifestation of the myth would expand the parameters of the known variants: 'We define the myth as consisting of all its versions; or to put it otherwise, a myth remains the same as long as it is felt as such. . . . Therefore, not only Sophocles, but Freud himself, should be included among the recorded versions of the Oedipus myth on a par with earlier and seemingly more "authentic" versions.'[24] Each impression, whether it builds on or contradicts what is already there, is part of a character that is the sum of its particular presentations. Contrary to popular conception, not all Don Juans are inveterate seducers. In eighteenth-century puppet-plays Don Juan is rarely amorous, in nineteenth-century musical comedy he is sometimes an oaf. In the twentieth-century versions of George Bernard Shaw and Max Frisch he distrusts and even dislikes women. Yet such versions as these perpetuate the legend all the same. Even aberrant versions of the legend will rely on our knowledge and acceptance of the myth as a fixed point of departure for themselves. Each version of the legend will

---

[24] Claude Lévi-Strauss, *Structural Anthropology*, tr. Claire Jacobson, Brooke Grundfest Schoepf, and Monique Layton, 2 vols. (New York: Basic Books, 1963), ii. 217.

necessarily provoke a dialogue, albeit at times an implicit one, with other existing or surviving representations: 'each myth taken separately exists as the limited application of a pattern, which is gradually revealed by the relations of reciprocal intelligibility discerned between several myths'.[25]

Byron's *Don Juan* is certainly not strictly equivalent to Tirso de Molina's 'original' work or to the hypothetical tradition of the legend sketched by myth-criticism, but this only makes an examination of the differences all the more necessary. In part, we should expect these differences to be representative of its historicity. The composition of Byron's *Don Juan* was contemporaneous with an increasingly moralistic hegemony: the prevailing virtue 'much in fashion' was that of chastity (*Don Juan*; VIII, 128). Dr Bowdler darkly hinted that adultery should be capitally punished and in 1800 a bill was introduced to strengthen the financial penalties for adultery (the Bishop of Rochester remarking that eternal damnation was no longer proving to be an adequate deterrent).[26] Byron's Don Juan courts the danger of being entrapped within the legal charge of adultery, brought by the husband upon the seducer of his wife: 'Or whether he was taken in for damages | For being too excursive in his homages' (XI, 89). The necessity of retelling, defended throughout Byron's poem, is evident locally in the revision of the 'myths' of Noah's sending of the dove from the ark (which would have been devoured by the inhabitants of this ark, the *Trinidada*; II, 95), of Odysseus (who returns to an unfaithful Penelope, two or three illegitimate children, and a far from trusty Argus; III, 23) and, among Byron's notes to the poem, in the suggestion that the emancipation of black slaves might have been more easily effected if Christ had been born mulatto.[27] These particularized examples of the deliberate and motivated misreading of traditional narratives are embodied throughout the poem in the treatment of the Don Juan legend and figure.

[25] Claude Lévi-Strauss, *The Raw and the Cooked: Introduction to the Science of Mythology*, i (1964), tr. John and Doreen Weightman (Harmondsworth: Penguin, 1986), 13.
[26] This point is taken from William St Clair, *The Godwins and the Shelleys* (London: Faber & Faber, 1989), 193: *Substance of the Bishop of Rochester's Speech* (1800), 8, 19.
[27] Byron's note to *Don Juan*, XV, 18, is quoted in *Complete Works*, v (1986), 763.

Tacit assumptions concerning Don Juan were a controlling principle for Byron's poem as a whole because, despite its lengthy serial publication (15 July 1819–26 March 1824), each of its six instalments was entitled *Don Juan*. That the title in itself was of considerable importance to the reception of the work is evident from Murray's original manner of advertising its first publication in the *Morning Chronicle*: 'In a few days DON JUAN'.[28] The title was of talismanic significance because of its ability to generate a network of allusions—sexual, political, and personal. *The Literary Chronicle* (24 July 1819), for example, condemned the choice of theme as sufficiently scandalous: 'the very subject of the tale is censurable'. Yet while Byron's title is the most obvious facet of his epic poem, it is also the one most frequently overlooked by 'modern' criticism. To neglect the work as a version of the legend is to ignore the importance of its differences from a perceived tradition and consequently to deny its political nature. And because these differences are clearly intentional, it is to ignore the specific ideology of the text and the provocation it extends as a reaction to the popularly conceived legend.

Contemporary accounts do not support criticism's judgement of a rather desultory or arbitrary adoption. The question of Byron's new poem was a source of considerable interest and speculation among his friends: Shelley urged the subject of the French Revolution as a suitable theme for an epic, Hobhouse suggested the Fall of the Goths in Italy.[29] Both proposals suggested subjects of which Murray, Byron's publisher at that time, would have approved, since his own advice was that Byron should write 'some great work worthy of his reputation'.[30] These ambitious projects were indicative of more than individual hopes, for they were also repeated in the popular press. The *Edinburgh Review* and *Morning Chronicle* of August 1818 exhorted Byron to further British claims to excellence in writing

[28] Quoted in Peter W. Graham (ed.), *Byron's Bulldog: The Letters of John Cam Hobhouse to Lord Byron* (Columbus, Ohio: Ohio State University Press, 1984), 275.

[29] *The Letters of Percy Bysshe Shelley*, ed. Frederick L. Jones, 2 vols. (Oxford: Clarendon Press, 1964), i. 507, letter 363 (29 Sept. 1816). For Hobhouse's suggestion, see Leslie A. Marchand, *Byron: A Biography*, 3 vols. (London: John Murray, 1958), ii. 720.

[30] Samuel Smiles, *A Publisher and His Friends: Memoirs and Correspondence of the late John Murray*, 2 vols. (London: John Murray, 1891), i. 401.

and in politics. Byron knew of these linked appeals.[31] His reply
was to write *Don Juan.*

This book is therefore an attempt to uncover the debates—of
sexual and class politics, among others—within which Byron's
poem was automatically implicated. This study has been largely
inspired by, and certainly draws widely upon, the readings of
Byron's contemporaries. Indeed, the response of the audience
to myths was important to Lévi-Strauss's non-hierarchical
theory. People do not choose between versions, they do not
usually criticize or decree that one is truer than the others; they
accept them all at the same time and the differences are not
troublesome. It has been claimed that Byron's *Don Juan* is entirely different from the formal structure of previous versions of
the myth of Don Juan. While most critics concur on this point,
very few have questioned why it should be so. Northrop Frye
wrote of the potential ideological force of 'myth' in *The Anatomy
of Criticism* (1957): 'A myth being a centripetal structure of
meaning, it can be made to mean an indefinite number of
things, and it is more fruitful to study what in fact myths have
been made to mean.'[32] This book might therefore be summa-
rized as an attempt to combine an awareness of what the legend
of Don Juan makes Byron's *Don Juan* mean, with a consideration
of what in turn Byron's *Don Juan* makes the legend mean.
And if *Don Juan* is accepted as an interpretation as much as a
version of the legend, its ideological claims become all the more
apparent.

Chapter 1 outlines a history of the Don Juan legend until
1824. Differences between versions argue for a more generous
understanding of what constitutes a version of the legend. Similarities between versions cumulatively build up a picture of a
hypothetical 'traditional' form of the legend—a theoretically
imperfect prototype, but an attempt to discover the popular
understanding of Don Juan in each period and, for the purposes of this book, particularly that current in Regency
England. While this 'traditional' Don Juan is undoubtedly
largely irrecoverable, the attempt needs to be made because it is

[31] See Hobhouse's letters to Byron in *Byron's Bulldog,* ed. Graham, p. 243 (17 Aug.
1818).
[32] Northrop Frye, *The Anatomy of Criticism* (Princeton: Princeton University Press,
1957), 341.

Don Juan's reputation as much as his individual embodiments which continues to structure new versions of the legend and which dictates how Byron's own version will be interpreted. The currency of, and the debates surrounding, the legend at this time demonstrate that no reader would have approached the text of *Don Juan* with neutrality.

Chapter 2 attempts to recreate the constitutive presence of the historical reader by continuing with suggested readings of *Don Juan* as a version of the legend. Contemporary reviews of *Don Juan* openly declared their expectation that the work was linked with the popular theme. And this assumption was compounded by the suspicion which readers entertained concerning Byron's reputation as a philanderer. The powerful conjunction of these predispositions—to expect a work about the legendary seducer, Don Juan, and moreover one written by the Don Juan-like author, 'Byron'—dictated the ways in which many readers interpreted the text. This reading recognizes the overt links with the Don Juan tradition as it would have been accepted by the public and therefore reads the poem's allusions, puns, and innuendoes programmatically. *Don Juan* thus becomes a dialectical work whose meaning is not intrinsic but rather is generated by its argumentative relationship with the reader.

While the first two chapters sketch a more inclusive definition of the tradition of the Don Juan legend and argue that Byron's *Don Juan* ought to be included within it, the following two chapters consider the implications of the legend for the reception of the poem. Molière's *Dom Juan* was conventionally didactic, in that the libertine was ultimately punished. Yet the censors criticized the play as being 'irreligious', irrespective of this plot. They were outraged, and particularly by Sganarelle's final and apparently blasphemous cry of 'Mes gages! mes gages!' Such a detail is accorded only a marginal status within myth-criticism as being extraneous to the traditional story of Don Juan. Yet it was a crucial element of the play's reception, and thus synonymously, 'meaning'. In the same way, the textual attributes of Byron's poem cannot be considered as operating independently of their reception because they constitute forms of rhetoric, or ways of addressing its readers. Text and context operate together in the production of meanings, as the readings are generated in the conditions of the reception of the work.

This book therefore also considers Byron's *Don Juan* as a 'speech act', that speech performance which is examined with reference to its context. This definition is taken from Shoshana Felman's work upon speech-act theory, *Le Scandale du corps parlant* (1980), in which the expression of Don Juan is seen as exemplary of the performative utterance, a 'perlocutionary' act which produces such effects upon the reader as surprising, convincing, deceiving, misleading.[33] Chapters 3 and 4 demonstrate how the text of *Don Juan* itself contains the force which the figure of Don Juan conventionally exploits. They illustrate how the choice of Don Juan extended an invitation to specific categories of readership—those of the working classes and of women. The active dimension of their participation in the 'meaning' of the text ensured that *Don Juan* was performative as much as referential. And this in turn was demonstrated by subsequent reviews of the poem which exclaimed against the pernicious consequences of the poem's dissemination, especially among these two 'classes' of readership whose autonomy was most feared.

The first four chapters of this book share a reconstruction and subsequent consideration of the context of the Don Juan legend—that which gives the legend its proverbial status and its repetitive reputations for scandal and populism (Chapter 1), or which renders the devices of innuendo meaningful (Chapter 2), that which explains the class political (Chapter 3) or the sexual political (Chapter 4) implications of the work. They also refute the critical claims that 'Don Juan' was only a name, a pretext, a legendary figure who is entirely dissimilar from Byron's hero. Chapter 5 continues the book's commitment to recovering the context of the Don Juan legend in considering Byron's most notorious revisionism—that his Don Juan is not the seducer, but seduced. And because the political issue of seduction remains problematic, this chapter considers the importance for feminism of remembering the work's implication within the legend.

[33] Shoshana Felman, *The Literary Speech Act: Don Juan with J. L. Austin or Seduction in Two Languages*, tr. Catherine Porter (Ithaca, NY: Cornell University Press, 1983).

Chapter 5 therefore continues the book's critique of more traditional forms of myth-criticism—this time in its attempt to avoid retelling the story of Don Juan and capitulating to its meaning. The priority of Lévi-Strauss's approach to the analysis of myth is that of finding a strong coefficient of generalization which can be uncovered by analysis. This approach means that questions of the chronological priority of one version of a myth over another are quite irrelevant. The existence of a privileged textual basis is denied and even the interpretation itself becomes another version of the story it purports to study. Myth-criticism has traditionally masqueraded as being purely descriptive and has never acknowledged its capacity for being, or rather its tendency to be, prescriptive. But, in drawing up a list of versions, and denying the ideologies of the texts themselves in focusing exclusively on 'plot', myth-criticism has frequently perpetuated its own ideology. Lévi-Strauss's method cannot be exempt from this danger even in its attempt to escape it. His interpretations of symbolic elements in myth are not fixed and immutable but are determined by the place they occupy within the economy of that particular myth. This, in turn, is to interpret myths from within, to allow the system itself to dictate the meaning. In disposing of the exclusive and hypo-thetical unity of the myth, Lévi-Strauss replaced it with the unity of myth-criticism itself:

the unity of the myth is never more than tendential and projective and cannot reflect a state or a particular moment of the myth. It is a phenomenon of the imagination, resulting from the attempt at inter-pretation; and its function is to endow the myth with synthetic form and to prevent its disintegration into a confusion of opposites.[34]

The unity of the myth is thus a 'projection', the act of interpre-tation itself, the unity brought to the myth by the critic.

In *Don Juan and the Point of Honour* (1992), James Mandrell criticized both the assumptions of Lévi-Strauss's own myth-criticism, and those of Maurice Molho, who applied Lévi-Strauss's procedures to the Don Juan 'myth'. Mandrell ques-tioned the heuristic base on which each critic had constituted his reading, arguing that the 'confusion of opposites' so de-scribed is itself a result of interpretation: 'The rejection of the

---

[34] Lévi-Strauss, *The Raw and the Cooked*, 5.

syntagmatic disposition of the plot as embodied in the text engenders . . . not a paradigm, as Molho and Lévi-Strauss would have it, but another syntagma, *another* story.'[35] Both Lévi-Strauss and Molho would claim that the higher level of critical analysis sublates the syntagmatic and paradigmatic versions so as to represent and subvert, to include and discount, the material under scrutiny. However, they do not explore the possibility that their own versions might in turn be sublated. And it is in this way that myth-criticism perpetuates the 'myth' as much as it represents it. Thus this book, while agreeing with and enjoying the relative flexibility of myth interpretation enabled by Lévi-Strauss's redefinition, also attempts to do so with a critical awareness of how 'interpretation' itself is political. This is also why I have preserved a conscious distinction between 'myth' (largely perpetuated by myth-criticism) and the preferred term, 'legend', as representative of the continuing dialogue with myth-criticism.

One further influence on the project of this book has been deliberately delayed until this section's questioning of the ideology of myth-criticisms: Jane Miller's *Seductions* (1990). Miller's work is exemplary of the kind of reading which this book has attempted to recreate, illustrated in the following sentence concerning Byron's *Don Juan*: 'Men have wanted and needed to hear women tell them, as Byron gets Donna Julia to, that it is all right for men to love them and leave them, for how else would the world's business—*whatever that might be for a Don Juan*—get done?' (my emphasis).[36] This kind of feminist reading is critical, suspicious, and sceptical, and thus is similar to the reading of Byron's contemporaries. Of course the moral censoriousness of the poem's most vocal readers of 1817–24 is a rather uneasy alliance for contemporary feminisms to make. Jane Miller also addressed this implication when she wrote of the difficulties of resisting the seduction and speaking of it: 'Murderer, bandit, burglar he may be, but to see through his seductions, to deny him ourselves, is to spoil the fun—his fun, our fun, and the

---

[35] Mandrell, *Don Juan and the Point of Honour*, 20. Mandrell discusses Maurice Molho, 'Trois mythologiques sur Don Juan', *Les Cahiers de Fontenay*, 9–10 (Mar. 1978), 9–75.
[36] Jane Miller, *Seductions: Studies in Reading and Culture* (London: Virago Press, 1990), 29.

complicity of the won-over audience.'[37] Miller's worry is not only a modern one however. Even in 1818, Charles Lamb attempted to prevent his displeasure with Leporello from being interpreted as moral conservatism. When he declared: '[w]e cannot sympathise with *Leporello*'s brutal display of the *list*' in Mozart's *Don Giovanni*, he added hastily in parenthesis: 'no strait-laced moralists either'.[38] Indeed, humour is a test-case for speech-act theory because the distinction between 'saying' and 'doing' is clearly elided in its production of 'making (someone) laugh'. This, explicitly, was the criticism made of Molière's *Dom Juan*—not that its hero-villain ridiculed principles but that he made his spectators do so. Politically, the ironist is extremely difficult to assail, precisely because it is virtually impossible to fix his or her text convincingly.

The need to expose the contradictions of the sexual politics of *Don Juan* remains. The epilogue examines what is at stake in recent critical readings which would define Byron's work as 'progressive'. If the modern reader's association with the once notorious figure of Don Juan is increasingly tenuous, the context of the Don Juan legend for an understanding of Byron's *Don Juan* is no less important. For Don Juan's reputation was, and is, as a literary seducer of women, and those who forget merely collude in their own, more tacit, seduction. In the prologue to *El hermano Juan* (1934), Miguel de Unamuno indicated the distinctly political nature of the Don Juan figure, because he is an embodiment not only of an individual, but of a rhetoric which we should not allow to become a monologue: 'If Don Quixote says: "I know who I am!", Don Juan tells us the same thing, but in another way: "I know what I represent! I know (but) what I represent!"'[39]

---

[37] Ibid. 27.

[38] *The Works of Charles and Mary Lamb*, ed. E. V. Lucas, 7 vols. (London: Methuen, 1903–5), i, review of *Giovanni in London*, from *The Examiner* (22 Nov. 1818), 372–3, 373.

[39] Miguel de Unamuno, *El otro, El hermano Juan* (1934; repr. Madrid: Colección Austral, Espasa-Calpe, 1981), 56. 'Si Don Quijote dice: "¡Yo sé quién soy!", Don Juan nos dice lo mismo, pero de otro modo: "¡Yo sé lo que represento! Yo sé qué represento!"'

1

The Don Juan Legend

Everyone knows that wretched Spanish tragicomedy which the Italians call *Il Convitato di Pietra* and the French *Le Festin de Pierre*. I have always regarded it with horror in Italy, and I could never understand why this farce should have maintained itself so long, attracting crowds of spectators and being regarded as the delight of a cultivated nation. Italian actors held the same opinion, and either in jest or in ignorance, some said that the author had made a bargain with the Devil to have it kept on the stage.[1]

Carlo Goldoni's disdain for the subject of Don Juan was principally directed against the popular and farcical versions of the legend contemporaneous with the writing of his *Memoirs* in 1787. It demonstrates the extent to which the legend had become identified with popular appeal, an appeal moreover which extended throughout European culture: Spain, Italy, and France are mentioned, but so too might have been Germany, Scandinavia, Ireland, and England. Goldoni's fastidious approach to the vulgar appeal of the Don Juan theme is also interesting because, despite this professed dislike of current versions of the legend, he himself had written a dramatic version, *Don Giovanni Tenorio* (1736). This ambivalence towards the legend is shared with the authors of many versions, divided between contempt for a work which was increasingly identified with the 'lowest' forms of art and audience, and the attraction of recreating it in their own fashion. Despite the attempts of myth-criticism to perpetuate an archetypal Don Juan to which all representations worthy of the name must conform, the history of the legend displays a surprising degree of variety. This is a characteristic of its very popularity, since new representations had to compete with one another,

---

[1] Carlo Goldoni, *Memoirs* (1787), i. 39. Quoted in Edward J. Dent, *Mozart's Operas* (1913; repr. Oxford: Oxford University Press, 1973), 123.

first to attract an audience and then to sustain interest. The following history demonstrates the heightened popularity of versions of the Don Juan legend in specific clusters of periods and nations—in France in the mid-seventeenth century; in Italy, particularly Venice, in the 1780s; and, most significantly for a consideration of Byron's *Don Juan*, in London between 1817 and 1824. Adaptors of the legend have always striven to create their own novelties. Where similarities do occur, they are frequently to be found in less apparent areas than narrative, and instead in more 'marginal' details such as setting, the aristocratic status of the protagonist, and in reception. Myth-criticism continues to be significant however, not so much because of its accuracy regarding the versions of the legend themselves, but as an indication of the preconceptions and expectations which surrounded the notorious figure. This chapter demonstrates and begins to question the popularity of the legend and to provide explanations other than the 'jesting' or 'ignorant' theory that it maintained its success due to a pact with the devil.

THE HISTORY OF THE DON JUAN LEGEND 1630–1788

The very popularity of the Don Juan figure has made the task of ascertaining literary origins uncertain. Oral narratives alone might seem to account for its extraordinary hold over the popular imagination, while twentieth-century critics have quarrelled over 'claiming' his original nationality.[2] Ignoring these difficulties, this literary history begins in Spain where, in 1630, Tirso de Molina published his *El burlador de Sevilla*.[3] From this time many versions of the legend retained at least one connecting thread, that of the Spanish setting and character. Nearly all Juans are 'Dons' born in Spain, if not in Seville, even, incongruously, the Italianate Don Giovanni

---

[2] See Leo Weinstein, *The Metamorphoses of Don Juan* (Stanford, Calif.: Stanford University Press, 1959), 6.

[3] The privileging of Tirso de Molina in the history of the legend is complicated with difficulties, including the question of authorship, the date of publication, and textual priority. See James Bennet Mandrell, *Don Juan and the Point of Honour* (Philadelphia: Pennsylvania State University Press, 1992), 1–2.

of Mozart and da Ponte's opera.[4] When the narrator of Byron's Don Juan claimed that Seville is famous for oranges and women (I, 8), he thus excluded the (literary) reason for Seville's renown.

Tirso's 'original' story has largely been used as the constant of myth-criticism and therefore an outline of its narrative is important to this study. After the opening seduction of Isabela, who has mistaken him for her lover Octavio, Don Juan Tenorio flees the court of Naples, and, flouting his exile from Spain (a consequence of previous seductions), returns to Seville. On his journey there he and his servant, Catalinón, are shipwrecked. Washed up ashore, Don Juan Tenorio is tended and nursed by Tisbea, a fishergirl whose haughty condescension to potential suitors does not reflect her lowly status. Don Juan succeeds because his aristocracy and compliments flatter Tisbea's sense of her own superiority. Deserting Tisbea, Don Juan continues on his way to Seville where he tricks a former friend, the Marqués de la Mota: disguised in Mota's red cape he steps into an assignation between Mota and Doña Ana. She, however, discovers the ruse and raises the alarm. Her father, the *comendador* Don Gonzalo de Ulloa, attacks Don Juan but is murdered by him. Fleeing Seville, Don Juan then interrupts the country wedding of a peasant couple, Aminta and Batricio. Aminta is less susceptible than Tisbea to his flattery but she is eventually persuaded to succumb by the encouragement of her father and the suspicion of Batricio. She is duly deserted by Don Juan Tenorio. Thus his seductions seem to promise to continue until Don Juan encounters the stone statue of the murdered Don Gonzalo and facetiously invites him to dinner, an invitation which the stone guest keeps and reciprocates. When Don Juan returns to the chapel to enjoy the *comendador*'s hospitality, he courageously accepts the statue's challenge of a handshake and is instantaneously dragged to hell. Tirso's Don Juan is finally repentant, but the theological didacticism of the play dictates that such a belated repentance is ineffectual because his past

---

[4] Molière's *Dom Juan* is set in Sicily, although his protagonist is evidently Spanish. In Bertati/Gazzaniga's opera, *Don Giovanni*, the setting is Villena; the characters bear Italianate names, yet Donna Elvira has, traditionally, followed Don Giovanni from Burgos; and Matturina, Biagio, and the peasants first enter singing and dancing a tarantella accompanied by castanets.

conduct complacently relied upon an always future date at which to reform: Don Juan's motto is *Qué largo me lo fiáis* ('plenty of time to pay that debt'). Because this narrative has largely been the basis of the hypothetical unity of plot constructed by myth-criticism, it has dictated that all Don Juans worthy of the name shall be inveterate seducers whose only punishment can be a supernatural, or at least an extraordinary, one.

Although Tirso's intention was undoubtedly that his play should be morally didactic, this also dictated that it be satirical: Don Juan could only succeed in a flawed society. He succeeds in seducing Isabela and Ana, for example, by exploiting their illicit affairs with other men. Clandestine marriages had been prohibited by the Council of Trent in 1563 but Isabela and Ana's secrecy appears to be unnecessary—both the duque Octavio and the Marqués de la Mota are eminently 'suitable' lovers. These surreptitious assignations would seem to allow both couples an escape from the constraints and boredom which the codes of aristocratic life imposed upon them. *El burlador de Sevilla* suggests that such risks are taken for the pursuit of vicarious thrill. In the following excerpt Octavio illustrates this in his response to Ripio's pointed questioning:

RIPIO: But if the two of you love each other equally, tell me, what other objection can there be to your settling down together?
OCTAVIO: Apart from, stupid, that being the way a footman or a laundry woman would marry.[5]

This exchange also demonstrates how sexuality was differentiated according to class, a division which Don Juan exploits and reinforces in his varying strategies towards lady and serving girl. While wealthy ladies such as the duquesa Isabela and Doña Ana are seduced through subterfuge and disguise, peasant girls like Tisbea and Aminta are seduced by flattery and the dazzling power of Don Juan's status. Tisbea succumbs through pride and self-conceit, as she is flattered by the attentions of the nobleman which reflect her own ambition. Aminta's initial reluctance is

---

[5] Tirso de Molina, *El burlador de Sevilla* (1630; repr. Madrid: Espasa-Calpe, 1989), I, ll. 227–33; p. 87: Ripio: '. . . mas si los dos os queréis | con una mesma igualdad, | dime, ¿hay más dificultad | de que luego os deposéis?' Octavio: 'Eso fuera, necio, | a ser | de lacayo o lavandera | la boda'.

tested by the mean and grasping ambitions of her father, who is eager to encourage the match, and by the too quick jealousy of her husband, Batricio, who suspects his wife before she has been unfaithful.

Both figures of authority in the play, the Kings of Naples and of Castile, prove to be hopelessly ineffectual in controlling Don Juan Tenorio. Their susceptibility to the influence of favourites was a topical criticism, since it was allusive of the prominence enjoyed by the Duke of Lerma and the Count-Duke of Olivares. Lack of resolution was widely alleged to be characteristic of the reigns of Kings Philip III (1598–1621) and Philip IV (1621–55). Both criticisms are implied in the play's portrayal of the King of Naples, who evades the issue of Don Juan's seduction of Isabela within palace walls, principally because Don Juan is nephew to the Spanish ambassador.[6] Inadequate authority was a necessary part of early treatments of the legend, since the didactic impulse of these versions dictated that only supernatural intervention could punish a Don Juan. Tirso's exile from Madrid in 1625 was ordained by the Junta de Reformación on the pretext of moral aberrancy. However, political disfavour is the more likely, and deliberately obscured, explanation. Tirso de Molina's political views concerning the contemporary Spanish courts led to enmity with the influential Duke Olivares. Thus it is also with Tirso de Molina's *El burlador* that the first of many instances of suppression and censorship associated with versions of the legend occurs.[7] However, the frequent censorship of the legend is a constant which has been overlooked by myth-criticism, because the history of the legend's reception has been judged extraneous to the details of plot and character upon which such criticism excessively concentrates.

These examples of satire are important because in each case the object of attack is a character or convention other than Don Juan himself—yet only Don Juan is punished. Performances of the play might therefore deflect sympathy onto the very figure whom the play was designed to censure. This risk was

[6] For the King's response, see e.g. Tirso de Molina, *El burlador*, p. 79, ll. 33–4: 'Y con secreto ha de ser, | que algún mal suceso creo, | porque si yo aquí lo veo | no me queda más que ver'.

[7] The ban is quoted in Ruth Lee Kennedy, *Studies in Tirso*, i. *The Dramatist and his Competitors, 1620–26* (Chapel Hill, NC: North Carolina Studies, 1974), 85.

compounded by the seducer's dashing behaviour which, it was feared, might charm female dramatis personae and spectators alike, especially if they too were female. Of course many spectators resisted the seduction which the performance of a Don Juan promised to effect. This more conservative tradition of interpretation has persisted throughout the history of the legend and is evident in the later considerations of the Restoration and Regency stages. Indeed it is still apparent in Elizabeth Boyd's interpretation of the legend (in *Byron's* Don Juan, 1945) as an uncomplicated morality play: 'the traditional Don Juan is a libertine, a man of endless and heartless seductions, a monster *fitly* consigned to the Devil in a blast of thunder' (my italics).[8] However, while this would have been true of some receptions of Don Juan, for example, perhaps that of the Junta de Reformación in 1630 or of feminist criticism in the 1990s, it is certainly not true of all audiences nor of all versions. The necessary attractiveness of Don Juan would always risk the subversion of the ostensible morality of the Don Juan theme, the audience might regret rather than applaud his demise. Indeed, the versions of the legend current on the English Regency stage at the time of Byron's adoption of the theme exhibit this desire to exonerate the seducer, or at least to reclaim him.

When Tirso's play transferred to Naples, at this time Spanish territory, it quickly inspired a new adaptation by Giacinto Andrea Cicognini, *Convitato di pietra, opera esemplare* (written between 1630 and 1650). The legend was already changing: Don Juan's servant became more farcical, missing the macaroni of Naples when he is in Seville and farting in jest. It is not surprising therefore that in 1641 an Italian poetaster referred to the *Convitato di pietra* as a 'vulgarissima tragedia'. In *Convitato di pietra, rappresentazione in prosa* by Onofrio Giliberto (1652) the clowning of the valets, in this case Passarino and Arlequino, became even more farcical, while Don Juan himself became more brutal, a ravisher rather than a seducer, perhaps as an attempt to alienate potential sympathy for the character. Because these early Italian versions were performed by *commedia dell'arte* companies, no texts survive of their plays. Indeed performances would have been characterized by indeterminacy.

---

[8] Elizabeth Boyd, *Byron's* Don Juan: *A Critical Study* (New Brunswick, NJ: Rutgers University Press, 1945), 37.

The variations on the 'original' theme are unsurprising given the nature of improvisation associated with *commedia dell'arte*. By the mid-seventeenth century the legend had entered the French repertory, transported there by the Italian *commedia dell'arte* companies which played at the Petit-Bourbon among other venues. French authors exploited the current fashion and five French Don Juan plays appeared within twenty years: *Le Festin de pierre ou le Fils criminel* by Dorimon (1658); *Le Festin de pierre ou le Fils criminel* by Claude Deschamps, Sieur de Villiers (1659); *Dom Juan ou le Festin de pierre* by Molière (1665); *Le Nouveau Festin de pierre, ou l'Athée foudroyé* by Claude Rose, Sieur de Rosimond (pseudonym of Jean-Baptiste Du Mesnil; 1669); and Thomas Corneille's verse adaptation of Molière's play, *Le Festin de pierre* (1677).[9] The subject of Don Juan had fallen so low in the estimation of polite society that all approached the theme with a degree of fastidiousness. In the dedication of his play, Villiers defensively argued that the decision to write on Don Juan had been dictated by the demands of his fellow actors at the Hôtel de Bourgogne: 'in the belief that the ignorant, who are far more numerous than those who understand the theatre, would take a greater pleasure in the figure of Dom Pierre [the Commander] on his horse than in the verse and management of the play'.[10] By the mid-seventeenth century therefore, the association of the theme with the 'ignorant' was already established. Villiers claimed that the company had been reduced to treating this subject and that he had conceded to write it only in order to make money for them. He was painfully aware of the irregularity of the play, which violated every rule of classical decorum, and he promptly disclaimed any originality, stressing—perhaps honestly, or perhaps in order to save his reputation—that he had merely translated the text from the Italian. The versions of Dorimon and Villiers both display a new caution. Villiers set the action in heathen times so that the 'atheist' could brag against Jupiter with impunity. Both dramatists strenuously attempted to turn support away from the seducer by

---

[9] Dates are of first performances. For further details of the authors and productions see *The Complete Works of Thomas Shadwell*, ed. Montague Summers (London: Benjamin Blom, 1968), i, introduction, p. cxxix.

[10] Quoted in Oscar Mandel (ed.), *The Theatre of Don Juan* (Lincoln, Nebr: University of Nebraska Press, 1963), 105.

making him a violent rebel against his father, even to the point of striking him. Although this blow does not kill, the father later dies of grief, and the insinuation of parricide is reinforced by the subtitle, *le fils criminel.*

Molière's version was more daring in portraying a Don Juan with considerable charm and swagger—but at a cost. His character's outspoken justifications of his behaviour led to rigorous censorship. *Dom Juan* played to full houses at the Palais-Royal for fifteen performances (25 February–20 March 1665) but pamphlets denouncing the play as shocking to religion led to its ban:

Who can endure the boldness of a clown who makes a joke of religion, who preaches libertinism, and who makes the majesty of God fair game on stage for a master and a servant—for an atheist who laughs at it, and for a servant, even more impious than his master, who makes the audience laugh at it?[11]

This denunciation illustrates that the play's critics were more alarmed by the audience's response than by the theme itself. The play is denounced not because it itself mocks religion, but because, through its encouragement of laughter, it manipulated the spectators to do so, demonstrating its perceived performative rather than referential effect. Censors of the Don Juan story feared its subversive power, a power intricately linked with its traditional form of theatre and its direct appeal to all classes.

Particular scenes which caused offence in Molière's version included Dom Juan's attempt to bribe a beggar to blaspheme and his 'credo' of rationalist Cartesian philosophy (that he believed only that two and two equal four, four and four, eight). However, the most excessive indignation was reserved for Sganarelle's final cries for the wages he has lost with Dom Juan's sudden punishment: 'Mes gages, mes gages, mes gages!' The moral of the traditional story implied that the wages of sin are death—Sganarelle implies otherwise. It is significant that the most vehement denunciation was levelled not, as might have been anticipated, at the central figure, but at a detail which is marginal to the main theme, or at least to that elaborated by myth-criticism. Moreover, since a similar cry had

[11] Sieur de Rochemont, *Observations sur une comédie* (1665), tr. ibid. 112.

been overlooked in Cicognini's earlier *Convitato di pietra*, the historicity, not only of the versions, but of their interpretations is evident.[12] Although there was no official prohibition, such was the vehemence of the pamphlets that Molière himself withdrew the piece from the theatre.[13] This example of censorship corroborates the sense that the legend could be appropriated for radical impulses, despite its conventionally religious ending. Molière's version, like that of Tirso de Molina before him, was denounced because the spirit of the work was judged to be seductively subversive of the plot's apparent message.

Corneille's alexandrine adaptation significantly cut the most offensive scenes of Molière's version. Sganarelle's final mercenary complaints were altered to an expression of traditional piety: '. . . je cours me rendre Hermite; | L'exemple est étonnant pour tous les Scélerats; | Malheur à qui le voit, et n'en profite pas'—although it is an amendment which nevertheless retained the language of capitalist economy.[14] Like Villiers, Corneille was careful in his *Avis* to abdicate responsibility for the choice of theme ('Quelques Personnes qui ont tout pouvoir sur moi, m'ayant engagé à la mettre en vers')—while he also explained the changes to the text as dictated by his greater delicacy ('je me reservay la liberté d'adoucir certaines expressions qui avoient blessé les Scrupuleux').[15]

Rosimond's *Le Nouveau Festin de pierre* attempted within its title to validate its status as yet another version of the legend. Rosimond, like Villiers and Corneille, also disclaimed responsibility for the choice of theme. In a preface to the play, the author claimed that he undertook the work because his was the only company in Paris which had not given a Don Juan play and that it had lost money as a consequence of disdaining the current fashion. This was a rather disingenuous way of reserving some credit for 'taste' while succumbing to the expediency of market forces. It was a rhetorical gesture which would be frequently repeated.

---

[12] Cicognini, quoted in Shadwell, *Complete Works*, i, introduction, p. cxxxii. Cicognini's phrase however did not close the play.

[13] Although Molière's play was published posthumously in 1682, it was not performed in France again until 17 Nov. 1841 when it was revived at the Odéon.

[14] Corneille's ending is quoted in Shadwell, *Complete Works*, i, introduction, p. cxxxiii.

[15] Quoted ibid. i, introduction, p. cxxxiii.

The first English version of the Don Juan legend, Thomas Shadwell's *The Libertine* (1675) was influenced by Rosimond's version. The Don Juan plays of Rosimond and Shadwell both display a more condemnatory attitude towards their protagonist by increasing his brutality and violence, certainly beyond what was strictly necessary for the mechanisms of the plot. Shadwell's depiction of Don John is that of a monster, a variation which would have decreased his sense of borrowing while also playing safe with the moral censors in England. His Don John has not only been married six times and engaged sixteen times in one month, but, when his wives claim their rights, he turns them over to his companions; then, having given his servant orders to bring him the first woman he meets in the streets, he rapes this one, an old and very ugly maid, with obvious displeasure. To these outrages are added assassination, pillaging churches, raping a nun—'I could meet with no willing dame, but was fain to commit a Rape to pass away the time'—poisoning a former lover (Leonora), parricide, and the massacre of a band of shepherds.[16]

After Tirso de Molina no author stumbled accidentally upon the theme of the legend. Instead the inherent reputation of the Don Juan figure became a forceful controlling element in any new variation. This enabled Shadwell, not entirely disingenuously, to abdicate authorial responsibility for its present form: 'I hope the Readers will excuse the Irregularities of the Play, when they consider, that the Extravagance of the Subject forced me to it: And I had rather try new ways to please, than to write on in the same Road, as too many do.'[17] The apparent contradiction of this statement is illustrative of the difficulties in inheriting an already scandalous theme. There is the impulse to treat it with originality and novelty. This would not only justify its existence, but also reflect the pressure of the market, and the theatre was an especially ruthless one. But in an age of censorship this was compounded by the temptation to disclaim responsibility for a potentially immoral production with the argument of expediency—that of blaming the source. Shadwell continues by suggesting why the play has, erroneously, been interpreted as irreligious, that by demonstrating and

---

[16] The quotation is from ibid. iii, Act I, p. 32.
[17] Ibid. iii, preface to *The Libertine*, 21.

performing vice, Don Juan was effectively teaching it: 'I hope that the severest Reader will not be offended at the Representation of those Vices, on which they will see a dreadful punishment inflicted . . . and some, not of the least Judgement and Piety here, have thought it rather an useful Moral, than an incouragement to vice.'[18]

In the quarrels concerning the immorality of the stage which followed the publication of Jeremy Collier's *A Short View of the Immorality and Profaneness of the English Stage* (1698), several, unsuccessful, defenders of the theatre cited *The Libertine* as an outstanding example of morality because, they argued, Don Juan is punished at the end. It certainly was an unfortunate, because not entirely convincing, choice for their defence: many spectators remembered the appeal of the character's performance throughout rather than his abrupt demise. These arguments remained contentious at the time of Byron's composition of *Don Juan*. Coleridge defended the legend's moral didacticism in *Biographia Literaria* and the theatrical controversy of the final years of the seventeenth century, and the specific example of the Don Juan legend, were explicitly reinvoked by Hazlitt in his 'Lectures on Restoration Drama' in 1818. Shadwell's play would have been widely known to Regency readers of all classes through its dissemination in 6*d.* chapbook form (*The History of Don Juan, or the Libertine Destroyed*, published in 1815) and it is with quotations from this play that Coleridge defends the Don Juan legend.

The popularity of Shadwell's play is important in that it made the legend proverbial in England: in Wycherley's *The Plain Dealer* (1676), the coxcomb Novel described his dinner at Lady Autum's as 'like eating with the Ghost in the Libertine'.[19] The greatest indication of Don Juan's fame in England is evident in its new form, that of the 6*d.* chapbook. This demonstrates how popular the legend had become, since the cheapness of the edition and its inscription in the colloquial tradition of the chapbook with its sensational subject-matter and presentation would have made it available to the poorest of readers and to women with some degree of literacy. This is a significant

---

[18] The quotation is from Shadwell, *Complete Works*, iii, preface to *The Libertine*, 21.
[19] Wycherley, *The Plain Dealer* (1676; repr. London: Methuen, Swan Theatre Plays Series, 1988), Act II, scene 1, p. 18.

feature of the legend's early history when such communities would have been excluded from the written sphere of high culture.

The same kind of familiarity was also a controlling feature of Don Alonso de Córdoba y Maldonado's *La venganza en el sepulchro* (1690s). In this piece the many adventures of Don Juan are not enacted, but merely related in rapid narrative when the hero retrospectively tells the story of his life. Only with the invitation to supper by the Stone Statue does the play revert to more traditional representation. This divergence represents the familiarity of the legend to the audience: a repetition of by-now-conventional events was unnecessary. The legend had become so familiar that in 1669 when Queen Christina of Sweden attended a production in Rome of *L'empio punito*, an opera by Acciaindi and Melani, she was reportedly overheard as complaining 'Why, this is just the Stone Guest!'.[20]

Throughout the eighteenth century, the theme's notoriety continued as it was adapted by popular forms such as the puppet-theatre, vaudevilles, and pantomimes. In Germany sensational stories based on the French texts were popularized in puppet-plays which further exaggerated the level of Don Juan's villainy. In *Laufen*, Donn Joann murders the proprietress of an inn because her bill is exorbitant. The extreme villainy of Don Juan in another puppet-play is obvious from its title: 'Don Juan or the Quadruple Murderer'. Don Juan was also a familiar hero of melodramatic farces, pantomimes, and vaudevilles at the fairs of Paris. The director of one production of the *Grand Festin de pierre ou l'Athée foudroyé* made this pitch at the crowd: 'This way! This way! Mister Pompey will change costumes twelve times. He will carry off the Commander's daughter in a frogged jacket and will be struck down by lightning in a spangled coat!'[21] In 1713, at the Théâtre de la Foire in Paris, a vaudeville comedy composed by Le Tellier was performed—*Le Festin de Pierre, en vaudeville sans prose*. Despite public enthusiasm, the production was banned because of its representation of hell in the final scene. The scandalous hint of blasphemy thus continued to surround the ostensibly

[20] Quoted in Nino Pirotta, 'The Tradition of Don Juan Plays and Comic Operas', *Proceedings of the Musical Association*, 107 (1981), 60–70, 60.
[21] Quoted in Mandel (ed.), *Theatre of Don Juan*, 251.

religious work. Despite, or perhaps because of, this scandal, Le Tellier's piece inspired more than a hundred subsequent versions, many of them burlesques and extravaganzas which drew huge crowds.

Antonio de Zamora's play of 1735 continued the trend of adding sensations. New additions included thunder and lightning, a female character who plots Don Juan's assassination, an attempted rape on stage, a statue disappearing spectacularly through the floor, skeleton masks, a supper of ashes and fire in the final scene and the introduction of a company of students to provide more riotous entertainment. The play was entitled *No hay plazo que no llegue ni deuda que no se pague, o El convidado di piedra* ('A day of reckoning always arrives and debts must be paid; or, The stone guest'). Both it and the *sainete* version of the legend continued to be performed when Tirso's *El burlador* was banned from the Spanish stage during the late eighteenth and early nineteenth centuries, and contemporaneously with Byron's visit to Spain in 1809.[22] Zamora's play may have influenced the later version of Zorrilla and other 'Romantic' treatments of the legend in its suggestion of Don Juan's contrite repentance at the close of the play.

The continuing and irresistible popularity of the legend is demonstrated in its adoption by the favourite Venetian playwright, Carlo Goldoni, for, if we are to judge by his words quoted at the beginning of this chapter, it was a 'choice' made involuntarily. The character Lelio in Goldoni's story *Il teatro comico* (1760) provides one explanation of why Goldoni succumbed to the impulse to retell the Don Juan story:

I will have my comedies acted in spite of them, if it is only by a troupe of strolling players at a village fair. Who are these people who are going to reform the theatre? Do they think that by producing two or

---

[22] In 1801 and 1802, several of Tirso's plays were placed on the 'lista de las piezas dramaticas que conforme a la real orden de 14 de enero de 1800, se han recogido prohibiendose su representación en los teatros publicos de Madrid y de todo el reyno'. These certainly included *Convidado de piedra*. *Teatro nuevo español* (Madrid, 1800–1), i, pp. xxvi–xxvii. Quoted in A. S. Bushee, *Three Centuries of Tirso de Molina* (Philadelphia: University of Pennsylvania Press, 1939), 13. However the prohibition suggests that *El burlador* had not entirely vanished from the stage. Moreover Moratín, the eminent Spanish playwright of that time, had seen a performance of Tirso's play in Naples. Quoted in Mandel (ed.), *Theatre of Don Juan*, 41. (See also the consideration of Byron's visit to Spain below.)

three new plays they have killed all the old ones? Never! and with all their novelties they will never make as much money as was made for so many years with *Il Gran Convitato di Pietra*.[23]

Goldoni's motivation, like, for example, the French dramatists of the mid-seventeenth century, appears to have been the temptation of a 'sure-thing' success with the audience. This might explain the tendency on the part of adaptors to both censure the theme as tawdry and vulgar and to write their own version.

In his *Don Giovanni Tenorio* (1736), Goldoni transformed the legend into a comedy about commonsensical, practical life, in which there was no place for passion or miracles. He attempted to rationalize the supernatural by portraying Don Giovanni shot down by a bolt of lightning. However, this 'rational' solution to the problem posed by Don Giovanni still demonstrated the inadequacy of human authority to confront and deal with such an offender. Goldoni's play has largely been vilified by traditional myth-criticism, in one case because Don Giovanni's request of poison demonstrates a cowardice which deviates from, and which it would prefer to exclude from, its archetypal Don Juan.[24] Goldoni himself however boasted of his changes:

At the first representation of this piece, the public, accustomed to see in the *Convitato di Pietra*, Harlequin save himself from shipwreck with the assistance of two bladders, and Don Juan make his escape from the waves of the sea perfectly dry, and his clothes quite untouched, did not know what to make of the air of dignity which the author had given to an old piece of buffoonery.[25]

Goldoni's comment permits a glimpse of the popular forms of the legend at this time, versions which otherwise remain unknown even though they represented the most pervasive dissemination of the legend.

Two years prior to Goldoni's play, the first Italian opera of the century was performed: *La pravità castigata* (Brno, 1734) by A. Mingotti and Eustachio Bambini. In this work the part of Don Giovanni was sung by a woman, a practice which was to become common in the Regency burlesques of 1817 to 1824. Musical adaptations of the legend had by now become the most popular

[23] Quoted in Dent, *Mozart's Operas*, 127–8.
[24] See e.g. Charles Minguet, *Don Juan* (Paris: Éditions Hispaniques, 1977), 17.
[25] Carlo Goldoni, *Memoirs* (1787), tr. John Black, 2 vols. (London: Henry Colburn, 1814), i. 262.

form. In 1761 Gluck wrote the music for the ballet *Don Juan*, with a scenario by the imperial ballet-master in Vienna, Gasparo Angiolini. Angiolini chose the subject because of its currency— a pantomime version was performed in Vienna each year on All Souls' Day until 1772. However he hoped to bring the theme to aristocratic audiences, estranged from the 'vulgarity' of the popular forms. He therefore removed the farcical elements: his Don Juan was a seducer, murderer, and mocker of divine justice, whose punishment was intended to serve as a warning.[26]

Like the concentration of versions in mid-seventeenth-century France, the Mingotti/Bambini opera was followed thirty years later by a cluster of operatic versions. Nine operas by Italian composers appeared within eleven years.[27] Goethe told his friend Zelter that he remembered a time in Rome (which he visited between 1786 and 1788) when:

. . . an opera called Don Juan (not Mozart's), was played every night for four weeks, which excited the city so much that the lowliest grocers' families were to be found in the stalls and boxes with their children and other relations, and no one could bear to live without having fried Don Juan in Hell, or seen the Commendatore as a blessed spirit, ascend to heaven.[28]

Goethe significantly specified the 'lowliest grocers' families' to demonstrate the opera's phenomenal popularity.

Since the chronology of the legend is now within only thirty years of Byron's adaptation, it is significant that this rush of operatic forms reveals a geographical concentration in Venice, where Byron began his own version. The popularity of these versions of the Don Juan legend in the Venetian *carnivales* might explain why this Italian city gave the first professional performance of Mozart's opera rather belatedly in

[26] For details of this version, see Charles C. Russell, 'The Libertine Reformed: "Don Juan" by Gluck and Angiolini', *Music and Letters*, 65 (Jan. 1984), 17–27.

[27] Vincenzo Righini, *Don Giovanni ossia il convitato di pietra* (Vienna, 1777); *Il convitato di pietra*, by Calegari (Venice, 1777); Cimarosa (Venice, 1777); Giacomo Tritto (Naples, 1783); Vigano (Rome, 1784); Giachino Albertini (Venice, 1784); Gazzaniga, *Il Don Giovanni ossia il dissoluto* (Venice, 1787); Gardi, *Il nuovo convitato di pietra* (Venice, 1787); Vincenzo Fabrizi, *Don Giovanni Tenorio ossia il dissoluto* (Fano, 1788).

[28] Quoted in Abert, *Mozart's* Don Giovanni, p. 33.

1833.[29] Alhough little is known of most of these operas, the concentration of competing versions of the Don Juan legend demonstrates its tendency to invite cross-referentiality and competition, both of which are implied within the title of Gardi's opera, *Il nuovo convitato di pietra*.

The Gazzaniga/Bertati opera is the most notable of these Italian productions in that it almost certainly inspired da Ponte's choice of *Don Giovanni*, in addition to providing him with much of his text. In the Gazzaniga opera the cast unite in a hectic final song: 'Tran, tran trinchete . . . Flon, flon, flon . . . Pu, pu, pu', alias guitar, contrabass, and bassoon, avoiding final moralizing for a suitably frivolous ending to a carnival evening. This opera also shares with the earlier plays of Villiers, Corneille, Rosimond, and Shadwell an explicit apology for its choice of theme. The one-act opera was preceded by a dramatic capriccio which introduced the audience into the midst of a group of players: the troupe's affairs are in a sad state, in fact they are facing bankruptcy. The shrewd impresario, Policastro, suggests that they revive the story of the Stone Guest, admittedly 'una bella e stupenda porcheria', but one whose noise and bustle might appeal to the German provinces. Immediately the cast complain of sore throats, although they are eventually cajoled into performing through promises of increased salaries and Policastro's appeal to the more reputable precedents of Tirso de Molina and Molière.

It is in the context of this continuing populism that Mozart and da Ponte adopted the theme for their opera in 1787. They restored something of the original Don Juan of Tirso de Molina by imbuing their character with vitality, charm, and the same ambiguity. All of these qualities would have increased the ambivalence of the audience's reception of the seducer, in direct contrast to the more recent tradition of creating a thoroughly villainous character, apparent in the plays of Villiers, Dorimon, Rosimond, Shadwell, the puppet-plays of eighteenth-century Germany and the English 6*d.* chapbook. This was reinforced by the opera's ending. As in the Gazzaniga opera, the musically sophisticated grandeur of the punishment scene potentially makes of the final, and

---

[29] Mozart's *Don Giovanni* was first performed in Florence in 1798, Rome in 1811, Naples in 1812, Milan and Turin in 1814, Bologna in 1818, and Parma in 1821.

more conventional, sextet a hollow victory—'Questo è il fin di chi fa mal'—not quite 'tran, tran, tranchete', but similarly jaunty. Indeed, so hollow was the victory considered that the final scene was omitted in the 1788 Vienna production, and the characters merely entered to witness Don Giovanni's fate in silence. This practice continued in the majority of nineteenth-century productions which performed the opera as a tragedy.

Obviously, such tolerance towards Don Juan/Don Giovanni was not shared by all, especially not by those audiences who were used to the melodramatic villain of the pantomimes, vaudevilles, puppet-shows, and burlesques. One contemporary response to Mozart's opera displays this prejudice: 'Don Juan combines all the nonsensical, extravagant, contradictory and unnatural features that ever qualified a poetic absurdity of a human being for the role of an operatic hero. He is the stupidest, most senseless creature imaginable, the misbegotten product of a crazed Spanish imagination.'[30] Underlying this attack is a literary snobbery which was a predictable reaction to the increasing popularity and sensationalism of the legend. The respective success and failure of Mozart's *Don Giovanni* in Prague and Vienna has been attributed to the former's intellectually unpretentious public. Prague's prosperity had declined since its heyday as Imperial Court in the seventeenth century and its more provincial public also received *Le nozze di Figaro* (1786) with considerably greater enthusiasm than the moderate reception which Vienna had given it. *Don Giovanni* was dropped from Vienna after only fourteen performances, possibly because the sophisticated audience felt that the subject was rather beneath them. One contemporary observer complained: 'The common people still flock to see *Il Convitato di Pietra* . . . And it is no excuse that educated persons are well aware of the improprieties of such comedies, which please only the ignorant lower classes; for in the theatre the taste of the common people upheld by the educated masses is the national taste.'[31]

Da Ponte also continued the tradition of the legend's political subversiveness in giving the phrase 'Viva la libertà!' (Finale

[30] Quoted in O. E. Deutsch, *Mozart: A Documentary Biography*, tr. E. Blom, P. Brascombe, and J. Noble (London: Simon & Schuster, 1961), 353–4.
[31] Quoted in Dent, *Mozart's Operas*, 129.

Act I), not only to Don Juan, but to the full cast. And since the Don Juan legend is one which increasingly addressed the responses of the audience to itself, it is significant that this cheer was sometimes echoed by the audience. At the beginning of Act II Don Giovanni and his servant argue on absolutely equal terms, a scene which would have been inconceivable to the tradition of *opera seria*. The theatre historian, Simon Williams, suggested that *Don Giovanni* may have met with some resistance at its first production in Vienna because of its unorthodox treatment of social relationships.[32] Mozart's opera narrowly escaped the censure which had plagued the earlier versions of Tirso de Molina and Molière: on 7 August 1791 the opera fell under the censor's ban in Munich, which was later revoked by an influential authority who, it was rumoured, had personally enjoyed the opera.[33] Byron would have enjoyed this example because within *Don Juan* he attempted to highlight the discrepancy between official dogma and seduced, personal response.

This early history of the Don Juan legend has already demonstrated how the popularity of Don Juan might be described as phenomenal and the cult of the Regency Don Juan burlesques has yet to be considered. It also illustrates those characteristics which versions of the legend did share—not, as myth-criticism would imply, the character of Don Juan, or the interpretation of the theme—but characteristics which are a consequence of the legend's notoriety: how the imputation of scandal and the danger of censorship were risked by all versions, for example, or of the legend's currency throughout Europe and among all classes. An increasing number of versions are also prefaced with embarrassed disclaimers. These betray the authors' increasing sensitivity to accusations of plagiarism and of shameless appeals to financial expediency, accusations which they risked merely by adopting the theme of the Don Juan legend. Don Juan had come to represent lucrative investment for those companies and theatres which increasingly relied upon the market for their survival—a consideration

[32] Simon Williams, ' "No Meat for the Teeth of my Viennese": *Don Giovanni* and the Theatre of its Time', *Theatre Research International*, 14/1 (Spring 1989), 23–40.
[33] Quoted in Hermann Abert, *Mozart's* Don Giovanni, tr. Peter Gelhorn (London: Eulenberg, 1976), 92.

which Byron would be forced to acknowledge within his role of
committee member for Drury Lane Theatre.

THE DON JUAN LEGEND IN LONDON 1788–1824

The first professional performance of Mozart's *Don Giovanni* in
England was not given until 1817 because London audiences
were in thrall to opera's rival genre—the pantomime. On 10
May 1782, Drury Lane offered the pantomime *Don John; or, The
Libertine Destroyed*, an anonymous production which was later
revised and arranged by Delpini with songs, duets, and choruses
by Reeve and instrumental music borrowed from Gluck's ballet
score. *Don Juan; or the Libertine Destroyed: A tragic Pantomimical
Ballet* was first performed at the Royalty Theatre, Wells Street on
23 June 1788 and its libretto was sufficiently popular to warrant
three octavo editions in 1788. These expensive editions demonstrate that, whatever its popular appeal, the legend was not
solely reserved to the lower classes. *Don Juan; or the Libertine
Destroyed: A Grand Pantomimical Ballet* was first performed at
Drury Lane Theatre on 26 October 1790 and published also in
the same year.[34] Da Ponte's residence in London led to a performance of his libretto at the King's Theatre in 1794. Although the music was a medley of Gazzaniga, Sarti, Federici and
Guglielmi, it did include Mozart's 'catalogue aria'. This *Don
Giovanni* was first performed on 3 January of 1794 and repeated
on 8 March. The second performance caused a furore, with
spectators in the pit striking each other and even, across the
stage, 'Don Juan' himself. *The Times* (10 March 1794) reported
the disturbance at length:

So determined an opposition to this kind of entertainment we have
never witnessed; . . . till the fall of the curtain, . . . all was noise and
uproar; and the scene of *Hell*, magnificent and terrific as it was, had so
far the characteristic accompaniments of *groans*, not of the damned
but of those troubled spirits who wished to torment the Manager.
    The Procession, as we recommended, was totally omitted and sev-
eral other judicial alterations made, but as the sense of the subscribers,
as well as the public, seems decidedly against a repetition of this

[34] All of these publications are listed in Frederich L. Beaty, 'Harlequin Don Juan',
Journal of English and Germanic Philology, 67/3 (1968), 396.

Opera, we have no doubt but the Manager will submit respectfully to their *fiat*—comforting himself with the reflection, that his liberal exertions deserve—though it is not always in the power of mortals to command success.

This review demonstrates the vocal power and considerable demands of the English theatrical audiences at this time. No consideration of stage history can ignore the formative influence of the English 'mob' of spectators. In this case, the audience objected to the cast. Several dancers had been prevented from leaving France and Italian singers had been unable to reach London because of their necessary route through France. The riot which ensued was said to have been preconcerted. It certainly reflects the tumultuous history and patriotism of 1794. Many reviewers would later scorn the British public's blatant xenophobia and patriotism manifested in their noisy abuse of dramatic representations of Don Juan, others blamed the pernicious tendency of Byron's *Don Juan* on foreign influences.

A further example of the legend's incorporation within political debates is apparent in the role it played in the 'Old Price riots' of autumn 1809. A fire at Covent-Garden in September 1808 forced the theatre to close for a year. When the new theatre was reopened on 18 September 1809, the management raised the admission prices in an attempt to recoup the expense of the building. However, James Boaden claimed that the real objection of the rioters was to the new segregation, 'the absolute seclusion of a *privileged order* from all *vulgar contact*'.[35] Seating which had once accommodated the public was now transformed into costly private boxes, sold at the prohibitive price of £300 per year. Separate staircases only exacerbated the impression of exclusivity. Although the gallery was excluded from the new price rises, it was so far up and so steep that from there only the legs of the performers could be seen. The rioters also protested against the exorbitant fee which Angelica Catalani was able to command from the management, a protest exacerbated by the chauvinism of some of the British spectators. In the first night of the riots, in fact the first night of the reopening, 500 soldiers were dispatched to the gallery. After

[35] James Boaden, *Memoirs of the life of John Philip Kemble*, 2 vols. (1825), ii. 492. Quoted in Joseph Donohue, *Theatre in the Age of Kean* (Oxford: Basil Blackwell, 1975), 53.

this night, many rioters entered the theatre only at the interval, known as the half-price time, when spectators paid a lower price to attend the popular after-piece, or, as was the case during the disturbances, only to see the ritual Old Price war dance.

The popular clown, Grimaldi, delayed his appearance until the forty-ninth night of the furore: on 20 November he appeared before the rioting audience in the pantomime of *Don Juan*, a deliberate alteration to the original programme. Covent-Garden was as noisy as ever, but Grimaldi himself, in the role of Scaramouch, was given a great reception by the rioters. The following week *Don Juan* supplied the Old Price demonstrators with a popular banner. During the play, Don Guzman's statue appeared with its traditional inscription in letters of 'blood':

> Don Juan, by thee
> Don Guzman bleeds,
> Heaven will avenge
> Thy bloody deeds!

At this moment a contingent of men with Old Price symbols on their hats raised a placard on which was written in huge letters:

> What are Don Juan's bloody deeds
> Compared with Don John's bloody deeds?[36]

While the moral relativism used to condemn the managerial decisions of John Harris was facetious, this inscription illustrates how sympathetic portrayals of Don Juan were not only becoming possible, but were being used to reveal and attack hypocrisy. The Old Price riots also illustrate the vigour, energy, and tyranny of the Georgian and Regency audiences and suggest one reason for the enormous popularity of the harlequinade in which Grimaldi was the incarnate rebel. The riots lasted three months, after which Kemble, who had been attacked with the greatest venom, was forced to accept the rioters' terms and deliver a public apology from the stage. When he attempted to maintain half the number of private boxes at the beginning of the next season, the riots briefly, because successfully, flared again.

---

[36] Richard Findlater, *Grimaldi, King of Clowns* (London: Macgibbon & Kee, 1955), 126. *Memoirs of Joseph Grimaldi*, ed. 'Boz' (Charles Dickens) and Revd. Charles Whitehead, 2 vols. (2nd edn.; London: Richard Bentley, 1846), 73.

The 'Grand Pantomimical Ballet' of *Don Juan; or the Libertine Destroyed* was widely performed during Byron's years in London. It was particularly associated with Drury Lane, a connection which is evident in its published title of *An Historical Account of the Tragi-Comic Pantomime Intituled Don Juan, or The Libertine Destroyed, As it is Performed at Drury-Lane Theatre*. It supplemented the overture from Mozart's *Don Giovanni* and music from Gluck's setting for the ballet with additions by Reeve.[37] The playbills boast of the 'universal applause' which it enjoyed. More authoritative support for this claim is provided by the play's crossing the traditional divide of the theatres into 'major' and 'minor' venues. The major or 'patent' Houses were those of Covent-Garden and Drury Lane which enjoyed the favours originally bequeathed to Sir William Davenant and Thomas Killigrew by Charles II in 1662. Parliament later added support to the royal privilege when it passed the Licensing Act of 1737, in which the 'minor' venues were forbidden from representing straight tragedy or comedy and were strictly limited in their use of dialogue, in an attempt to suppress political dissent. The minor houses relied instead upon farce, burletta, ballet, pantomime, and a range of spectacles which might include anything from boxing to the exhibition of mummies, astrological lectures to circus animals, rope-dancing to fireworks. The segregation increasingly extended also to the contracts of the performers themselves. The *Theatrical Inquisitor* of September 1816 argued that principal actors should be exempted from the clause obliging them to perform in all genres, especially the dreaded pantomimes, ballets, and after-pieces. The grander neo-classical theatres were decorated with statues of muses and poets ancient and modern as symbols of their exclusive place in the nation's culture. Yet the true deities of both Drury Lane and Covent-Garden were Harlequin and Columbine, the Bleeding Nun and the Spectre Knight, the Wild Man and the Clown. These temples of drama were kept alive by the popular nature of pantomime and melodrama, despite their

[37] Adeline's song 'I am a friar of Orders Grey' (*Don Juan*, XVI, 40ff.) was composed some time in 1802 by William Reeve, with words originally written by John O'Keefe. See *The Complete Poetical Works of Lord Byron*, ed. Jerome J. McGann, v (1986), 766, XVI, l. 304.

pseudo-Greek facades, an irony which did not escape Byron and which he duly noted in his 'Address, Spoken at the Opening of Drury Lane Theatre' (1812). The division between the houses became increasingly internecine as the patent theatres resorted to the lures of their competitors in order to reclaim defecting audiences and shrinking receipts, while still maintaining their monopoly over the 'great' plays of the past. So while the legend of Don Juan retained its notoriety as suitable entertainment for the lowest classes, performances of Don Juan versions were not restricted to the 'minor' theatres.

The only theatre in London which did not stage a pantomime of Don Juan was the King's Theatre, Haymarket, the chief theatrical haunt of the aristocracy and the venue for the first professional performance of Mozart's *Don Giovanni* (12 August 1817). Although the theatrical history of Don Juan in London has already been demonstrated as significant, it is unlikely that it would have created the mania which did occur if it had not been for Mozart's opera. The success of *Don Giovanni* in London is evident in the number of its performances: twenty-six in 1817, fifteen in 1818, and twenty-two in 1819. These figures far exceed those of Mozart's other operas which were performed between 1806 and 1819. Indeed in its first three years, *Don Giovanni* already exceeded the total number of performances of these other Mozart operas, one of which (*La clemenza di Tito*) had first been performed some eleven years previously.[38] The

TABLE. *Performances of Mozart's operas in London*

	1806	1811	1812	1813	1816	1817	1818	1819
La clemenza di Tito	6		16	5	9	4	3	
Cosi fan tutte				12			11	2
Die Zauberflöte		1						15
Le nozze di Figaro			8	5	4	11	12	5
Don Giovanni						26	15	22

Source: Frederick C. Petty, *Italian Opera in London, 1760–1800* (Ann Arbor, Mich.: UMI Research Press, 1980), 271.

[38] Performances of Mozart's operas in London up to 1820 are shown in the Table.

King's Theatre even had to throw open disengaged boxes to the public in order to accommodate the crowds demanding admission.[39] Many memoirs from this period testify to the work's considerable popularity.[40]

Further proof of the success of Mozart's opera in London was its rapid translation into a more vernacular tradition. John Harris, the proprietor of Covent-Garden, authorized an English version entitled *The Libertine* which was performed almost within a week of Mozart's opera (20 May 1817). This was largely adapted from Shadwell's play of the same name by Pocock and its music, mostly that of Mozart, was arranged by Bishop. Something of the character of this piece can be glimpsed in the reaction of one foreign visitor, Prince Pückler-Mushau, to a similar adaptation of Mozart's *Le nozze di Figaro*:

neither the Count, the Countess, nor Figaro sang; these parts were given to mere actors, and their principal songs, with some little altera-tion in the words were sung by the other singers; to add to this, the gardener roared out some interpolated popular English songs, which suited Mozart's music just as pitch-plaster would suit the face of the Venus de Medici. The whole opera was moreover 'arranged' by a certain Mr Bishop... that is, adapted to English ears by means of the most tasteless and shocking alterations.[41]

In Pocock's *The Libertine* 'Là ci darem' was sung by Zerlina and Masetto in place of Don Giovanni because Charles Kemble was not a singer. This change made no dramatic sense since the duet of adulterous seduction then became one of conjugal fidelity. And because Mr Chapman did not sing either, Don Pedro's aria of 'Di rider finirà pria della Aurora' was omitted. Both these changes were derided by Hazlitt in his review of the piece for *The Examiner* (25 May 1817). He also denounced the xenophobia of the audience which entailed

[39] William C. Smith, *The Italian Opera and Contemporary Ballet in London, 1789–1820* (London: Society for Theatre Research, 1955), 143.

[40] For examples from contemporary memoirs see Lady Sydney Morgan, *Passages from my Autobiography* (London: Richard Bentley, 1859), 85 (10 Sept. 1818), and *The Life of Mary Russell Mitford*, 3 vols. (London: Richard Bentley, 1870), ii. 4 (23 May 1817).

[41] Prince Pückler-Mushau, *Tour in Germany, Holland and England in the years 1826, 1827 and 1828... series of Letters by a German Prince* (London: Effingham Wilson, 1832). Quoted in Eric Walter White, *A History of English Opera* (London: Faber & Faber, 1983), 251.

that the songs were loudly prevented from being encored, simply because their composition was not British.[42] However despite Hazlitt's reservations about the reception of the piece, it was sufficiently popular to be performed on twenty more nights.

The phenomenal success of Mozart's *Don Giovanni* in England is also apparent in the overwhelming cult of burlesques and parodies which it inspired: Thomas Dibdin's *Don Giovanni; or, A Spectre on Horseback!* (first performed 26 May 1817, at the Royal Circus and Surrey Theatre); *Harlequin's Vision; or, The Feast of the Statue* (26 December 1817, at Drury Lane); W. T. Moncrieff's *Don Giovanni in London, or The Libertine Reclaimed* (26 December 1817, at the Olympic Theatre); G. Smith's *Don Giovanni, Being an accurate account of his peregrinations in Hell, Italy, Paris, London, and the Country* (July 1820, at Sadler's Wells); *Giovanni in the Country; or A Gallop to Gretna Green!* (31 July 1820, at Astley's Amphitheatre); *Giovanni the Vampire; or How shall we get rid of him?*, a title which indicated tedium while perpetuating the cult (15 January 1821, at the Adelphi Theatre); *Don Giovanni in Ireland* (22 December 1821, at Drury Lane); *Giovanni in Botany Bay; or The Libertine Transported* (11 March 1822, at the Olympic); and *Giovanni in Paris* (East London Theatre). The air of hack-work continued to surround the Don Juan legend as these competing versions appeared sometimes within weeks of each other. Pocock's English version was produced just over a month after the first night of Mozart's opera in London. Even more impressively, Thomas Dibdin attended Mozart's opera on a Tuesday and wrote his piece for rehearsal the following Monday.[43]

One way in which these parodies and burlesques could strive to outdo one another was in increasing sensationalism and buffoonery. *Harlequin's Vision; or, The Feast of the Statue* particularly takes its lead from the most 'licentious' of the pantomime productions. Its equestrian statue, toppling to crush the Don Giovanni harlequin, falls instead into a large bowl of macaroni. Yet its farcical nature is framed within classical allusions to

---

[42] Reprinted in *The Complete Works of William Hazlitt*, ed. P. P. Howe, 21 vols. (London: J. M. Dent, 1930–4), v. 370–2, 370.

[43] Thomas Dibdin, *The Reminiscences of Thomas Dibdin*, 2 vols. (London: Henry Colburn, 1827), ii. 135, ch. 1.

ancient Roman myth. The pantomime begins in the council hall of Pluto, where the audience learns that the business of the pantomime is a dream, which Mercury has conjured up in order to warn Don Juan from his evil courses. When Don Juan, just on the point of being consigned to hell, awakes, he hastily repents of his former follies, begs forgiveness of his wife, Donna Elvira, whom he had abandoned, and, accompanied by her, proceeds to the Palace of Pleasure, where all the classical gods and goddesses receive the happy pair with shouts of congratulation. These epic correlations might have suggested to Byron that he should make of his new poem a modern epic in the style of the ancients. Certainly both exploit the humour of such a seemingly incompatible coupling: the populism and vulgarity associated with the legend is combined with the grandeur and high culture of classical mythology.

Between 26 December 1817 and 22 January 1818 this pantomime ran for twenty-four consecutive nights, excepting Sundays. That this represented a considerable degree of success may be inferred from the benefit system: on the twenty-first night, any additional profit would be given to the author's family. Such phenomenal popularity was crucial to the theatre's fortunes. According to Harris, the proprietor of Covent-Garden (1809–21), no profits were cleared from the regular drama. It was the profit made on the annual Christmas pantomime that offset other losses and enabled the theatre to realize a net gain. Between 1810 and 1820, for example, the annual profit cleared from the pantomime averaged £16,767.[44]

Keats's review of this pantomime in *The Champion* (4 January 1818) did not attempt to speak elegantly of the production but instead rivalled the plot in whimsy. It mimics the language of the nursery: moo-cows, hunt the slipper, knitting needles, the secret memoirs of a ladybird, Punch and Judy, and the milky way are all included in the 'cast' of the article. Such elements are introduced as a reflection upon the work's most suitable audience: 'As to the pantomime, be it good or bad, a child should write a critique upon it.'[45] Despite the legitimization of

---

[44] Donohue, *Theatre in the Age of Kean*, 56; Dewey Ganzel, 'Drama and the Law in the Early Nineteenth Century', *PMLA* 76 (1961), 384–96, 389.

[45] Reprinted in *The Poetical Works and Other Writings of John Keats*, ed. Harry Buxton Forman, 5 vols. (New York: C. Scribner's Sons, 1938–9), v. 252–6, 256.

the Don Juan legend by Mozart's opera, the degeneration of the character's serious reputation continued apace. In fact, it is hard to believe that the following excerpt from a review in *The Theatrical Inquisitor* (January 1818) is of a version of the Don Juan legend at all, since the clowning and effects completely dominate:

Amongst the best tricks in the piece was the transformation of an old woman into a table and a couple of chairs. The transformation of a chest into a sofa, on which the Clown seats himself, and which is immediately afterwards converted into a kitchen-grate, with a fire briskly burning in it, which gives the Clown an unpleasing hint, *a posteriori*, was also cleverly executed. A tournament scene, in which the combatants are deprived of their head and legs displayed considerable ingenuity. The Clown formed a sort of army out of the disjointed materials, by placing a head on each pair of legs, and setting the trunks upright. This extraordinary battalion, one-half consisting of heads and legs, the other of bodies and thighs, paddled off the stage with more gravity than grace.[46]

The rush of Don Juan productions meant that each new work tried to entice an audience with the promise of novelty. Keats's zany review is evidence that this applied equally to the reviewers and their interpretations. The following notice for *Giovanni in London* displays how the defence of originality was important to those theatrical representations competing financially against one another:

It has been erroneously imagined by those persons who have not witnessed the performance of GIOVANNI IN LONDON that it is 'a tale twice told' and founded on the old worn out Piece of 'Don Juan', it may therefore be necessary to add, that this DRAMA begins where the Italian opera finishes—that the HERO and LEPORELLO are placed in situations entirely NOUVELLE—and that the incidents arising from those situations are entirely original.

Giovanni the Vampire was similarly billed as 'an old acquaintance, considered in a new light'. The emphasis of the playbills was always upon *new* scenery and *new* costumes. The playbill of *Giovanni the Vampire* ingenuously proclaimed its originality in the advertisement itself by mocking this conventional ploy and

---

[46] *The Theatrical Inquisitor and Monthly Mirror* (Jan. 1818), 51, review of *Harlequin's Vision* at Drury Lane Theatre.

exposing the plea as being absurdly specious: 'for the first Time, AN ENTIRELY NEW, (with the exception of the Music, some Part of the dialogue, and a few Scenes, Dresses, and Decorations) Operatic, Burlesque BURLETTA . . . Giovanni the Vampire!' The convention is also mocked within Byron's *Don Juan* in the narrator's boast: 'I've got new mythological machinery I And very handsome supernatural scenery' (I, 201).

The 'draw' for prospective audiences continued to be spectacle, with each theatre striving to outdo one another in special effects if not in novelty of plot or character. The emphasis on spectacle was also demanded by the increase in size of the patent theatres. Their managements' desire for larger capacity houses, or rather the greater receipts which would then ensue, was in fact counter-productive, for the theatres in turn were forced to greater expense in special effects which those spectators towards the back of the theatres could at least see. The apotheosis of this tradition must surely have been that of W. T. Moncrieff's show *Cataract of the Ganges! or, The Rajah's Daughter* in which a real waterfall was created on stage. Eluned Brown, who edited extracts from the diary of Henry Crabb Robinson concerning the London theatre of 1811–66, noted that Robinson unashamedly admitted to his enjoyment of stage scenery, which, if stunning or ingenious, would compensate for the inadequacy of a play.[47]

The Don Juan burlesques and pantomimes were not exempt from such ambitious staging, especially when the plot maintained the tradition of a statue transforming to life. The playbills for *Don Giovanni; or, A Spectre on Horseback!* consistently advertised 'The Marble Horse, by a Real Pony'. One of its early announcements declared that 'on account of the *stupendous* Preparations for Don Giovanni, Who's the Murderer is unavoidably postponed' (playbill for 12 May 1817). *The Theatrical Guardian* (Saturday 12 March 1791) loudly applauded the impressive design of the pantomime at Covent-Garden:

The vessel that is seen in the Pantomime of Don Juan unfurling her sails, and going out to sea, is a charming piece of mechanism. The efforts of genius in this line should be patronised by our Theatres, as

[47] Henry Crabb Robinson, *The London Theatre, 1811–1866: Selections from the Diary of Henry Crabb Robinson*, ed. Eluned Brown (London: The Society for Theatre Research, 1966), 23.

an encouragement to an art to which we are principally indebted for
the superior advantages we enjoy.[48]

Hazlitt's criticisms of *The Libertine* did not extend to the 'splendid car brought to receive him by the devil, in the likeness of a
great dragon, writhing round and round upon a wheel of fire—
an exquisite device of the Managers, superadded to the original
story' (*The Examiner*, 25 May 1817). Similarly, while Hunt's
review of the Harlequin Don Juan pantomime was highly censorious, it did single out for praise the storm at sea in which the
Clown was tossed about (*The Examiner*, 11 January 1818).
Giovanni in London finished with ladies and gentlemen in rich
dresses, a backdrop of a splendid fancy pavilion, a grand display
of fireworks, and the name of 'Giovanni' illuminated in large
characters. The playbills usually listed the scene changes in
detail which might strike the modern theatre-goer as verging
on the pedantic. However the staging was evidently judged to
be one of the major attractions of the piece to prospective
spectators, for the playbill was forced to use its limited space
profitably. The history of the legend has already demonstrated
the popularity of the hell-fire scenes. All of the playbills of the
burlesques, whether at the Olympic, Surrey, Covent-Garden,
Sadler's Wells, Lyceum, or Drury Lane theatres, ended with the
identical enticement: 'To conclude with a view of the Infernal
regions, and a shower of Fire!'

The most successful of the many burlesques were undoubtedly *Giovanni in London* and *Don Giovanni; or, A Spectre on Horseback!*, both of which were performed across the divisions of the
theatres. *Giovanni in London* was especially popular, largely because of the infamy of its 'breeches role': Madame Vestris
played the part of the libertine and attracted considerable attention by displaying her legs. The songs from this piece were
published separately and the play itself ran into many reprints.
It accompanied Moncrieff to Drury Lane in 1820, was acted
twenty-nine times that season, and was still being performed
there, although less frequently, in 1827. It was subtitled 'a
grand moral, satirical, tragical, comical, operatical, melo-
dramatical, pantomimical, critical, infernal, terrestrial, celestial,
GALLYMAUFRICALOLLAPODRIDACAL, Burletta Spectacle'. Byron

recognized his own poem's tendency to such heterogeneity by describing it as an *olla podrida* in the preface to Cantos I and II.

Giovanni in London opened in Hades where two female demons, Tartarus and Succubus, and Proserpine quarrel over Don Giovanni, thus continuing the epic allusions previously deployed by Drury Lane's pantomime, *Harlequin's Vision*. Pluto, jealous of his wife's adulterous favour, exiles Don Giovanni from hell. On earth, Leporello is now married to Donna Anna and stepfather to Giovanni's illegitimate child. At a masquerade, Don Giovanni meets Constantia, a £30,000 heiress and ward of Deputy English. Giovanni duels with Finikin, suitor of Constantia, and is sued for damages by the husbands of the 'shrews' he accompanied on his return from hell (sued for bringing them back rather than for seducing them). Meanwhile, Constantia has declared her intention to marry Giovanni since 'I've heard an old proverb, which says, a reformed rake always makes a good husband' (Act II, scene 2). Because Giovanni is unable to pay the £10,000 damages, he is taken to the Kings' Bench, where he is conventionally 'fleeced' by his fellow debtors and where Leporello, disguised as his lawyer, is humiliatingly tossed in a blanket. Once acquitted, Giovanni announces his intention to compensate for his temperance in prison with a life of renewed dissipation. Leporello's simulation of a speaking statue frightens him into 'repentance', defined by Giovanni as the intention to marry a wealthy old maid. However, making love in dumb show to the disguised Mrs Leporello, he recalls Constantia and renounces wealth for love, a decision which is revealed as being a most fortunate one: 'Know, to reward your love and constancy, Constantia still is rich and worthy of you' (Act II, scene 7).

The piece includes conventional satire—principal targets are wives and lawyers—and much buffoonery. Leporello's tossing in the blanket, Giovanni's stealing of Charon's boat and of Mercury's light heels (or 'Murky' as Giovanni calls him; Act I, scene 2) are all typical of this kind of pantomimic farce. The piece has, unsurprisingly, been derided by literary criticism. Frederick Beaty, for example, describes it as having 'reduced the legend to a domestic cockney farce with suggestive

overtones'.[49] However, it is interesting as an attempt to translate
the legend into the popular vernacular of Regency England. It
was in fact one of the first pieces of the time to employ the
actual city of London for a series of settings. The statue of the
Commander becomes the equestrian statue of King Charles II
at Charing Cross and the threatening invitation of the Commendatore becomes Leporello's nursery-like feint:

> Pluto put the kettle on,
> Pluto put the kettle on
> To supper once I asked the Don
> I ask him now to tea.[50]

   Pocock and Bishop's adaptation of *The Libertine* and Dibdin's
Don Giovanni; or, A Spectre on Horseback! also attempted to accommodate the legend within a specifically English context. In
Dibdin's burlesque, Act I, scene 3, opens with the obviously
paradoxical setting 'Blackfriars Bridge—Gondolieri plying'.
(This stage direction illustrates the association of Venice with
the legend, possibly because of the city's scandalous reputation.) The bill of fare for supper with the Stone Guest includes
beef-steak and onions or bacon and beans. Leporello's list of his
master's conquests consists entirely of English female names:
Sally, Agatha, Alice, Georgina, Joan, Mabel, Mildred . . . And
the statue's voice is described as 'something like a paviour when
he is ramming the roads'. Like *Giovanni in London*, the entire
piece renders the tradition of the legend into jolly vernacular,
most absurdly so in the murder of Don Guzman:

> *Air—Jacky returned from Dover*
> GIOVANNI: With my tierce and carte, sa, sa!
> GUZMAN: Which I repel so smart, ha, ha!
> GIOVANNI: I think I've touch'd the heart—
> GUZMAN: [*Having received a thrust*] Oh, la!
>   From the stream of life I'm ferried,
>   With my tierce and carte, sa, sa!
> GIOVANNI: Which I repel so smart, ha, ha!
>   [*Kills Guzman*
>   I think I've touch'd his heart—
> GUZMAN: Oh, la!

[49] Beaty, 'Harlequin Don Juan', 402.
[50] Mandel (ed.), *Theatre of Don Juan*, 443: Act II, scene 6.

GIOVANNI: So go, now go, and be buried   [*Exit*
Don Guzman blows out his light and dies.[51]

Faithful to the spirit of levity, Guzman is not dead and merely stage-manages his return as the Stone Guest. However, this simulation is later deliberately underplayed as Giovanni is surrounded by 'furies', a concession to the need of impressive spectacle in the finale.

Clearly, one way to curry favour with the English audience was to Anglicize the work. This would have been unthinkable prior to the flourishing cult of Don Juan in 1817–24. In its review of *Letters from England, by Don Manuel Alvarez Espriella*, the magazine *La Belle Assemblée* (1807) mocked the pretence of Spanishness in the name of Espriella: 'which is no wise Spanish, no more than *Don Juan Bull*'.[52] The years of peace after 1815 and the almost unanimous patriotism of the audiences made such a metamorphosis not only possible but necessary. This is certainly suggested by the following review in *Cumberland's Minor Theatre* of 1822: 'It became necessary to invest the Don with certain *national* qualities that peep beneath his Spanish cloak and doublet, like the *curling-irons* out of the fashionably cut pocket of honest Tom King, ere it could be relished by an audience purely *English*.'[53] Charles Lamb's review of *Giovanni in London* also wrote of the audience's patriotic partiality: 'The *Leporello* of the Olympic Theatre is not one of the most refined order, but we can bear with an English blackguard better than with the Italian one'.[54]

These Don Giovanni burlesques demonstrate how well-known the traditional plot had become, for they implicitly drew upon presupposed knowledge. For example, in *Giovanni in London* the audience is first introduced to Mrs Leporello with an allusion which they would have recognized from other versions: 'Oh, false Giovanni to desert me thus, and leave none but Leporello as the husband of your Anna, and the

---

[51] *Don Giovanni; or, A Spectre on Horseback! A comic, heroic, operatic, tragic, burletta, Spectacular Extravaganza, in Two Acts; Adapted to Hodgson's Theatrical Characters and Scenes in the Same* (London: Hodgson, 1817), 6.

[52] *La Belle Assemblée*, supplement for vol. 3 (1807), 49.

[53] *Cumberland's Minor Theatre* (1822), 4.

[54] Charles Lamb, *The Examiner* (22 Nov. 1818), repr. in *The Works of Charles and Mary Lamb*, ed. E. V. Lucas (London: Methuen, 1903), i. 372–3, 'Miscellaneous Prose 1798–1874', 373.

father of your baby' (Act I, scene 4). This speech, in referring
to a liaison with Don Giovanni, identifies Mrs Leporello with
the Donna Anna of previous versions. Her history is not literally
true of previous plots, since no earlier version, or at least none
that has survived, considered that Don Juan might father
children, despite his notorious promiscuity. The 'birth' of her
child thus occurs, the audience presumes, within that imaginative space of time between the more traditional plots of
other versions and this of W. T. Moncrieff. Leporello's reference to the statue is similarly allusive: 'he must pass by this
statue, so, like the commandant upon his horse—I have it—
in this blue light 'twill answer certainly: just so he looked who
asked the Don to sup where he was supped on' (Act II, scene
6)—since no encounter with a commandant has been enacted
in this version. Such references are stated elliptically, for
they need not be otherwise: 'My name's Don Giovanni, O! |
Well known to a good many, O!' (*Don Giovanni; or, A Spectre
on Horseback!*).

The burlesques also became increasingly inter-referential as
the proliferation of Don Juan productions caused a considerable degree of mutual awareness and cross-comparison between
literally competing versions. Hazlitt criticized the actors in
Pocock's *The Libertine* for not entering fully into their parts
because they compared themselves too consciously with their
counterparts in the opera at the King's Theatre, Haymarket.[55]
Such self-consciousness was increasingly visible in versions of
the legend as individual performances were forced to compete
for appraisal in the minds of spectators who had attended a
version of the legend before and would, most probably, attend
one again. Since it was therefore futile to attempt to ignore
competition, the playbills often foregrounded other productions in an attempt to advertise their own. The following playbill
for *Giovanni in Botany Bay; or The Libertine Transported* demonstrates this kind of overt cross-referencing:

It is respectfully presumed that, notwithstanding this celebrated character has been already so often before the Public, and although some
affirm him to be on *his last legs*, he is yet capable of *standing* another
trial and that *malgre* his having been *destroyed* in *Spain*, *resuscitated* in

---

[55] Hazlitt, *The Examiner* (25 May 1817), repr. in Hazlitt, *Complete Works*, v. 370–2.

Drury Lane, *Vampirized* in the Adelphi, and *damned* in Ireland, this final attempt to *transport* him, to the Olympic will not fail to delight!

The playbill for a production of the pantomime *Don Juan* at Sadler's Wells (25 July 1820) exploited the same extensive notoriety of the legend: 'Being an Accurate Account of his Peregrinations in HELL, ITALY, PARIS, LONDON, and the COUNTRY'. This extensive cross-referencing of the Don Juan versions would have extended to Byron's *Don Juan*.

Although the surviving playbills are incomplete, those of 1817 for performances of *Don Giovanni; or, A Spectre on Horseback!* advertise the number of successive evenings it has played as its major attraction to potential theatre-goers. For example, that of 12 September 1817 announces that it will be the 107th performance that season (that is, since its opening on 12 May 1817). This was announced to be the last evening, excepting benefit performances. However, it continued in the repertory and on 15 August 1818 the playbills justified its continuance by citing popular demand: 'Notwithstanding the frequent Repetitions of Don Giovanni which has been acted upwards of two hundred Nights, the Enquiries after it are so numerous . . .'. It is within this context—of hundreds of successive performances—that the popularity of the Don Juan legend on the Regency stage might justifiably be described as phenomenal.

BYRON AND THE DON JUAN LEGEND

> Whereas this story's actually true.
>
> If any person doubt it, I appeal
> To history, tradition, and to facts,
> To newspapers, whose truth all know and feel,
> To plays in five and operas in three acts.
> All these confirm my statement a good deal,
> But that which more completely faith exacts
> Is that myself and several now in Seville
> Saw Juan's last elopement with the devil.
>
> (I, 202–3)

Byron visited Seville and Cádiz with the invasion of French troops imminent. This has led most English commentators and biographers to presume that cultural activity was limited.

Indeed the editors of both modern editions of *Don Juan* (Penguin and Clarendon) annotate these stanzas by quoting the same source—W. A. Borst, *Lord Byron's First Pilgrimage 1809–1811* (1948)—in support of their claim that Byron could not have seen Tirso de Molina's *El burlador de Sevilla*.[56] This takes account of the professional stage, but not the prevalence of an active, if amateur, cultural life which flourished under, and indeed as a result of, the oppressive political regime and its prohibition of professional companies.

We might expect Byron to have been interested in theatrical life during his stay in Seville because the attempted suppression of the theatres in 1800 was referred to in Lord Holland's book, *Some Account of the Lives and Writings of Lope Felix de Vega Carpio* (1817). Holland records that the Sevillians voluntarily renounced the theatre as an attempt to appease divine justice.[57] Byron owned a copy of the first edition of this book which had been published anonymously in 1807. And, because this copy was later sold in the sale of his library in 1816, his letter to Samuel Rogers in April 1817 states that he was expecting a new copy of the book from Lord Holland and looking forward to 'reperus[ing]' it. It is quite possible that Byron read this book before or shortly after his visit to Spain.[58]

When Byron visited the city in July 1809, he would have heard of a recent theatrical history which was even more scandalous than that of Holland's account. The principal acting company had been disbanded as a consequence of the marital bickerings of their directors, the Calderi-Sciomeri couple. Lazaro Calderi had accused his wife of adultery and had himself been imprisoned for theft. On 11 July 1808 the town hall decreed its ban on the company with a combination of political and moral censure.[59] In May 1809 Ana Sciomeri's request that the theatre be reopened was denied and again the justification was patriotic, for the liberty of Spain was linked with its moral qualities of 'catolicismo, seriedad y nobleza'.[60]

[56] *Don Juan* (1973), 589 n. 203, pp. 3–4 and *The Complete Poetical Works*, v (1986), 681, n. 1624.

[57] Lord Henry Richard Holland, *Some Account of the Lives and Writings of Lope Felix de Vega Carpio and Guillen de Castro* (London, 1817), 132.

[58] *Byron's Letters and Journals*, v. 206 and n. (to Samuel Rogers, 4 Apr. 1817).

[59] Francisco Aguilar Piñal, *Sevilla y el teatro en el siglo XVIII* (Oviedo: Universidad de Oviedo, 1974), 224, quotes the edict.   [60] See ibid. 224–5.

Accepting these religious and patriotic arguments, *la Junta Suprema* ordered the demolition of the Teatro Cómico on 27 January 1810, although this destruction was in fact never carried out: on the following day the people fled to Cádiz in advance of the French troops. Soult and his troops arrived in Seville on 1 February 1810 and remained for thirty-one months. During this period theatrical performances continued to flourish and private entertainments proliferated as a consequence of the theatre's ban. Existing records of the professional theatre show that between 1808 and 1811 Antonio Zamora's *El convidado de piedra* was performed eight times; 13, 14, 29 February 1808; 5, 6 January 1811; 24 February 1811; 18 September 1811; and 26 December 1811.[61] Existing theatrical records for Cádiz demonstrate that between 1810 and 1812 Tirso de Molina's *El convidado de piedra* was performed on 18 June 1812, and the *sainete, El burlador burlado,* on 6, 7, 13 April and 16 May 1812.[62]

None of these performance dates, in either Seville or Cádiz, are particularly auspicious since they do not include the year of Byron's stay in Cádiz, where he certainly attended the opera (on 2 August 1809).[63] However, the available theatrical records indicate that the two Don Juan plays were still a part of the performance repertory even more than a century after their composition. And these records exclude the more prolific amateur performances. Byron attended the *tertulias* of both cities where theatrical presentations were always a feature of the evening's entertainment. In Cádiz this was an especially strong tradition due to the lack of a professional theatre. Byron visited the salons of the Retortillo family, where the habanos-smoking Margarita López de Morla presided over her liberal circle. It is therefore quite probable, though not definitively provable, that Byron, as an interested visitor to Andalucia, would have been entertained with the region's most infamous legend, and especially given the context of increased Spanish nationalism: 'During the French invasion, and as a reaction and affirmation of

[61] Francisco Aguilar Piñal, 'Cartelera Prerromantica Sevillaña Años 1800–1836', *Cuadernos Bibliograficos XXII* (Madrid: Artes Gráficas Clavileño, 1968), 17.

[62] Ramon Solís, *El Cádiz de las Cortes: La vida en la ciudad en los años 1810 a 1813* (Madrid: Instituto de Estudios Politicos, 1958), 395, 400.

[63] See Esteban Pujals, *Lord Byron en España y otros temas Byronianos* (Madrid: Editorial Alhambra, 1982), 15.

national character, all performances of a popular nature were received with delirious enthusiasm; at that time balls, dance and folksong flourished with notable vigour.'[64] Any representation of the legend Byron might have witnessed in Spain, perhaps in excerpts or snatches of song, would have been a fiercely political statement of national and local pride.

Prosper Mérimée's *Les Ames du Purgatoire* (1834) was inspired by his visit to Seville in 1830 and the opening pages of his novel relate the various tales of Don Juan which he heard during his stay there. Mérimée claimed that the truth of these stories was indisputable, since one would offend the Sevillians if they were doubted. Their tales of Don Juan are of a 'real, live' character who asks for a light from a passer-by on the right bank of the Guadalquivir.[65] The professed certainty of Don Juan's existence is similar to Byron's profession of authenticity in actually witnessing Don Juan in Seville (I, 203, quoted above), both of which may represent, as indeed Mérimée claims, a passionate account of the figure by the Sevillians themselves. Mérimée's novella was more specifically based on the life of Don Miguel Mañara, who was born in Seville in 1626. Mañara reputedly encountered his own funeral procession and thereafter repented and led a life of strict sanctity and charitable works, including the erection of a church and hospital. Mérimée saw Mañara's tomb at Seville in 1830 and may well have based his story on oral tradition rather than written sources.[66] The painting of Miguel de Mañara by Juan Valdés Leal (in about 1672) was and is still displayed in the Hospital de la Caridad which Mañara had founded.[67] Gendarme de Bévotte claimed that in 1855 a street in Seville still bore the name of the family

[64] Santiago Montoto, *El teatro, el baile y la danza en Sevilla* (Archivo Hispalense, 103–4; Seville: Imprenta Provincial, 1960), 14: 'Tras la invasión francesa y como reacción y afirmación del carácter nacional, todas las manifestaciones de índole popular fueron acogidas con delirante entusiasmo; entonces el baile, la danza y los Cantos folklóricos se desarrollaron con notable pujanza'.

[65] Prosper Mérimée, *Colomba et dix autres nouvelles* (Paris: Gallimard, 1964), 'Les Ames du Purgatoire', 209–78, 212.

[66] See A. W. Raitt, *Prosper Mérimée* (London: Eyre & Spottiswoode, 1970), 177n. 11: Mérimée, *Romans et nouvelles*, ii. 10. That Mérimée heard of Don Miguel Mañara through oral accounts would explain the deformation of his name to Maraña in Mérimée's story.

[67] Weinstein, *Metamorphoses of Don Juan*, 212, catalogue no. 463. This hospital is also referred to in Mérimée's novella.

of the *comendador* of Tirso's version and that the tomb of Ulloa himself was in the convent of the Franciscans.[68] The respective visits of Byron and Mérimée to the city are divided by twenty-one years (1809 and 1830) but one aspect which remained unchanged was the city's nationalism. Certainly as a visitor to Seville, Byron is unlikely to have been a stranger to the legendary name of Don Juan.

This 1809 visit to Spain would have been Byron's only opportunity to know the Spanish tradition, whether that of Tirso de Molina or that of Antonio Zamora, directly. However, this native tradition had resurfaced to an extent in the English pantomimes of the late eighteenth and early nineteenth centuries. Samuel Chew, quoting Gendarme de Bévotte, claimed that Delpini's pantomime of 1787 was taken directly from the Spanish. The libretto of da Ponte's *Il Don Giovanni*, published in London in 1817, included a brief history of the play's migrations through Europe, including the original *El burlador de Sevilla, y combidado [sic] de piedra* by Gabriel Téllez of Madrid.[69] It is likely that Byron would have known *Letters from England: by Don Manuel Alvarez Espriella, Translated from the Spanish* (1807), although he may not have seen through the alias (the original writer was in fact Robert Southey). The 'Spanish' writer mocks the boast of the superiority of English taste because of the popularity of 'one of the most monstrous of all our dramas', the legend of Don Juan. He attends a performance of the legend at Drury Lane, possibly the 'Grand Pantomimical Ballet' of *Don Juan; or the Libertine Destroyed*. The criticism of blatant commercialism and the tone of condescension which have been typical throughout the legend's history remain: 'Nothing could be more insipid than all the former part of this drama, nothing more dreadful, and indeed unfit for scenic representation than the catastrophe; but . . . this is a favourite spectacle everywhere.'[70] Byron's incomplete, and unpublished, preface to the first edition of his

---

[68] Georges Gendarme de Bévotte, *La Légende de Don Juan*, 2 vols. (1906; repr. Pairs: Hachette, 1929), ii. 17.

[69] *Il Don Giovanni* (London: W. Winchester, 15 Apr. 1817). The history of the play continues with references to the plays by Cicognini, Giliberto, Molière, Corneille, Shadwell, and Goldoni. The author of this history was William Ayrton.

[70] *Letters from England: by Don Manuel Alvarez Espriella, Translated from the Spanish* (1807; repr. London: The Cresset Press, 1951), 101.

poem, that of Cantos I–II, may allude to this work in suggesting
that the reader ought to think of the narrator as 'either an
Englishman settled in Spain, or a Spaniard who had travelled in
England'. In Don Juan *and Regency England* (1990), Peter W.
Graham considered *Don Juan* as having being influenced by this
text, an ironic influence given the considerable and notorious
hostility between the two authors.[71] Certainly, the Spanish origin of the myth was never overlooked despite other varied
metamorphoses. Byron himself refers to the 'Spanish tradition'
in suggesting to Murray that Don Juan's ultimate fate might be
banishment to hell.[72] He also gives the honour of Don Juan's
birth to Seville (I, 8), despite his own avowed preference for
Cádiz.[73] (Like Byron, Juan will shortly travel to Cádiz, and there
embark for the eastern Mediterranean.) In this way Byron's
version conforms with one of the few narrative details which
(almost) consistently recurred throughout the history of the
legend.

Many of the earlier versions of the legend also remained
current within Byron's London, including Molière's *Dom Juan*.
When *A Tale of Terror* by Henry Siddons was performed in
Covent-Garden on the 12 May 1803, the dramatist acknow-
ledged his debt to Molière's play in the advertisement to the
published piece: 'Molière's play of the "Feast of the Statue"
furnished the idea of the characters of Valdarno and Donna
Mercia in this little attempt. Some of the speeches in the First
Scenes are almost literal translations from that play.'[74] Claire
Clairmont records in her diary entry of 10 February 1818 that
she had read Molière's plays, including *Le Festin de pierre*.[75]
Teresa Guiccioli was later to contrast Molière's Don Juan directly with Byron's own, with evident unease.[76] Byron's *Don Juan*
itself contains a reference to Molière's play: Don Juan 'who
cared not a tobacco stopper | About philosophy' (X, 60) allu-

[71] See Peter W. Graham, Don Juan *and Regency England* (Charlottesville, Va.:
University Press of Virginia, 1990), ch. 2, 'Two Dons, a Lord, and a Laureate'.

[72] *Byron's Letters and Journals*, viii. 78 (16 Feb. 1821).

[73] See ibid. ii. 216, 217, 220, and *Don Juan* (I, 8).

[74] Quoted in Shadwell, *Complete Works*, iii. 14, 'Theatrical History'.

[75] *The Journals of Claire Clairmont*, ed. Marion Kington Stocking (Cambridge,
Mass.: Harvard University Press, 1968), 90 (Friday 10 Apr. 1818).

[76] Teresa Guiccioli, *Lord Byron jugé par les témoins de sa vie*, 2 vols. (London:
Richard Bentley, 1869), i. 442.

sively recalls the opening line of *Dom Juan* in which Sganarelle enters saying: 'Aristotle and the philosophers can say what they like, but there's nothing to equal tobacco'.

It was not only individual versions of the legend which were recognized and known. Early reviewers of Byron's *Don Juan* elaborated histories of the legend which rival my own in comprehensiveness. For example, *The Miniature Magazine* (October 1819) dispensed with recounting the traditional story of the legend because it is 'well known'. Instead the reviewer plotted the course of the legend's history. *El burlador de Sevilla, y Combidado de Piedra* is cited as the first version of the legend and ascribed to 'Gabriel Tellez/Tyrso de Molina'. Other versions referred to are those of Cicognini, Giliberto, Goldoni, Molière, Corneille, Shadwell, Mozart/da Ponte, and the more contemporary pantomimic forms. Corneille's advertisement to his piece, which included his concession to the 'scrupulous', is quoted in translation, and the reviewer claims that Molière was 'strongly solicited' by his troupe to write the piece, a reflection of the continuing embarrassment of the theme for highly regarded writers.[77] *The Gentleman's Magazine* (January 1822) also cited the original *El combidado de Piedra* by Tirso de Molina and Molière in its review of Cantos I–II.[78] Other reviews explicitly defended their omission of an explanation of Don Juan by claiming its redundancy—the legend, they argued, would already be familiar to their readers.[79] Those publications which had accompanied the first productions of the pantomimes in the 1780s also sketched comprehensive histories of the legend.[80]

In addition to these many versions was the proverbiality of the name Don Juan itself and its evocation in disparate contexts. The anonymously written poem, *Don Juan, or, The Battle of Tolosa* (1816) was quoted by Weinstein as a possible source for Byron's poem, although this theory is radically undermined by

[77] *The Miniature Magazine*, 3 (Oct. 1819), 236–9.
[78] *The Gentleman's Magazine* (Jan. 1822), 48–50.
[79] See *The Literary Gazette* (17 July 1819), 449–51. *The Literary Chronicle* (17 July 1819), 129–39. *The European Magazine*, 76 (July 1819), 55–6—all of which are quoted in Ch. 2.
[80] *An Historical Account of . . . Don Juan, or The Libertine Destroyed* (London: G. Bigg, No. 20 Strand, 1782). *The History of Don Juan, or the Libertine Destroyed* (London: J. Roe, c.1815).

Weinstein's grave inaccuracies about its plot.[81] Byron would
certainly have shared the public recognition of the designation
of 'Don Juan' as a by-word for villainous seduction. He had read
Les Liaisons dangereuses (1782), whose Vicomte de Valmont ac-
cuses the Chevalier Danceny of being a Don Juan.[82] He had also
read Madame de Staël's *De l'Allemagne* (1810) which quotes
'The Banquet of the Statue' as an example of the perfect marriage of music and words.[83] Goldoni's *Memoirs* was valued so
highly by Byron that, having sold his first copy in the 1816
auction of his library, he traded Thomas Moore an edition of
Ariosto for a replacement three years later. In these memoirs,
Goldoni talks at length about his own decision to write a Don
Juan play and comments upon the popularity of the subject
(see above).[84]

On Byron's return to England in July 1811, he was immediately catapulted into society life with the publication of
Childe Harold Cantos I–II in March 1812. This in turn facilitated
his 'theatrical' life with his appointment as management sub-
committee member for Drury Lane in May 1814 (although
Byron's reference to having seen Master Betty perform in 1804
indicates that he had been a theatre-goer for a considerable
period in advance of his nomination).[85] This position entailed,
among other duties, sifting through 500 dramas.[86] One
play which he might have considered is that by his friend
'Monk' Lewis—*Adelmorn: The Outlaw*—which had first been performed at Drury Lane on 4 May 1801. It had been criticized
as 'irreligious' because heaven and hell were represented.
The author replied to this allegation in his preface to the
octavo edition by citing the same audience's acceptance of
Don Juan, whose 'devils have exhibited their flame-coloured
stockings and black periwigs in every theatre throughout the

    [81] *Don Juan: or, The Battle of Tolosa* (London: James Harper, 1816). Weinstein,
Metamorphoses of Don Juan, 199, catalogue no. 230.
    [82] Choderlos de Laclos, *Les Liaisons dangereuses* (1782), tr. P. W. K. Stone
(Harmondsworth: Penguin, 1981), letter 155.
    [83] Quoted in Peter Le Huray and James Day (eds.), *Music and Aesthetics in Eight-
eenth and Early Nineteenth Centuries* (Cambridge: Cambridge University Press, 1981),
302.
    [84] Byron was reading Goldoni and seeing his plays in 1816–17. See *Byron's Letters
and Journals*, v. 238 and 274, and Boyd, *Byron's Don Juan*, 10, 35.
    [85] *Byron's Letters and Journals*, ii. 192.
    [86] Ibid. v. 150. See also ix. 35.

kingdom'.[87] Byron was also acquainted, and indeed corresponded, with Thomas Dibdin, who was later to write *Don Giovanni; or, A Spectre on Horseback!* Dibdin was known to Byron through their mutual involvement in Drury Lane, since Dibdin and Alexander Rae succeeded Samuel Whitbread as managers of the theatre after Whitbread's suicide in 1815.[88]

Byron's residence in London coincided with performances of the pantomime of *Don Juan* at the Lyceum Theatre in October–December 1811; August–September 1813; and July 1814. Those performances of 1811 had in fact been staged by Drury Lane: in 1809, after the fire at Drury Lane, the theatre took its patent to Samuel Arnold's previously unlicensed Lyceum Theatre in the Strand and remained there until its own reopening in 1812. The 'Grand Pantomimical Ballet' of *Don Juan; or the Libertine Destroyed* evidently remained within the repertory of Drury Lane—Southey's publication in 1807 of the *Letters from England* referred to this production. Certainly the 500 plays which Byron pored over on the shelves of Drury Lane's library would have included *An Historical Account of the Tragi-Comic Pantomime Intituled Don Juan or, The Libertine Destroyed, As it is Performed at Drury-Lane Theatre* (1782).

Byron criticized the fervour for pantomime in his early *English Bards and Scotch Reviewers* (1809).[89] However, Grimaldi's memoirs boast of Byron's enthusiasm for his performances and the authenticity of his claim is supported by Byron's regular subscriptions for Grimaldi's benefit performances at Covent-Garden and his gift to him of a snuffbox.[90] The part of Scaramouch in the pantomime of *Don Juan* was a particular favourite of Grimaldi's and it formed an essential part of the repertory with which he chose to tour the provincial theatres (hence the currency of the Don Juan legend extended beyond London). Despite his pretended disdain, Byron also knew of the pantomimes at the Royal Circus—he nicknamed Douglas Kinnaird and his actress-mistress the 'Dog & Duck', a pantomime which

[87] Quoted in Shadwell, *Complete Works*, iii. 14.
[88] See *Byron's Letters and Journals*, iv. 304 (July 1815), 316 (27 Sept. 1815), 335 (1 Dec. 1815).
[89] *English Bards and Scotch Reviewers* (1809), ll. 586–607.
[90] See Grimaldi, *Memoirs*, ii. 106 and 128 and Ernest J. Lovell (ed.), *His Very Self and Voice: Collected Conversations of Lord Byron* (New York: Macmillan, 1954), 624 n. 37.

shared evening performances with *Don Juan* in the autumn of 1816.[91] Many of the reviewers of Byron's *Don Juan* contrasted his poem with the pantomime tradition: *The Monthly Magazine* (September 1821) referred to the poem as 'his serio-comic melo-dramatic harlequinade'.[92] Byron himself demonstrated the allusive familiarity of the tradition in describing Suwarrow as 'Harlequin in uniform' (VII, 55) and in describing Don Juan's dancing as excelling in 'the eloquence | Of pantomime' (XIV, 38).

Byron's close association with Drury Lane continued to exercise an influence even after his removal from England. He continued a liaison—this time by correspondence—with Miss Susan Boyce, a minor actress at Drury Lane with whom Byron had a brief affair before going abroad. Indeed, we know that she must have written to him, not only of amatory, but also of financial affairs at Drury Lane because Byron repeated to Hobhouse her complaint that her salary had been reduced.[93] The success of the 1817 Christmas pantomime at Drury Lane would probably have secured its fortunes for the following year. Byron's continuing interest in the fate of Drury Lane theatre would therefore suggest that he knew of this success. It is a piece of news which his correspondents— and particularly Douglas Kinnaird—would have been unlikely to omit. It was Kinnaird who had been responsible for Byron's appointment to the committee in 1815. In Byron's desire for news of London from Kinnaird, chronological priority was given to the theatre: 'P.S. If you write to me—pray—do not refer to any *persons* or *events*—except our own *theatrical—political—personal—attorneycal—poetical—& diabolical*—concerns.'[94] And Kinnaird was certainly well qualified to reply. It is also likely that Byron's many English correspondents and visitors would have told him of the proliferation of Don Juan productions. The visits of 'Monk' Lewis, who stayed with Byron in Venice during the first week of July 1817, and of Douglas Kinnaird, Lord Kinnaird, and W. S. Rose in September 1817, would

[91] See e.g. *Byron's Letters and Journals*, vi. 20, 21.

[92] *The Monthly Magazine*, 102 (Sept. 1821), review of Cantos III–V: 124–9, 124.

[93] *Byron's Letters and Journals*, vi. 97 (to Hobhouse, 26 Jan. 1819).

[94] Ibid. v. 136 (to Douglas Kinnaird, 27 Nov. 1816). A few months after Byron left England, Kinnaird himself was ousted from the Drury Lane Committee. Byron sent condolences and counsel, ibid. v. 158–9 (to Douglas Kinnaird, 12 Jan. 1817).

probably have included news of the theatrical rage which had consolidated since the first professional performance of Mozart's *Don Giovanni* on 12 April 1817. And, after 1819, such informants would have had additional motivation to speak of the current fashion of Don Juan burlesques since these productions then shared their titles, despite variations, with Byron's own poem. The notoriety of these performances is implicit in the narrator's description of his own poem as what was once romance turning 'burlesque' (IV, 3). Cantos III–V were first published on 8 August 1821, by which time many of the burlesques and parodies were flourishing and competing.

Byron left England before the first public performance of Mozart's opera in London, but he is certain to have heard of this production and its phenomenal success while abroad. For example, Peacock introduced Shelley to opera through this very performance and claimed that from this time until he finally left England Shelley was an 'assiduous' frequenter of the Italian opera.[95] Indeed, Claire Clairmont's journal testifies to the popularity of the work among their group: the Shelleys, Hogg, Peacock, and Claire Clairmont attended four performances together within one fortnight (Tuesday 10 February, Saturday 14 February, Saturday 21 February, and Tuesday 24 February 1818) and Mary Shelley's journal records that in addition she and Shelley had previously attended *Don Giovanni* on 23 May 1817.[96] Peacock further added, though such a comment now seems self-evident, that Shelley particularly delighted in the music of Mozart. Mary Shelley's letter to Marianne and Leigh Hunt, written in Leghorn in May 1818, testifies to her continuing enthusiasm for opera and operatic news from London: 'tell me if you go often to the opera and if any changes have taken place in that singing Paradise'.[97] Leigh Hunt was hardly uninformed about such matters—he had reviewed Mozart's *Don Giovanni* three times for *The Theatrical Examiner*

[95] *Peacock's Memoirs of Shelley*, ed. H. F. B. Brett-Smith (1858; repr. London: Henry Frowde, 1909), 39–40.

[96] Clairmont, *Journals*, 83–5. *Mary Shelley's Journal*, ed. Frederick L. Jones (Oklahoma: University of Oklahoma Press, 1947), 80.

[97] *Letters of Mary W. Shelley (Mostly Unpublished)* (Boston, 1918), 52 (Leghorn 13 May 1818).

(18 May 1817; 17 August 1817; 19 April 1818), as well as a performance of the Drury Lane Christmas pantomime, *Harlequin's Vision; or, The Feast of the Statue* for *The Examiner* (11 January 1818). In a later letter to the Hunts, Mary Shelley demonstrated their continuing familiarity with the opera: she referred without contextual explanation to the opening aria of *Don Giovanni*, Leporello's 'Notte e giorno faticar' (27 July 1823).[98]

Shelley's introduction to and passion for Mozart thus occurred between periods spent abroad in Byron's company: in June–August 1816 Byron and Shelley first became acquainted by the shores of Lake Geneva and Shelley visited Byron at intervals during August–October 1818 in Venice. This latter period coincided with the first months of the composition of *Don Juan*: the manuscript of Canto I was marked by Byron as having been written between 3 July and 6 September 1818.[99] Although no existing records prove that the legend of Don Juan, Mozart's opera *Don Giovanni*, or any of the other burlesques, pantomimes, and farces on the subject of Don Juan were discussed by Byron and the Shelleys, it is probable that they were so.

The only explicit reference by Byron to Mozart's opera is that given to explain his interruption in writing the poem: 'Someone has possessed the Guiccioli with a notion that my Don Juan and the Don Giovanni of the opera are the same person; and to please her I have discontinued his history and adventures.'[100] Jerome McGann noted that Byron's mockery of opera in *English Bards and Scotch Reviewers* (1809) must have been at least partly affectation, and that 'in any case, he was an avid opera-goer during his years in Italy'. While this is certainly the case, no research has as yet fully ascertained which specific operas Byron did see or could have seen during his years there.[101] This history of the legend has demonstrated the particular association be-

---

[98] *The Letters of Mary Wollstonecraft Shelley*, 2 vols. (Baltimore and London: Johns Hopkins University Press, 1980), i. 353, letter to Leigh and Marianne Hunt (27 July 1823).

[99] *Complete Poetical Works*, v. (1986), 663.

[100] *Medwin's Conversations with Lord Byron: Noted during a residence with His Lordship at Pisa, in the Years 1821–1822*, ed. Ernest J. Lovell (Princeton: Princeton University Press, 1966), 164.

[101] *Complete Poetical Works*, v. (1986), 705: Canto IV, l. 700. In *Shelley and his Circle: 1773–1822*, ed. Donald Reiman (Cambridge, Mass.: Harvard University Press, 1986), vii, some details of opera performances in Venice are noted (p. 173).

tween Don Juan operas of the late eighteenth century and
Venice, but this did not include Mozart and da Ponte's version.
Teresa's comparison might refer, for example, to the Bertati/
Gazzaniga opera of the same name which was intimately linked
with Venice. In the penultimate scene, Don Giovanni and
Pasquariello raise a toast to Venice, and especially to Venetian
women (although other praises of the city are introduced to
further the claim).[102] Byron, as a foreigner in Venice, and as
with his visit to Spain in 1809, at a time of heightened nationalism and local pride, might have known the popular aria
even if he did not see a complete performance.

The narrator of *Don Juan* slyly connects the hero with
Mozart's Don Giovanni and his ability to fit his charms to the
occasion:

> . . . He danced and sung and had
> An air as sentimental as Mozart's
> Softest of melodies and could be sad
> Or cheerful without any 'flaws or starts'
> Just at the proper time . . .

(XI, 47)

That such references were made obliquely may be an indication
of the reader's familiarity with the figure in his most famous
incarnation. That the obliqueness was a deliberate ploy can be
seen in the humour which it creates, a humour which relies
upon, while also drawing attention to, the shared knowledge of
the narrator and his readers. The very openness of the secret is
flaunted: 'though young—I see, Sir—you | Have got a travell'd
air, which shows you one | To whom the opera is by no means
new' (IV, 88). Similarly, during the siege of Ismail Don Juan is
described in passing as 'a child of song' (VIII, 24) and because
Byron's readers would have known of the legendary figure
mostly through musical genres, their interpretation of such an

---

However the editor adds: 'We have made no attempt to collect all Byron's references to the musical and theatrical performances he attended during his time in
Venice' (175 n. 35).

[102] Bertati, *Don Giovanni*, booklet for Orfeo Recording (C 214 902 H), tr. Lionel
Salter (1990), e.g. scene, 23: Pasquariello: 'With pleasure I raise a toast | To
matchless Venice | The heart of Augustus | is precisely to be found in the men; | in
the civil order | there is the utmost kindness | and even the lower classes | are good-
hearted and well-mannered.'

apparently 'innocent' statement would have made it one of implication. Because of the allusiveness of the legend, and the reader's predisposition to remember other Don Juans, it does not seem entirely fanciful to imagine the description of the baritone on board the ship Juan takes from Greece as the sort of baritone to play Don Giovanni:

> A pretty lad, but bursting with conceit . . .
> Forsooth, scarce fit for ballads in the street.
> In lovers' parts his passion more to breathe,
> Having no heart to show, he shews his teeth.

> (IV, 89)

The reader might have understood the second of these lines as referring to Don Giovanni's serenade to a servant girl in the window above, 'Deh vieni alla finestra', one of only three solo arias by Mozart's Don Giovanni.

Two further publications concerning the Don Juan legend of these years remain to be considered—Lady Caroline Lamb's *Glenarvon* (1816) and Coleridge's 'Critique of *Bertram*' (1816). These shall now be discussed at greater length because both are illustrative of the biographical and political implications of the choice of Don Juan which will be important throughout this book.

GLENARVON

In 1816 Lady Caroline Lamb published *Glenarvon*, a novel which has been described by Peter Graham (1990) as 'an English version of the Don Juan myth told from a woman's viewpoint'.[103] The description seems just. Certainly Glenarvon charms every woman in the novel, while proclaiming the imperviousness of his own heart:

Wherever he appeared, new beauty attracted his worship, and yielded to his power; yet he valued not the transient possession, even whilst smiling upon the credulous being who had believed in his momentary affection. Even whilst soothing her with promises and vows, which he meant not for one hour to perform, he was seeking the means of extricating himself from her power.[104]

---

[103] Graham, Don Juan *and Regency England*, 9. See also ch. 4, 'A Don, Two Lords, and a Lady'.

His seductions include the otherwise formidable Elinor St Clare who has lived in a convent since her birth, and who thus has affinities with Molière's Done Elvira who returned to confront Dom Juan from her convent. The married Lady Calantha is likewise seduced by his tender professions of love—and subsequently abandoned. The allusive presence of the Don Juan legend remains throughout, but it is especially apparent in the depiction of Glenarvon's death. 'Visions of punishment and hell pursued him', as he hears a voice address him:

Hardened and impenitent sinner! the measure of your iniquity is full: the price of crime has been paid: here shall your spirit dwell for ever, and for ever. You have dreamed away life's joyous hour, nor made atonement for error, nor denied yourself aught that the fair earth presented you. You did not controul the fiend in your bosom, or stifle him in his first growth: he now has mastered you, and brought you here: and you did not bow the knee for mercy whilst time was given you: now mercy shall not be shewn. O, cry upwards from these lower pits, to the friends and companions you have left, to the sinner who hardens himself against his Creator—who basks in the ray of prosperous guilt, not dreams that his hour like your's is at hand. Tell him how terrible a thing is death; how fearful at such an hour is remembrance of the past. Bid him repent, but he shall not hear you. Bid him amend, but like you he shall delay till it is too late.[105]

This is certainly evocative of the traditional legend's didacticism and its condemnation of an evasive immorality which continually postpones repentance.

Byron was soon told of this novel's publication, and he was also quick to read it, because of its obviously biographical intent. It was rumoured for example that the letter Glenarvon sent to Lady Calantha in which he announced his desertion of her—'I am no longer your lover . . .'—was reproduced *verbatim* from that which Byron had sent to Lady Caroline in November 1812. Indeed early readers of the novel identified the fictional with real characters by entering a 'key' on the flyleaves of their copies. *Don Juan* itself includes a covert reference to this epi-

---

[104] Lady Caroline Lamb, *Glenarvon* (1816), *Revolution and Romanticism 1789–1834* (Oxford and New York: Woodstock Books, 1993), ii. 93, ch. 9.
[105] Ibid. iii. 320–1.

sode: 'Some [women] play the devil, and then write a novel' (II, 201).[106]

This publication is important because it demonstrates how scandalous Byron's reputation was after 1816. Deserted by his wife for unmentionable reasons, involved in continuing affairs, publishing a selection of poetry which was received as being a combination of moral and political subversion, Byron was notoriously vilified by the English press and public. André Maurois in his biography of Byron recounted how in 1816 the Tory journals compared Byron to Nero, Heliogabalus, Henry VIII, and the devil. These accusations do not, however, include the archetypal figure whom this Byron most clearly did resemble— although Maurois himself implicitly acknowledged the connection in entitling his book *Don Juan, ou la vie de Byron*.[107] And in *Ada Reis* (1823), Caroline Lamb described the protagonist, who was again recognizably a representation of Byron, as 'the Don Juan of his day'.[108] Byron's reputation as a Don Juan is also evident in two drawings by Cruikshank: 'Fare Thee Well' portrays Byron declaiming the poem on board a boat to the disappearing figures of his wife and child on shore, while he embraces three rather immodestly dressed women, two of whom lewdly embrace his thighs and 'The Separation: a sketch from the Private Life of *Lord IRON* who panegyrized his wife, and satirized her confidante!!', in which Byron is depicted with his arm around Mrs Mardyn, an actress with whom he was reputed to have had an affair.[109]

[106] For the letter, see Lamb, *Glenarvon*, iii. 81–3. For Byron's partial acknowledgement of the letter as his own, see Lovell (ed.), *Medwin's Conversations*, ii. 79. One example of a biographical key is reprinted in Lady Seymour, *The Pope of Holland House* (London: Fisher & Unwin, 1906).

[107] André Maurois, *Byron: Don Juan, ou la vie de Byron*, 2 vols. (Paris: Bernard Grasset, 1930), ii. 59.

[108] Quoted in Bernard Grebanier, *The Uninhibited Byron: An Account of his Sexual Confusion* (London: Peter Owen, 1971), 147. Byron dramatized himself as the two-timing Macheath in a letter to Douglas Kinnaird (20 Jan. 1817), *Byron's Letters and Journals*, v. 162. One of Caroline Lamb's names for Byron in a letter to him (3 June 1814) was 'Valmont'—see George Paston and Peter Quennell, '*To Lord Byron*': *Feminine Profiles Based upon Unpublished Letters, 1807–1824* (London: John Murray, 1939), 63. Compare Mary Shelley's implicit comparison of Byron to Don Giovanni in describing Fletcher as a 'Leporello': *The Letters of Mary Wollstonecraft Shelley*, i. 437 (letter to Edward John Trelawney, 28 July 1824).

[109] Cruikshank's 'Fare Thee Well' is reproduced in Joanna Richardson (ed.), *Lord Byron and Some of his Contemporaries* (London: The Folio Society, 1988), 109. 'The Separation' is reproduced in Grebanier, *The Uninhibited Byron*, 294.

Certainly the caution urged by Byron's friends concerning the publication of *Don Juan* was a consequence of the anticipated biographical readings which, it was feared, would automatically ensue. Hobhouse advised that the 'half real hero' of *Don Juan* would only ruin Byron's reputation as a man, and as a poet. His letters on the subject reflected the unanimity among Byron's circle of friends: 'But do not do it [publish]—all the stories about your Venetian life will be more than confirmed, they will be exaggerated . . . I am not preaching to you of the deeds themselves but merely of the inexpediency of even appearing to make a boast of them' (5 January 1819).[110] Byron however had already been boasting—he wrote to James Wedderburn Webster that he had enjoyed 200 ('—perhaps more— for I have not lately kept the recount') conquests in Venice (letter of 8 September 1818). His letter to Hobhouse and Kinnaird of 19 January 1819 narrated his own 'catalogue', which, like the 'catholic' tastes of the legendary Don Juan, emphasized its inclusiveness: 'some of them are Countesses—& some of them Cobblers wives'.[111]

What his friends did not consider however, was that Byron not only anticipated such an interpretation, but had partly chosen the figure of Don Juan for this very reason. That Byron himself understood and provoked the biographical reading is evident from *Donna Josepha: A Fragment of a Skit on the Separation* (1817). This is a short fragment of the novel which Byron was working on simultaneously with the first Cantos of *Don Juan*.[112] It is largely a transcription of the events of his wife's separation from him in 1816 into a Spanish setting. Lady Byron becomes Donna Josepha; her father Sir Ralph Milbanke becomes Don José di Cardozo; London becomes, significantly, Seville; and Kirkby Mallory, the Milbankes' home in Leicestershire, Arragon. The narrator's condemnation of himself, albeit ironically, in the phrase —'all Spain could produce nobody so blameable'—is reminiscent of Don Juan Mañara (whose tombstone at Seville was notoriously engraved *Aquí yace el peor hombre que fué en el mundo*). And the threatened punishment—'little

[110] Peter W. Graham (ed.), *Byron's Bulldog* (Columbus, Ohio: Ohio State University Press, 1984), p. 258 (5 Jan. 1819).
[111] *Byron's Letters and Journals*, vi. 66 and 92.
[112] See Byron, *Miscellaneous Prose*, nn. 346–8.

less than an auto-da-fé'—reinforces the impression of seven-
teenth-century Spain, contemporaneous with the 'original'
Don Juan.[113]

Clearly this biographical imperative was one reason for
Byron's choice of the figure of Don Juan. However, as this
chapter has demonstrated, the often ambivalent legend did not
offer a certain tradition of interpretation but rather a compli-
cation of responses. This history of the versions is important for
the moral and political considerations raised by Coleridge's
response to the legend, a response which is far from, though it
is disguised as being, typical. The influence of Coleridge's essay
in turn is crucial because it demonstrates how Byron was reacting against one type of reading of the legend and that Byron's
work itself was to a great extent inspired by an *interpretation*
of the legend.

COLERIDGE'S 'CRITIQUE OF *BERTRAM*'

A significant influence upon Byron's choice of Don Juan
was undoubtedly Coleridge's 'Critique of *Bertram*', first published as a series of five letters to *The Courier* between 29 August
and 11 September 1816 and subsequently published as an
additional chapter in *Biographia Literaria* in 1817.[114] Coleridge
compares Charles Maturin's play *Bertram* unfavourably with
the Spanish play of Don Juan and devotes much of the essay
to praising the traditional play, quoting extensively from
Shadwell's *The Libertine*, or rather from a pantomime closely
based upon the play.

Coleridge's essay is yet another attempt to explain the
phenomenal popularity of the figure and to give this curiosity concerning such a populist figure some respectability:
'A popularity so extensive, and of a work so grotesque and
extravagant, claims and merits philosophical attention
and investigation.'[115] Although he applauds the thrilling treat-

---

[113] See Byron, *Miscellaneous Prose*, 77–8 and 346–8 nn.
[114] This influence has been widely acknowledged. See e.g.: Boyd, *Byron's* Don
Juan, 36–7; *Complete Poetical Works*, v. (1986), note on Canto I, st. 1, l. 7; Michael
Foot, *The Politics of Paradise* (London: William Collins, 1988), 226; Caroline
Franklin, *Byron's Heroines* (Oxford: Clarendon Press, 1992), 99: Neil Barry, *The
Times Literary Supplement* (23 Jan. 1987).

ment of the figure, Coleridge really uses the example of the play to applaud its intended moral value and deride the present 'spirit of modern jacobinism' which he claims is apparent in *Bertram* (p. 229). The charge of immorality, as a result of the English interpretation of and counter-propaganda against the French Revolution, had become a political accusation. We would certainly expect Byron to react to such arguments. He himself had been a victim of such twinning disrepute in 1816. The publication of *Lord Byron's Poems On His Own Domestic Circumstances* (1816), with its inclusion of poems both personal—'Fare Thee Well', 'A Sketch from Private Life'—and political—'On the Star of the Legion of Honour' and other poems ostensibly 'from the French'—was reviewed by *The Champion* (14 and 28 April 1816) as exhibiting the connection between domestic and political conduct, commonly conflated in the accusation of 'French morals'.[116]

In addition (perhaps one might say, as always), there was a personal stimulus. Maturin's *Bertram* had been preferred by the Drury Lane committee to Coleridge's own *Zapolya* and Byron had been one of the committee members at that time. Indeed, Byron had strenuously supported Maturin in a personal capacity. So far as we know, Byron only gave his unconditional support to two new plays during his membership of the sub-committee for Drury Lane: Maturin's *Bertram* and William Sotheby's *Ivan*.[117] This last was never staged at Drury Lane though it was performed at Covent-Garden. *Bertram* however was performed at Drury Lane and its first night was given on 9 May 1816, three weeks after Byron left England. The play was, by the standards of its time, very successful: it was performed twenty-two times that season and the text ran into seven editions before the end of 1816.[118] And Byron enquired after its fortune with interest in Italy.

---

[115] *The Collected Works of Samuel Taylor Coleridge*, ed. Walter Engell and W. Jackson Bate, 16 vols. (Princeton: Princeton University Press, 1983), vii. *Biographia Literaria: II*, 212–13. Future references are from this edn. and are quoted in the text.

[116] Quoted in *Shelley and his Circle: 1773–1822*, ed. K. N. Cameron (Cambridge, Mass.: Harvard University Press, 1970), iv. 643.

[117] However, prior to his membership of the Committee, Byron had supported Coleridge's *Remorse* which was finally produced in Drury Lane in 1813.

[118] Richard Lansdown, *Byron's Historical Dramas* (Oxford: Clarendon Press, 1992), 36.

Maturin's Bertram was a recognizably Byronic hero, for example, in the Prior's description:

> High-hearted man, sublime even in thy guilt;
> Whose passions are thy crimes, whose angel-sin
> Is pride that rivals the star-bright apostate's—
> Wild admiration thrills me to behold
> An evil strength, so above earthly pitch—
> Descending angels only could reclaim thee.[119]

Predictably, the charge of Maturin's literary borrowing from Byron was pervasive among the periodical reviewers.[120] And the misrecognition of the Byronic hero was also made by contemporary audiences who mistook the appearance of Byronic style as equivalent to his signature. When Hobhouse wrote to Byron on 26 May 1816 about the début of *Bertram* at Drury Lane, for which event he had expressly visited London, he recounted how the audience confidently attributed its authorship to Byron:

From the outset there was a notion that the play was yours—and these lines in the prologue,

> *Through dark misfortune's gloom condemn'd to cope*
> *With baffled effort and with blighted hope*

occasioned a great allusive roar—as if forsooth there was no greater misfortune in life tha[n] being left at peace to take a tour up the banks of the Rhine.[121]

This excerpt also reflects the issue raised in the consideration of *Glenarvon*—namely, the extent to which biographical readings of Byron's work were exacerbated after the scandal of 1816 and his removal from England, and by an increasingly antagonistic public.

Reviews of the 'Critique of *Bertram*' in both *Blackwood's Edinburgh Magazine* (October 1817) and the *Edinburgh Review* (August 1817) were highly censorious, accusing Coleridge of jealousy and envy. The review in the *Edinburgh Review* is especially interesting in that it adopts the metaphor of the sensualist

---

[119] Revd. Charles Maturin, *Bertram; or the Castle of Maldobrand* (London: John Murray, 1816), Act III, scene 1. p. 41.

[120] See *The Monitor: A Collection of Essays on Various Subjects*, 20/1 (Simpkin & Marshall, 1817), 125.

[121] Graham (ed.), *Byron's Bulldog*, 221.

whose repentance is only a hypocritical screen for masochistic delights:

The cant of Morality, like the cant of Methodism, comes in most naturally to close the scene: and as the regenerated sinner keeps alive his old raptures and new-acquired horrors, by anticipating endless ecstasies or endless torments in another world; so, our disappointed demagogue keeps up that 'pleasurable poetic fervour' which has been the cordial and the bane of his existence, by indulging his maudlin egotism and mawkish spleen in fulsome eulogies of his own virtues, and nauseous abuse of his contemporaries.[122]

Coleridge's stance of moral fervour is thus translated into a self-indulgence which is not dissimilar from the figure whom he defends. Of course, Coleridge defends Don Juan only because his ultimate punishment demonstrates a condemnation of his lifestyle, however appealing the process of that life might have appeared when enacted on the stage. *Don Juan* is regarded as moral and *Bertram* as 'jacobinical' because in the latter the immorality of the character appears to be applauded. (Bertram commits suicide, robbing any power, human or supernatural, of the privilege of meting out justice.) However, as we have seen, contemporary versions of the legend were themselves to deal more sympathetically with the once-villain, but now potential hero, Don Juan.

That the figure of Don Juan was a test-case for moral-political debate is apparent in Hazlitt's singling out of the legend in his criticism of Jeremy Collier's *A Short View of the Immorality and Profaneness of the Stage*:

He does not think it enough that the stage 'shows vice its own image, scorn its own feature', unless they are damned at the same instant, and carried off (like Don Juan) by real devils to the infernal regions, before the faces of the spectators. It seems that the author would have been contented to be present at a comedy or a farce, like a Father Inquisitor, if there was to be an *auto da fé* at the end, to burn both the actors and the poet.[123]

Hazlitt's argument is that an extraneously added ending of moral righteousness can only be a sop to convention which

---

[122] *Edinburgh Review*, 56 (Aug. 1817), 488–516, 515.
[123] Hazlitt, *Complete Works*, vi. 90.

excuses the pleasure enjoyed in the wickedness itself. An audience which delights in the exploits of Don Juan and then unquestioningly delights in his punishment is an audience unaware of its own act of hypocrisy.

That Byron was roused by Coleridge's attack is evident in his letter to John Murray from Italy on the subject.[124] It is also evident in *Don Juan*, in which Byron, like Hazlitt, would attempt to explain to the English public the inconsistency of their moral code. The poem proposes an analogous example to the reception of Don Juan in that of St Augustine's *Confessions*: 'Which make the reader envy his transgressions' (I, 47), transgressions which were enticing *because* they were forbidden. The concerted campaign against Byron was consolidated with Coleridge's claim in the pages of *The Courier* in August 1816, just before the articles on *Bertram*, that Byron had reached new heights of immorality by failing to punish his transgressive heroes. The figure of Don Juan was just such a hero. In choosing the legendary figure of Don Juan, Byron adopted a theme which had already proved to be highly problematic. It had been applauded by moral censors as worthy didacticism. English examples of this tradition included those who defended the Restoration stage from the accusations of Jeremy Collier and the eighteenth-century 6*d.* chapbook. And in the early nineteenth century this tradition was maintained by Coleridge. However, the figure had also been applauded by audiences who were undoubtedly seduced by the charisma and sheer theatricality of the figure. The same version of the legend which is morally applauded by Coleridge was described by Hazlitt as exhibiting 'the spirit of licentiousness and impiety'.[125] It is this ambivalence which Byron exploited. *The Gentleman's Magazine* (January 1822) reviewed *Don Juan* Cantos III–V by referring to its concern over traditional stage versions of the legend. It significantly did not distinguish between those versions and that of Byron:

For our part, we never could vindicate the taste with which Don Juan has been brought upon our stage, and heartily wish that it had from

---

[124] *Byron's Letters and Journals*, v. 267 (12 Oct. 1817).
[125] Hazlitt, *Complete Works*, vi. 54.

the first been prohibited by the Lord Chamberlain. It seems to us just
as disgusting as fitting up a charnel-house like Vauxhall; as taking
the history of the villanies, debaucheries, murders, trial, execution,
and judgement after death of an accomplished impenitent criminal, and decorating these horrors with all the fairy charms of pleasurable and attractive embellishments, the awful sympathy excited by a
ghost, and the sportive tricks of an ingenious buffoon. This jumble
may be accounted for, first, by its derivation from the middle ages,
having been first written under the title of 'El combidado de Piedra' by
Tirso de Molina; and secondly by its being in the Spanish taste ...[126]

This chapter has shown how Byron was not alone in aesthe-
ticizing and even defending the scandalous libertine. Increasingly, theatrical representations of the legend were
exonerating and reforming the 'hero'—and in this context
the designation is not incongruous. Although Byron did not
witness these productions, he did partake of the same impulse to explain and at least partially defend the previously
designated 'villain'.

Myth-critics usually invoke E. T. A. Hoffmann's *Don Juan*
(1813) as an example of the heroization or defence of the
legendary seducer. It is a tale of a traveller who watches a
performance of Mozart's *Don Giovanni* from an opera box. After
the performance he is visited by the ghostly presence of Donna
Anna who tells of her secret love for Don Giovanni. This story
also epitomizes an increasing tendency of the variations in explicitly acknowledging that the legend is being interpreted
rather than merely retold. This was evident in Alonso Cordova
y Maldonado's short-hand method of narrating the exploits of
Don Juan, but it is also implicit in all of the variations which
make their own adjustments to the legend. Mozart and da
Ponte were succeeding to Gazzaniga and others; later Zorrilla
would consciously write his *refundición* of Zamora and Tirso de
Molina, *Don Juan Tenorio* (1844); and George Sand would write
her feminist interpretation of the male 'myth' in *Lélia* (1833).
As Lévi-Strauss's work defended a more generous definition of
'myth' in posing the question of what kind of analysis of the
Oedipus myth would refuse to include Freud, so too these
'reinterpretations' are versions in their own right.

[126] *The Gentleman's Magazine*, 92/1 (Jan. 1822), 48–50.

Because audiences and readers were fully aware of divergences and reaffirmations, they were not excluded from the full implications of any new version. This public debate secured the legend's political nature. Indeed, the very popularity and familiarity of the legend entailed that all of the public was enabled to engage in this dialogue—an unusual feat in centuries in which most of the population (that is the lower classes and most women of all classes) were excluded from cultural debate. This dissemination merely compounds the already intrinsically political nature of the legend. This chapter has begun to recreate those debates in suggesting versions which might have inspired both Byron's and his readers' *reactions* to his poem, *Don Juan*.

2
Byron's Don Juan

Those critics who have dismissed the significance of the Don Juan legend to Byron's poem have usually done so for one reason: they have interpreted Byron's Don Juan as being so unlike the traditional seducer that extended comparison between the two is judged to be futile. They view Byron's Don Juan as innocent, naïve, vulnerable to the initiating passions of the women he meets, relatively chaste, and of basically good intentions.[1] Countless examples of this interpretation could be cited because it is assumed throughout twentieth-century criticism of Byron's *Don Juan*. Anne Barton's recent book, *Byron:* Don Juan (1992), for example, continues the critical tradition of the impeccable Don Juan: 'a Don Juan who is gentle, tender-hearted and, although amorous, forever being seduced by women rather than seducing, with none of the traits of his treacherous archetype'.[2]

It is this understanding of Don Juan's character which is most directly contrary to the comments and reviews of Byron's contemporaries. Indeed, the differences between the respective critical interpretations are so striking that the historical perspective of altered social values is insufficient to explain them. While it is true that *Don Juan* was written at a time of increased moral conservatism—a time when Dr Bowdler petitioned Parliament for increased penalties for adulterers with the fire-breathing oratory of such statements as, 'With regard to adultery . . . as it was punished capitally by the Jewish law, some think it ought to be so . . . among us'—the

---

[1] Examples include: Leslie A. Marchand, *Byron: A Biography* (London: John Murray, 1958), ii. 750; Claude Bergerolle, 'Révolte sexuelle et liberté individuelle dans le "Don Juan"', in *Romantisme: Revue de la Société des Études romantiques*, 7 (1974), 44–59, 48. See also introduction and notes.

[2] Anne Barton, *Byron:* Don Juan (Cambridge: Cambridge University Press, 1992), 3.

differences cannot entirely be so accounted for. It is the very
character who is discussed, not the judgement itself, which is
altogether different.[3]

Contemporary reviews display their own unanimity in
interpreting Byron's Don Juan as the traditional, amoral Don
Juan of legend. Hobhouse for example spoke continually
of 'the Rake Juan' and the belated review of *Don Juan*, Cantos
I–II, in *The Investigator* (October 1821) illustrates the reviewers'
dislike of the character: 'Don Juan, the hero of his lordship's
tale, is as complete a rake, as entire a sensualist, as the world
ever saw, or the prurient imagination of the most abandoned
writer ever formed, or could form, in its wildest fits.'[4] The dating
of this review suggests that this interpretation was not reserved
to the early reception of the poem but continued even after
Byron's attempt to 'tame' subsequent Cantos, particularly in
the Don Juan–Haidée episode of Cantos III–IV. The reviewer
of *The Literary Chronicle* in the same year wrote of Cantos
III–V: 'The volume now before us is a continuation of the
adventures of that vivacious libertine, Don Juan.'[5] Although in
this example Don Juan is praised as 'vivacious', the epithet of
'libertine' represents the more constant accusation of the
reviewers. *The Ladies' Monthly Museum* (January–February
1822), for example, described the poem as retelling 'the exploits of a libertine' and the review of Cantos I–II in *The Literary
Gazette* (17 July 1819) depicted Don Juan as much more villainous than the work itself would seem to authenticate: 'Even when
we blame the too great laxity of the poet, we cannot but feel
a high admiration of his talent. Far superior to the libertine
he paints, fancifulness and gaiety gilds his worst errors, and
no brute force is employed to overthrow innocence.'[6] Of
course, it might be argued that the libertine referred to is not
Byron's own but a prototypical character. Yet the review illustrates the automatic association between the text and the reader's preconception of the legendary figure. It ironically

---

[3] Quoted in E. P. Thompson, *The Making of the English Working Class*
(Harmondsworth: Pelican, 1963), 443.

[4] Peter W. Graham (ed.), *Byron's Bulldog* (Columbus, Ohio: Ohio State University
Press, 1984), 258 (5 Jan. 1819). *The Investigator*, 3 (Oct. 1821), 353–60, 357.

[5] *The Literary Chronicle* (11 Aug. 1821), 495–7, 495.

[6] *The Ladies' Monthly Museum* (Jan.–Feb. 1822), 86–91, 90. *The Literary Gazette* (17
July 1819), 449–51, 451.

juxtaposes the writer who insidiously charms and seduces his readers, with the Don Juan who rapes, because the latter has at least the 'virtue' of openness. This review illustrates both how the interpretation of Don Juan was often a matter of the reader's own perversity and how that interpretation was thoroughly political. Although this review in the notoriously Tory *Literary Gazette* represents an extreme instance of this, it clearly demonstrates how it is the reader who to some extent creates Byron's Don Juan.

This at least begins to explain the considerable divergence between the contemporary and modern readings of the character. Modern readers tend to underestimate Don Juan's rakish qualities, often because they neglect the poem's extensive use of innuendo, either because the sexual innuendo is no longer current or because they do not realize how the most apparently 'innocent' of statements was interpreted more sceptically by the contemporary reader. What differentiates our reading from our Regency predecessors is the missing context of the Don Juan legend, the cause of continuing controversy. In forgetting the poem's interaction with a subject of public and popular discussion, we no longer recognize the political import of a work which was consciously written both in imitation and in subversion of an existing tradition. This chapter applies the context of the legend to Byron's poem and thus begins to uncover the contemporary responses to the poem as demonstrations of the debate which has been neglected by modern criticism—the interpretation and judgement of the legendary Don Juan.

THE CONTEMPORARY RECEPTION OF *DON JUAN*

'Our readers will . . . be surprised at our thus bringing to their notice Don Juan, of which the very name is construed to be the watchword of Licentiousness.'[7] The 'very name' of *Don Juan* was sufficient to scare the Newcastle Literary and Philosophical Society: when the first two Cantos were published on 15 July 1819, the Society ordered the work to be removed from its

---

[7] *The Gentleman's Magazine*, 92/1 (Jan. 1822), 48–50, review of Cantos III–V.

library as an immoral publication.[8] Some booksellers refused to
handle the book, including Murray's Scottish distributor,
William Blackwood of Edinburgh, who had benefited from Byron's earlier publishing successes.[9] The precipitousness of these
actions suggests that the work was banned even before a first
reading—a fear which the poem itself acknowledges and attempts, in vain, to prevent.[10] Certainly Murray exploited the
sensationalism of the title in the manner of the work's advance
publicity. Advertisements in the newspapers merely announced:
'In a few days, DON JUAN'. Hobhouse wrote to Byron of this
sensational marketing: 'And now I shall go to London this day
to hear what the world say—you may depend upon a great
sensation—It was announced thus: *Don Juan . . . to morrow* [twice
underlined]. There's a way for you!! *To morrow* [twice under-
lined] *The Comet! to morrow!*'[11] Hobhouse's letters also demonstrate how successful the commercial appeal of the title alone
proved to be. Many bought up *Mazeppa*, which was deliberately
published early by Murray, mistakenly thinking that they were
buying the advertised volume of *Don Juan*, the 'mysterious' work
which rivalled the imminent comet in the portentousness of its
announcement.[12]

    The periodical reviewers were duly alarmed—'merely' by the
title: 'Don Juan (as the title might lead one to expect) is a tissue
of all immoralities' (*The Champion*, 25 July 1819); 'The very
title, "Don Juan", furnishes but too much reason for a conviction that the author selected the progress of a *Libertine* as a fit
vehicle for licentious description' (*New Monthly Magazine*, August 1819); 'The very subject of the tale is censurable' (*The
Literary Chronicle*, 24 July 1819).[13] Although the currency of the

    [8] See Samuel C. Chew, *Byron in England* (London: John Murray, 1924), 28, and
William Ruddick, 'Byron and England', in Paul Graham Trueblood (ed.), *Byron's
Political and Cultural Influence in Nineteenth-Century Europe* (London: Macmillan,
1981), 25–47, 27.
    [9] William St Clair, 'The Impact of Byron's Writings: An Evaluative Approach', in
Andrew Rutherford (ed.), *Byron: Augustan and Romantic* (London: Macmillan,
1990), 1–25, 14.
    [10] See e.g. *Don Juan*, I, 207; IV, 7; XII, 87.
    [11] Graham (ed.), *Byron's Bulldog*, 275–6 (15 July 1819). Hobhouse collapses
notices in *The Morning Chronicle* concerning *Don Juan* with daily reports called
'Authentic Observations of the Comet'.
    [12] Ibid. 276.
    [13] *The Champion* (25 July 1819), 472–3, 472. *The New Monthly Magazine*, 12 (Aug.
1819), 75–8, 78. *The Literary Chronicle* (24 July 1819), 147–9, 149.

Don Juan legend was undoubtedly pervasive, this did not prevent the reviewers' hostility, but rather caused its influence to be feared. The burlesque of *Giovanni the Vampire*, for example, ironically justified its performance as an attempt to prevent all others. The apparently contradictory claim in its playbill (January 1821) was a facetious attempt to anticipate and encourage moral approbation: 'to preclude the Possibility of his Adventures being extended by other Pens, is the design of the present Production, and will doubtless meet the hearty Concurrence of the Suppressors of Vice, whether officially or privately situated, to whom it is most respectfully dedicated by the Author.'

And because this statement formed part of its advertisement, the hint of indecorous immorality was presumably part of its attraction. Indeed the playbill for the Don Juan play at the Adelphi Theatre (15 January 1821) used the legend's controversial notoriety as a bait to entice audiences. It declared that the theatre had put on the production only because it was the sole theatre which had not done so—a familiar argument, as the considerations of the versions of Villiers, Rosimond, and Gazzaniga/Bertati in Chapter 1 demonstrated. The playbill thus argued 'that they have been instigated by no paltry spirit of opposition to a LARGER *though not more respectable concern*' (my italics). When the later Cantos of Byron's *Don Juan* were sold in cheap editions, *Blackwood's Edinburgh Magazine* (July 1823) disdained its popularity by claiming: 'of course, it has all the advantage of being believed to be a licentious thing'.[14] The 'licentious' subject of Don Juan compounded the scandal of its cheap price and aroused prurient curiosities.

Since Don Juan had become a figure of scandalous notoriety, a contemporary reader could not have approached the text with any degree of detachment or neutrality. In direct contrast to the disregard of the legend by twentieth-century criticism, a great many of the contemporary reviewers did make particular reference to the Don Juan of popular tradition. Those of *The Miniature Magazine* (October 1819) and *The Gentleman's Magazine* (January 1822) have already been cited for their avowals of the

---

[14] *Blackwood's Edinburgh Magazine*, 14 (July 1823), review of Cantos VI–VIII, pp. 88–92, 92.

history of the legend (see Chapter 1). *The Literary Gazette* (17
July 1819) dispensed with such an introduction because 'the
hero is well known by means of play, opera, and pantomime'; as
did *The Literary Chronicle* (17 July 1819): 'The story of Don Juan,
or the Libertine, is one with which all classes, in all countries,
are familiar'; and *The Monthly Review* (July 1819): 'Our Opera-
house and other theatres have made Don Juan, the libertine,
perfectly familiar to the British public.'[15] In all, seventeen periodicals invoked the theatrical Don Juan legend in their reviews
of Byron's poem between 1819 and 1823, and many more
referred consistently to the character of Don Juan as that of a
libertine.[16] Even the common abbreviation of 'the Don', frequently used in reviews of *Don Juan*, demonstrates the figure's
familiarity. Byron's opening denomination of Don Juan as 'our
hero' was therefore neither far-fetched nor new: Charles Lamb
had also spoken thus of the figure in his review of *Giovanni in
London*. It is certainly interesting that the reviewers' references
to the legendary figure did not entirely disappear after the
publication of the first two Cantos, so that evidently something
other than 'just' the title is at issue.

The history of the legend, while demonstrating that versions
had often been subject to censorship, does not allege that the
legend itself was intrinsically objectionable. *El burlador* was written by a monk as a didactic morality play. Many commentators,
from those Restoration writers who defended the stage from
Collier's strictures to Coleridge's more contemporary disapproval of *Bertram*, urged the moral efficacy of the Don Juan
legend. However, there was also a tradition of rendering the

---

[15] *The Literary Gazette* (17 July 1819), 449–51, 443. *The Literary Chronicle* (17
July 1819), 129–30, 129. *The Monthly Review*, 2nd ser. 99 (July 1819), 309–
21, 315.
[16] *The Literary Gazette* (17 July 1819); *The Literary Chronicle* (17 July 1819);
The Champion (25 July 1819); *The European Magazine*, 76 (July 1819) 53–6; *The
Monthly Magazine* (Aug. 1819); *The New Monthly Magazine* (Aug. 1819); *The Literary
Chronicle* (11 Aug. 1819); *The Miniature Magazine* (Oct. 1819); *The Examiner* (31 Oct.
1819), 700–3; *The Edinburgh Monthly Review*, 2 (Oct. 1819) 468–86; *The Monthly
Magazine*, 52 (Sept. 1821), 124–9; *The Investigator*, 3 (Oct. 1821), 353–60; *The
Gentleman's Magazine*, 92/1 (Jan. 1822), 48–50; *The Literary Examiner* (5 July 1823),
6–12; *British Critic* (Aug. 1823). The parodies of Byron's *Don Juan* also frequently
made the legendary context of the poem explicit, e.g. Alfred Thornton, *Don Juan*
(1821) and its sequel, *Don Juan: Volume the Second, Containing his Life in London*
(1822).

Don sympathetic—indeed the contemporary versions of the burlesques, parodies, and pantomimes were beginning to forgive the 'hero' in conformity with their comic status. The outcry which greeted Byron's *Don Juan* and its choice of subject was therefore not solely the consequence of the legend itself but specifically of Byron's adoption of it. It was not only a question of the contemporary reader's preconceptions concerning the Don Juan figure but also those concerning Byron himself. *Don Juan* seemed to represent the tale of the legendary seducer told by an author with a reputation for libertinism. Thus, many of the reviewers and readers, including the reviewer of *The Miniature Magazine* (October 1819), combined their distaste for the figure of Don Juan with their suspicions concerning Byron himself: 'What Lord Byron's real motive could be for chusing such a worn-out subject for his genius to work upon, I cannot say; unless the known character of Don Juan was considered as the most convenient for uttering blasphemy, and spreading pollution with impunity, in language at once elaborate and beautiful.'[17] This excerpt is typical of many contemporary reactions and proves the extent to which Byron's choice of hero was considered to be a provocative one.

Although Byron first published *Don Juan* anonymously, the association of his name with that of the libertine was quickly made. *'Don John' or 'Don Juan' Unmasked; Being a Key To the Mystery Attending that Remarkable Publication with A Descriptive Review of the Poem and Extracts* (1819) was quickly published by William Hone after the initial publication of *Don Juan*, Cantos I–II. Its title refers to the 'mystery' with which the work had supposedly been surrounded. But Hone's work, like many of the initial reviews, treated its authorship as an open secret. The reviews exploited this association of Byron with libertinism: 'Will *he* descend to the composition of a work, linked to the celebrity of his name by a thousand palpable relations, which the more scrupulous delicacy of his bookseller refuses to avow?' (*Edinburgh Monthly Review*, October 1819).[18] These 'palpable relations' were Byron's celebrity as a Don Juan-like libertine and the rumours surrounding the notorious

---

[17] *The Miniature Magazine*, 3 (Oct. 1819), 236–9, 238.
[18] *The Edinburgh Monthly Review*, 2 (Oct. 1819), review of Cantos I–II, pp. 468–86, 469.

break-up of his marriage. When *The Investigator* declared that 'even to the titled profligate before us justice must not be denied', it would have been difficult for the paper's readers to avoid the allusive sense of a pun—the Don, Juan, and the Lord, Byron.[19]

To add what the readers thought they knew of the character of the author to the already existing preconceptions of a Don Juan was to raise the expectation that the seducer would be defended—an expectation which, as will become apparent, would be fulfilled. The parody *Don Juan: Canto the Third* (1819) demonstrates the suspicion that *Don Juan* would be a poem of self-defence, in choosing the following quotation from *Richard II* as epigraph:

> But in this kind, to come in braving arms,
> Be his own Carver, and cut out his way,
> To find out right with wrongs . . . it may not be.[20]

The frequently contradictory stances of *Don Juan* towards its readers can be explained by the differences which the poem anticipated between those readers who were like-minded and were therefore addressed conspiratorially and those readers who were expected to be antagonistic and were therefore deliberately provoked. However, both types of reader would have shared one predisposition—to read *Don Juan* as a poem about the legendary Don Juan.

When the first edition of *Don Juan*, Cantos I–II, was published in July 1819, it lacked the Preface, which Byron had not completed, and the Dedication, which he reluctantly agreed to suppress. (The Dedication was first published in 1832, the Preface not until 1901.) Thus Byron's final choice of epigraph, from Horace's *Epistola ad Pisones*, was the sole introduction to the poem proper: 'Difficile est proprie communia dicere'. In the *Ars Poetica*, Horace counsels Pisones on the choice of appropriate material for writing and recommends either the invention of a story which would be internally consistent, each element thereby contributing to the consonance of the whole,

---

[19] *The Investigator*, 3 (Oct. 1821), review of Cantos I–II, pp. 353–60, 357. See also *The Literary Chronicle* (6 Dec. 1823), 769–71, 769: 'Lord Byron is, generally speaking, the hero of his own tale'.

[20] *Don Juan: Canto the Third* (London: William Hone, 1819), frontispiece.

or the adherence to a sure tradition: 'Aut famam sequere aut sibi convententia'.[21] An author who wants to demonstrate his worth can best do so by undertaking a project previously attempted by another, by infusing familiar material with originality so as to make that which is common, personal: 'publica materies privati iuris erit'. Byron had translated Horace's *Epistle to Pisones* in 1811 under the title *Hints from Horace*, and the lines which were later chosen as the epigraph for *Don Juan* were then transcribed as: ' 'Tis hard to venture where our betters fail, | Or lend fresh interest to a twice-told tale' (ll. 183–4). Although a description of Don Juan legend as a 'twice-told tale' would be a conservative estimate, it does suggest its proverbiality, as indeed the playbill for *Giovanni in London* (1817) had done (see Chapter 1 above).

Byron's choice of the character of Don Juan as literary hero is sketched in the first five stanzas of Canto I. The catalogue of possible heroes, all of whom are rejected in turn, is a valid, if oblique, comment on the final choice itself. The dismissal of military heroes is a denial of the conventional cult of heroism which swept through England during the years of the Wars with France and which further intensified after the victory at Waterloo. In *Britons: Forging the Nation, 1707–1837* (1992), Linda Colley examined how this was used as an ideological aid in the cultural reconstruction of an élite at a time when the aristocracy was increasingly under threat from the burgeoning middle classes. It was a highly selective cult which never focused on the heroism of ordinary soldiers or seamen but only upon those commanding them. It was promoted through the painting of heroic battlefields (as, for example, in the art of West, Copley, and Devis) and through the erection of statues of military and naval officers in St Paul's Cathedral in London, funded by state revenue. And this cult of heroism flourished in large part because of the enthusiasm of Englishwomen.[22] Byron's extensive cataloguing of such likely popular heroes is deliberately a mere list, the contents of which will be summarily forgotten, as expendable as Don Juan's infamous list of

---

[21] Horace, *Satires, Epistles, and Ars Poetica*, tr. H. R. Fairclough (Cambridge, Mass.: Harvard University Press, 1926), 460–1, *Epistola ad Pisones*, i. 119.
[22] Linda Colley, *Britons: Forging the Nation, 1707–1837* (New Haven and London: Yale University Press, 1992), esp. 166–91 and 257–8.

conquests. There is great show in the 'arbitrary' rejection of so many.

These stanzas were sent to Murray in a letter of 8 December 1818, after he had taken the decision to publish the first two Cantos without the Dedication and Preface.[23] Byron used the additional material to restate and reformulate the satirical intent of his poem and also to provoke further in his choice of 'hero' by summarily dismissing so many, more conventional, heroes.[24] Thus the first five stanzas of Byron's *Don Juan*, when read in conjunction with the epigraph from Horace, demonstrate the extent to which Byron valued Don Juan as an immediately accessible and recognizable dramatic character, a character who would bequeath to his text an existing sense of tradition, however mixed its reputation might be.

READING *DON JUAN*

> We all have seen him in the pantomime
> Sent to the devil somewhat ere his time.

(I, 1)

In the first stanza of the poem proper, Byron chooses the course of provocation. The demise of Don Juan was most usually presented as a moral sermon: Don Juan must be punished, or at least repent. Yet the history of the legend had been shadowed by accusations of impiety, if not outright blasphemy. If the exploits of the seducer were entertaining, their enjoyment threatened to overwhelm the ending, the brevity of which could seem to ironize its own gesture. Those who criticized Coleridge's moral fervour—and such critics included Hazlitt and Byron—derided the ostensible duplicity of combining an enjoyment of the seducer's bravura with approval of his punishment.

Early readers of the poem hoped that, however impious the

---

[23] See *The Complete Poetical Works of Lord Byron*, ed. Jerome J. McGann (Oxford: Clarendon Press), v (1986), 673.

[24] This section on the epigraph is indebted to James Bennet Mandrell, *Don Juan and the Point of Honour* (Philadelphia: Pennsylvania State University Press, 1992), 35–7.

poem might be or become, it would finally have to satisfy common morality in conforming to the didactic ending of the tradition. *The Literary Examiner* (5 July 1823) admitted the latitude which the legend offered the author, but rather complacently assumed that the final destination would be the conventional one: 'we can scarcely conceive an outline more capable of excursion *ad libitum* than the pilotage of a Don Galaor of headlong courage and boundless adventure to the gates of hell'.[25] *The New Monthly Magazine* (August 1819), whose suspicions concerning Byron's motives in choosing the theme of Don Juan have already been noted, clung hopefully to the glimpse of conventional religiosity offered by Canto I, stanzas 200 and 207, by adding: '*although* he promises to conduct his hero to a place of final punishment' (my italics).[26] The literal interpretation of these stanzas was, however, rather tenuous. The narrator had in fact only promised to portray hell not to transport his hero there. The expression used by *The Edinburgh (Scots) Magazine* (August 1821) more ambiguously positioned itself between these two perspectives—the expectation due to the legend and the hope that Byron would conform to it: '*Don Juan* . . . was poured abroad, thick and threefold upon us—like the fiery flakes of that eternal element to which he is to be ultimately consigned.'[27] Because Byron's reputation was certainly not conducive to moral confidence, such hopes reflect the expectation that the author would necessarily conform to the traditional ending because it was conventional. However, current burlesques and parodies did not always justify such hopes, and in *Harlequin's Vision, Giovanni in London,* and even in performances of more conventional versions, benevolent interpretations of Don Juan were engaging audience sympathies.

Other readers feared from the outset that traditional morality would be subverted. *The Examiner* (31 October 1819), for example, placed no faith in the possibility of a conventional ending and instead suspected that traditional morality was being sent up:

[25] *The Literary Examiner* (5 July 1823), review of Cantos VI–VIII, pp. 6–12, 9.
[26] *New Monthly Magazine*, 12 (Aug. 1819), 75–8, 78.
[27] *Edinburgh (Scots) Magazine*, 2nd series 9 (Aug. 1821), review of Cantos I–II and III–IV, pp. 105–8, 106.

And he adds, with a hit at the 'moral' conclusion of hell-fire,—that 'comfortable creed' (as he elsewhere stiles it) of some Christians:

> I've got new mythological machinery
> And very handsome supernatural scenery.[28]

When Byron submitted his intentions for later Cantos to Murray in January 1819, his publisher was already urging him to use Don Juan more traditionally: 'Your history of the plan of the progress of *Don Juan* is very entertaining, but I am clear for sending him to hell, because he may favour us with a description of some of the characters whom he finds there.'[29] Given the phenomenal commercial pull of the pantomimes' scenes of hell, such caution was probably a mixture of business-like acumen and moral timidity. With the threat of censorship, denial of copyright, and subsequent piracies, the two were not unrelated.

The reviewer of *The New Monthly Magazine* (August 1819) mirrored Murray's general fears about *Don Juan*. He anticipated a final denouement which would punish the hero—but he feared the latitude and relish which would be permitted before then:

The play upon the stage was subject, from the opening scene, to instant condemnation by the audience, if, in the execution, the writer of the drama had not restrained himself within due limits. But the author of the poem is under no such control; and, we fear that the concluding moral in the twelfth or twenty-fourth, will prove but a feeble antidote to the poison in the other eleven or twenty-three Cantos.[30]

As was evident in the examples of the 1794 production of the Don Juan pantomime at Covent-Garden and of the Old Price riots of 1809, contemporary theatrical audiences were certainly never passive consumers. This review expresses the frustration of the reader who feels he cannot exercise the vocal influence which is available to him in the theatre. His 'boo' or 'hiss' or cry of 'shame' is completely redundant in the reception of the poem. This literalizes the problem of

---

[28] *The Examiner* (31 Oct. 1819), 700–2, 702.
[29] Samuel Smiles, *A Publisher and his Friends* (London: John Murray, 1891), i. 401 (Jan. 1819).
[30] *New Monthly Magazine*, 12 (Aug. 1819), 78.

responsibility within the moral argument which *Don Juan* provokes.

To these readers, the first stanza of *Don Juan* would have both frustrated and confirmed expectations. The deliberate, and early, statement that Don Juan's punishment came too quickly was both contrary to the traditional moral didacticism of the legend and exactly what the reader might have expected of Byron: namely that he should embrace the notorious seducer as a 'friend' (I, 1, l. 5). The reasoning is that of a traditional Don Juan, complacent that there is always a later time for repentance: 'tan largo me lo fiáis'. The fears of *The New Monthly Magazine* writer are fully realized in the first couplet of *Don Juan*, the pace of which not only makes of the statement a seeming inevitability, but naturalizes the provocation: the reader's moral response is implicated with that of the narrator, and involuntarily. In the same way, the narrator will later express the ostensibly tentative hope that Don Juan has become 'Our hero (and I trust, kind reader, yours)' (IX, 23). However the use of 'our' and the insinuating blackmail of 'kind' give the reader a choice which is effectively no choice, much in the manner of the first stanza. The provocation of the first stanza is exacerbated by a blasphemous allusion to Christ: Don Juan's designation as the 'true' hero would have been interpreted as an oblique reference to the biblical 'true Messiah'.[31] It is appropriate, therefore, that these various kinds of subversions are reinforced by the immediately aural subversion of the reader's preconception—the sound of 'Juan'.

Byron's Don Juan is first portrayed as the child of a failed marriage and the son of a rake. For the first time in the history of the legend, the upbringing of a Don Juan is sketched. Interest in the figure of Don Juan had become so fanatical by 1818 that only his 'past' remained untouched by the many versions. Keats ridiculed this excessive interest in the figure by mocking a curiosity about every facet of his life in his review of the Drury Lane pantomime for *The Champion* (4 January 1818):

Your great antiquaries now would pronounce his whole history from the day of his birth to this present, not omitting the gradual changing of his hair from flaxen to black, nor any little choice of conversation or

[31] *Complete Poetical Works*, v (1986), 673, l. 4.

riddle me ree between him and his nursery maid on the day he was breeched; nor how fond he was of rabbits, and pidgeons, and cockchaffers, and moo-cows, and hunt the slipper, nor how he volunteered among the little tambour workers for weeks and weeks, so breathing in an intoxicating air, sucking in poison from a sampler, and forgetting himself at a red morocco slipper. Unfortunate Don! unthinkingly didst thou treasure up the forms of things in thine imagination—the storm, the fatal storm was mustering by little and little till it burst to the utter astonishment of a certain fair playmate. Then were his eyes opened, he forgot his kite, his top, and what is more his knitting needles—for now that happy time was gone where with a luxurious patience he would frame and fashion delicately a pair of garters for a being made of light. Aye happy and yet not happy was that May morning on which the young Giovanni and the fair little Silentilla walked forth—but this is no place for a fairy tale; suffice it to say, that in consequence, has the poor youth been thrown into Tartarus from every stage in Europe.[32]

Previous Don Juans had often exploited mystery and ambiguity as seduction tactics. Increasing explication of the figure is a reflection of how saturated the Don Juan 'market' was becoming. Keats's review stresses the absurdity and seeming incongruity of a childish Don Juan, playing with spinning-tops and kites. It was a spectacle which the middle classes, who celebrated the sanctity of childhood, would not willingly have confronted. Of course, Keats was also criticizing the increasingly 'infantile' versions of the legend popular in the pantomime. The review does emphasize, however, how surprising and comical Byron's first undertaking was—to portray the childish and teenage Don Juans.

Contemporary readers seem to have welcomed such a novel aspect of the legend. The Anglicization of Don Juan had been attempted in the burlesques and parodies of Mozart's opera. Byron attempts the domestication of the figure. Byron's psychological realism and the burlesques' Anglicization of the figure both created a vernacular, or more ideologically, a 'real' Don Juan. To Kierkegaard, it was an unfortunate effect: 'Byron has ventured to bring Don Juan into existence for us, to tell us of his childhood and youth, to construct him out of the context of his

---

[32] Repr. in *The Poetical Works and Other Writings of John Keats*, ed. Harry Buxton Forman (New York: C. Scribner's Sons, 1938–9), v. 252–6, 252–3.

finite life-relationships. But Don Juan thereby became a reflective personality who loses the ideality he has in the traditional picture.'[33] To the authors of the parodies and to Byron, however, it was an effect which was deliberately cultivated.

What did horrify many contemporary readers was that the sins of the son should be compounded by those of his father, and in her own way, of his mother. This criticism was voiced both by *The Literary Chronicle* (17 July 1819): 'The author of this poem has not been satisfied with making Don Juan only a libertine, but he has assigned the same character to his father, and not spoken very respectfully of the mother' and by *The Investigator* (October 1821): 'Yet his debaucheries are not enough to satisfy the depraved taste of Lord Byron, but he must e'en paint the father and mother nearly as bad as their hopeful son.'[34] Byron ascribes his figure's personality, not, as might have been expected, to the example set by his father, but primarily to the most 'moral' of upbringings. His is an education highly censored and disciplined—in the narrator's terms, repressive. Only one action of the young Juan is noted, but it is one of illicit spontaneity, flinging a pail of 'house-maid's water' upon the narrator (I, 24), a conventional slapstick device of the burlesques, parodies, and pantomimes. After a diet of expurgated Ovid and St Augustine, Don Juan becomes uncharacteristically anodyne. That such 'model' behaviour is judged to be insipid by the narrator is evident in his use of literary cliché and archaism: 'Juan waxed in goodliness and grace; | . . . He studied steadily and grew apace' (I, 49). (There is also a hint, again blasphemously, of biblical allusion.) These conventional epithets would have permitted the reader the option of approval. Byron might have expected that the most moral readers of the poem would applaud such an upbringing. However, the narrator slyly inserts his own doubts as to the efficacy of this education:

> At six, I said, he was a charming child,
> At twelve he was a fine but quiet boy.
> Although in infancy a little wild,

---

[33] Søren Kierkegaard, *Either/Or: Part I* (1843), ed. and tr. Howard V. Hong and Edna H. Hong (Princeton: Princeton University Press, 1987), 106.
[34] *The Literary Chronicle* (17 July 1819), 129–30, 129. *The Investigator*, 3 (Oct. 1821), 357.

> They *tamed him down* amongst them; *to destroy*
> *His natural spirit* not in vain they toiled,
> *At least it seemed so* . . .

(I, 50, my italics)

The narrator's doubts will of course prove to be entirely vindicated: for the little boy grows up to be Don Juan. The narrator clearly insinuates that what Donna Inez is attempting to stifle is his sexuality. When he reaches 16, the thought that he is almost a man has her flying into a rage, even biting her lips to prevent a scream (I, 54), and the associative repetition of 'precocious' (I, 54 and V, 157) makes the specifically sexual nature of Juan's growing up apparent. Inez's attempt to suppress Juan's sexuality is shown to be fatally mistaken, for it is Don Juan's very naivety which leads him into an affair with the married Donna Julia. Don Juan is too innocent, a very new condition for the legendary character—but then Don Juan had, as yet, never been portrayed at such a premature stage of his development. The stirrings of Don Juan's sexual desire for Donna Julia are associatively linked to his education and its fruitless exclusion of Ovid as a 'rake' in the respective references to Medea (I, 42 and 86). Don Juan is forbidden to read of 'quick feelings', but this ban, the poem argues, will not prevent him from experiencing what is 'natural'.

A contemporary solution to the social problem represented by Don Juan might have suggested an alternative and stricter upbringing, just such a one as Donna Inez provides. *Don Juan* demonstrates how oppression will ultimately lead to rebellion, even in the domestic sphere. This censure of sexual repression also subverts the moral superiority of northern countries over those of the south, a philosophy espoused by Madame de Staël, Montesquieu, and the German theoreticians. The so-called 'morality' of the north is exposed as a hypocritical veil for a sexual sphere in which marriage is marketable (I, 64). Such an argument is important for the reception of Don Juan, the very embodiment of Latin sexuality to theatre-goers throughout Europe. Blame for Juan's fall in Canto I is repeatedly attributed to the sun and the June setting (I, 102–4, 121). However, given the context of the Canto's argument hitherto—that it is Donna Inez's education which contributes to Don Juan's early and sinful manner of losing his virginity—the culpability of the weather is only a pose of speciousness which reflects the reasoning and explanations which English readers might traditionally have been expected to make. This new 'explanation' for Don Juan was accepted by a rather unlikely reader. When Murray's lawyer, Sharon Turner, consulted Mr Shadwell on the likelihood of the Chancellor granting *Don Juan* copyright, he was surprised by his indulgent reading of the poem. In Turner's account, Shadwell 'added that one great tendency of the book was not an unfair one. It was to show in Don Juan's ultimate character the ill effect of that injudicious maternal education which Don Juan is represented as having received . . .'.[35]

Don Juan's effective disobedience of his mother leads to a new independence and introspection which is pilloried by the narrator as self-indulgent (I, 87–96). Although the satirical thrust against Wordsworth and the Lake poets has been widely recognized, a second debt has been overlooked—that of Beaumarchais's young page, Chérubin, here confessing his amorous propensity to Susanna: 'I feel such a need to say "I love you" to someone that I catch myself saying it to myself walking in the park, to your Mistress, to you, to the trees, to the clouds, to the wind which wafts them away with my fleeting words.' This is an apposite parallel because Kierkegaard discussed Mozart's Cherubino as the first of 'The Immediate Erotic Stages', which effectively makes of him a juvenile Don Juan.[36] Byron's Don Juan is '[a]ctive, though not so sprightly as a page' (I, 54). Like Cherubino, Byron's Don Juan is young enough to be allowed liberties and old enough to exploit them.

Although Don Juan is certainly ridiculed in these stanzas, he is implicitly exonerated by compensating naivety and susceptible puberty. The narrator argues that the young Don Juan cannot be guilty of the sexual debauchery of which he is accused, although this defence is not always conducted with pleas of which the moral reader would approve. The sexual innuendo

---

[35] Smiles, *Publisher and Friends*, i. 407–9.
[36] Beaumarchais, *The Marriage of Figaro* (1784), tr. John Wood (Harmondsworth: Penguin, 1964), 117. Lorenzo da Ponte, *Le nozze di Figaro*, Deutsche Gramophon booklet 429869-2, tr. Lionel Salter, pp. 60 and 62. Kierkegaard, *Either/Or: Part I*, 75-7.

of 'He did the best he could I With things not very subject to
control' (I, 91) would be an example of this. The narrator's
following attempt to criticize Don Juan's sinning is a deliberately cultivated sham:

> And secondly, I pity not, because
> He had no business to commit a sin,
> Forbid by heavenly, fined by human laws,
> At least 'twas rather early to begin . . .
>
> (I, 167)

The first three lines begin by placating the moral reader. The
qualification is reserved until the fourth line where it is hastily
inserted as if as an after-thought. The narrator is thus able to
translate his exoneration of Don Juan's conduct into the appearance of compassion after strident condemnation. The
stanza then appropriately modulates into an allusion to Don
Juan's famous motto:

> But at sixteen the conscience rarely gnaws
> So much as when we call our old debts in
> At sixty years and draw the accounts of evil
> And find a deuced balance with the devil.
>
> (I, 167)

Any thoughts of repentance are postponed: 'tan largo me lo
fiáis', plenty of time to pay that debt.

Interrupted by Don Alfonso, Don Juan and Donna Julia
resume their caresses after his departure, while Antonia advises
him to leap from the window (I, 137). Continuing the association with Mozart's *Le nozze di Figaro*, this mirrors the correspond-
ing scene and triangle of the married Countess, her maid
Susanna, and the youthful Cherubino—although Tirso's Don
Juan Tenorio had also escaped from Naples by leaping from a
balcony. Byron's Don Juan is discovered through a pair of
masculine shoes—'(No one can tell how much I grieve to say)'
(I, 181), though whether the narrator laments the discovery or
the fact is uncertain. When Don Alfonso, clearly in the role of
the *comendador*, threatens death, Juan knocks him down and
blood does flow—although the narrator adds bathetically:
'('twas from the nose)' (I, 186). The episode becomes 'one of
the most circulating scandals I That had for centuries been

known in Spain' (I, 190), an obvious, if indirect, reference to the legend itself.

Byron's *Don Juan* therefore begins with the incident which precipitates the legend—a confrontation between the seduced lady's male relation (here her husband) and Don Juan. Appropriately, the elder man swears he'll be revenged, while Don Juan blasphemes (I, 184). Antonia allusively scolds 'The devil's in the urchin' (I, 171). And Donna Julia, like Molière's Done Elvira, enters a convent. Don Juan is exiled from Spain, as was the 'original' Don Juan Tenorio and other Don Juans within this tradition. He sails on the 'most holy *Trinidada*' (II, 24), a covert, and potentially blasphemous, allusion to the triangular situation of Don Juan, Donna Julia, and Don Alfonso. Thus, within the first Canto, Byron's Don Juan already bears significant traces of his legendary ancestors: he escapes the doctrines of his mother's oppressive education to live according to his feelings and inclination, involves himself in a case of adultery, duels with the offended male party, and is exiled from Spain as punishment.

The correspondence of this opening episode with the Don Juan legend did not escape contemporary readers. For example, *The Champion* (25 July 1819) commented that: 'the injured husband, instead of having his throat cut, in the old Don Juan style, escapes with a good pummelling'.[37] However these deviations from the prototypical legend struck contemporary readers as relatively trivial. They were not diverted by the difference in detail from accepting the subject of the poem as the legendary Don Juan. *The Literary Chronicle* of 17 July 1819 acknowledged the divergence from the traditional story while simultaneously accepting it as a version: 'Don Juan's first amour, too, is with the wife and not the daughter of the Spanish Hidalgo, at Seville.'[38]

The first trial for this Don Juan is of his constancy to the memory of Donna Julia and this comes in the rather unlikely test of sea-sickness, representing the exigencies of the moment, in this case, of the weather. His professions of love are parenthetically juxtaposed with the exclamations and sounds of near-retching, to the detriment of the former: Don Juan's

[37] *The Champion* (25 July 1819), 473.
[38] *The Literary Chronicle* (17 July 1819), 129.

sea-sickness sounds genuine (II, 20). Don Juan has therefore quickly succeeded in the first rule of Don Juan-like behaviour— amnesia concerning his past lovers. Subsequent stanzas describe a scene which often passed off-stage, the sea journey of Don Juan. They portray the hero as courageous in adversity and principled when faced with cannibalism. (In Act III of Shadwell's *The Libertine* the storm at sea is extensively described, the Captain exclaiming at its extraordinary ferocity, while Don John alone remains without fear.) In this episode of *Don Juan*, the moralistic reader who would condemn the savagery of those who succumb to eating their fellow survivors, is simultaneously encouraged to admire the, in this case, abstemious Don Juan.

Don Juan alone survives, is washed ashore, and duly rescued—by two females. Again this is strictly in accordance with the Spanish/pantomime tradition. Indeed, Gendarme de Bévotte, in his history of the legend of Don Juan (1906), made the rather surprising claim that this episode is the poem's most direct reference to the traditional story.[39] The narrator continues to imply a more cynical interpretation of Juan's arguably moral behaviour: 'He was in love, as you would be no doubt, | With a young *benefactress*' (II, 167, my italics). If Don Juan's love for Haidée is tinged with mercenary motives then the darker insinuations of Byron's Don Juan as the traditionally heartless seducer gather ground. The reader is prevented from moral condemnation by being forced into a position where this condemnation would seem like hypocrisy. The careful placing of 'as you would be no doubt' fulfils just this purpose. Haidée's eyes are also described as 'the finest eyes that ever made a youthful heart *less steady*' (II, 171, my italics), an allusion to Donna Julia which is extremely covert. The feelings of Don Juan and Haidée are clearly differentiated: Haidée visits Don Juan every morning at day-break, 'Rather early | For Juan, who was somewhat fond of rest' (II, 168). The contemporary reader was programmatically suspicious, for (s)he already expects the worst—at least as far as Don Juan's behaviour is concerned. In this way, even Don Juan's religious fervour becomes suspect—to those alert to such nuances:

[39] Georges Gendarme de Bévotte, *La Légende de Don Juan* (1906; repr. Paris: Hachette, 1929), 268.

For woman's face was never formed in vain
For Juan, so that even when he prayed
He turned from grisly saints and martyrs hairy
To the sweet portraits of the Virgin Mary.

(II, 149)

The narrator's choice of pejorative ('grisly', 'hairy') and approbative ('sweet') adjectives is an indication of his own internalization of the sentiment, as it also excuses Don Juan's preference. Similarly, regarding 'Both were so young and one so innocent I That bathing passed for nothing . . .' (II, 172)—the sceptical reader might question: if one is 'not innocent' can bathing pass for nothing? Or is the narrator subtly hiding Don Juan's sexual pleasure behind the screen of Haidée's innocent response?

The consummated relationship between Haidée and Don Juan, like that of Donna Julia and Don Juan, would have been condemned by orthodox morality as illicit, because the lovers are unmarried (III, 12). At this point, their love affair is described in terms which clearly echo the Don Juan legend:

Alas, they were so young, so beautiful,
So lonely, loving, helpless, and the hour
Was that in which the heart is always full,
And having o'er itself no further power,
Prompts deeds eternity cannot annul,
But pays off moments in an endless shower
Of hell-fire, all prepared for people giving
Pleasure or pain to one another living.

Alas for Juan and Haidée! They were
So loving and so lovely; till then never,
Excepting our first parents, such a pair
Had run the risk of being damned forever.
And Haidée, being devout as well as fair,
Had doubtless heard about the Stygian river
And hell and purgatory, but forgot
Just in the very crisis she should not.

(II, 192–3)

It is significant that only Haidée is addressed in the second part of this last stanza, perhaps because Don Juan is already, and given his ancestry has been from the beginning, a lost cause.

While the narrator might seem to concur with the moralistic reader in describing their 'illicit | Indulgence', the line continues with the more approving 'of their innocent desires' (III, 13). Indeed the presentation of the couple is much too sympathetically and idyllically portrayed to admit any validity to lines of condemnation, whose deliberate harshness exposes the commonly didactic reading as cruel:

> If she loved rashly, her life paid for wrong;
> A heavy price must all pay who thus err,
> In some shape. Let none think to fly the danger,
> For soon or late Love is his own avenger.

(IV, 73)

When Haidée's father returns, Don Juan confronts, for a second time, the irate male relation of his lover. This time, however, the episode more exactly mirrors the legend, in that Lambro is the offended father and appears as if 'risen from death' (IV, 36). Don Juan is outnumbered by Lambro's servants and thus once again finds himself put to sea, exiled this time from Greece.

Don Juan's next sexual encounter follows quickly, for in the boat he is tied up with an Italian soprano whose charms ('And she had some not very easy to withstand') he spurns. A benevolent reading of Don Juan's nature would suggest that his disinclination is due to fresh memories of Haidée. The narrator, however, enjoys hinting at more suggestive and involuntary reasons: 'Perhaps his recent wounds might help a little' (IV, 95). The contemporary reader would have understood the innuendo that only Don Juan's physical incapacitation prevented him from succumbing. This sceptical interpretation is reinforced by the description of his love for Haidée—'no knight could be more true; | And firmer faith no ladye-love desire' (IV, 96)—an obviously clichéd and anachronistic description of old-fashioned chivalry. This episode is a missed opportunity for sexual liaison but its force in the text is as an encounter that remained potential: the Italian soprano was almost one of the 'catalogue'. The poem itself claims that it might have developed this episode, ironically as a 'chaste description', if the reviewers had permitted (IV, 97). Cantos III–V were published on 8 August 1821, that is, two years after the publication and subse-

quent outcry which greeted Cantos I–II, a response which is
explicitly evoked in this stanza. The abrupt ending of the encounter is therefore not a consequence of Don Juan's sexual
abstemiousness, but of the reviewers' censures: '*Therefore* I'll
make Don Juan leave the ship soon' (IV, 97; my italics).

Byron increased the poem's provocation in the frank sexuality of the Turkish episode, despite, or rather because of, the
narrator's depiction of the harem as a convent and its
odalisques as nuns. The theme of Don Juan had already tra-
versed this erotic/spiritual divide: in Shadwell's version the Don
surreptitiously entered a convent. It was also an accomplishment which was included among Don Juan's early education (I,
38). Of course, the anxious safeguarding of chastity within a
harem is not without its irony, since the harem itself is a form of
institutionalized Don Juanism: Shadwell's Don John proclaimed, 'nor will I ever give over, till I have as many wives and
concubines as the *Grand Signior*'.[40]

Don Juan's actions continue to counter the darker implications of the narrator. He weeps as he recollects Haidée; he is
incredulous that Johnson should already have been married
three times; he refuses, at first adamantly, the sexual favours of
Gulbeyaz. However, the narrator's insinuations of libertinism
remain sufficient to remind the reader of one possible interpretation of Don Juan's behaviour, one which would feed from
prejudices regarding his lineage. Examples of this include the
extremity of his reaction to the prospect of circumcision, an
excessiveness which is offset by Johnson's cool and expediently
diplomatic compliance (V, 71). (Circumcision punishes too
close to the 'heart' of a Don Juan's body!) Similarly Don Juan
only agrees to dress in female clothes when threatened with
castration (V, 75). And he engages in mock simpering with
Johnson, insisting upon a virgin marriage like a Richardson
heroine, a female coyness which he clearly derides (V, 84).
Although Don Juan is a suitable case for transvestism with his
beardless chin and 'half-girlish face' (I, 171), Baba advises him
against his manly stride, which is a rather rakish swagger (V,
91). Don Juan's refusal of Gulbeyaz is delivered in a panegyric
to the freedom of love, a speech which his ancestors would

[40] *The Complete Works of Thomas Shadwell*, ed. Montague Summers (London:
Benjamin Blom, 1968), iii. 43.

certainly have approved of, even if the narrator does not (V,
127–8). The narrator pretends to be dismayed at Don Juan's
loss of 'virtue' in yielding to Gulbeyaz's tears, while obviously
praising his compassion and simultaneously defending his
'weakness' in yielding. The insinuation of the libertine is carried as a narrative aside: Don Juan stands resigned 'Rather than
sin—except to his own wish' (V, 141).

The arrival of the Sultan prevents Don Juan from completing
this transformation from resistant to compliant lover so that
once again an affair is disrupted by the sudden reappearance of
the woman's male relation, and Don Juan quickly encounters
the next female in his catalogue of adventures, Dudù. His yielding to Gulbeyaz has already performed a preliminary function
in that Don Juan has now forgotten Haidée, immediately evident in his ogling of the odalisques (VI, 29). This 'ogling'
recalls that of the bidder's appraisal of the slaves (V, 26–7) and
it is sufficiently sinister here to be acknowledged as a sin in
'moral England'. Like his legendary fathers, Byron's Don Juan
is irresistible to all women and thus the concubines are unanimously seduced by his magnetism or 'devilism' (VI, 38). Yet
Byron's Don Juan is not devilish enough to accept Dudù's
assistance in undressing (VI, 61). Perhaps he would rather not
be discovered, not yet at any rate, since the belated discovery of
his true sex facilitates his bedding with Dudù. The narrator's
telling of the affair that night implies that Juan is a conventional, skilfully duplicitous libertine:

> But what is strange—and a strong proof how great
> A blessing is sound sleep—Juanna lay
> As fast as ever *husband by his mate*
> In holy matrimony snores away,
> Not all the clamour broke her holy state
> Of slumber, ere they shook her—*so they say*
> *At least*, and then she too unclosed her eyes
> And yawned a good deal with *discreet* surprise.
>
> (VI, 73; my italics)

Conventionally Don Juan effected his seductions by promises of
marriage, playing upon the distinction between sexual consummation and marriage which moral and legal codes rendered
synonymous. Here Don Juan has more immorally abolished the

difference: 'As fast as ever husband by his mate'. Juan is offered a new bed, and a potential new affair with Lolah (VI, 81). However, this Don Juan, it must be admitted, is not quite so promiscuous.

Don Juan's next adventure—the Siege of Ismail—is a 'new one' for the legendary libertine. This was recognized by *The Monthly Review* (August 1823) in a review which demonstrates the importance of the traditional legend as a continuing standard with which Byron's version was compared: 'Here the employment of Don Juan is certainly changed, from making love to making war.'[41] Although the Ismail Cantos certainly diverge from the usual settings for the Don Juan legend—a point which the poem itself acknowledges in Suwarrow's statement that Don Juan's name is a 'new one' (VII, 60)—the contamination of Don Juan's character by the narrative voice continues. In popular culture and slang, military and sexual metaphors were linked (as in Russia Don Juan's illness is ascribed to 'the fatigue of the last campaign'; X, 40). Therefore the poem's motif of sexual innuendo continues, even on the exclusively male field of battle, where opportunities for (hetero)sexual liaison are rare.

As noted at the beginning of this chapter, the narrator had from the first declared his intention to portray hell (I, 200 and 207), an episode which would clearly follow the pattern of the Don Juan legend and fulfil the pious hopes of the poem's most moral readers. The theme of the siege of Ismail allowed Byron to realize his intention of setting hell within a naturalistic framework, the battlefield. Suwarrow is described as 'the greatest chief | That ever peopled hell with heroes slain' (VII, 68). It is therefore appropriate that in the hell-flames of war Don Juan becomes more explicitly the deliberate seducer of legendary fame. The narrator's asides concerning Don Juan are now more solemn: Juan's bluster in consoling Dudù and her companion is openly ridiculed as exaggeration (VII, 75). This more overt treatment of Don Juan as similar to his legendary ancestors is possible because of the satire against war, for Juan's rakishness can be received more indulgently when the alternative is cruel brutality. As in the episode of

---

[41] *The Monthly Review* (Aug. 1823), 319–20.

cannibalism, Don Juan's sin of womanizing seems tame in the comparison:

> And here he was, who upon woman's breast
> Even from a child felt like a child, howe'er
> The man in all the rest might be confest.
> To him it was Elysium to be there.
> And he could even withstand that awkward test
> Which Rousseau points out to the dubious fair,
> 'Observe your lover when he leaves your arms';
> But Juan never left them *while they had charms.*
>
> (VIII, 53; my italics)

If Byron's Don Juan considers the field of battle to be an Elysium, then, judged by the anti-war ethic of these Cantos, he ought to be condemned. However the placing of the line within this stanza allows for a more comic reading with its bawdy portrayal of the Don Juan who is never happier than when he is on a woman's breast. Despite the narrator's 'attempt' to defend Juan's constancy—he never leaves a lover—the attempt fails with the necessary qualification—at least, while they still have charms. The following stanza continues 'Unless compelled . . .', but the final line of stanza 53 exploits the break by leaving the accusation as an, albeit momentary, single unit.

If Don Juan's action of saving the little girl Leila from slaughter is a new addition to the adventures of a Don Juan, the deliberate emphasis of reassurance to the reader is necessary: he makes a vow to shield her 'which he kept' (VIII, 141). A Don Juan, of course, does not always keep his promises. The hints of a 'man' lurking beneath his appearance become more sardonic as Don Juan becomes a cupid personified (IX, 44–7; later he becomes a 'full-grown Cupid', XIV, 41). In Russia his youthfulness continues to attract and to divide marriages, a consequence shared with other Don Juans and, in more epic style, with Paris (IX, 53). In Russia Juan has for the first time prostituted himself, because he does not reciprocate, though he indulges in, Catherine's lust. He is now revealed as being quite clearly in the 'dissipated' (X, 23) mould of the traditional libertine:

> Besides, he was of that delighted age
> Which makes all female ages equal, when

We don't much care with whom we may engage,
As bold as Daniel in the lion's den,
So that we can our native sun assuage
In the next ocean, which may flow just then
To make a twilight in, just as Sol's heat is
Quenched in the lap of the salt sea or Thetis.

(IX, 69)

This wide-ranging taste had traditionally been the attribute of Don Juans, most famously expressed in Leporello's 'catalogue' aria which lists women young and old, fat and thin. The imagery of this stanza portrays the impulse as both mythical and natural, and in this way taunts and defies moral censure of promiscuity, as, in the earlier affair with Haidée, Edenic images of nature had been employed to support the 'natural' morality of their love (IV, 19). In addition, the use of the first person plural pronoun prevents the reader from disassociating *him*self from the ranks of lustful sinners. Love is depicted as freely available only to the young man and therefore the more elderly narrator urges him to enjoy the expendable commodity while he can (X, 9 and 22).

Don Juan's acquiescence to the desires of Catherine is portrayed as merely dutiful and his growing unhappiness is possibly a result of boredom with a lady with whom he is certainly not in love and whom he would prefer to exchange for some 'beauty' (X, 37). The narrator hints that pleasing Catherine is hard work: the disparity between them is reconciled only by Juan's 'skill' (IX, 66) and the diamond bestowed upon him is judged to have been 'fairly earned' (XI, 39). Thus Don Juan in Russia has effectively become a professional lover. The narrator's distaste at Juan's voluntary servitude is implicit in the vulgarity of the consistently obscene innuendoes which characterize this episode: 'the duty waxed a little hard, | To come off handsomely in that regard' (X, 22); 'but most | He owed to an old woman and his post' (X, 29); 'at times | He felt like other plants called sensitive' (X, 37). (Both 'post' and 'sensitive plant' were contemporary slang terms for penis.) There is a suggestion that Don Juan's 'illness' is a declining of sexual potency: 'The cankerworm | Will feed upon the fairest, freshest cheek, | As well as further drain the withered form' (X, 38, ll. 2–4).

The Russian Cantos also contain a brief affair which has been neglected in criticism of Byron's poem, that with Catherine's *éprouveuse*, Miss Protasoff. The reason for its neglect has probably been its short duration—it lasts for only one stanza. But this very brevity is, of course, entirely apposite to the subject of a Don Juan. The affair is certainly consummated, because of the hint contained in her title of office, an *éprouveuse*. Suspicions are only further raised when the narrator attempts to pretend ignorance of the significance of the French phrase ('A term inexplicable to the Muse'; IX, 84). The tactical ending of the Canto is also euphemistic: 'With her then, as in humble duty bound, | Juan retired, and so will I' (IX, 85). And in a typical gesture of the poem, blame is deflected from Juan by the suggestion that his involvement is involuntary.

Don Juan's first adventure in England echoes 'The Tyrolese to Liberty' from *Giovanni in London* (1817), which was published both with other songs from the burlesque and as part of its complete libretto:

> GIOVANNI: . . . Now Giovanni's freedom soundeth,
> Merrily oh! merrily oh!
> Here the pistol's balls fly more fleetly
> Here the syllabubs eat more sweetly,
> Every joy Chalk farm surroundeth,
> Merrily oh! merrily oh! . . .

> MRS ENGLISH: Over Primrose Hill we'll sally,
> Cheerily oh! cheerily oh!
> If a charming girl, won by bravery,
> Sweeter be than one kept by knavery,
> Round Giovanni's pistol rally,
> Cheerily oh! cheerily oh![42]

Certainly Giovanni's eulogistic verse resembles Juan's paean to English freedom, a praise which Byron was to subvert in having him accosted by the freedom of one particular type of individual—a highwayman. The relative 'simplicity' of the legendary Don Juan's life was interrupted by his perpetration of murder. Tirso's Don Juan Tenorio was reluctant to fight with the *comendador*, disdaining to fight with such an elderly adver-

---

[42] Act II, scene 1. Repr. in Oscar Mandel (ed.), *The Theatre of Don Juan* (Lincoln, Nebr.: University of Nebraska Press, 1963), 431.

sary. Mozart's Don Giovanni appeared especially troubled since the music associated with the murder is still faintly discernible in Giovanni's words in the second scene.[43] Byron's Don Juan also murders, and in rather precipitate self-defence: 'This made him meditative' (XI, 18). Don Juan is now referred to as 'our young sinner', rather than hero (XI, 29).

Despite his rather shady background, Juan is perceived to be an 'inveterate patrician' and is quickly assimilated into English society (XI, 45). The legendary Don Juan was always highly born, a *caballero*, a *cavaliere*, or a *dom*, and it was in flashing his aristocratic status that he both achieved his successes with peasant girls and remained largely untouchable by the law. In eighteenth- and early nineteenth-century society the seducer becomes the gallant, an easily imitable figure. In W. T. Moncrieff's *Giovanni in London* (1817) Leporello instructs Giovanni in the art of incarnating a beau: what to wear (not only 'Cossacks you like sacks must wear, | In a brutus cock your hair | And wear of wellingtons a pair' but also stays, an eyeglass, a sham collar, brass heels, and false calves); where to go (the Opera, ball, and play); what to do ('Drink, game, swear, and lie all day, | Protect some graceless chere amie, | Yourself to ruin bringing').[44] Such accoutrements as fashion and leisure pursuits can quickly be cultivated and the simulation of gentility can be bought. Indeed, Jane Austen's *Sanditon* (written in 1817) demonstrates how the role of seducer was becoming a fashionable pose: 'Sir Edward's great object in life was to be seductive'.[45] Don Juan's talents for charm and flattery thus become useful accomplishments in the drawing-rooms of the gentry and their coteries. There, to resist female attraction would be tantamount to bad manners (XI, 48, ll. 4–6). The consciously insinuating and assimilating Don Juan of the English Cantos is also 'a little superficial' (XI, 51) but he quickly becomes renowned among the country set for his 'vivacity among the fair' (XVI, 91).

The dashing and popular representatives of Don Juan and Don Giovanni on the Regency stage also increased the figure's

[43] Da Ponte, *Don Giovanni*, tr. William Mann (Hayes, Middlesex: EMI Ltd., 1987), Act I, pp. 44–5.

[44] Repr. in Mandel (ed.), *Theatre of Don Juan*, 423–4.

[45] Jane Austen, *Lady Susan/The Watsons/Sanditon* (Harmondsworth: Penguin, 1963), 191.

social respectability. In its review of *Don Juan*, Cantos I–II, *The European Magazine* (July 1819) introduced Byron's poem by referring to the successful theatrical hero, Don Juan: 'With so much éclat has he been personified by Sig. Ambrogetti, at the Opera, Charles Kemble, at Covent Garden, and Short, at the Surrey, that his name has reached the *ne plus ultra* of gallantry.'[46] The quick assimilation of Byron's Don Juan into English society was thus mirrored in the burlesque versions of the legend. English patriotism was flattered by this image of their generosity, evident in *Giovanni in London* where Deputy English's immediate response to Giovanni is one of benevolence and generosity. He certainly overlooks Giovanni's more notorious celebrity as a villainous seducer: 'Do you know this is the famous Giovanni? And, from what I have heard, a foreigner and a singer. So sir, like a true John Bull, I am glad to see you; and, though I may not understand you, sir, I like you; and any service I can render you, you may freely command.' (Act II, scene 1)[47] This inspires a rousing response from Giovanni, Mrs English, and the full chorus in a rendition of 'The Tyrolese to Liberty'. As Sir Henry Amundeville's treatment of Juan demonstrates however, such benevolence may not be without its condescension (XIII, 20, ll. 3–6).

When the narrator conjectures as to what might become of his hero in the following Cantos, all suggestions are amatory. Juan's future risks the penalty which awaited Moncrieff's Don Giovanni: 'Or whether he was taken in for damages | For being too excursive in his homages' (XI, 89). Don Juan's experience with women is now obvious rather than the innocence which had been emphasized in earlier scenes with Donna Julia and Haidée (see, for example: XII, 67, 69, 81). There is even an ominous hint of Juan's intentions for Leila, despite the narrator's attempts to deny any sexuality in his feelings for her. Knowing the scandalous rumours of incest which surrounded the very public break-up of Byron's marriage, the reader may not accept the argued innocence of their relationship:

> He was not quite old enough to prove
> Parental feelings, and the other class,

[46] *The European Magazine*, 76 (July 1819), 53–6, 53.
[47] Repr. in Mandel (ed.), *Theatre of Don Juan*, 431.

Called brotherly affection, could not move
His bosom, for he never had a sister.
Ah, if he had, how much he would have missed her!

(X, 53)

—especially since Donna Julia's self-delusions included a justification of her preference for certain men as 'so many brothers'
(I, 77). The following stanza consolidates the darker implications with its increasingly explicit doubt as to the innocence of
Don Juan's feelings towards Leila:

And still less was it sensual, for besides
That he was not an ancient debauchee
(Who like sour fruit, to stir their veins' salt tides,
As acids rouse a dormant alkali),
Although ('twill happen as our planet guides)
His youth was not the chastest that might be,
There was the purest platonism at bottom
Of all his feelings—only he forgot 'em.

(X, 54)

The innuendo of this stanza is compounded by the continuation in the following line, the first of stanza 55: '*Just now* there
was no peril of temptation'. Stanza 54 blurs its own contradictions—'he was not . . . Although . . . There was . . . only he forgot'. Confounding the reader in this way is typical of the
narrative strategy of *Don Juan*. The more sinister hint that
the relationship is safe only for the present recurs later in the
decision of the English ladies that Leila ought to be educated
and lodged with someone other than Don Juan: 'Howe'er our
friend Don Juan might command | Himself for five, four, three,
or two years' space' (XII, 29). The diminishing projected years
may have reflected the reader's unease regarding trust in or
predictions of Don Juan's future behaviour.

Suspicions of alternative interpretations of the Don Juan–
Leila relationship are confirmed by Byron's own intentions for
the poem: 'In his suite he shall have a girl whom he shall have
rescued during one of his northern campaigns, who shall be in
love with him, and he not with her.'[48] Similarly, when Johnson

---

[48] E. J. Lovell (ed.), *Medwin's Conversations with Lord Byron* (Princeton: Princeton
University Press, 1969), early 1822, pp. 164–5.

at first contemplated dissuading Juan from saving the girl, he
weighed up her claims: 'The child's a pretty child—a very
pretty— | I never saw such eyes...' (VIII, 101). The sexual
insinuation is less surprising in the context of *The Confessions*
(1781) in which Rousseau purchases a part-share in a young
Venetian girl, a guaranteed virgin of 11 or 12. Rousseau justifies
the agreement as 'an arrangement which is not rare in Venice',
although in his case, like that of Juan for the moment, it arouses
parental solicitation rather than carnal desire.[49] It is also a joke
which Byron had enjoyed sharing with Lady Melbourne concerning Lady Oxford's daughter, Lady Charlotte Harley.[50] And
within *Don Juan*, some of the Sultan's daughters were wed at the
age of 6 (V, 152). This is not one of the poem's many fictions,
for its authenticity was reinforced by Moore's note in his edition
of Byron's works. Moore quoted from Baron François de Tott,
Memoirs . . . Concerning the State of the Turkish Empire (1786), in
which the 6-year-old princess exclaimed against her forced marriage to a decrepit old man.[51] In England, the age of consent
until 1875 was only 12.[52]

Adeline, Juan, and Aurora form a ménage of intrigue in
Canto XV which closely parallels that of the Marquise de
Merteuil, Valmont, and the formidable challenge of Madame
de Tourvel in *Les Liaisons dangereuses*. Juan, obviously aware of
Adeline's attraction to him, deliberately rouses her jealousy in
emphasizing Aurora's suitablity in outrageous terms—her Catholicism (XV, 50). Because Adeline knows that Aurora is her
greatest rival, she derides the young girl as 'prim, silent, cold',
in other words, as an impossible conquest. Thus when Aurora
does indeed treat Juan with indifference his pique is roused
(XV, 77). His increasingly overt Don Juan-like behaviour might
be a consequence of his growing age and corruption, or, given
his already long-corrupted state, a new tactic necessary for the
exigency of an excessively timid heroine. Adeline's subsequent
triumphalism spurs Juan's pride sufficiently for him to tender

[49] Jean-Jacques Rousseau, *The Confessions* (1771), trs. J. M. Cohen (Harmondsworth: Penguin Classics, 1981), 202–3.
[50] *Byron's Letters and Journals*, ed. Leslie A. Marchand (London: John Murray,
1973–82), iii. 42 (letter to Lady Melbourne, 22 Apr. 1813).
[51] See *Don Juan* (1973), 646.
[52] See Keith Thomas, 'The Double Standard', *Journal of the History of Ideas*, 20
(Apr. 1959), 195–215, 198.

some attentions to Aurora: 'just enough to express | To females of perspicuous comprehensions | That he would rather make them more than less' (XV, 80). The sexual insinuation here is certainly explicit, a lucidly oblique style of reference which is 'perspicuous' to all. Similarly when Juan refuses Adeline's suggestion that he marry, his explanation might easily be overlooked. Yet it is not without its significance, since it is a reply most appropriate for a Don Juan—he pleads a predilection for already married ladies (XV, 30). As Juan muses on 'mutability | Or on his mistress', the statement that they are 'terms synonymous' deflects from the suggestion that Juan has a mistress at this time (XVI, 20).

The contortions of judgement throughout these last Cantos become more extreme as the narrative veers between outright condemnation and attempted defence: 'Now grave, now gay, but never dull or pert, | And smiling but in secret—cunning rogue' (XIV, 37); 'A little spoilt, but by no means so quite; | At least he kept his vanity *retired*' (XIV, 41; my italics). The duplicity of his behaviour is reflected in the text's shadowing of his Don Juan-like nature. Throughout *Don Juan* the voice of the hero has been directly, if infrequently, quoted. Now, as Juan's increasing corruption becomes more overt, the distance between narrator and character diminishes, and more of the narrative lines might be ascribed to an 'interior monologue' of Don Juan's. For example, because we are already aware of Juan's displeasure at Aurora's indifference, the irritability of the following, unascribed, lines would appear to suit the voice of someone who is intimately involved in the delicate subject of Aurora's consent. Its impatient tone certainly suggests someone with more at stake than the narrator: 'The devil was in the girl! Could it be pride | Or modesty or absence or inanity?' (XV, 78). In the scene of Juan's apprehension of a ghost, when he is suddenly scared by a cat, the following lines again suggest that the speaker might be Juan:

> And not in vain he listened. Hush, what's that?
> I see—I see—oh no—'tis not—yet 'tis—
> Ye powers, it is the—the—the—pooh, the cat!
> The devil take that stealthy pace of his!
> So like a spiritual pit-a-pat
> Or tiptoe of an amatory Miss,

> Gliding the first time to a rendezvous
> And dreading the chaste echoes of her shoe.
>
> (XVI, 112)

If so, they suggest that he is accustomed to assignations with virginal young ladies. That these lines are not quoted directly as belonging to the voice of Don Juan is an indication that the responses of the narrator and hero have effectively become identical. The effect, once again, is to shield Juan from a full display of his Don Juan-like behaviour, because there is an uncertainty in distinguishing between the narrator and the character. It would certainly have been difficult for the moral reader to level accusations when the object of criticism was, as here, itself unclear. If these examples are accepted as typical of Don Juan's thought, the figure can hardly be the same as that entirely innocent and amiable character delineated by more recent criticism.

The professed 'chasteness' of Juan is now so ambivalent that Byron is able to exploit the mystery of the meeting with her Grace Fitz-Fulke: 'Whether his virtue triumphed, or at length | His vice—for he was of a kindling nation— | Is more than I shall venture to describe' (XVII, 12). The implications of his nationality, a 'kindling' one, and the sexual innuendo of the 'length' of vice enjoy the hint of scandal which they raise. The narrator can now openly reprimand Juan for failing to seize the opportunity raised by Aurora's softening smile towards him. His failure is expressed as an inexplicable dereliction of his libertine duty: 'Juan should have known' that he had accomplished the first of the stages towards Aurora's seduction, her attention (XVI, 93). (Later his sullen silence at dinner is valued positively by the narrator as at least gaining Aurora's esteem: XVI, 107.) Don Juan, however, is perturbed by the recollection of the ghost. Whether Juan will escape the figurative flames of passion with her Grace Fitz-Fulke might remain ambiguous but here, at the inadvertent close of the poem, the reader is reminded of the legendary Don Juan:

> It opened with a most infernal creak
> Like that of hell. *Lasciate ogni speranza*
> *Voi che entrate!* The hinge seemed to speak,
> Dreadful as Dante's *rima* or this stanza,

Or—but all words upon such themes are weak.
A single shade's sufficient to entrance a
Hero, for what is substance to a spirit?
Or how is't matter trembles to come near it?

(XVI, 116)

'A single shade', in the guise of the stone statue, was sufficient to entrance the legendary hero, Don Juan. The terror of Byron's Don Juan at the 'spectre' makes of him a deathly figure: like the *comendador* he is 'petrified' (XVI, 22) and stands like a statue on its base (XVI, 23). And, with all the superstition of his Spanish ancestors, he trembles at the spectre of the ghostly, hooded, sable Friar (XVI, 118). Like Don Juan Tenorio, however, bravery overcomes fear as he brandishes carte and tierce, an echo of Dibdin's Giovanni killing Guzman (XVI, 119; see Chapter 1 above). The ghost stands 'stone still' (XVI, 119), like 'stony death' (XVI, 121—the *comendador* of the ballads and burlesques was dubbed 'Old Stoney') and Juan's first touch reaches the wall, which he mistakenly supposes is the Friar (XVI, 120 and 122).[53] Like the contemporary burlesques, *Don Juan* rationalized the supernatural, with the Stone Guest becoming a human figure disguised (in *Giovanni in London*, for example, the 'statue' is merely the voice of Leporello, delivered from behind the statue of King Charles II at Charing Cross) and, in being female, parallels the penultimate scene of Molière's *Dom Juan* in which the hero encounters 'Un Spectre en femme voilée'.[54]

BYRON'S *DON JUAN* AS A VERSION OF THE LEGEND

This programmatic reading of Byron's poem is an attempt to recreate the presuppositions of a contemporary reader, given the pervasive tradition of the legend which was sketched in Chapter 1. And, as the examples of Swinburne and John

---

[53] This episode has been acknowledged as reflecting the stock legend. For example, by Graham (ed.), *Byron's Bulldog*, 14 and by Peter Conrad, *Shandyism* (Oxford: Basil Blackwell, 1978), 62. David Punter's essay in Nigel Wood (ed.), Don Juan: *Theory in Practice* (Buckingham: Open University Press, 1993) considers Aurora as a displaced representation of the Stone Guest (pp. 122–53, 135).

[54] Molière, *Dom Juan*, Act V, scene 5, p. 101.

Addington Symonds demonstrated (see Introduction above), this type of reading was evident only in the years of the poem's first publication. These years coincide with those in which the Don Juan burlesques continued to flourish (1817–24) after which time the burlesques disappeared as quickly as they had first appeared. In 1825, for example, no revivals of the Don Juan pieces occurred, and the figure's place among the harlequinades was superseded by that of Faust. It therefore does not seem unduly tenacious to argue that all the products of the legend mutually influenced the extreme interest of the public in an increasingly self-aware manner, and that Byron's work was one of this group.

Thomas Moore attended a Don Juan pantomime on 10 July 1819 and it is quite possible that he did so in conscious anticipation of the publication of Cantos I–II of Byron's poem on 15 July 1819. After all, the pantomime version of Don Juan was hardly a new one and it is likely that Moore had seen many previous performances. His own play *M.P. or The Blue Stocking* shared the bill with *Don Juan* at the Lyceum on 23 October 1811.[55] The characters of *Giovanni in Ireland* (22 December 1821) were drawn from novels set in Ireland, and included Caroline Lamb's Glenarvon, a hero-villain who was notoriously modelled upon Byron himself. On 10 January 1820, as one of its 'Soirees Amusants', the Lyceum Theatre staged its first production of *Dr Faustus in London, or Lecture on Living Heads* in which Faustus was shown in his laboratory at midnight 'where appear in various large bottles the heads of *Lady Midnight, Don Giovanni,* and several other ludicrous characters'. The Don Giovanni head, played by Miss Stevenson in a medley of dialogue and songs, details a series of whimsical adventures 'since she came out of the third Canto of a Noble Lord's Poem'. The 'character' of *Don Giovanni* is billed as 'a new edition'. The bill of 19 January 1821 elaborates upon these allusions to Byron with its description of the author of *Don Juan* as 'the poetical punster, who keeps a menagerie of wild beasts' and who is titled Mr Apollo Stir-em-up, a poetical showman.

The frequency and cross-referentiality of these allusions to

---

[55] *Memoirs . . . of Thomas Moore* (London: Longman, Green, Longman & Roberts, 1860), i. 213.

the Don Juan legend lead us to assume that the poem's audience would have read it in an inter-textual context. The poem throughout addresses not only the responses of its readers but also their preconceptions and rash judgements. For example, in the description of Lambro's reaction to the hedonistic lifestyle everywhere apparent on the island on his return, consecutive stanzas start: 'Perhaps you think . . .', and, 'You're wrong . . .' (III, 40, 41). And when the narrator launches a general tirade against 'Bills, beans, and men', he adds 'and—no! *not* womankind' (VI, 22). The recognition of the reader's preconception of what a Don Juan is and does works in the same way, with the text sometimes opposing, sometimes insinuating or even reinforcing the preconception. The poem, that is, directly appealed to the shared knowledge of its readers concerning the legendary figure, a knowledge which gave them access to the moral and political debate in which *Don Juan* participates. Their understanding of an already existing tradition and the automatic presumptions which it entailed contribute to the dialogue of the poem. For example, in Canto XIV, the narrator warns the reader against being too complacent as to the poem's outcome:

> Above all, I beg all men to forbear
> Anticipating aught about the matter.
> They'll only make mistakes about the fair
> And Juan too, especially the latter.
>
> (XIV, 99)

Predictions concerning the poem were especially made of the notoriously named Don Juan. An early example of the unwritten element of *Don Juan* is the deliberately interrupted sentence: 'Jóse, who begot our hero, who | Begot—but that's to come' (I, 9). The possibility of Don Juan becoming a father is tantalizing because of his legendary ancestor, who was not usually portrayed as having children. The reader would automatically have suspected the worst of Don Juan, especially where amatory affairs were concerned. Thus when the love-sick young Juan thinks 'unutterable things' (I, 90), the reader may have expected them to be scurrilous rather than sublime. That the narrator anticipates the knowing response of his readers is illustrated in the following lines in which he qualifies the description of a 'dish' to make it clear to the reader that this encounter is not sexual:

> Don Juan sate—next an *à l'espagnole*—
> No damsel, but a dish, as hath been said,
> But so far like a lady that 'twas drest
> Superbly and contained a world of zest.
>
> (XV, 74)

Yet, the reader's suspicions are confirmed to a certain extent—in the eroticized world of *Don Juan*, even a culinary dish is described in sexual terms. The initial possibility of a sexual personification is strengthened by the following stanza's description of Juan seated between Aurora and Lady Adeline and the comment, some stanzas earlier, that the younger men are poor gourmands, preferring the 'dish' of 'some pretty lisper' if she is seated adjacently (XV, 70).

The deliberate deployment of innuendo also includes Byron's exploitation of serial publication. For example, *The Literary Museum* (6 December 1823), reviewing Cantos XII–XIV, demonstrates the programmatically corrupt reading which Byron both anticipated and provoked: 'We are left to all sorts of conjectures as to the progress of this friendship, by the abrupt termination of the Canto' (where the 'friendship' referred to is that between Don Juan and the Lady Adeline).[56] The encounters with Miss Protasoff and with Fitz-Fulke also exploited their positioning at the close of Cantos IX and XVI. Although Canto IX was serially published in conjunction with the following two Cantos, the narrator uses the close of the Canto to veil its outcome, teasingly.

The reader's predisposition to corrupt readings makes of such tactics as innuendo, insinuation, and doubting qualification a controlling principle for understanding the poem. These devices rely upon context, in this case that of the legend, since, given the title and figure of Don Juan, innocent readings of sexual allusion were precluded. While this chapter has argued that there is more similarity than difference between Byron's and other, more traditional, versions of the legend, to a great extent this was a consequence of the reader's predisposition to

---

[56] *The Literary Museum* (6 Dec. 1823), 769–70, 770.

make it so. The contrast between contemporary and successive readings of the poem has therefore been considerable, while the causes of this difference have been overlooked. The vehemence of the contemporary reviewers' attacks on the poem do not greatly surprise the modern reader, who explains it as a form of moral hegemony and premature 'Victorianism'. However, the programmatically suspicious interpretation of Don Juan reveals, not a different moral perspective, but an entirely different 'hero'. This character is a rakish figure, such as that sketched in the interpretations of the poem's contemporary reviewers, who were scandalized by his behaviour, not just that of 'Byron', the author.

BYRON'S RAKE

Byron's Don Juan has been criticized as a shoddy example of his illustrious predecessors and frequently because of an underestimation of the sexual content of the poem. W. H. Auden, for example, was disappointed by Byron's comparatively chaste Don Juan: 'As a libertine, his Don Juan, who sleeps only with four women, and either because they take the initiative or because they happen to be around, makes a poor showing beside the Don Giovanni of the opera's "Catalogue Aria" or even of Byron himself, with his two hundred Venetian girls.'[57] The initial premiss behind Auden's complaint is that any Don Juan worthy of the name ought to have an inexhaustible and exhausting catalogue of affairs. However this a priori argument need not be accepted, since, as the Introduction has already considered, not all 'Don Juans' have been inveterate seducers, indeed not all have even liked women. However, waiving the issue of how many seductions constitute a 'true' Don Juan, Auden's remains a conservative estimate. His 'four' are probably Julia, Haidée, Dudù, and Catherine, those with whom the relationship with Juan is obviously consummated and whose encounters with Don Juan are considered at some length. However such critics as Auden already do read 'programmatically', for few exclude the relationship with Dudù from a catalogue of

---

[57] W. H. Auden, *The Dyer's Hand* (London: Faber & Faber, 1948), 392.

Don Juan's liaisons. The 'facts' of the Dudù case include only
that she and Don Juan sleep in the same bed, that Dudù has a
nightmare, and that she awakes screaming (VI, 85). Yet the
relationship is clearly more than this and Baba's withholding
of the information about the dream (VI, 104) is as much
symptomatic of their guilt as it is illustrative of the poem's
strategy as a whole. Indeed, the more Baba tries to hide, the
more he discloses (VI, 100). Baba claims ' 'twas certain' Don
Juan's behaviour had been pure because the penalty for his
behaving otherwise was death. A sceptical response might retort
that that had never prevented any Don Juan from seducing (VI,
104).

Those critics who underestimate the extent of Don Juan's
sexual encounters have ignored the significance of innuendo.
The list ought to include Catherine's *éprouveuse* and might also
include Gulbeyaz, whose offer of herself to Juan was clearly
sexual and on the point of being accepted. Then there are
those encounters, with the Italian soprano, her Grace Fitz-Fulke
and even Leila, which are expressed with considerable sexual
innuendo. Indeed, given the insinuation of post-coital sadness
at breakfast the next morning, the affair between Don Juan and
Fitz-Fulke would appear to have been consummated (XVII, 14).
The threat of possible adultery with Adeline is one which the
poem itself acknowledges as being the express suspicion of the
reader, in the very act of attempting to deny it: 'It is not clear
that Adeline and Juan | Will fall . . .' (XIV, 99). The reviewer of
The Literary Museum (6 December 1823, see above) was one
such reader. Byron's plans for the poem suggested that Adeline
would compromise her married and chaste reputation.[58] The
softening of even Aurora in her behaviour towards Juan makes
a new tally of at least eleven romantic or flirtatious adventures.
Recent criticism would strenuously deny Don Juan the conquest
of Aurora because she is portrayed as a feminist heroine who
resists his vacuous charms. Byron's contemporary readers, however, were more disposed to suspect sexual misdemeanours. For
example, *The Examiner* (14 March 1821) was certain that Aurora's behaviour proved an acquiescence: 'this all-conquering

[58] E. J. Lovell (ed.), *His Very Self and Voice* (New York: Macmillan, 1954), 355;
Byron, *Complete Poetical Works*, v (1986), 761, ll. 479–80; and *Letters and Journals*, viii.
78.

adept contrives to win the attention'.[59] And Mary Shelley proph-
esied not that Aurora would succumb, but rather that she would
entrap Don Juan.[60] The contamination of Aurora is less surprising when the narrative treatment of the Virgin Mary is recalled:
it is suggested that Don Juan's piety towards Mary might be
libidinous rather than religious (II, 149). Thus, of Don Juan's
relationships with women, five are without doubt sexually consummated, a figure which rivals those actually represented in
other Don Juan versions. The hint of other sexual liaisons, as in
other versions, is contained within his reputation. And in the
case of Byron's *Don Juan* this reputation is sufficient to make the
suggestions, allusions, and innuendoes contaminate the interpretation of, for example, his affair with Leila, or with Gulbeyaz,
Adeline, Aurora, Fitz-Fulke, and even with the Virgin Mary. The
list is certainly sufficient to represent an indefinite number, and
perhaps most importantly because it remains open.

This sceptical interpretation of Don Juan's affairs is supported by contemporary readings. In direct contrast to Auden's
criticism, *The Monthly Review* (August 1821) complained that
the serial encounters were the only substance of the 'entire'
poem (that is, Cantos I–V):

We are disposed to ask what benefit can accrue to the reader of a series
of *love-intrigues*,—not the worship of the *casta Venus*—not the pure love
which God and nature ordain and sanctify—but the mere repetition of
sensual and 'casual fruition'—varied in attendant circumstances, but
still the same in origin, termination and tendency? Yet such has hitherto been, and such apparently will continue to be, the whole employment of Don Juan.[61]

Indeed Kierkegaard argued that Byron's *Don Juan* failed as a
version of the legend because it depicted too many seductions.
While the 'immediate' Don Juan (whose medium is music) can
seduce *mille e tre*, the 'reflective' Don Juan (whose medium is

[59] *The Examiner* (14 Mar. 1821), review of Cantos XV–XVI, pp. 163–4, 164. For
recent appraisals of Aurora, see Caroline Franklin, *Byron's Heroines* (Oxford:
Clarendon Press, 1992), 156–64, and Bernard Beatty, 'Fiction's Limit and Eden's
Door', in Beatty and Vincent Newey (eds.), *Byron and the Limits of Fiction* (Liverpool:
Liverpool University Press, 1988), *passim*.

[60] *The Letters of Mary Wollstonecraft Shelley* (Baltimore and London: Johns Hopkins
University Press, 1980), 324 (letter to Byron, 30 Mar. 1823).

[61] *The Monthly Review*, 2nd ser. 95 (Aug. 1821), review of Cantos III–V, pp. 418–
24, 420.

language) needs to seduce only one, 'and how he does it is what occupies us'.[62]

When the Reverend George Burges labelled Byron's poetic characters by their prevailing vices, Harold was judged proud, Cain blasphemous, and Juan licentious (*Cato to Lord Byron on the Immorality of his Writings*, 1824).[63] And when Hazlitt coyly decided against describing 'simple girls' in *Table Talk*, he did so with an expression of Don Juan's infidelity: 'Oh! might I but attempt a description of some of them in poetic prose, Don Juan would forget his Julia ...'. Hazlitt's insinuation is illustrative of the contemporary reader's preconceptions because it was made before the publication of Cantos III and IV, in which Juan so obviously 'forgets' Julia in his affair with Haidée. Byron's Don Juan was still relatively 'innocent' of the later serial seductions (although Canto II, stanza 208, had already suggested that Julia might be forgotten).[64]

The plot which these writers imply is, of course, entirely consonant with the premisses of a conventional Don Juan play. Juan's original naivety concerning relationships with women perversely led him into an affair at the rather premature age of 16, and this enabled him to embark on a series of affairs while he still retained his youthful attractiveness. Julia's letter predicted that he would be beloved and love 'many' (I, 195). Certainly Juan is seldom without a partner or possible partner, his adventures are structured by Byron around an amorous interest: 'As our hero can't do without a mistress ...'.[65] The females, meanwhile, remain merely dispensable or at any rate numerical: 'We left our hero and third heroine ...' (VI, 7). This disposal of the heroines is also reflected in Don Juan's forgetting of his past lovers: Haidée is remembered as far as the encounter with Gulbeyaz, although when Don Juan weeps at the slave-market the narrator ascribes his tears to causes which include, only in passing, the loss of a mistress. Haidée's significance to Juan is subverted by being included in a list which also

[62] Kierkegaard, *Either/Or*, 108. See also Otto D. Rank, *The Legend of Don Juan*, tr. David G. Winter (Princeton: Princeton University Press, 1975), 100.

[63] Quoted in Chew, *Byron in England*, 38.

[64] *The Complete Works of William Hazlitt*, ed. P. P. Howe (London: J. M. Dent, 1930–4), viii. *Table-Talk*, essay 23, 'On Great and Little Things': 'Simple Girls', pp. 226–42, 236. First published in *The London Magazine* in 1820–1.

[65] Lovell (ed.), *Medwin's Conversations*, 164.

comprises the losses of blood, wealth, and comfortable quarters (V, 8). She is then forgotten until the meeting with Aurora rekindles a faint remembrance in his act of comparing the two (XV, 58), and even here there is some doubt as to whether it is the narrator or Don Juan who remembers. The Don Juan–Haidée episode is thus ironized by its positioning within the structure of the poem.

If some of these encounters seem to strain credibility as *amours* worthy of a Don Juan, what have been forgotten are the reader's predisposition to think the worst of the character, at least where amorous events are concerned, and the narrator's conspiratorial innuendoes. Because of the character's very name, the distinction between an archetypal Don Juan and that of Byron's hero could never be fully effected. In a conversation with Byron, Dr William Kennedy complained that 'the hero goes on, prosperous and uncontrolled, from one vice to another, unveiling and mocking the crimes and vices of mankind'. Byron's reply was ambiguous as to the distinction between his hero and the traditional Don Juan: 'I take a vicious and unprincipled character, and lead him through the ranks of society.'[66] Although both Kennedy and Byron were primarily attacking the vices of society, this exchange demonstrates the necessary confusion which the shared name engendered, the doubt as to whether the 'character' was the legendary Don Juan or Byron's own. After all, Byron's description is not dissimilar from the many interpretations of the licentious protagonist depicted by the reviewers. This blurring also occurred between the title of the poem as a whole and its eponymous hero. *The Monthly Review* (February 1824), for example, claimed that '*Don Juan* is now voted a bore, and to see him figuring *ad infinitum* . . .'—a confusion which creates a synonymity between 'it' (the text) and 'him' (the character).[67]

The indistinction was partly a consequence of the poem's style and mode of address, both of which were themselves 'Don Juan-like'. That the narrator of Byron's poem displays the cynicism, facetiousness, and libertinism made typical of the legendary Don Juan by myth-criticism is a modern critical concession

---

[66] Lovell (ed.), *His Very Self and Voice*, 442.
[67] *The Monthly Review*, 2nd ser. 103 (Feb. 1824), review of Cantos XII–XIV, pp. 212–15.

to the importance of the legend.[68] The narrator's adoption of a prototypical Don Juan-like pose certainly exacerbated the fury of the reviewers. Many examples of this persona might be cited: his profession of direct knowledge of a harem (VI, 51; see also I, 87); his postponing of penitence for present pleasure: 'Let us have wine and women, mirth and laughter, | Sermons and soda water the day after' (II, 178, and see also IV, 25); his defence of being unable to resist instinctual compulsion (IX, 21); his specious attempt to attack sexual inconstancy (II, 209–15). The continual leers and ribaldry of the narrator also blur the distinction between his and his character's behaviour until there is a dizzy doubt as to which is really committing the 'sin'—Juan in his actions, which are perhaps only apparently innocent, or the rhetoric of the narrator. Is the narrator or the character, or indeed the reader, 'responsible' for the insinuations? The ribaldry of the narrator is also perfectly compatible with the theme. Byron defended *Cain* from Murray's suggested alterations by claiming that Lucifer could not be made to speak like the 'Bishop of Lincoln'.[69] In the same way the theme of Don Juan could not escape sexual knowingness. The choice of theme was responsible for the text's degree of lewd suggestiveness, since it encouraged and predisposed the reader to suspect ulterior, and corrupt, interpretations.

That readers also blurred the contours between narrator and author is unsurprising, especially given the context of already prevalent biographical readings, from Childe Harold to the protagonists of the oriental Tales. Byron's preface to Canto IV of *Childe Harold* described his previous attempts to draw a line between himself and his creations as 'unavailing'. So much so that in *Don Juan*, far from refuting this approach, he positively encouraged it by sprinkling his text with tantalizingly biographical details. We have already seen how many of Byron's readers thought of him as an English Don Juan, a judgement which was circulated by Caroline Lamb's *Glenarvon* (1816) and the many

---

[68] e.g. Conrad, *Shandyism*, 104. For a Regency equivalent, see Smiles, *Publisher and Friends*, i. 414: 'the Protean style of "Don Juan", instead of checking (as the fetters of rhythm generally do) his natural activity, not only gives him wider limits to range in, but even generates a more roving disposition' (letter of Croker to Murray, 26 Mar. 1820).

[69] See *Byron's Letters and Journals*, ix, 53 (3 Nov. 1821) and ix. 60 (15 Nov. 1821).

moral condemnations directed at Byron after the separation from his wife and from England in the same year. The parody *Jack the Giant Queller; or Prince Juan* (1819) characterizes Prince Juan as Byron, including a parody of his lyric 'Fare Thee Well' (stanza xxxviii). Only the public perception of Byron as a Don Juan might provide the stimulus for this poem's accusation: 'Juan prov'd a raving libertine | Worse than Don Juan in the Pantomime' (stanza xxv). Again there is a deliberate play upon the two possibilities of interpreting Juan: the personification of Byron ('Prince Juan') or the hero of his own poem (Don Juan).[70] When *The Edinburgh Monthly Review* (October 1819) complained that *Don Juan* systemized Byron's tendency to profanity, it was the inter-related contaminations of subject, theme, expression, and author to which it objected:

the occasional profanity which defiled his graver, and the indecency which stained his lighter productions, are here *embodied* into the compactness of a system, and have been madly exalted from their station as humble though repulsive accessories of his theme, to be its avowed end, purpose, and consummation—that we have here, for the first time in the history of our literature, a great work, of which the very basis is infidelity and licentiousness, and the most obtrusive ornaments are impure imaginations and blasphemous leers.[71]

Modern criticism has been unable to explain the extremity of such responses because it has failed to understand the network of allusions which the text *Don Juan* automatically and necessarily engendered: that an author with the reputation of a libertine writes a work about the infamous seducer Don Juan, indeed audaciously entitles that work, *Don Juan*, and composes it with a bravura display of 'smut', insinuations, and obscenity. The reviewer of *The Literary Chronicle* (24 July 1819) who complained that the 'very subject' was in itself censurable added 'but particularly so when it is made the vehicle of indecent allusions, *double entendres* and a mockery of religion'.[72] The radical publisher, William Benbow, stated that *Don Juan* was composed 'in the spirit of an epicure and a libertine' and Harriette Wilson wrote to Byron: 'don't make a mere *coarse* old libertine of

[70] *Jack the Giant Queller; or Prince Juan*, printed in *Political Satires 1810–1819* (London: W. Horncastle, 1819).
[71] *The Edinburgh Monthly Review*, 2 (Oct. 1819), 468–86, 482.
[72] *The Literary Chronicle and Weekly Review* (24 July 1819), l. 49.

yourself'.[73] Such narrative devices as insinuation, innuendo, and bawdy pun are appropriate for the subject-matter but they are not merely expressions of it. Instead they serve a tactical purpose.

THE DEFENCE OF DON JUAN

The reading proposed in this chapter dramatically alters the character of Byron's Don Juan who has been unanimously interpreted as innocent by modern criticism. Those critics who have conceded the significance of the legend to Byron's poem do so only as a consequence of the 'inversion' of the legend which Byron's poem, they argue, represents. The importance of the legend is acknowledged only in so far as it provides an ironic reversal or point and counterpoint dynamic with Byron's inauthentic seducer, facilitated by Lévi-Strauss's stressing of inversion as the way in which a myth survives.[74] But such critics actually concur with those to whom they are ostensibly opposed. The Don Juan which they portray—entirely innocent, amiable, and passive, a victim rather than a predator—is exactly that of those critics who deny that Byron's *Don Juan* is a version of the legend. This chapter has demonstrated that reading programmatically, that is responding to the insinuations which surround the character, prevents such an interpretation of Don Juan. When the poem is read unprogrammatically, that is, uncomprehending both the sexual humour and the irony, an innocent Don Juan does appear since the 'facts' support this interpretation. Considering only such 'facts', it might be argued that Don Juan is as chaste as he might be—given the circumstances. He has no opportunity to return to Donna Julia (who is in a convent in the country from which he has been exiled), or to Haidée (who is dead, although this is unknown to Don Juan himself); he resists the temptations of the Italian soprano and of

[73] Benbow's statement is quoted in St Clair, 'Impact of Byron's Writings', 23; Harriette Wilson's in George Paston and Peter Quennell, '*To Lord Byron*': *Feminine Profiles Based Upon Unpublished Letters* (London: John Murray, 1939), 159.

[74] See e.g.: J. W. Smeed, *Don Juan* (London: Routledge, 1990), 35; Lilian Furst, *Fictions of Romantic Irony in European Narrative* (London: Macmillan, 1984), 99 and 103; James D. Wilson, 'Tirso, Molière and Byron', *The South Central Bulletin*, 32/4 (Winter 1972), 248.

Gulbeyaz; he has no choice but to share his bed with one of the harem, the alluring Dudù; he is commanded by the Empress of Russia, Catherine, and thus also by her *éprouveuse*; and merely flirts with the numerous English ladies, mostly married, who literally fall at his feet. Lady Pinchbeck's defence of Don Juan is exemplary of these kinds of argument. She judges him to be: '[a] little spoilt, but not so altogether, | Which was a wonder, if you think who got him | And how he had been tossed, he scarce knew whither' (XII, 49).

This defence of Don Juan was later echoed in George Bernard Shaw's short story, 'Don Giovanni Explains' (1887), in which the ghost of Mozart's seducer claims that, contrary to his reputation, he was pious and chaste; and his notoriety as a seducer was a result of a series of misunderstandings and of women's compulsive attraction towards him. It thus recreates the traditional narrative from an altered perspective. It elaborates the kinds of arguments which Mozart's Don Giovanni might make in his own defence, and in this way is not dissimilar from Byron's *Don Juan* in which Don Juan is defended by the narrator's telling of his career and by the author's structuring of it.[75]

The very reading which modern critics have argued for the hero's character is thus in fact the basis for Byron's defence of Don Juan. Although it is unaware both of the poem's suggestiveness and of its political challenge, it is the one, indeed the only, interpretation which Byron would have acknowledged. Because the hints of a more sinister Juan almost always originate in the narrator's innuendoes, cynical taggings, and doubting qualifications, the darker insinuations which surround Don Juan's character are attributed to the narrator or, as the narrator often argues, to the reader. The use of innuendo allowed the narrator to remain uncontaminated by it, since he could always argue innocence and deflect the blame on to the reader. This is obvious in the narrator's bawdy insinuation about the 'one vent' of the convent: 'And what is that? Devotion, doubtless—how | Could you ask such a question?' (VI, 33). These frequently abrupt terminations coyly tease the reader in confounding the ethical with the artful. Lady Byron wrote that her husband's

---

[75] George Bernard Shaw, 'Don Giovanni Explains' (1887), in *Short Stories, Scraps and Shavings* (London: Constable, 1932), 95–116, 107 and 108.

insinuations were 'much more convincing than the most direct
assertion' of his unnamed 'crime', to which Doris Langley
Moore commented that it was 'marvellously typical of Lady
Byron to be more convinced by insinuations than by direct
assertion'. Jerome Christensen added that it was also marvellously typical of every reader of Byron.[76]

The characteristic narrative devices of *Don Juan*—innuendo,
doubting qualifications, sly hints, asides, and contradictory
taggings of lines—are thus central to the poem's rhetorical
strategy. They often assume the form of narrative asides, or
after-thoughts, 'tagged' to the end of a line. For example, Juan
delights the chaste 'and those who are not so much inspired', a
euphemism for the promiscuous, from whose contamination he
is in this way at least rhetorically shielded (XIV, 41). The accuracy of the assertion 'Sincere he was' (XV, 13) is subverted by
the continuation of the line: 'at least you could not doubt it | In
listening merely to his voice's tone'. The final couplet of this
stanza further undermines Don Juan's virtuous sincerity: 'The
devil hath not in all his quiver's choice | An arrow for the heart
like a sweet voice.' However innocent the narrator might pretend Juan is, he is here, again, associatively linked with the devil,
a significance which would be unlikely to escape the suspicious
reader. When Don Juan is pampered and indulged by
Catherine, the narrator qualifies his apparent certainty that this
did not spoil him with a more doubtful after-thought: 'Though
this might ruin others, it did not him, | At least entirely' (XII,
49).

The very practice of qualification highlights the easiness of
lying. Almost without thinking one could tell an untruth, by a
mere slip of phrase: 'Gulbeyaz and her lord were sleeping, or |
At least one of them . . .' (VI, 24). Like many other versions of
the legend, *Don Juan* foregrounds questions of the deceptions
of appearance and the difficulty of determining a 'reality' which
would be both definitive and readily distinguishable from appearance. It thus highlights the provisionality of language, its
inability to sustain such concepts as 'truth' and 'falsity'. This
relativism also includes the determination of ethical judgement,

---

[76] Doris Langley Moore, *Lord Byron: Accounts Rendered* (London: John Murray,
1974), 444. Jerome Christensen, *Lord Byron's Strength* (London and Baltimore:
Johns Hopkins University Press, 1993), 80.

a parallel difficulty to that of ascertaining 'truth', since the act
alone is insufficient to deserve the attribution of vice or virtue.
Don Juan's action of resisting the obvious attractions of the
Romagnole singer might earn him the praise of the poem's
most moral readers. However, the same readers would be unlikely to applaud if the cause of his resistance was not that he
was unwilling, but only that he was physically unable, to re-
spond. Don Juan's actions may belong to the world of the
poem's 'facts' but it is his motivation and intentions which will
decide the moral judgement of him. Byron's preoccupation
with this issue is apparent elsewhere: for example in Adah's
questioning of Lucifer, 'Can circumstance make sin | Or vir-
tue?', or in Werner's advice to his son, 'there are crimes | Made
venial by the occasion'.[77] Since Don Juan, like Lucifer, was a
commonly recognized 'sinner', Byron's defence of him engages
throughout with such arguments. The varying responses of the
poem's dissimilar readers therefore literalize the provisionality
and relativism of judgement which are embodied within the
narrative.

While the use of these narrative devices often shields Don
Juan from censure, Byron also rendered Don Juan more sympathetic in portraying his comparative ordinariness. That this
emphasis is ideological is evident in the direct address to the
reader: Don Juan's behaviour is frequently compared to how
anyone, including the reader, might react in that given situation (see, for example, II, 167; V, 43). This automatically forces
the censorious reader into a position of hypocrisy. George
Bernard Shaw's criticism of Byron's Juan for being too commonplace is therefore both entirely accurate and inapposite:
'In fact he is not a true Don Juan at all; for he is no more an
enemy of God than any romantic and adventurous young sower
of wild oats. Had you and I been in his place at his age, who
knows whether we might not have done as he did.'[78] Don Juan's
very ordinariness forms part of his defence: 'Youth, ceruse |
Against his heart preferred their *usual* claims' (XI, 48, my italics). Shaw's statement portrays himself as a man of the world
who is indulgent towards the inevitable sowing of wild oats, his

---

[77] *Complete Poetical Works*, vi (1991), 245 (*Cain*, ll. 381–2) and p. 432 (*Werner*, ll. 147–8).

[78] Shaw, Epistle Dedicatory to *Man and Superman* (1903), 12.

worldliness and tolerance both expressed in his deployment of the proverbial and jovial phrase. This stance is mirrored throughout *Don Juan*, and reflected most particularly, both in content and style, in Lord Henry's approbation of the youthful lapses of Don Juan: 'He knew the world and would not see depravity | In faults which sometimes show the soil's *fertility*' (XIII, 22, my italics). Such 'liberalism' is typical of the narrative stance of *Don Juan* which, Don Juan-like, confounds liberty with licence.

The narrator maintains that criticism has misjudged the poem throughout *Don Juan*, preserving both it and its character's innocence and transferring the accusation of corruption onto the misinterpretation of the readers.[79] The narrator's statement, 'I'll try | To tell you truths you will not take as true, | Because they are so' (X, 84), plays upon the sense that the reader is free in his interpretation and the sense that the reader is just too headstrong, if not opinionated. By such strategies his hero is relatively immured from censure because the plot or Juan's actions in themselves are largely insufficient to condemn him. The insinuations of a more cynical interpretation of Juan's nature rely instead upon a predisposition in the reader to think badly, or stereotypically, of him. In *The Deformed Transformed*, Lucifer, who has taken the form of 'Caesar' claims: 'The Devil speaks truth much oftener than he's deemed: | He hath an ignorant audience.'[80] In the benevolent readings of modern criticism, Byron might be said to have found a competent audience for *Don Juan*.

To a certain extent the dichotomy between contemporary and modern readings represents moral tensions which were existent at the time of the poem's composition. Chapter 1 illustrated how ambivalent responses to the legendary, if charming seducer could be, while more recent portrayals of Don Juan on the London stage had begun to treat Don Juan more sympathetically. *Harlequin's Vision, Giovanni in London, Giovanni in Botany Bay, Giovanni in the Country*—all culminated in happy

---

[79] Examples of the explicit criticism of the reader for precipitate or erroneous judgement include: I, 207; IV, 7; VI, 56, 88; VII, 3–4; IX, 22; X, 11; XI, 88, 90; XII, 86; XIII, 25.

[80] *Complete Poetical Works*, vi (1991), 568–9, *The Deformed Transformed*, Part II, scene 3.

endings. In *Don Giovanni; or, A Spectre on Horseback!* the final punishment of the seducer is deliberately obscured so that there is some doubt as to whether the devils are simulated or 'real'. *Giovanni in London* demonstrated the new enthusiasm for reforming the libertine. Its Leporello exclaims 'Oh! if we could but reclaim this libertine, it would immortalize us' (II, vi). The finale became an appeal to the tolerance and humanity of the audience rather than a moral sermon delivered for their edification:

LADIES:	Worthy patrons,
GENTLEMEN:	Kindly shield him
LADIES:	Do not blame him
GENTLEMEN:	Pardon yield him
ALL:	Here's success to Don Giovanni!
	Though his follies have been many,
	Overlook his errors past.[81]

Even within the more traditional versions of the legend—the pantomimes based upon Shadwell and the Spanish tradition, or Mozart's opera—performances of the infamous seducer had become markedly more sympathetic. Within the pantomime tradition, Don Juan became a variation of the English Harlequin and endeared himself to the audience in his attempts to win some attractive Columbine, struggling against an obnoxious Pantaloon in the form of a husband or father, and succeeding through his own ingenuity or through the aid of his companion Scaramouch.[82] In productions of Mozart and in other operatic versions, performances of Don Giovanni also became markedly more sympathetic. Hazlitt criticized Kemble's portrayal of Don Giovanni in *The Libertine* (25 May 1817) as being so tame that his punishment seemed entirely unjustified. That this response was not idiosyncratically Hazlitt's own is evident in the agreement between his review and that of Henry Crabb Robinson, who also complained that Kemble played the part 'very tamely'.[83]

[81] Mandel (ed.), *Theatre of Don Juan*, 442, 445–6.
[82] See Beaty, 'Harlequin Don Juan', 405.
[83] William Hazlitt, review of 'The Libertine' at Covent-Garden Theatre in *The Examiner* (25 May 1817), repr. in *The Complete Works*, v. 370–3, 371. Henry Crabb Robinson, *The London Theatre*, ed. Eluned Brown (London: Soc. for Theatre Research, 1966), 76 (20 May 1817).

Coleridge's approval of the strict didacticism of more traditional versions of the legend was therefore not reflected in
contemporary stage productions. While his stout defence of the
morality of the legend and its fitting conclusion preceded the
performance of Kemble in *The Libertine* and the composition of
the burlesques, its vehemence betrays his fear that such interpretations might occur. Critical interpretations of the theatre
were so intertwined with pleasure that reviewers had long been
praising those Don Juans and Giovannis who were entertaining.
A review of a pantomime Don Juan in 1801 spoke of its
portrayal of 'the dauntless daring and awful punishment of a
libertine'.[84] Mr De Camp's performance of Don Juan in a
pantomime of 1801 was censured because it did not delineate
an elegant libertine: 'his figure is altogether too insignificant
and his deportment by no means significantly graceful for the
part'.[85] Later, Ambrogetti's performance of Mozart's Don
Giovanni was widely praised as 'vivacious', 'dashing', and a
fitting representation of 'a dissolute but finished cavalier'. Such
attributes were insufficient for Hazlitt's praise, who, admitting
that Ambrogetti possessed 'considerable life and spirits', and
was a 'successful and significant intriguer', was disappointed
because he was not 'an intriguer—in love' and lacked the
groundwork of 'sensibility'.[86]

These contemporary reclamations of the Don Juan figure
were possible to a certain extent because authenticity had become one of the most esteemed virtues. This was already apparent in Shadwell's portrayal of Don John, who was somewhat
exonerated by his Hobbesian appeals to 'nature'. When the
statue asks Don John if he will repent, his response offered the
possibility of a benevolent interpretation, as being a heroic
denial of hypocrisy according to his claims to live 'naturally':
'Could'st thou bestow another heart on me, I might; but with

[84] *The Theatrical Repertory*, review of the pantomime of *Don Juan* at Drury Lane
(Friday 4 Dec. 1801), 192.
[85] *The Theatrical Repertory*, 13 (14 Dec. 1801), 209.
[86] *The Theatrical Inquisitor* (Aug. 1817), 137: 'Ambrogetti as a dissolute
yet finished cavalier'. *Autobiography of Leigh Hunt*, ed. J. E. Morpurgo (London:
The Cresset Press, 1949), 128: 'Ambrogetti . . . was a fine dashing representative
of Don Juan, without a voice'. *The Theatrical Inquisitor* (Aug. 1817), 137: 'Never
was *Ambrogetti* more vivacious, more characteristic in the profligate hero'. Hazlitt,
review of *Don Giovanni* in *The Examiner* (20 Apr. 1817), repr. in *Complete Works*, v.
365.

this heart I have, I cannot.'[87] The contradiction inherent within this characterization means that Don John lives according to an instinct which refuses compromise, and yet, in order to achieve his acknowledged desires he must use art. Similarly, Molière's Dom Juan hypocritically adopted the mask of piety in order to satisfy an impulse which may certainly have been reprehensible but 'at least' was honest: 'Such conduct carries no stigma nowadays, for hypocrisy is a fashionable vice and all vices pass for virtues once they become fashionable.'[88] The confusions between appearance and reality, performative and referential speech, are frequently integral to portrayals of Don Juan, who exploits such indistinctions as strategy. Once society began to value its heroes according to the integrity of their actions, however reprehensible in themselves, it was able to envisage a 'heroic' Don Juan.

By the early nineteenth century the glorification of passion and sensibility further supported those writers who attempted to defend or 'rationalize' the seducer. Laurence Sterne's portrait of the amorous Yorick in *A Sentimental Journey through France and Italy* (1768) exploited this new valorization, and, like Byron's *Don Juan*, demonstrated how it could be used to excuse and even heroize the former libertine. Yorick argues that he can be philanthropic only when he is in love.[89] Many turn-of-the-century debates distinguished the passionate lover who was carried away by excessive emotion from the cold and calculated seducer-as-strategist. We would expect the Hunts' interpretations of *Don Juan* to be sympathetic (John Hunt published Cantos VI–XVI) and, indeed, Leigh Hunt distinguished Byron's Don Juan from 'the unfeeling vagabond in the Italian opera'.[90] The distinction between the two kinds of seducer was also carefully maintained by Mary Wollstonecraft, and the comparison, in *A Vindication of the Rights of Woman* (1792), led her into rather surprising praise of the 'libertine':

---

[87] Shadwell, *Complete Works*, iii. *The Libertine*, Act V, p. 91.

[88] Molière, *Dom Juan*, Act V, scene 2, p. 95: 'Il n'a plus de honte maintenant à cela: l'hypocrisie est un vice à la mode, et tous les vices à la mode passent pour vertus.'

[89] Laurence Sterne, *A Sentimental Journey* (1768; Harmondsworth: Penguin, 1972), 57.

[90] *Leigh Hunt's Literary Criticism*, ed. Lawrence Huston Houtchens and Carolyn Washburn Houtchens (New York: Columbia University Press, 1956), 158.

'I have endeavoured' says Lord Chesterfield, 'to gain the hearts of twenty women, whose persons I would not have given a fig for'. The libertine who, in a gust of passion, takes advantage of unsuspecting tenderness, is a saint when compared with this cold-hearted rascal— for I like to use significant words.

How much more modest is the libertine who obeys the call of appetite or fancy than the lewd joker who sets the table in a roar.[91]

Coleridge's essay on Don Juan also did not deny the charisma of the central character. Indeed, in admitting the grandeur of Don Juan's behaviour, he even confessed a desire to *be* him: 'Who also can deny a portion of sublimity to the tremendous consistency with which he stands out the last fearful trial, like a second Prometheus?'[92] The inclusion of even the morally conservative Coleridge within this trend of heroizing Don Juan demonstrates its prevalence. Coleridge excused his apparent praise of Don Juan by claiming that the stage Don Juan was merely an abstraction, not because of his wickedness, but predominantly because of his unique and 'impossible' combination of entire wickedness with desirable qualities. It is this very configuration which Byron claims for his 'real' Don Juan.

Byron's *Don Juan* differed significantly from these other versions and interpretations. However sympathetic their libertine might be, however engaging and vital the dramatic personification of their Don Juan or Giovanni, he was nevertheless to be duly punished—unless, that is, he were to reform (as indeed he did in, for example, *Harlequin's Vision* and *Giovanni in London*). Coleridge's moral quarrel with the 'jacobinism' of the theatre was that its villains were exonerated: 'mysterious villains, (geniuses of supernatural intellect, if you will take the authors' words for it, but on a level with the meanest ruffians of the condemned cells, if we are to judge by their actions and contrivances)'.[93] This specific accusation—that villains were exonerated—had also been the focus of Coleridge's criticism of Byron in *The Courier* in 1816. The didactic ending of the tradi-

---

[91] Mary Wollstonecraft, *A Vindication of the Rights of Woman* (1792; repr. Harmondsworth: Penguin, 1992), ch. 4, p. 148.
[92] *The Collected Works of Samuel Taylor Coleridge*, ed. Walter Engell and W. Jackson Bate (Princeton: Princeton University Press, 1983), vii. *Biographia Literaria: II*, 219.
[93] Ibid. 211.

tional legend was the compromise which accommodated both the theatrical expediency of a dashing actor and the moral stipulation of edification. It also remained the most proverbial and immediately recognizable feature of the legend.[94] The pantomimes and burlesques of the London stage attracted their audiences with bold advertisements of presentations of hell-fire. Some of the early responses to Byron's poem quoted at the beginning of this chapter demonstrated that this was an ending which many of his readers wished for the poem. However, Byron consciously distinguished his own Don Juan version from that of others only in the case of the ending. Murray wrote to Byron of Lady Caroline Lamb's fancy dress at Almack's masquerade in 1820 where she appeared as Don Juan surrounded by a host of devils. Byron recognized the allusion to his own poem (if not to himself) and only wondered 'that she went so far as "the *Theatre*" for "the Devils"'—a detail studiously avoided in his own interpretation.[95] The distinction was repeated by Byron in quoting Teresa Guiccioli's objection to his poem: 'She says in the P.S. that she is only sorry D.J. does not *remain* in Hell (or go there).'[96]

Byron's intentions for the poem remained ambiguous. He once teased that Don Juan would reform by turning 'methodist' (see also III, 66). This 'moral' ending, however, was not without its own ambivalence, for 'methodism', or rather 'methodist*e*', was a euphemism for homosexuality understood between Byron, Hobhouse, and Matthews.[97] He also deliberately played with the possibility of the conventional ending, Don Juan's dramatic capture by hell. In *Don Juan*, Canto I, he anticipated moral censure of his poem and quickly defended his poem by arguing '*Besides*, in Canto twelfth, I mean to show | The very place where wicked people go' (I, 207, my italics) and he later implied that the book would ultimately frustrate its critics in their suspicious expectations (XII, 87). This teasing is also evident in his comparatively late conversation with Kennedy, re-

---

[94] See e.g. *The Letters of Thomas Moore*, ed. W. S. Dowden (Oxford: Clarendon Press, 1964), ii. 645 (July or Aug. 1829).

[95] *Byron's Letters and Journals*, vii. 169 (to John Murray, 31 Aug. 1820).

[96] Ibid. viii. 145 (to John Murray, 4 July 1821).

[97] For Don Juan becoming Methodist, see Lovell (ed.), *His Very Self and Voice*, 332 and 363. For the innuendo of 'methodiste' see Louis Crompton, *Byron and Greek Love* (Berkeley: University of California Press, 1985), 127–9.

called in Teresa Guiccioli's *Lord Byron jugé par les témoins de sa vie*.
When Kennedy argued that Byron was merely displaying, not
curing, vice, Byron replied: 'But I shall not be so bad as
that; . . . you shall see what a winding up I shall give to the
story.'[98] Lady Caroline Lamb's verse imitation *Gordon: A Tale*
(1822) also defended the poem from moral censure by partially
quoting *Don Juan* (I, 207), and by advertising its own final view
of hell as being like that promised by Byron in his 'Canto
twelfth' (*Gordon*, II). The following defence of Byron's poem by
'John', a ghost-like appearance, continues the argument:

> You judge the subject long before the time;
> The whole is not yet published, as you know;
> And you condemn the author for a crime
> Not yet committed—this you must allow;
> Remember, Juan has scarce reached his prime,
> We have but two Cantos, then pray forego
> Your bitter judgement till the tale is ended,
> And Juan's pleasures also are suspended.[99]

One of *Don Juan*'s most subversive effects was therefore that of
form, for in being inconclusive, it both teased and frustrated
the reader's anticipation for either final justice or reformation.[100] Thus, like the prototypical Don Juan, the effect of the
poem was to delay a reformation of his morality (by punishing
or reclaiming its hero) until it was too late to do so.

The continual postponement of any moral conclusion is mirrored in the treatment of Don Juan throughout the text. The
description of the 'hero' is poised between two tendencies: a
Don Juan with enough characteristics to resemble the traditional figure and provoke the usual admonitions and pious
platitudes concerning just deserts, and a Don Juan whom the
narrator can defend from such censure. Thus Byron's Don Juan
is an ambivalent mixture of proofs of 'innocence' and sly insinuations of something more 'wicked'. The following lines are

[98] Guiccioli, *Lord Byron* (London: Richard Bentley, 1869), i. 20.
[99] Caroline Lamb, *Gordon: A Tale* (London: T. & J. Allman, 1821), Canto II,
stanza 13.
[100] See Hazlitt's recognition of this narrative tactic: 'Mr Bowles has numbers of
manuscript sermons by him, the morality of which, we will venture to say, is quite as
pure, as orthodox, as that of the unpublished cantos of Don Juan', in 'Pope, Lord
Byron, and Mr Bowles', *The London Magazine* (June 1821), repr. in *Complete Works*,
xix. 62–84, 66.

illustrative of several of the narrator's tactics, here working in conjunction:

> About this time, as might have been anticipated,
> Seduced by youth and dangerous examples,
> Don Juan grew, I fear, a little dissipated.
>
> (X, 23)

The quoted lines begin by acknowledging the reader's constitutive reading. The confirmation of this preconception is deliberately delayed by the intermediary second line, a prefacing of justification and excuse. Within the accusation itself the narrator preserves a space of moral innocence ('I fear').

The portrayal of Don Juan strives to counteract anticipated moral condemnation. Instead the narrator, deploying innuendo and understated asides, forces his reader to read in a corrupt manner, whilst reclaiming the innocence as his, and Juan's, own. Thus Byron exploited a deliberately hypocritical style as a rhetorical weapon with which to attack the 'cant', that is hypocrisy, which explicitly motivated the poem—and in the same way that the traditional Don Juan exploits the illusion of truth in an 'authentic' behaviour which is duplicitous. The nephew of Leigh Hunt recognized Byron's tactic and appropriated its argument for his own review of Cantos III–V: '[Byron] is particularly successful in his careless contempt of the canting moralists who, by the help of their own polluted imaginations, found many hidden indelicacies to cry out against in the two former Cantos.'[101]

The use of innuendo was especially seductive because it enticed readers into corrupt readings through humour, a strategy which is openly admitted in the comparison of the poem's readers with children who are encouraged to cut teeth with a coral (I, 209). The reader is faced with alternative responses—a ribald laugh or solemn censoriousness—responses which would have been equivalent to those facing the audiences at performances of the traditional stage representations of the legend, and which feminist analyses of the legend still face. The anonymous writer in *The Eclectic Review* (August 1819) recognized this danger in referring to *Don Juan*, Cantos I–II, with

---

[101] *The Examiner* (26 Aug. 1821), 538.

readerly unease: 'There are cases in which it is equally impossible to relax into laughter or to soften into pity, without feeling that an immoral concession is made to vice.'[102]

Innuendo depends on a sense of context—in the case of Byron's poem, the expectations aroused by the very figure of Don Juan. Innuendo is also neatly emblematic of the relative powers of the author and the reader: in *Don Juan*, it facilitates a lewdness which is both encouraged (by the author) and understood (by the reader). And because it only becomes 'existent' when it is 'effected', both author and reader were able to argue the responsibility of the other in evading their own. Innuendo also incorporates the possibility of several readings. In fact its full power depends to a great extent on its ability to alienate as much as to share intimacy.

[102] *The Eclectic Review* (Aug. 1819), 3.

3

The Political Implications of a Don Juan

'The last thing Juan is doing in Europe is raising stones against tyrants. These libertarian outbursts have no correspondent action in the poem.'[1] By focusing exclusively upon Don Juan's action *within* the poem, Malcolm Kelsall underestimated the politically subversive challenge *of* a poem whose subject was Don Juan. The allusive appeal of the title *Don Juan* was not only that it would portray a philanderer, its politics were not solely sexual. It also invoked specific class configurations which the figure represented, for Don Juan was an aristocratic figure whose story was popular among the lower classes. And the poetry of Lord Byron, whose former publications had previously entertained the upper classes, was more widely read when the working classes bought his new poem—*Don Juan*.

The poem's own references to the 'mob' and the 'people' indicate that it did not foresee speaking to them, however it might speak of them (see for example, VIII, 50–1; IX, 25; and X, 63). The narrator may claim that he is writing only for the initiated, and do so by quoting Latin: '*Vetabo Cereris sacrum qui volgarit,* | Which means that vulgar people must not share it' (XIV, 21), but the open invitation which a book entitled *Don Juan* automatically effected was a 'mystery' which the most uneducated of theatre-goers could have penetrated. Working-class readers seem to have relished the opportunity to read the poetry of Lord Byron, the subject of so much notoriety, vilification, and prohibition among 'superior' circles, and in a work whose theme and diction was comprehensible to them. The poem was therefore in the unusual position of attracting just about the only readers which it ostensibly neglected to address—other than in the obvious significance of title and hero. This chapter considers the extent to which the poem was seen to be

---

[1] Malcolm Kelsall, *Byron's Politics* (Brighton: The Harvester Press, 1987), 151.

politically subversive and the extent to which the Don Juan legend made it so.

THE POPULARITY OF DON JUAN AMONG THE LOWER CLASSES

'After the stately music of Mozart, and the imposing machinery of Covent-Garden Theatre, this representation had at least the merit of boldness, and we are not sure that it had not the more important merit of bringing back to the class in which its effect is most natural, a work which belongs to Pantomime.'[2] This review of a Don Juan pantomime at the Lyceum Theatre betrays the unease which was at the heart of the reception of the Don Juan legend in 1817. Chapter 1 demonstrated that the legend steadily achieved such popularity that new versions were anxious to justify their choice of theme as involuntary. The accusation of pandering to the public in a spirit of crass commercialism was anticipated and feared. In addition, the popularity of the Don Juan theme was tainted by its association with the lower classes. This was apparent throughout its early history and continued to be the case in England during the late eighteenth and early nineteenth centuries. While all the Don Juan publications of this time were inexpensive, that of the 6d. chapbook, *The History of Don Juan,—or the Libertine Destroyed* (1815), particularly demonstrates the legend's frequently specific address to an uneducated audience.[3] The English pantomimes of Don Juan regularly entertained the crowds in the minor and provincial theatres. However, both patent theatres also regularly performed a version of the popular legend as an after-piece, that production which closed the evening's entertainment and which was permitted as a sop to the 'second-price' visitors. These spectators gained admission to the upper gallery after the interval at a considerably reduced entrance fee and were frequently berated by the reviewers for the disruption and noise they caused in the theatre.[4]

---

[2] *The Examiner* (30 June 1817).
[3] Other cheap publications included: *An Historical Account . . . Don Juan, or The Libertine Destroyed* (1s.); *The Libertine; an Opera* (2s. 6d.); Dibdin, *Don Giovanni; or, A Spectre on Horseback!* (1s. 6d.).
[4] *The Theatrical Inquisitor* (Nov. 1818), 368.

The major theatres' inclusion of such after-pieces as *Don Juan* in their repertories was a cause of considerable complaint among the theatrical reviewers. In 1814 when Covent-Garden produced three farces in one bill it was denounced as representing 'the degradation of the stage' and the comparative frequency of performances of tragedies, comedies, and farces was regularly tabulated with horror.[5] The reviewers' principal argument was that only the major venues could uphold standards, unconstrained by the financial expediency which dictated what was performed elsewhere.[6] The argument of standards disguised another concern at the heart of the debate—the desire to maintain a division of the classes according to their 'taste'. Pantomime was for the working classes and it was censured as vulgar and coarse. The 'classics', for example the plays of Shakespeare, Otway, and Massinger, were for the upper and aspiring middle classes. *The Theatrical Inquisitor* of November 1813 demonstrates that class division was automatically assumed when considering dramatic genres: 'It is certainly an indication of the improving taste of the theatrical world, especially among the middling class, to find the rage for pantomime and buffoonery declining, and the preference inclining to dramatic dialogue.'[7] However, such statements were unquestionably prescriptive, for in 1813 this 'dramatic' segregation is unlikely to have been apparent. The inclusion of entertainments such as farces, after-pieces, melo-dramas, and even rope-dancing at the patent theatres testifies to the hypocrisy of the reviewers' arguments: Carlo the performing dog appeared at Drury Lane for forty nights in 1803. *The Times* of 1823 lauded Grimaldi's career with a more honest appraisal of the pantomime: 'Everybody "pooh-poohs" the pantomime, but every body goes to see it. It is voted "sad nonsense", and played every night for two months.'[8]

The legend's contamination as a disreputable though popular entertainment was also evident in a dispute between Mr Taylor, manager of the King's Theatre, and one of his contracted singers, Tramezzanni, which was publicly conducted

---

[5] *The Theatrical Inquisitor* (Jan. 1814), 9n.
[6] See ibid. 118.
[7] *The Theatrical Inquisitor* (Nov. 1813), 198.
[8] *The Times* (27 Dec. 1823), quoted in Mayer, *Harlequin in his Element*, 17–18.

through *The Times* in 1813. Tramezzanni argued that his en-
gagement was limited to serious operas and he claimed an extra
£200 to perform in comic operas. When this was denied,
Tramezzanni refused to appear in *Enrico IV* and the theatre was
forced to close. In a letter to *The Times*, Mr Taylor sarcastically
cited the opera of Don Juan as an example of a work which
would be 'beneath [the] dignity' of his leading tenor, knowing
this would offend the taste of the majority of theatre-goers. It
was specifically this accusation which provoked Tramezzanni's
reply to the paper in which he denied refusing the part on
grounds of artistic discrimination, that is, snobbery. Instead he
claimed that the part had never been offered to him, and that
the Don Juan part in the opera was scored for a bass and not a
tenor voice (although Mozart's Don Giovanni was frequently
sung by tenors in early performances). Tramezzanni evidently
feared that he might insult his audiences by allowing the claim
concerning their favourite, Don Juan, to stand.[9]

Mr Taylor cleverly exploited the ambivalence of the Don Juan
theme in his choice of that work as an example. Don Juan was
traditionally associated with low-brow, popular entertainment.
In 1817, however, the legend appeared in London in the more
legitimate form of Mozart's opera and was performed in the
most respectable venue of all—the King's Theatre, Haymarket.
This was an altogether new venue for the Don Juan legend—
this theatre alone in London never having staged a pantomime
version of Don Juan—and also therefore a new audience. One
contemporary source demonstrates how the popularity of the
King's Theatre, Haymarket, the chief theatrical haunt of the
aristocracy, was a consequence of the immorality and vice which
were associated with the other theatres, both patent and minor:
'The most striking thing to a foreigner in English theatres is the
unheard-of coarseness and brutality of the audiences. The consequence of this is that the higher and more civilised classes go
only to the Italian opera, and very rarely visit their national
theatres.'[10]

---

[9] *The Theatrical Inquisitor* (Apr. 1813) quotes from *The Times* (16 Mar. 1813).
[10] Prince Pückler-Mushau, 'Tour'. Quoted in Eric Walter White, *A History of
English Opera* (London: Faber & Faber, 1983), 251. For the reputation of the other
theatres, see Allardyce Nicoll, 'The Theatre', in G. M. Young (ed.), *Early Victorian
England* (London: Oxford University Press, 1934), ii. 279.

The ambivalence towards the legend of Don Juan, a theme
which was adopted by such disparate and socially distant genres
as after-piece and Italian opera, is reflected in the review of the
pantomime at the Lyceum Theatre in *The Examiner* (30 June
1817; quoted above). Only when the vulgarity of Don Juan had
been 'redressed' in operatic 'state' could the middle and upper
classes greet the performances with uninhibited enthusiasm:

The celebrity of this performance is a proof that public feeling is
sometimes excited by an adequate cause, and may occasionally follow
the efforts of genius, with correct and unabating ardour. That every
man had 'music in himself' who cried *bravo* and *encore* to the sweet
sounds of Mozart, we most religiously disbelieve, and assert, without
fear of contradiction, that music of this divine order, if commensu-
rately felt, would have produced a very different impression.[11]

This reviewer, writing for *The Theatrical Inquisitor* (August
1817), attempts to reserve Mozart's *Don Giovanni* for the middle
and upper classes alone: the riotous response of those who are
most vociferous in their enjoyment of the opera betrays that it
comes from the galleries and not from the circle. In *The Theatrical Inquisitor* of July 1817, the reviewer of *The Libertine* at the
Royal Circus censured Fitzwilliam's performance of Don
Giovanni as 'playing to the gallery', in this case quite literally.[12]
Hazlitt's criticism of Jeremy Collier demonstrated that he was
alert to potential hypocrisy within interpretations of the legend
(see Chapter 2). His review of *Don Giovanni* is also scathing
about the snobberies of the opera-going audience: for example,
he mocks the audience's tendency to attend only on Saturday
evenings, since that was the 'fashionable' night to attend the
opera.[13] His review of *The Libertine* (25 May 1817) similarly
compared the enthusiastic demands for encores at the King's
Theatre with the polite applause at Covent-Garden because
'etiquette' decreed it at the opera house.[14] These criticisms
were obviously common enough. *Giovanni in London* also

[11] *The Theatrical Inquisitor* (Aug. 1817), review of *Don Giovanni*, Saturday 9 Aug.
1817, 136.
[12] *The Theatrical Inquisitor* (July 1817), 80.
[13] Hazlitt's review of *Don Giovanni* for *The Examiner* (20 Apr. 1817), repr. in *The
Complete Works of William Hazlitt*, ed. P. P. Howe (London: J. M. Dent, 1930–4), v.
362–6, 364.
[14] Ibid. 370–71.

mocked the upper-class pursuit of opera-going as a form of exhibitionism:

> To the Opera you must go,
> Don Giovanni, Don Giovanni,
> And talk as fashionables do,
> Most loudly while they're singing.[15]

In this case the satire would have had the additional motivation of rivalry between the theatres.

Hazlitt also taunted that the work was popular only because the composer was dead and now revered. His review is motivated in great part by the excesses of the praise which greeted the opera, since it had been spoken of as 'Shakespearean' and 'tragic'. He was evidently bemused by the extraordinary degree of praise lavished upon it, remembering especially the same reviewers' condescension towards other stage versions of the Don Juan legend. He certainly berates the talismanic quality of the word 'Mozart', a word which, like 'Don Juan', or 'Byron', entailed an automatic response, and, because Mozart was revered, this was an assumption of quality.[16] The review of Byron's *Don Juan* in *The Literary Chronicle* (17 July 1819) which included a brief sketch of the theme's history, pointedly specified that the story was 'dignified with the divine music of Mozart'.[17] Leigh Hunt's criticism of the Drury Lane pantomime, *Harlequin's Vision*, also maintained a careful distinction between the legend and the music of Mozart. He attributed its failure largely to 'fastening itself upon the story and *not* the music of an attractive opera, which story has been exhausted at all ends of the town'.[18] However, the success of Mozart's *Don Giovanni* was so phenomenal that the distinction between this mania and the cult for the Don Juan of the pantomimic forms became increasingly difficult to assert. *Cumberland's Minor Theatre* of 1829 remarked that the tale of Don Juan 'did not disgust the vulgar; who, in

---

[15] Repr. in Oscar Mandel (ed.), *The Theatre of Don Juan* (Lincoln, Nebr.: University of Nebraska Press, 1963), 424.

[16] Hazlitt's review of *Don Giovanni* for *The Examiner* (20 Apr. 1817), repr. in *Complete Works*, v. 362–4.

[17] *The Literary Chronicle* (17 July 1819), 129–30, 129.

[18] *The Examiner* (11 Jan. 1818). Quoted in Frederick L. Beaty, 'Harlequin Don Juan', *Journal of English and Germanic Philology*, 67/3 (1968), 403.

emulation of their betters, are ever awake to wonders and impossibilities'.[19] We might guess that Byron would have enjoyed the element of hypocrisy which surrounded the reception of Don Giovanni but he too exploited the newly ambivalent status of the Don Juan legend, with its legitimization by Mozart's opera, by writing a work entitled *Don Juan*.

Byron plays a significant role in this discussion of theatrical history because many of the expectations for the improvement of the patent theatres rested upon his election as sub-committee member for Drury Lane Theatre. Those reviewers who censured the frequency of farces at the patent theatres caustically reminded Byron of his address at the opening of Drury Lane in 1812 and frequently quoted entire sections of it. In his *Address, Spoken at the Opening of Drury Lane Theatre*, Byron celebrated the theatre's upholding of national standards:

> If e'er frivolity has led to fame,
> And made us blush that you forbore to blame;
> If e'er the sinking stage could condescend
> To soothe the sickly taste it dare not mend,
> All past reproach may present scenes refute,
> And censure, wisely loud, be justly mute![20]

And in *English Bards and Scotch Reviewers* (1809), he had given a condescending dismissal of pantomime.[21] Byron's election at Drury Lane Theatre in May 1815 intensified expectations of 'reform'. For example, *The Theatrical Inquisitor* of September 1815 quoted from his opening address and added:

The name of Byron authorises us to look with confidence to a succession of entertainments worthy of the first theatre in the world. With such a leader, the happiest results may assuredly be expected.

> *Nil desperandum Teucro duce, et auspice Teucro.*

In proportion, however, as the expectation of the public has been excited by the noble Lord's having undertaken the direction of this theatre, proportionably great will be their disappointment should he fail to produce any reform in the *sound* and *shew* system which has so

---

[19] *Cumberland's Minor Theatre* (1829), ii. 3.
[20] *Address*, ll. 56–61. *The Complete Poetical Works of Lord Byron*, ed. Jerome J. McGann (Oxford: Clarendon Press), iii (1981), 20–1.
[21] *English Bards and Scotch Reviewers* (1809). See especially ll. 586–95. Compare also 'Opening Address', variant ll. 55–63, *Complete Poetical Works*, iii (1981), 20.

long prevailed within its walls, and contentedly imitate the examples and errors of his predecessors.[22]

This is the context for Coleridge's opening sally against the expectations invested in the new Drury Lane Theatre committee, which forms the preliminary section of his 'Critique of *Bertram*':

Could an heroic project, at once so refined and so arduous, be consistently entrusted to, could its success be rationally expected from, a mercenary manager, at whose critical quarantine the *lucri bonus odor* would conciliate a bill of health to the plague in person? No! As the work proposed, such must be the work-masters. Rank, fortune, liberal education, and (their natural accompaniments, or consequences) critical discernment, delicate tact, disinterestedness, unsuspected morals, notorious patriotism, and tried Mæcenasship, these were the recommendations which influenced the votes of the proprietary subscribers of Drury Lane Theatre, these the motives that occasioned the election of its Supreme Committee of Management.[23]

Coleridge ironically echoes the expectations which the public invested in public figures like Byron. The manager, Mr Whitbread, is disqualified by his concern with the Juvenalian *lucri bonus odor* or 'good smell of profit'—although Whitbread's notorious advocacy of parliamentary reform undoubtedly contributed to Coleridge's political animosity towards him.[24] Chapter 1 considered how, in Coleridge's singling out the choice of *Bertram* for ridicule, Byron would undoubtedly have felt that much of the criticism was directed specifically at him. Not only had he promoted *Bertram* before leaving England, but the specific qualities mockingly outlined by Coleridge in this excerpt would have applied in Byron's case. He certainly possessed the necessary combination of rank, fortune, and liberal education. Drury Lane's declining fortune appeared to call for drastic measures and Whitbread had suggested that all the committee should retire and the theatre be leased to a manager with sole responsibility. Douglas Kinnaird firmly opposed this proposition and resolved to save the committee system and preserve the

---

[22] *The Theatrical Inquisitor* (Sept. 1815), 217–18.
[23] *The Collected Works of Samuel Taylor Coleridge*, ed. Walter Engell and W. Jackson Bate (Princeton: Princeton University Press, 1983), vii. *Biographia Literaria: II*, 209.
[24] Ibid. 257–8.

theatre's reputation as the national theatre. Whitbread's attempt to 'privatize' the theatre was outmanœuvred precisely by Kinnaird's 'trump' of Byron's appointment.[25] Coleridge was evidently aware of the extent of popular opinion's trust in the election of Byron who was doubly esteemed as a potential reformer of the theatre in his capacities of peer and of revered national poet. These were years in which his poetic reputation, especially among the upper classes, flourished with the enormous successes of *Childe Harold*, Cantos I and II (1812) and the Tales.

In the years after Byron's departure from England, Drury Lane Theatre was increasingly burdened with financial difficulties and Covent-Garden became known as the more 'fashionable' of the theatres. The administrative difficulties of Drury Lane were detailed at length in *The Theatrical Inquisitor* of August–November 1818, and in 1819 the theatre was forced to close temporarily with debts of over £90,000.[26] The reviewers claimed that Drury Lane's decline had lowered its reputation to that of a minor theatre and urged the theatre to trust in the natural superiority of high standards of excellence.[27]

Drury Lane's financial troubles were not unusual. All the London theatres competed in an increasingly ruthless market. The King's Theatre was the sole exception because of the monopoly it enjoyed as a venue for an élite audience. Its successes were a continual source of envy to the other theatres. Indeed, the seating alterations which Covent-Garden made in 1809 and which resulted in the riots had been an attempt to imitate the King's Theatre's reputation for exclusivity. Similarly, the spectacular success of *Don Giovanni* at the King's Theatre was obviously the motivation for the ensuing spate of Don Juan burlesques, pantomimes, and parodies which proliferated on the Regency stage between 1817 and 1824. *The Drama; or Theatrical Pocket Magazine* of November 1821 suggests that the financial security of the King's Theatre was due to *Don Giovanni*: 'Mozart's opera ran through the whole season with the greatest

[25] See Richard Lansdown, *Byron's Historical Dramas* (Oxford: Clarendon Press, 1992), 29–30.
[26] See ibid. 13–14 for the dwindling receipts at Drury Lane between 1812 and 1818.
[27] See *The Theatrical Inquisitor* (Sept. 1818), 226–7 and (Dec. 1818), 441.

applause, proving the most profitable speculation that house had entered into for many years.'[28] Clearly the other theatres' real ambition was to emulate its financial rather than its artistic success. This might explain why cross-references to other Don Juan productions were so apparent in playbills and reviews, openly encouraging comparisons, which, it was claimed, would be in their own favour. *The Examiner* (30 June 1817), for example, reviewed the Lyceum Theatre's production of the pantomime *Don Juan* as representing the legend in its 'regular and antique shape': 'The celebrity which has made *Il Don Giovanni* the favourite of the Winter Theatres, has revived Don Juan in his regular and antique shape at the English opera.'

The spring and summer seasons of 1817 sported rival productions of the Don Juan theme. *Don Giovanni* at the King's Theatre, *The Libertine* at Covent-Garden, *Don Giovanni; or, A Spectre on Horseback!* at the Surrey, and *Don Juan; or the Libertine Destroyed* at the Lyceum all ran concurrently. When, in December of that year, *Giovanni in London* opened at the Olympic and *Harlequin's Vision* at Drury Lane, the legend's monopoly of the theatres was complete, with six different productions playing simultaneously in the early season of 1818. Indeed, on 16 June 1818, Covent-Garden attempted to trump even this spectacular record by billing within the one evening 'Acts from Shakespeare's plays—The Libertine—Don Juan'. Doubtless, Byron would have been amused by Drury Lane's degeneration, in that the version written originally and specifically for that venue— *Harlequin's Vision*—was a pantomime farce, an even more lowly form than the earlier Drury Lane commission, the ballet pantomime of *Don Juan; or The Libertine Destroyed.*

These burlesques and parodies unashamedly appealed to the taste of the 'masses', as opposed to that of the cultural élite. *Giovanni in London* replaced the more customary didacticism of the legend's final scene with an appeal to the applause of the audience: 'Since our efforts now are o'er, | Let us hope we've pleased the many | And we often will go o'er | The wondrous tricks of Giovanni.' Illustrative of this flattering of the audience is the bizarre and seemingly inapposite inclusion of the popular air 'Oh! the Roast Beef of England!' in both *Giovanni in London*

---

[28]   *The Drama; or Theatrical Pocket Magazine* (Nov. 1821).

and *Don Giovanni; or, A Spectre on Horseback!* In Dibdin's work it is included among the fare at the final supper. In Moncrieff's burlesque Deputy English sings the air as a paean to all things good and English. In his *Musical Memoirs* (1830), W. T. Parke compared this air unfavourably with the music of Mozart:

It is gratifying to observe the advance music has made in this country during the last fifty years, particularly in our English theatres, where now it is listened to with attention, and its beauties felt and applauded, even by those in the galleries, who formerly were so coarse in their manners, that the respectable part of the audience were stunned with their continued and vociferous calls of 'Roast Beef' and 'Play up, Nosey!'[29]

Since this account was written in 1830, the 'improvements' it refers to were probably more recent than the claimed fifty years. Certainly the effect of dragging the 'Roast Beef of England' into the Don Juan burlesques, whatever its inappositeness, is indicative of the tastes and demands of the 'galleries' in 1817–18, that section of the audience which the managers ignored or slighted only at their peril.

Byron would have been well aware of Don Juan's reputation as a crowd-pleaser, especially since, as a member of the sub-committee for Drury Lane, he had had to be conscious of how the market dictated the repertory. He remarked in a letter to John Herman Merivale (1 July 1815): 'We are really in want of opera and comedy—particularly the former which when successful draws more than fifty Shakespeares—excuse the blasphemy—but it is really the case.'[30] John Harris, the proprietor of Covent-Garden, openly admitted that the theatre cleared its debts each year only through the receipts of the Christmas pantomime. The success of *Harlequin's Vision* at Drury Lane would therefore have been crucial to the theatre's 1818 season. It is probable that Byron knew of this, possibly from Kinnaird. Both Kinnaird and Byron had enjoyed participating in the masquerade scene of the Christmas pantomime at Drury Lane in

[29] W. T. Parke, *Musical Memoirs*, 2 vols. (London: Henry Colburn & Richard Bentley, 1830), ii. 146–7.
[30] *Byron's Letters and Journals*, ed. Leslie A. Marchand (London: John Murray, 1973–82), iv. 301 (letter to John Herman Merivale, 1 July 1815).

1815.[31] The lucrative promise of the Don Juan legend was also fulfilled in indirect ways: Hazlitt's review of the Drury Lane production of *Giovanni in London* was included as one of the articles on 'The Drama' which he wrote for *The London Magazine* (July 1820). These articles, like the articles on Kean for *The Morning Chronicle*, reputedly saved the theatre from bankruptcy. Madame Vestris's performances as Don Giovanni were also spoken of as having saved the credit of Drury Lane.[32]

In choosing the Don Juan legend Byron therefore adopted a theme which was connected with financial profiteering and indulgence to the market. In 1821 Byron, arguing that *Marino Faliero* had never been intended for the stage, derisively claimed his own aloofness from the theatrical audience and wrote to Murray that: 'Had I sought [the public's] favour it would have been by a Pantomime.'[33] Although *Don Juan* was evidently not a pantomime, it did adopt a theme whose notoriety was due to its populist theatrical forms. And this would have influenced how the poem was received. It certainly struck many of his previous readers as an unexpected and unwelcome development. *The Ladies' Monthly Museum* (August 1817), for example, strongly urged that *Manfred* should be read rather than performed on a stage: 'Lord Byron is not to be comprehended by everyone, and least of all by the *crowd*.'[34] This review suggests that the majority of his former readers would have disapproved of the choice of Don Juan. Byron's early successes among the upper classes had to a great extent been a consequence of his appeal to an élitism which complimented such readers. They had enjoyed accepting the ambivalent 'heroes' of the Tales with an indulgence which flattered their self-esteem and seemed to differentiate them from others who might not understand the 'hero' and would philistinely fail to appreciate his qualities.[35] The Don Juan of the

---

[31] See *Byron's Letters and Journals*, ix. 36–7, no. 70, 'Detached Thoughts'.

[32] See *The Life of Mary Russell Mitford*, ii. 67 n. and *Memoirs of the Life, Public and Private Adventures of Madame Vestris* (London, 1939), 18.

[33] *Byron's Letters and Journals*, viii. 90 (letter to Murray, 22 Jan. 1821). *Marino Faliero* shared the bill with *Giovanni in London* at Drury Lane on 3 and 4 May 1821.

[34] *The Ladies' Monthly Museum*, 3rd ser. 6 (Aug. 1817), 91.

[35] See e.g. *The Giaour* (1813), ll. 866–9; *The Corsair* (1814), Canto I, st. 9, ll. 199–202, and *Lara* (1814), Canto I, st. 21.

London stage in contrast was a figure created for the consumption of the 'crowd'.

Byron was especially sensitive to the charge of making lucrative profits from his writing. Throughout his years in London, he had always denied that he wrote for financial gain and in 1819 his letters defensively denied that he was flattering public opinion.[36] Indeed, *Don Juan* was written in a presumed spirit of antagonism towards his audience. In anticipating the charge of pandering to the tastes of his audience, Byron may therefore have been referring to his appropriation of a figure who was at the height of theatrical fashion—Don Juan. Within *Don Juan* he allowed the dangerous admission that the continuation of the poem depended on the public's desire for more (see I, 199 and 221). However facetious this claim might have been, it skirted dangerously close to the accusation that in choosing Don Juan he was directly appealing to the public.[37] The poem's narrator derided the new poetic conventions of orientalism and picturesque descriptions of abroad (V, 42 and 52). In this way Byron acknowledged his own responsibility for creating literary fashion. With *Don Juan* it might have been said that he was following it.

Byron, therefore, cannot have been entirely surprised at the accusation of financial prostitution which was widely levelled at his poem. In particular, the anonymous mode of its publication was suspected as being a ruse to generate interest in what was, according to the reviewers, a hackneyed subject. Illustrative of such charges is the early review which appeared in *The European Magazine* (July 1819):

It was, doubtless, this uncommon celebrity that induced the author to bring him forward in a new dress—though it's rather an *expensive* one; a circumstance which may, not improbably, account for the whimsicality of the advertisement; the publisher, very justly, deeming a guinea and a half too much for a repetition of stale incidents, resorted to this novel experiment to excite curiosity.[38]

[36] For denial of flattering the public see *Byron's Letters and Journals*, vi. 101 (letter to Douglas Kinnaird, 6 Mar. 1819); vi. 192 (letter to John Murray, 1 Aug. 1819). Compare however vi. 61 (to Murray, 17 July 1818) and vi. 77 (to Hobhouse, 11 Nov. 1818).

[37] See ibid. vi. 67–8, 168, 235, 256.

[38] *The European Magazine*, 76 (July 1819), 53.

The accusation that the book's mystery was a trick to excite curiosity and enhance the sale also occurred in the review by *The Champion* (25 July 1819).[39]

Byron's adoption of the theme of Don Juan was widely perceived as compromising his fame as a national poet. Like the patent theatres, he was expected to be above the vagaries of popular appeal and the sense of betrayed expectation was exacerbated by his status as aristocrat. Many of the poem's reviewers drew comparisons between Byron's poem and the pantomime legend—but none compared it to Mozart's opera.[40] Instead the choice of subject was termed 'humiliating' (*The Edinburgh Monthly Review*, October 1819), and was interpreted as a betrayal of his ability and status: 'It is really lamentable to see such powers . . . employed to such purposes: for Don Juan (as the title might lead one to expect) is a tissue of all immoralities' (*The Champion*, 25 July 1819).[41] Remembering the genre segregation of actors, it is interesting that, when Caroline Lamb feared for Byron's poetic reputation in choosing such a theme, she declared that Edmund Kean could not have impaired his own reputation more if he had played the role of Harlequin.[42] The accusation that Byron had compromised his artistic credibility in prostituting his talent to the vagaries of public opinion is also implicit in his billing as 'Mr Apollo Stir-em-up, a poetical Showman' in *Dr Faustus in London* (10 January 1820). The rhymes of this 'poetical punster' display 'the prevailing follies, prejudices and *bad tastes* of the current times' (my italics). When the author of a later imitation, *Juan Secundus* (1825), questioned why Don Juan had been chosen as a hero, the accusation remained that of poetic sensationalism: 'Perchance I'm a *young poet*, and if so I The *very name* may make the people pant.'[43]

Such criticisms were not reserved to the reviewers. Many of Byron's friends also regretted his poetic humbling in adopting

[39] *The Champion* (25 July 1819), 472.

[40] See e.g. *The Monthly Magazine*, 52 (Sept. 1821), 124–9, 124: 'Like his prototype in the pantomime', and *The Gentleman's Magazine* 92/1 (Jan. 1822), 48–50; 'For our part, we never could vindicate the taste with which Don Juan has been brought upon our stage'.

[41] *The Edinburgh Monthly Review*, 2 (October 1819), 482. *The Champion* (25 July 1819), 472.

[42] *Byron's Letters and Journals*, iv. 366n.

[43] *Juan Secundus* (London: John Miller, 1825), v. 7.

such a scurrilous subject. The Reverend Dallas wrote of *Don Juan*: 'Until then his truly English muse had despised the licentious tone belonging to poets of low degree. But, in writing "Don Juan" he allied his *chaste and noble genius* with minds of that stamp.'[44] Dallas's comment reveals both a submerged literary snobbery (poets of 'low degree' might have been expected to produce such a work) and xenophobia (for Byron is portrayed as having abandoned his distinctly 'English' muse). Harriette Wilson also wrote to Byron of the work's vulgarity: 'I would not, even to *you*, who in a wrong-headed moment wrote it, lie under the imputation of such bad taste as to admire what in your cool moments, I am sure, you must feel to be *vulgar* at least . . .'.[45] And Hazlitt spoke of Byron having 'prostituted his talents' in writing *Don Juan*.[46] Such readers referred and objected to the alliance of subject, tone, and expression of the poem, all of which were judged to be equally scandalous and demeaning. It was also impossible to disentangle this alliance, as those reviewers found who strove, in vain, to select passages which they would permit to be reprinted in vindication of their condemnation.

When, in 1823, Cantos VI–XIV of *Don Juan* were published by John Hunt, the critics claimed that the work had at last found an appropriate publisher. John Murray's name had always been cited as one ill-suited to a work of the nature and title of *Don Juan*. William Hone's pamphlet, *'Don John' or 'Don Juan' Unmasked* (1819), rhetorically juxtaposed the extremes of propriety and scandal within one sentence: 'Not the least extraordinary circumstance connected with the history of this singular poem, is, that the Publisher—the Bookseller to the Admiralty, and a strenuous supporter of orthodoxy and the Bible Society, is the publisher of Don Juan.'[47] The title 'Don Juan' alone was again sufficient to illustrate the perceived disparity between Murray's publications. This unease was shared

---

[44] Quoted in Teresa Guiccioli, *Lord Byron jugé par les témoins de sa vie* (London: Richard Bentley, 1869), i. 417.

[45] Quoted in George Paston and Peter Quennell, *'To Lord Byron'* (London: John Murray, 1939), 160.

[46] Hazlitt, *Spirit of the Age* (1825), 'Lord Byron', repr. in *Complete Works*, xi. 69–78, 75.

[47] *'Don John' or 'Don Juan' Unmasked* (London: William Hone, 1819), 33.

by the publisher himself. When Byron finally broke with Murray in 1821 it was a result of Byron's irritation at the large number of printer's errors in the proofs of *Don Juan*, Canto V, and at what he perceived as a lack of generosity in Murray's proposed terms of payment. Murray offered the same amount (2,500 guineas) for three Cantos of *Don Juan* and the three plays *Sardanapalus*, *The Two Foscari*, and *Cain* as he had offered for only one (and in Byron's judgement decidedly inferior) Canto of *Childe Harold* (Canto IV).[48]

In addition, Murray's timid manner of publishing the first Cantos of *Don Juan*—with copious asterisks and blanks—was received by radical publishers as an open invitation to piracy. The very subject of Don Juan would have been another such invitation, for the same radical publishers knew that this was a theme which would be recognized by all classes and not only by the educated. Murray published the first two Cantos of *Don Juan* in a sumptuous quarto edition which was priced at £1. 11*s*. 6*d*. The format of this edition was in itself designed to forestall libel, a ruse which the radical publishers were acutely aware of. In *'Don John' or 'Don Juan' Unmasked* (1819), the author condemned the political double standards which allowed Murray's name and ostentatiously expensive publication to be used as safeguards against the legal redress which had attacked other publishers:

no other man but he who has Government support and Government writers to back him, *dare* publish *Don Juan* as it now stands. Mr Murray is too 'respectable' to fear attack, or even insinuation for the *immoral* tendency of the Poem. He and his quarto book of 227 pages, with only 16 lines in a page, and a magnificent circumference of margin, and a guinea and a half in price, may defy the Society for Suppression of Vice, and

> The very place where wicked people go.[49]

Murray's 'defiance' of hell is allusive of the Don Juan legend and makes the publication of the poem equivalent to the audacious daring of a Don Juan figure.

---

[48] See *Byron's Letters and Journals*, ix. 72 and *Complete Poetical Works*, vi (1991), commentary to *Cain*, 647–8.

[49] *'Don John' or 'Don Juan' Unmasked*, 41. The Birmingham bookseller, Russell, was tried and convicted in 1819 for selling Hone's parodies, despite Hone's own acquittal in 1817.

Murray's relatively small production of 1,500 copies of this edition proved to be an overestimation of demand. When it failed to sell out Murray was forced to sell the remaining 150 copies as waste paper. Lockhart spoke of the poem as being read in 'furtive quartos' which would suggest that those who did read it, and who were wealthy enough to afford its prohibitive price, were ashamed of being seen to do so.[50] The title alone may have shocked the more fastidious with its automatic association with popular culture. Their response might have been different if the poem had been titled *Don Giovanni*, a mistake which Keats casually made. The date of Keats's error, February 1819, five months before the first publication of *Don Juan*, reveals both the extent of the gossip about the new poem and the assumption many made that it would be linked with the more elevated example of Mozart's opera (although Byron's residence in Italy might also have contributed to this assumption).[51] The first pirate edition of Cantos I–II was published by Onwhyn and appeared within four days. It advertised itself as 'an exact copy from the quarto edition' and sold at a price of only 4s. Twenty pirate versions of *Don Juan* Cantos were published in the next ten years and thousands of cheap editions were sold. These editions were published and distributed by radical figures such as William Hone, William Benbow, Richard Carlile, William Sherwin, and William Dugdale.

Byron had urged Murray to beat the pirates at their own game by publishing in cheap editions. Murray was forced to concede to a certain extent: Cantos III–V were never issued in quarto format but in demy octavo at 9s. 6d., as were further editions of Cantos I–II. Cantos III–V were also published in two smaller and cheaper editions, crown and post octavo, priced at 7s. and 5s., and Murray published new editions of Cantos I–II in these two cheaper editions in the same year. However, since the pirate editions were already circulating, these actions were rather belated. Murray had hoped that the work might be granted a copyright which would save his profits from being

---

[50] Lockhart's phrase is from *John Bull's Letter to Lord Byron* (1821), quoted in *The Critical Heritage*, ed. Rutherford, p. 184.
[51] *Letters of John Keats*, ed. Robert Gittings (Oxford: Oxford University Press, 1970), 211 (letter to George and Georgiana Keats, 14 Feb. 1819).

taken by the pirates but copyright was consistently denied by the courts. It was not until John Hunt became Byron's publisher that the tactic of cheap editions was adopted as a concerted strategy. Cantos VI–VIII were sold at close intervals in 1823 in three different sizes—traditional octavo (1,500 copies), a fools-cap octavo edition (3,000 copies), and an extremely small and cheap version in 18mo. format which was available for a shil-ling. Sixteen thousand copies of this 'common edition' were sold, by far the biggest single edition of any Byron book at this time. John Hunt continued to publish the remaining Cantos of *Don Juan* in these three editions. The publication figures for the three editions of Cantos IX–XI were 1,500 in demy octavo, 2,500 in foolscap octavo, and 17,000 in duodecimo.[52] And, since Byron's earlier publishing successes had all been as a result of an exclusive readership of upper- and upper-middle-class readers, it is already apparent that the most radical aspect of Byron's *Don Juan* was its reception by the working classes.

The reviewers seized upon the new mode of publishing as a vindication of their criticisms of the poem. They literally 'val-ued' the poem at its new price of a shilling and announced that these, considerably cheaper, editions made the poem available to those people for whom it was originally intended. *The Literary Chronicle* (30 August 1823) announced: 'In thus lowering the price, the noble lord has so far acted judiciously, that he has suited the price to that class of society for whom he seems to have intended his poem, which is a tissue of vulgar oaths and indelicacies.'[53] *The Literary Museum* (6 December 1823) claimed that the new price indicated Byron's own consciousness that his verses were 'mere twelve-penny trash' and at least had the virtue of openly admitting the new readers for whom the poem was

---

[52] No specific record of the print run for Cantos XII–XIV and Cantos XV–XVI survive but it is likely that figures would have reflected those for Cantos IX–XI. All publication details are from Jerome McGann's commentary in *Complete Poetical Works*, v (1986), 666–7, Cantos I–II (Murray published a 2nd edn. of these Cantos in 1819 in demy octavo and this was reprinted as a 'New Edition' in 1820 and 1822. All were priced at 9s. 6d.); pp. 694–5, Cantos III–V; p. 716, Cantos VI–VIII; p. 736, Cantos IX–XI; p. 753, Cantos XII–XIV; p. 762, Cantos XV–XVI. See also William St Clair, 'The Impact of Byron's Writings', in Andrew Rutherford (ed.), *Byron: Augustan and Romantic* (London: Macmillan, 1990), *passim.*

[53] *The Literary Chronicle* (30 Aug. 1823), 553, review of Cantos IX–XI.

intended: 'the lowest and vulgarest classes'.[54] In Canto I, stanza 221, the narrator of *Don Juan* acknowledges the conventional gentility of addressing the 'gentle' reader, but only so as to illustrate in turn the new commercial hierarchy by qualifying this with: 'and | Still gentler purchaser'. With the cheap editions of *Don Juan* such 'gentle' readers included the lower classes.

Unfortunately very few individual working-class responses to the poem have survived. However, in 'The Impact of Byron's Writings' (1990), William St Clair illustrated through empirical research the increasingly working-class readership which *Don Juan* did attract. His 'evaluative approach' led him to conclude that *Don Juan* had, within ten years, penetrated 'far deeper into the reading of the nation than any other modern book, with the possible exception of Tom Paine's *Rights of Man*'. And that *Don Juan* was read, at least in part, by 'many thousands who did not read any of Byron's other works, and it was probably read by thousands who read no other books of any kind except the Bible'.[55]

It was the working-class reception of *Don Juan* to which the reviewers objected above all. Indeed it has been suggested that the critical outcry did not occur until after the first pirate editions of Cantos I–II appeared. The element of conjecture which this suggests is confirmed by the many examples of reviews which openly reveal double standards according to class. Among the most undisguised of such reviews is that of *The Quarterly Review* (April 1822):

a work which, if it had been the subject of copyright, would have been confined by its price to a class of readers with whom its faults might have been somewhat compensated by its merits . . . *Don Juan* in quarto and on hot-pressed paper would have been almost innocent—in a whity-brown duodecimo it was one of the worst of the mischievous publications which have made the press a snare.[56]

The same attempt to segregate the theatres according to a 'taste' that was distinctly class-based was evident in the reception

---

[54] *The Literary Museum* (6 Dec. 1823), 769–70, review of Cantos XII–XIV. See also *John Bull* (20 July 1823), 229, review of Cantos VI–VIII, and *Blackwood's Edinburgh Magazine*, 14 (July 1823), 88–92, review of Cantos VI–VIII.
[55] St Clair, 'Impact of Byron's Writings', 18.
[56] *The Quarterly Review* (Apr. 1822). Quoted in Hugh J. Luke, 'The Publishing of Byron's *Don Juan*', *PMLA* 80/2 (June 1965), 199–209, 202.

of the pantomimic Don Juans, since the theatrical critics considered the legend of Don Juan as properly belonging to the uneducated and 'their' form, the pantomime. Both Byron's poem and the stage versions enjoyed a popularity which extended across the class divisions which the reviewers attempted to effect. Mozart's opera alone was excepted from the widespread dismissal and since Byron's writing was hardly of the 'sublime' mode by which they characterized Mozart's music, his poem was instead interpreted as a joke written as if for the galleries. *The Ladies' Monthly Museum* (January–February 1822), speaking of the 'gloominess and vice' of Byron's heroes, certainly alluded to his currently most notorious hero in complaining: 'It is a bad compliment to the first poet of the age, that he feeds the vulgar mind "which delights in mystery". It is like an actor who debases himself by playing to the gallery.'[57] Byron's deployment of bawdy innuendo would only have exacerbated the feeling that, like the patent theatres, Byron was lowering his standards in order to appeal to the 'mob'. The reviewers of the established press criticized the poem's sexual innuendo as pandering to the earthy tradition which they characterized as typical of working-class culture. This is evident in the criticism of *The Literary Chronicle* (30 August 1823) which associated *Don Juan's* readership with its expression of 'vulgar oaths and indelicacies'. *The Literary Gazette* (6 September 1823) denounced the scenes between Don Juan and Catherine as an obscene betrayal of Byron's aristocratic status, being 'a subject described with so many of those brutal allusions which might be expected among the mean profligates in a drunken night-house'.[58]

Conversely, however, the poem's extensive deployment of insinuation, innuendo, and inference was also seen by some as written for a rather more select readership. This criticism was levelled against Byron's bawdy poem by many of the working-class journals. *The Green Man*, an independent weekly, exploited the numerous asterisks in the publication of Cantos I–II in arguing that the character of the poem was distinctly exclusive: 'The Volume is eked out with numerous stars, which, . . . I suppose mean something if one could but find it out. This, there-

---

[57] *The Ladies' Monthly Museum* (Jan.–Feb. 1822), 88.
[58] *The Literary Gazette* (6 Sept. 1823), 562–3, review of Cantos IX–XI.

fore, let us leave to the Illuminati' (17 July 1819).[59] More re-
cently, Philip Martin (1982) argued that the rhetoric of the
poem was equivalent to the *bons mots* and hauteur of the lordly
after-dinner speaker.[60] However, both perspectives polarize the
deployment of the poem's language in a way which is oversim-
plified. Martin, for example, overlooked the poem's frequent
colloquialisms (for example, 'in a crack', I, 137), ungram-
matical expressions ('you was . . .', IV, 88, and the intimate use
of 'your' in X, 47 and VIII, 113), popular phrases ('dished' and
'diddled': XI, 78; 'dead set': XIV, 42), the occasional mocking
of polite speech ('toilet': XVI, 16; and 'philo-genitiveness': XII,
22) and the innumerable examples of slang (including 'kick'/
'sixpence', V, 27, and 'affair'/'vagina', VI, 2) throughout the
poem. But nor can this idiom be categorized as exclusively
lower-class. In Canto I, the names 'Cazzani' and 'Corniani' are
bawdy word-plays on vulgar Italian usage (st. 149) and in Canto
V, 'pukes in' is rhymed with 'Euxine' (st. 5).[61] Both demonstrate
the curious mixture of low-life and learning, high and low
cultures which is typical of *Don Juan*. The elegiac stanza on the
death of the highwayman might seem to represent the language
of the streets (XI, 19) but Jerome McGann has remarked that
such flash language was 'chic' in Regency society. Byron's own
note to this stanza claimed that the 'advance of science and of
language has rendered it unnecessary to translate the above
good and true English, spoken in its original purity by the select
mobility and their patrons'.[62] Byron's coinage of the term 'mobility' neatly expresses the triple pun of the 'fluidity' between
the 'mob' and the 'nobility' (whose seemingly antithetical inclusion is reinforced by the reference to patronage). Many of the
poem's examples of slang are also sporting terms (for example,
'all neck or nothing' or 'venturing everything', VIII, 45, and 'all
game and bottom' for 'endurance', VIII, 110)—a male rhetoric
which would not have been class-specific. In the example of
Canto XI, stanza 19, Byron's note continued by referring the
reader to his boxing coach, John Jackson, for a translation of

[59] *The Green Man* (17 July 1819), 69.
[60] Philip W. Martin, *Byron: A Poet Before his Public* (Cambridge: Cambridge University Press, 1982), 186.
[61] See *Complete Works*, v (1986), 679, ll. 1185, 1187.
[62] Ibid. 747 (XI, 19).

the popular song from which the diction of the stanza was taken. Jackson, appropriately, was known as 'Gentleman Jackson'—as Hazlitt described Byron as an, apparently antithetical, 'vulgar lord'.[63]

In addition, the upper classes had long enjoyed a sexual libertinism which would have allowed them to comprehend and enjoy the kind of bawdy humour and sexual word-play which might otherwise be characterized as decidedly 'low-brow'. That the antithetical groupings outlined above could argue such contradictory positions—that bawdiness was typical of upper-/working-class culture—is an indication of the cultural stratification of class sexualities and the peculiar allegiance which it created of an equivalence in sexual behaviour between such socially and economically disparate sections of the public. And since the reputation of Don Juan has always been associated with his sexual behaviour, a consideration of the specific historicity of sexuality in 1819 is necessary for an understanding of the significance of Byron's *Don Juan* and the reasons for the middle-class outrage against both the figure and the poem.

CLASS SEXUALITIES

Byron intentionally backdated his narrative to the last decades of the eighteenth century. In fact, the narrative of events can be traced as specifically occurring between the mid-1780s and 1792 or 1793.[64] This is an entirely appropriate gesture for a work which reverted to an earlier tradition of the Don Juan legend, a tradition which might be said to have reached its apotheosis in eighteenth-century libertinism, and which was reversed in the early decades of the nineteenth century with the tendency of new versions to 'reclaim' the legendary seducer. While Byron's brand of radicalism might have been true of the sexual libertarianism of the 1780s and 1790s, it was an attitude which was fast becoming not 'conventionally' radical, but reactionary, or at least eccentric.

[63] For Hazlitt's comment, see *Complete Works*, xix. 65.
[64] See *Complete Poetical Works*, v (1986), introduction, p. xxiii.

Towards the end of the eighteenth century, the issue of personal morality was closely fought as the last preserve of subversion, that sphere where political control would be at its weakest. The late eighteenth century witnessed few personal restrictions on topics of an openly sexual nature. The success of various pornographic magazines is one indication of this sexual permissiveness.[65] The Reverend Martin Adan's eccentric *Thelyphthora* (1780–1), for example, advocated polygamy as scripturally justified for 'surplus' women and caused much controversy. In 1786 Richard Payne Knight wrote his *Discourse on the Worship of Priapus*, a work which comprehensively traced sexual motifs in ancient religion, and, more scandalously still, their survival in Christianity.[66] Between 1779 and 1784 James Graham lectured fashionable London society on 'generation'—allegedly with the aid of a naked woman—and rented out his 'celestial bed' as a cure for sexual impotence, claiming that sexual lethargy was both the symptom and cause of the sickness of nations.[67] English political radicalism also spoke openly of sexual freedom at this time. The political libertarianism and sexual libertinism of Wilkes is paradigmatic of this allegiance. William Godwin notoriously denounced marriage as the worst of monopolies in *Enquiry Concerning Political Justice* (1798), in rhetoric which is typical of many traditional Don Juans:

So long as two human beings are forbidden, by positive institution, to follow the dictates of their own mind, prejudice will be alive and vigorous. So long as I seek to engross one woman to myself, and to prohibit my neighbour from proving his superior desert and reaping the fruits of it, I am guilty of the most odious of all monopolies.[68]

While Godwin's writings might be interpreted as too idiosyncratic to represent any political community, such views were

---

[65] See Lawrence Stone, *The Family, Sex and Marriage in England, 1500–1800* (London: Weidenfeld & Nicolson, 1977), 539.

[66] See Marilyn Butler, 'Myth and Mythmaking in the Shelley Circle', *ELH* 49 (1982), 50–72, 69. Knight's book still has to be read under restriction in the Bodleian Library.

[67] See Stone, *Family, Sex and Marriage*, 535, and Roy Porter, 'Libertinism and Promiscuity', in Jonathan Miller (ed.), *The Don Giovanni Book* (London: Faber & Faber, 1990), 1–19, 8.

[68] William Godwin, *Enquiry Concerning Political Justice* (1798; Harmondsworth: Pelican, 1976), book viii, appendix, p. 762.

pervasively current throughout radical writing, from the poetic prophecies of William Blake which equated sexual with political freedom, to the pamphlets of William Spence which proclaimed: 'the chains of Hymen would be among the first that would be broken . . . in case of a Revolution'.[69]

The end of the eighteenth century, therefore, seemed to mark the apotheosis of a sexual libertarianism/libertinism, the genealogy of which might be traced within the Don Juan legend. Male debauchery had been excused as gentlemanly accomplishment throughout the seventeenth and much of the eighteenth century. The Restoration court of King Charles II certainly demonstrated such tolerance: it was claimed that Francis North, Lord Guilford, was seriously advised to 'keep a whore' because 'he was ill looked upon for want of doing so'.[70] One reason for this clemency was financially pragmatic, since upper-class gentlemen could afford to pay for the upbringing of illegitimate heirs. Don Juan, despite many variations, consistently retained his class distinction. Not only were all Don Juans aristocratic, but they exploited their rank in the pursuit and attainment of sexual conquests. Don Juan's behaviour was frequently either undetected or protected from accusation by the upper classes as a consequence of his status. Conversely, his sexual success with peasant women was achieved despite their suspicion which automatically equated his aristocracy with sexual opportunism and predatoriness.

In addition, until and including the seventeenth century, the female nature was commonly considered to be inherently promiscuous.[71] It is therefore not fortuitous that the legend of Don Juan originated and first flourished in the seventeenth century—the versions of Tirso de Molina (1630), Molière (1665), and Shadwell (1675) all date from this period. In such a con-

---

[69] See e.g. William Blake, *America: A Prophecy* (1793), ll. 21–5 and 196–9. Spence is quoted in E. P. Thompson, *The Making of the English Working Class* (Harmondsworth: Pelican, 1963), 178–9.

[70] Quoted in Keith Thomas, 'The Double Standard', *Journal of the History of Ideas*, 20 (Apr. 1959), 195.

[71] See Stone, *Family, Sex and Marriage*, 501–2. See also Robert Burton, *The Anatomy of Melancholy*, 2 vols. (1621; repr. Oxford: Clarendon Press, 1989), i. 414–18: part 1; sect. 3; memb. 2; subs. 2: 'Symptomes of Maides, Nunnes, and Widowes Melancholy', and Joseph Swetnam, *Arraignment of Lewde, Idle, Froward, and unconstant women* (1617).

text, Don Juan could be depicted as seducing comprehensively, for no woman was able to resist him. These early versions also reflected the feudal nature of their contemporary societies because all of Don Juan's conquests were divided between women of either comparative wealth or poverty. Indeed, the inequalities between Don Juan's victims were revealed and reinforced by the divergent methods used to enjoy their favours. Wealthy ladies were seduced by deceit and disguise and were vulnerable because of their boredom and fashionable languor: covert sexual relations provided a titillating escape from the tedium of polite society. Peasant girls were tempted by promises of grandeur and largess, susceptible to the tremendous flattery and potential betterment offered by an aristocratic suitor. In addition, working-class customs allowed a woman to engage in premarital sex and still retain her honour.[72] Peasant girls were considered easy prey and their promiscuity was so renowned that their seduction was often casually assumed. Byron appropriated the rhetoric of the opportunist seducer with his differing strategies of seduction according to class distinctions when he apologized to Sir Walter Scott for his belated and shy correspondence:

I can only account for it on the same principle of tremulous anxiety with which one sometimes makes love to a beautiful woman of our own degree with whom one is <in love> enamoured of in good earnest;— whereas we attack a fresh-coloured housemaid without . . . any sentimental remorse or mitigation of our virtuous purpose.[73]

The retrospection of Byron's poem towards a setting in the 1790s has been widely interpreted as a gesture of political nostalgia. Malcolm Kelsall, for example, noted that the dating of the poem immediately precedes the great Whig triumphs in the constructive treason trials of 1794 in which Thomas Hardy, John Thelwall, Thomas Holcroft, and John Horne Tooke, among other radical figures, were acquitted.[74] This nostalgia is interpreted as a particularly Whig reaction, since the party had been out of office for nearly all of Byron's lifetime. (The

---

[72] See Anna Clark, *Women's Silence, Men's Violence* (London: Pandora Press, 1987), 10, 13.
[73] *Byron's Letters and Journals*, ix. 85 (letter to Sir Walter Scott, 12 Jan. 1822).
[74] Kelsall, *Byron's Politics* (Brighton: The Harvester Press, 1987), 184.

'Ministry of all the Talents' of 1806–7 included Fox but it lasted only fourteen months. The Whigs did not regain office until Grey's ministry in 1830.) However, Byron may also have been remembering the comparative permissiveness of that period, when sexual libertinism and political libertarianism were radical allies.

Unsurprisingly, Tory polemic countered this twinning and adopted the arguments of orthodox religion in advocating 'moral standards'. Thomas Robert Malthus, in his *Essay on the Principle of Population* (1798), decreed that procreation without financial means was 'immoral': unmarried mothers sinned not just against orthodox morality but against economic principles too. Edmund Burke's political conservatism was rooted in, and frequently indistinguishable from, moral orthodoxy. In *Reflections on the Revolution in France* (1790) he argued that men required their passions to be bridled by a force outside of themselves and '[i]n this sense the restraints of men, as well as their liberties, are to be reckoned among their rights'.[75] Burke's moral conservatism was exacerbated by the murmurings of alternative definitions of liberty which were largely emanating from France. The newspapers whipped up patriotism by denouncing 'French morals'. Indeed, the first phase of the French Revolution was distinguished by its comparative sexual freedom. The Liberty tree and the Phrygian cap originated in Roman fertility rites and were often portrayed as phallic symbols in cartoons of the period.[76]

The French Revolution made political dissent difficult for English liberals and thus the consolidation of moral conservatism was steadily effected throughout the years of the Napoleonic Wars. Linda Colley, in *Britons* (1992), contrasted the mid-eighteenth-century careers of such politicians as Viscount Bolingbroke, Robert Walpole, and the Earl of Sandwich, with their Regency counterparts. They had frequently flaunted the fact that they were keeping mistresses, or at any rate were unconcerned at its discovery, while those politicians in office in 1800 cultivated displays of ostentatious uxoriousness. Spencer

---

[75] Edmund Burke, *Reflections on the Revolution in France* (1790; repr. Harmondsworth: Penguin, 1968), 151.

[76] See Caroline Franklin, *Byron's Heroines* (Oxford: Clarendon Press, 1992), 625.

Perceval, Lord Liverpool, George Canning, Lord Sidmouth, Lord Castlereagh, and Robert Peel all prided themselves upon their happy domesticity. 'As a life-long bachelor, William Pitt the Younger was the great exception to this trend. But he was careful to die a virgin.' Linda Colley adds two important qualifications: first, that this pattern did not include out-of-office Whigs and colonial officials, and secondly that, while it was not true that all Tory ministers led impeccable lives, they were certainly more conscious of the need to be seen to be doing so.[77]

Throughout the eighteenth century an increasingly capitalist society began to demarcate the specifically moral contours of the new middle classes. Class sexuality increasingly structured eighteenth-century society and reinforced the divisions within it: for, in contrast both with the libertine appetites of the landed aristocracy and with the promiscuous mob, was the sanctuary of the middle class. Female promiscuity was condemned as a threat to property and inheritance, for the legitimacy of the heir had to be legally unquestionable. Sexual virtue thus became a commodity in the transaction of marriage. The structure of Rousseau's new society relied upon the family and women's maternal role within it. Betrayal of the family was as subversive as betrayal of the state, and in *Emile* (1762), female adultery was literally equated with treason.[78]

In this way the redefinition of the female and her role in society was a crucial feature of the hegemony that brought the middle classes into power. Marriages between aristocratic land and merchant money sent middle-class daughters into the families of the upper classes. Such marriages benefited both classes in their own way. The aristocracy would have risked extinction without the injection of chosen outsiders and a revolution in social codes was accomplished as bourgeois values were infused into the less restrained 'high life' of the aristocracy. Caroline Franklin's consideration of Christoph Meiners's *History of the Female Sex* (1808) demonstrates the crucial role which women's sexual conduct played in the construction of civic society:

[77] Linda Colley, *Britons* (New Haven and London, Yale University Press, 1992), 189 and 400n. 101.
[78] Jean-Jacques Rousseau, *Emile* (1762), tr. Barbara Foxley (London: J. M. Dent, 1950), 324–5.

'Marriage is overtly linked by [Meiners] to the hereditary dynastic transmission of property . . . The sexual mores of the female sex are thus perceived by Meiners as determinant of the economic and political nature of the whole society. Upon female chastity rests the whole edifice of middle-class property, liberty and independence.'[79]

The configuration of three class sexualities began to lose ground as the moral influence of the middle classes infiltrated into those ranks above and below. The growing band of Evangelicals called for a revolution in 'manners and morals' which would simultaneously improve the dissipated upper orders and subdue the lower. Although its origins dated from the 1730s, the momentum of Methodism only gathered force in the 1790s, when the French Revolution was rhetorically appropriated as threatening an earthly damnation.[80] The rhetoric of puritanical sexuality was also a strategy the middle classes used effectively to undermine the authority of the old aristocracy. Mary Wollstonecraft's *A Vindication of the Rights of Women* (1792) is one example of such a deployment. She omitted sexual passion from the construction of civic virtue because of its association with aristocratic voluptuousness and decadence. Charles Pigot's *A Political Dictionary, Explaining the Meaning of Words* (1795) advised his readers that they would recognize the aristocratic male primarily by his behaviour of 'debauching your neighbour's wife or daughter'.[81]

The penetration of the middle-class ideology of decency and respectability into working-class culture was simultaneously effected by such disparate influences as religion and trade-union action.[82] Many working-class radicals saw the percolation downwards of birth-control methods as a sign that aristocratic decadence was spreading debasement and outraged articles on the sexual habits of the wealthy became a familiar feature of the popular press. In radical discourse of the last decades of the eighteenth century, sexual libertinism was an expression of individual freedom. In the increasingly conservative years after

[79] Franklin, *Byron's Heroines*, 114.
[80] See Jeffrey Weeks, *Sex, Politics and Society* (1981; repr. London: Longman, 1989), 69; Stone, *Family, Sex and Marriage*, 648.
[81] Quoted in Colley, *Britons*, 153.
[82] See Thompson, *Making of the English Working Class*, 63.

Waterloo it served as a reminder of aristocratic privileges. Certainly, at the time of *Don Juan*'s writing (1819–24), sexual libertarianism was becoming untypical of the radical movement as a whole, which increasingly spoke the language of sexual virtue and marriage. This is evident in William Hone's pirate edition of *The Corsair* (1817) in which the celebrated champion of the freedom of the press 'censored' Byron's original text. Changes which Hone made to the poem included depicting the marriage of the lovers, Conrad and Medora, and making Medora feel a revulsion against their 'mutual degradation' when she discovers Conrad's mode of raising cash. This edition proves that moral censorship was not restricted to conservative preachers such as the notorious Dr Bowdler.[83]

If radical thought in the 1790s exploited the rhetoric of individual liberty, including that of sexuality, by 1819 John Hookham Frere was cautioning Byron against the publication of *Don Juan* because as a 'friend of liberty', he ought to be the enemy of licentiousness.[84] However, the principle of liberty began for Byron, as for the *libertà*-proclaiming Don Giovanni, with the possibility of sexual fulfilment for each individual. Thus within *Don Juan*, the Spanish insurrectionists figuratively become the aphrodisiacal Spanish fly: 'None, save the Spanish fly and Attic bee, | As yet are strongly stinging to be free' (IX, 28). As freedom is linked associatively with sexual liberty, so too chastity is associated with bonds: 'Chaste were his steps, each kept within due bound' (XIV, 39). The prevalence of class stratification in sexual libertarianism is criticized in the description of the magistrate's power over the pregnant serving girl of Norman Abbey. Some have (a) 'licence' for such activity:

> Now Justices of Peace must judge all pieces
> Of mischief of all kinds and keep the game
> And morals of the country from caprices

[83] See Marina Vitale, 'The Domesticated Heroine in Byron's *Corsair* and William Hone's Prose Adaptation', *Literature and History*, 10 (1984), 72–94; Peter J. Manning, 'The Hone-ing of Byron's *Corsair*', in *Reading Romantics* (New York and Oxford: Oxford University Press, 1990), 216–37. See also Thompson, *Making of the English Working Class*, 815, on the attempts of radicals to counter conservative propaganda by portraying themselves as 'moral'.

[84] Peter W. Graham (ed.), *Byron's Bulldog* (Columbus, Ohio: Ohio State University Press, 1984), 258 (5 Jan. 1819).

> Of those who have not a licence for the same;
> And of all things, excepting tithes and leases,
> Perhaps these are most difficult to tame.
> Preserving partridges and pretty wenches
> Are puzzles to the most precautious benches.
>
> (XVI, 63)

The play on 'peace'/'piece' continues in the ambivalence of 'licence' (permission/debauchery) and culminates in the parallel of partridges and young girls. Byron chose a bird which accords perfectly with the sexual theme of the strophe: in classical literature the partridge was renowned for its intense sexual activity.[85] The judge's role of gamekeeper is therefore of the same nature as that of censor of morals. The suppression of poaching is paralleled by sexual repression, since both are subject to inflexible and archaically feudal laws. The poem's defence of the notorious seducer, Don Juan, reflected and reinforced these local examples of sexual libertarianism as a calculated provocation to moral conservatism.

In the context of this moral hegemony, the potential of Don Juan to practise subversion appeared to increase. By appealing directly to the woman herself, he disrupted the patriarchal control of women in which fathers determined marriages. And by appealing most particularly to her sexual nature, he subverted the predominantly bourgeois ideology of the chastity of the proper female. Don Juan seemed to articulate a refusal of the bourgeois manifesto of conjugal fidelity and felicity prior to its consolidation in the course of the nineteenth century. Many nineteenth-century versions of the legend included the virtuous middle-class woman by making their Don Juans fall in love with her. Even Moncrieff's burlesque *Giovanni in London*, which included wives as a conventional butt of the piece's satire, finally portrayed its Don Giovanni as 'saved' through his love for and marriage to the appropriately named Constantia. Byron's poem, however, in celebrating sexual freedom and condemning the moral hypocrisy which opposes it, has no position for middle-class morality, other than implicitly opposing it throughout. The anti-marriage motif of many of the earliest portrayals of Don Juan is a motif which runs throughout the

---

[85] See Robert Graves, *The White Goddess* (London: Faber & Faber, 1967), 328.

narrator's satire, as in Don Juan's predilection for already married women (XV, 30).[86] Indeed, Byron's intention for his poem included the caustic comment that Don Juan's 'hell' could be realistically portrayed as marriage.[87] And the narrator ridicules the ideological appropriation of women as agents of middle-class power: 'Their love, their virtue, beauty, education | But form good housekeepers, to breed a nation' (XIV, 24).

The sexual exploits of Byron's Don Juan nostalgically replicate the class configuration of the seductions of earlier versions of the legend, for they are all with either aristocratic or peasant women. The only particularized female character who might approximate to a middle-class woman is Donna Inez. Yet Inez is of the noblest pedigree, one, unlike Donna Julia's, without ancestral 'stain'. Her bourgeois appearance belies her status because she is a paragon of middle-class virtues and their prescriptive conduct books. 'Morality's prim personification' (I, 16), her status is ambivalent because the spheres of sexual conduct and social class intermesh. Does Inez appear bourgeois because of her morality or moral because of her bourgeois manners?

Because it adopted the theme of the Don Juan legend, Byron's poem examined contemporary political debates, especially class debates, through its foregrounding of sexuality. And because the middle class attacked the sexual freedom of upper- and working-class cultures, this particular configuration of class sexualities dictated the narrator's, sometimes uncharacteristic, political allegiances. Conservative commentators who criticized patrician degeneracy as spreading debasement risked destroying the order of hierarchy and tradition upon which their very political manifestos depended. Similarly, *Don Juan*, in opposing middle-class morality, was led into a more sympathetic treatment of the working classes than its author might otherwise have contemplated. Byron's letters and journals are full of the most shocking political snobberies, even if they might, rather disingenuously, be dismissed as mere bravura. Such statements as 'a Gentleman scoundrel is always preferable to a vulgar one' (15 October 1819) and 'If we must have a tyrant—let him at

---

[86] See e.g. vii. 49, viii. 27, xiv. 95.
[87] *Byron's Letters and Journals*, viii. 78 (16 Feb. 1821).

least be a gentleman who has been bred to the business, and let us fall by the axe and not by the butcher's cleaver' (21 February 1820)[88] are pronounced with the same kind of aristocratic outrageousness which is deployed by, for example, Molière's Dom Juan. His snobbish disdain of Done Elvira's unfashionable dress—'She must be out of her mind not to have changed her clothes and to come to town dressed for the country'—is entirely typical of the lordly facetiousness of other Don Juans as it is of Byron's letters and journals.[89]

These examples from Byron's letters are contemporaneous with the writing of *Don Juan*. So too is Byron's dissatisfaction with Hobhouse's particular brand of political radicalism, a reaction which Hobhouse himself felt keenly as a personal betrayal. However, *Don Juan* itself displays relatively little of this kind of deliberately flaunted aristocratic facetiousness and, while the poem continues to exclude the working-class reader in its references to the 'mob', it nevertheless portrays them with some degree of sympathy. This 'mob' is described as falling sick 'of imitating Job' (VIII, 50–1). 'Democracy' is referred to positively, humorously scolding in: 'And wrinkles (the damned democrats) won't flatter' (X, 24). Death is portrayed as a radical reformer (X, 25) who cannot be resisted. And the defence of the poor man's right to drink gin explicitly indicates how the impetus of this sympathy was an opposition to the moral puritanism of the new middle classes (X, 63).

Malcolm Kelsall described the Byron of *Don Juan* as 'caught between tyranny and the mob with nowhere to go'.[90] However, in *Don Juan* the narrator fears neither the *ancien régime* nor the mass. It was the now properly designated 'mass' of the middle class who preached sexual chastity, if not abstinence, and encouraged the upper classes to pretend to moral virtues they did not possess, which he feared and despised. The plebeian 'mob' at least did not exercise the moral hypocrisy which seemed to characterize the middle classes and which was steadily infecting the nobility, especially among its women. If *Don Juan* is an

---

[88] *Byron's Letters and Journals*, v. 228–9 (to Augusta Leigh, 15 Oct. 1819); vii. 44 (to John Murray, 21 Feb. 1820). See also Byron's comment on Burdett, vi. 166.
[89] Molière, *The Miser and Other Plays*, tr. John Wood (Harmondsworth: Penguin, 1953), 205.
[90] Kelsall, *Byron's Politics*, 168.

attempt to redefine the eponymous hero, it is also a redefinition of the very term 'morality'. The narrator repeatedly insists that his poem is exceedingly 'moral'.[91] In a letter to Murray Byron protested, with a rhetorical innocence which is typical of his poem as a whole: 'I maintain that it is the most moral of poems, but if people won't discover the moral that is their fault, not mine.'[92] It was not a morality of which most readers would have approved. As a defence of the traditional Don Juan, the poem argued for a new and benevolent understanding of the seducer: if Don Jóse's sexual infidelities were reprehensible, '[h]e had been ill brought up and was born bilious' (I, 35). The poem's own cure for such sexual libertinism would hardly have been popular:

> And as for chastity, you'll never bind it
> By all the laws the strictest lawyer pleads,
> But aggravate the crime you have not prevented,
> By rendering desperate those who had else repented.
>
> (XII, 80)

The poem's perceived celebration of immorality directly opposed those writers who argued that the political strength of Britain required moral rectitude. Such an opinion was not reserved to Evangelical preachers and moral cranks. Every classically educated schoolboy was taught the licentious cause of the downfall of the Roman empire. Among Hobhouse's notes for *Childe Harold* was a reference to the inevitable decline of dissolute societies. Byron himself, in the appendices of *Marino Faliero,* included an excerpt from Pierre Antoine Daru's *Histoire de la République de Venise* which cited the 'freedom of manners' which had degenerated into 'scandalous licentiousness' as one of the causes of the decline of Venice.[93] The following 'review' of the pantomime *Don Juan* at the Lyceum Theatre in 1817 reveals how the discussion of the Don Juan legend could

---

[91] See e.g. I, 207; XI, 87; XII, 39, 55, 86.

[92] *Byron's Letters and Journals,* iv. 279.

[93] *Childe Harold,* Canto IV, stanza 108, Hobhouse's note, quoted in *Complete Poetical Works,* ii (1980), 253–4 (n. 964). See also Thompson, *Making of the English Working Class,* 442: '[Wilberforce's] conviction as to the intimate correlation between moral levity and political sedition among the lower classes is characteristic of his class'.

become a cautionary political tale. Beginning with straightforward theatrical comment, it quickly becomes a treatise on the
fall of empires:

> The causes which broke down Spain and buried her with all her
> costliness, like a great Herculaneum, perhaps entire still, yet showing
> nothing above but ruins and ashes . . . may not slightly substantiate the
> truth, that the fall of all nations comes from within, and not from
> without, from the decay of morals, and not the force of armies.
>
>   The story of Don Juan has the characteristic of having been one of
> the most popular in the whole history of the drama. It is exaggerated,
> its hero a model of guilt, a lewd, remorseless, faithless, sanguinary
> villain. But the multitude of all countries have watched with delight the
> progress of this monstrous criminal through his whole fiery circle,
> shouted after crime on the stage which in the streets would have raised
> the whole population to hunt it from society, and even where the
> libertine perishes, see only the final resistance of a being to be intimi-
> dated neither by death nor hell.[94]

The associative logic of this review creates a causal relationship
between exculpating the criminal Don Juan and destroying the
country. Exactly this point was made by the reviewer of *The
British Critic* (1819) when he declared that the 'British nation'
would allow itself to be tricked out of 'that main bulwark of its
national strength, its sturdy and unbending morality', in reading Byron's *Don Juan*.[95]
    Many reviewers of the Don Juan productions feared the con-
sequences of their adulation because it seemed to provide a
glimpse of the power and autonomy of the masses. And this
political analysis was repeated by those critics who unanimously
denounced, not just the immorality of Byron's *Don Juan*, but its
dissemination among the working classes. The poem's attempt
to excuse its libertine hero was therefore in itself a political act
because it contradicted the increasing hegemony of moral and
political conservatism. It was an example of the 'jacobinical
drama', defined by Coleridge in his 'Critique of *Bertram*' as
being 'the confusion and subversion of the natural order of
things in their causes and effects: namely, in the excitement of
surprise by representing the qualities of liberality, refined feel-

---

[94] *The Examiner* (30 June 1817).
[95] *The British Critic*, 2nd ser. 12 (1819), 202.

ing and a nice sense of honour . . . in persons and in classes where experience teaches us least to expect them'.[96] Coleridge's political conservatism is revealed by his pointed reference to those classes which display 'refined feeling' (evidently not a property of the spectators who attended Don Giovanni burlesques and roared for 'The Roast Beef of England'). Although Don Juan belonged to this class, he was not expected to display 'qualities' other than the traditionally permitted one of courage, synonymous in his case with audacity. In *Don Juan* Byron confused the natural order of the legend when he excused his 'hero', Don Juan.

The deliberate subversion of the expected was a tactic adopted by radical pamphleteers in 1817–18. The adoption of a conventional position and its rewriting in an unexpected direction was characteristic of the parodies published by William Hone. These included pamphlets which deliberately misread the Creed (*The Sinecurist's Creed*), the Catechism (*The Late John Wilkes' Catechism*), the Litany (*The Political Litany*), nursery rhymes (*The Political House that Jack Built*), the fairground patter of showmen (*The Political Showman at Home*), and theatrical spectacles (*A Lecture on Living Heads*). By deliberately misreading conventional texts, these pamphlets parodied and inflicted 'semantic wounds' upon the language of the middle class and the aristocracy.[97] Byron imitated this practice in his poetic decalogue (I, 205–6), fully aware of its political risk.[98] Harriette Wilson, for example, wrote to Byron: 'what catchpenny ballad writer could not write a parody on them as you have done?'[99] In the 1817 trials for blasphemy of William Hone, the publisher argued that his prosecution was political, not religious, and in *'Don John' or 'Don Juan' Unmasked* (1819) he drew attention to the apparent double standards which allowed Byron to parody the Bible, but prosecuted Mr Russell, the printer of *The Political Litany*.[100] Hone won his own case through

---

[96] Coleridge, *Collected Works*, vii, *Biographia Literaria: II*, 313.

[97] See Jon P. Klancher, *The Making of English Reading Audiences, 1790–1832* (Madison, Wis.: University of Wisconsin Press, 1987), 98–134. The phrase 'semantic wounds' is from p. 100. See also Vitale, 'Domesticated Heroine', *passim*.

[98] *Byron's Letters and Journals*, v. 22 (letter to Murray, 8 Oct. 1820).

[99] *Memoirs of Harriette Wilson*, 4 vols. (2nd edn.; London: J. J. Stockdale, 1825), iv. 217.

[100] *'Don John' or 'Don Juan' Unmasked*, 39–40.

a display of erudition and the laughing responses which his recitation of literary precedents drew from the courtroom. He demonstrated that Martin Luther, Bishop Latimer, John Milton, and many others, had also used the device of parodying a religious form for political effect. An inclusive definition of such parodies would recognize Byron's *Don Juan* and not just two stanzas of it, for *Don Juan* also deliberately (mis)read a conventional story for political motives.

The connection between *Don Juan* and the parodies of William Hone is allusively present in the narrator's repetition of the epigraph from *The Political House that Jack Built* (1819), 'A straw—thrown up to show which way the wind blows', in Canto XIV, stanza 8. The political significance of Hone's radical citation is reinforced in the narrator's desire that his poetry should 'sail in the wind's eye', as a metaphor for the dangers which the poem will not shun (X, 3–4). Early posthumous editions of *Don Juan* claimed that the suppressed Dedication to Byron's poem had circulated in broadside issues, a distinctly radical format, although unfortunately no copies of this edition have survived.[101] On 6 February 1822 Byron suggested to Kinnaird that some of the marginal or radical publishers might want to publish *The Vision of Judgement*.[102] While this might have been due to pragmatism—Murray's caution over *Don Juan* would certainly have suggested that he would not touch *The Vision*—it also implies an acceptance on Byron's part of the political necessity of such non-, if not anti-, establishment publishers, and of his own writing's allegiance with them. It is therefore appropriate that in *Don Juan: Canto the Third*, a parody of Byron's poem published and possibly written by William Hone in 1819, the figure of Don Juan himself became a radical publisher of *The Devilled Biscuit* which is described as being 'Rubbish on Reform' (stanza xviii, l. 2). He is arrested and tried for 'treasonous practices suspected' (stanza xciv, l. 5):

> 'We've heard enough already of your pranks,
> There's not a town in Europe does not scout you;
> Expatriated first, the very Franks
> Have branded you, you bear the marks about you;

---

[101] See *Complete Poetical Works*, v (1986), 667.
[102] *Byron's Letters and Journals*, ix. 100: ' "Try back the deep lane" '.

To pour your venom thro' our lower ranks
You've now come here—but they can do without you;
Altho' you think in London here to winter
What's your profession?—tell me Sir?' '*a Printer!*'[103]

And in the pamphlet *Remarks Critical and Moral on the Talents of Lord Byron and the Tendencies of Don Juan* (1819), the consequences of Byron's poem were directly compared with the publications of Richard Carlile, who was imprisoned and fined in 1819 for republishing Paine's *Age of Reason* and other 'offences': 'We have a Carlisle [*sic*] with his *dram* for the ignorant, and his Lordship with his *liqueur* for the enlightened; poisons precisely adapted to their respective recipients; both equally sure, and equally dangerous; but differing from each other, only as the *grape* from the *grain*, or the *nut* from the *juniper*'.[104] It is therefore appropriate that Byron associatively linked the legendary figure of Don Juan (who 'sow[s] scepticism to reap hell') with 'demagogues' and 'infidels' (IX, 25).

These references and other moral-political dimensions have frequently been overlooked in readings which underestimate the radical dynamic of the poem. The political implications of the Don Juan legend, however, counter the criticism that *Don Juan*'s tone is consistently one of hauteur and reveal the links which connected Byron's poem with such a notoriously radical figure as William Hone. These political implications work also through the poem's expression. The narrative strategies of sexual insinuation and innuendo effectively provoked and outraged the poem's moralistic readers in forcing them to concede their understanding of such 'obscenity' before they could criticize it. And such moral readers were associated with the middle class even if they were not literally of it.[105] Within the thoroughly libidinized language of *Don Juan*, political comment and satire were often expressed through sexual innuendo and word-play. The denunciation of Castlereagh, for example, is almost entirely voiced as sexual insult. He is the 'intellectual eunuch' (Dedication, 11), a 'state-thing' (Dedication, 16), the 'vulgarest tool that Tyranny could want', 'cold-blooded, smooth-faced',

---

[103] *Don Juan: Canto the Third* (London: William Hone, 1819), stanza 96.
[104] *Remarks Critical and Moral* (London: G. Woodfall, 1819), 3.
[105] See *Engels: Selected Writings* (Harmondsworth: Penguin, 1967), 92.

'dabbling its sleek young hands in Erin's gore' (Dedication, 12). His indeterminate sexuality, reinforced by the reiteration of 'it', and his *lack* of passion are portrayed as troubling. The designation 'placid' becomes an insult. These insults were continued in the Preface to Cantos VI–VIII (published 1823), where he is described as 'emasculated to the marrow' and in Canto IX where there is an oblique reference to Castlereagh's childlessness (stanza 49, l. 8). In fact, political reputations were more frequently broken by sexual than military scandals, as exemplified in the fates of Anthony (VI, 4), and the Trojans (IX, 53). Castlereagh's surprising suicide in 1822 has since been attributed to his fear of blackmail, for rumours of homosexuality carried severe penalties.[106] The insinuations of Castlereagh's sexual indeterminacy in *Don Juan* might corroborate such a suggestion, although the gesture of sexual insult is characteristic of the poem. The denunciation of Southey is also expressed as sexual innuendo: he is described by the slang phrase 'dry bob' of coition without emission (Dedication, 3) and, in the figure of the trimmer poet, as 'Pindar' (III, 85), an allusion to 'pandar' through the auditory word-play created by adjacent short 'a' sounds.[107]

Many of the sexual innuendos which are politically allusive are deployed within the Siege of Ismail Cantos since in popular slang the imagery of sex and battle were intertwined; slang for condoms, for example, was 'armour' and, during the Napoleonic wars, it was rumoured that prostitutes, known as 'gallows bitches', enticed men into houses where they were then forcibly recruited for the army.[108] In *Don Juan*, military metaphors often blur the distinction between rape and seduction: the genteel lady who hides her desires under false airs of innocence, erects 'palisades' (XIV, 61) which are a feature of military campaigns (VII, 10 and VIII, 46). The bravery of the Turkish army is ascribed to their embrace of death with its expectation of a paradise of virginal houris (VIII, 112–14). The Turkish soldier can then meet death as a form of sexual orgasm:

[106] H. Montgomery Hyde, *A Tangled Web: Sex Scandals in British Politics and Society* (London: Constable, 1986), 58–60.

[107] *Complete Poetical Works*, v (1986), commentary p. 700, ll. 679–80.

[108] See Thompson, *Making of the English Working Class*, 88 n. 3.

So fully flashed the phantom on his eyes
That when the very lance was in his heart,
He shouted 'Allah' and saw paradise
With all its veil of mystery drawn apart,
And bright eternity without disguise
On his soul, like a ceaseless sunrise, dart,
With prophets, houris, angels, saints descried
In one voluptuous blaze, and then he died.

(VIII, 115)

The problem of recruiting for a continually depleted army is seen to be solved by the Turkish harem system because polygamy spawns recruits (VIII, 105). This is suggested to an English audience, many of whom had spent years attempting either to resist or promote mobilization to the devouring army of the Napoleonic Wars. The narrator similarly relishes his suggestion for political amity between Russia and Turkey—nothing less than a sexual affair between Catherine and the Sultan (VI, 95). However unlikely it might be as a political solution, it is a predictable narrative response. Both examples demonstrate the libidinous expression of *Don Juan*, which suggests, however facetiously, more sex as the cure to just about every problem, including political difficulties. Such bravura demonstrates the flippancy of the narrator's stance and yet it is also an entirely typical gesture of the poem's sexually charged context—part erotic banter, part political subversion. To the poem's middle-class reviewers the two were almost synonymous.

The new confidence of the moral reformers is evident throughout the reviews of *Don Juan*. Donald Reiman in his preface to *The Investigator*'s review of *Don Juan* (October 1821) drew attention to its authoritative tone. Earlier reviews of Byron's poetry had criticized Byron's work only tentatively and obsequiously. The title of this review declared that its subject was 'Licentious Productions in High Life', by which it designated the works of Sir Charles Hanbery Williams, *Don Juan*, Cantos I–II and III–V, *Sardanapalus*, and Shelley's *Queen Mab*. The reviewer urged the Society for the Suppression of Vice to prosecute Byron, Shelley, and Lady Morgan among others, as vigorously as it did middle- and lower-class radical authors and publishers, and attacked the *Edinburgh* and *Quarterly* reviewers for their partiality. Turning specifically to *Don Juan*, the

narrator's tolerance of promiscuity was condemned as displaying the perspective of Byron's aristocratic status. Quoting Canto
I, stanza 35, in which the narrator indulgently excused Don
Jóse's philandering, the reviewer continued: 'its morality, the
fashionable world, in its practice at least, does not condemn,
though those who have any regard to the mere decencies of life
will not venture openly to defend it'.[109] Such outright censure
displayed the gaining authority of the middle class. The power
of the Regency aristocracy to set the social tone for England had
been broken. And the aristocratic Don Juan was also under
attack.

THE ARISTOCRATIC DON JUAN

Despite the increasing domination of middle-class morality,
examples of licentious behaviour were not at all a thing of the
past. Fashionable Whig circles, such as that surrounding Holland House, continued to permit a considerable degree of
sexual licence.[110] Indeed English manners among the aristocracy during the Regency were probably the most libertine since
the Restoration. The Prince Regent and his brother dukes kept
many mistresses, an expense which was covered, it was rumoured, by the taxes of the people.[111] The famous liaison between Lord Nelson and Lady Hamilton was only one of many
notorious adulterous affairs. When Dr Bowdler's supporters
tried to carry new legislation for adulterers in the House of
Commons, their attempt was frustrated. Penalties had already
been passed upon Sabbath-breakers, vagrants, tinkers, stage-
dancers and tumblers, ballad-singers, free-thinkers, and naked
bathers. Legislation against adultery however was dismissed because it would have discriminated against the diversions of the
rich as well as the poor.[112] This opinion was voiced by Hazlitt in

---

[109] *The Investigator*, 3 (Oct. 1821), 353–60, review of Cantos I–II and III–V, and
foreword note in *The Romantics Reviewed*, part B, ed. Donald Reiman, 5 vols. (New
York: Garland, 1972), ii. 1166.
    [110] See Michael Robertson, 'The Byron of *Don Juan* as Whig Aristocrat', *Texas
Studies in Literature and Language*, 17/4 (Winter 1976), 714–16.
    [111] *Byron's Letters and Journals*, ii. 194. Carl Woodring, *Politics in English Romantic
Poetry* (Cambridge, Mass.: Harvard University Press, 1970), 196.
    [112] See Thompson, *Making of the English Working Class*, 443.

his essay on the increase of capital punishment in *The Edinburgh Review* (July 1821). He drily observed that whereas offences against property were severely punished (theft of any property worth more than 12*d.* attracted the death penalty), those of seduction, drunkenness, and gambling were overlooked because they were practised by the wealthy.[113] The review of *Don Juan*, Cantos I–II, in *The New Bon Ton Magazine* (1819) accused the poem of diffusing immorality among its specifically wealthy readers: 'No wonder that . . . divorces, and separations, are multiplied, when vice and immorality are so powerfully and sedulously inculcated, and when the lessons and seductive examples of depravity are laid upon the tables of the fair and rich . . . in splendid quartos.'[114] William Parry's response to Byron's *Don Juan*—one of the few working-class responses to have survived—singled out the shipwreck episode as 'something we mechanics and the working classes understand'.[115] Parry thus deliberately excluded the events of the bulk of the poem which are amatory. The implication is that only the aristocracy would enjoy such sexual adventures. While upper-class sexual looseness continued, what had changed was the new confidence to challenge their behaviour.

In the earliest versions of the Don Juan legend, the character, however engaging, was ultimately condemned as impious: Tirso de Molina's *El burlador de Sevilla* (1630) was a didactic play, written by a monk. This of course did not prevent it from being considered scandalous and consequently censored by ecclesiastical authorities. However, by the early nineteenth century, debates concerning Don Juan were political rather than religious. This was partly because attacks upon his aristocratic status were now possible. But it was also because the issue of personal morality had become thoroughly politicized. In this context, Don Juan became subversive because his behaviour struck at the very foundation of the new capitalist economy—marriage. Byron's poem, in deliberately offending and antagonizing its middle-class readership, is evidence of how the legend could be used on behalf of a radical cause.

---

[113] Reprinted in *Complete Works*, xix. 250. The detail of the theft of property over 12*d.* is taken from William St Clair, *The Godwins and the Shelleys* (London: Faber & Faber, 1989), 89.

[114] *The New Bon Ton Magazine*, 3 (1819), 238.

[115] E. J. Lovell (ed.), *His Very Self and Voice* (New York: Macmillan, 1954), 575.

Byron's hero is wholly consistent with the traditional Don Juan in retaining his 'inherent' aristocracy (I, 9). His 'breeding' is listed as the first of his attractions to potential bidders at the slave-market: his 'mien' alone demonstrates that he is above the 'vulgar' (V, 9) and his status is so conspicuous that Johnson perceives it more minutely in his eye (V, 14). His proud refusal to kneel and kiss Gulbeyaz's foot (V, 102–4) is acclaimed as a quality intrinsically linked to his birth. His privileged status also makes him a suitable ambassador for Catherine and ensures his easy assimilation into English society, where '[h]is manner showed him sprung from a high mother' (XIII, 24). Don Juan's invitation to the Amundeville estate is largely due to his birth, before which other considerations (like the more sinister rumours surrounding his life) are waived. The special configuration of Don Juan's Spanish aristocracy is also significant because this was a synecdoche for class despotism. In Maria Edgeworth's novel, *Patronage* (1814), for example, the English Colonel Hauton is described thus: 'not the stiffest, haughtiest, flat-backed Don of Spain, in Spain's proudest days, could be more completely aristocratic in his principles, or more despotic in his habits'.[116] Thus in *Don Juan*, Johnson ascribes the hero's proud look to his nationality (V, 14), and this specifically Spanish pride makes him refuse to bow at the feet of Gulbeyaz: 'The blood of all his line's Castilian lords | Boiled in his veins' (V, 104). Later the narrator hints at an association between his nationality and that of the despotic Russian: 'And Juan like a true born Andalusian | Could back a horse, as despots ride a Russian' (XIII, 23).

Because the seducer had always been highly born, the increasing confidence of the middle classes allowed political criticism of him to be expressed. Elinor's appraisal of the libertine figure of Willoughby in *Sense and Sensibility* (1811) is that his behaviour is a consequence of 'too early an independence and its consequent habits of idleness, dissipation and luxury'.[117] Stendhal's consideration of Don Juan in *De l'amour* (1822) explained the figure's moral ruthlessness in terms of his pride

---

[116] Maria Edgeworth, *Patronage* (1814; repr. London: Pandora Press, 1986), i. 29, ch. 3.

[117] Jane Austen, *Sense and Sensibility* (1811; repr. Harmondsworth: Penguin, 1969), ch. 44, p. 339.

of birth. Being aristocratic, the notion of justice is foreign to Don Juan:

> The idea of equality arouses in him the same horror that water gives to a man suffering from hydrophobia, and that is the reason why pride of birth suits Don Juan's character so well. And with the idea of equality of rights also founders the idea of justice; or rather, since Don Juan has sprung from illustrious stock, these common ideas have never even reached him.[118]

This retelling of the Don Juan figure parallels Tom Paine's denigration of the aristocracy's ability to be just legislators because they benefit from the very system which is unjust (in *The Rights of Man*, 1791–2). It directly opposes the incipient hauteur which is discerned in Coleridge's claim that the character's 'constant interpoise of wit, gaiety and social generosity . . . prevents the criminal, even in his most atrocious moments from sinking into the mere ruffian'.[119]

The increasing popularity of the legend among the lower classes is usually ascribed by myth-criticism to its adoption by new forms—the slapstick comedy and buffooneries of pantomime with its bawdy punning and bowls of macaroni; the popular tunes and hell-fire spectacle of the burlesques; or the folk-entertainment of the German puppet-plays. This judgement exactly replicates and perpetuates the segregation of taste which was evident among the Regency reviewers of Don Juan productions. The traditional ending of divine punishment is then interpreted as strictly didactic, a moral sermon delivered to the masses for their edification and the relish with which the audiences enjoyed the spectacle of the finale is explained as that of moral correctness vindicated, or, alternatively, sheer pleasure in spectacular fireworks. It may also have indicated that the crowd delighted to see the lordly Don, who always gets his way, receive his 'come-uppance'. The satisfaction provided by the finale could therefore have been equally interpreted as moral conservatism—or political subversion. Certainly the riotous Georgian audiences who demanded, and were rewarded

---

[118] Stendhal, *Love* (*De L'amour*, 1822), tr. Gilbert and Suzanne Sale (Harmondsworth: Penguin, 1975), 207.
[119] Coleridge, *Collected Works*, vii. *Biographia Literaria: II*, 220. Coleridge describes Don Juan as a 'highly bred gentleman'.

with, the old prices at Covent-Garden in 1809 provide an example of how the theatre was one arena where the upper classes were not always protected from revolution. In the following example the seemingly arbitrary explanation of the internal organization of the late eighteenth-century theatre dictated the political 'meaning' of the play. The socially stratified assembly was reflected in the tripartite physical entity of the theatre: pit, box, and gallery. In the pantomime of Don Juan which was produced at Drury Lane in 1791, obviously a sensitive time for class loyalties, the reviewer of *The Theatrical Guardian* was outraged by the piece's political subversion. In this production Scaramouch shamelessly mocked those spectators who were closest to him, to the general hilarity of the crowds in the lower priced, and more distant, galleries. This mocking included swinging a lanthorn precariously close to the heads of the ladies and gentlemen sitting in the pit, and displaying a fear that his dish of macaroni might be stolen by them. The easiest targets for satire were thus chosen for their proximity to the stage. The outrage was provoked by the spectacle of the galleries laughing *with* Scaramouch and *at* the gentry.[120] Hazlitt also explicitly connected his enjoyment of *Giovanni in London* with the inherent political subversion of its form: 'There is something in burlesque that pleases. We like to see the great degraded to a level with the little.'[121]

Thus the same Don Juan who was interpreted as radically subversive by some, conversely was to others the very embodiment of the special privileges of the old hierarchy enjoyed by the upper classes, a somewhat anachronistic epitome of old-fashioned aristocratic caddishness. The legend of Don Juan was never intrinsically partisan. Instead it could be appropriated for contrary arguments and indeed its ambivalent political status has enabled many varied political readings. In his *Histoire de France*, Michelet claimed that Molière's depiction of Dom Juan was so equivocal that, while his courtiers admired the libertine, Louis XIV himself was irritated by the figure and acted against the *grands Seigneurs libertins* of his court as a consequence of

---

[120] *The Theatrical Guardian*, 2 (Saturday 12 Mar. 1791), 13–14.
[121] Hazlitt's Lecture on 'The Drama: No. VII' for *The London Magazine* (July 1820), repr. in *Complete Works*, xviii. 343–52, 351.

their response to the play.[122] In *Man and Superman* (1903), George Bernard Shaw's 'modern' Don Juan, John Tanner, MIRC ('Member of the Idle Rich Class'), writes political pamphlets such as 'The Revolutionist's Handbook'. In Sylvia Townsend Warner's version, *After the Death of Don Juan* (1938), Don Juan is a representative of Spanish fascism, implicitly in the context of the Spanish Civil War. Ramiro de Maeztu's ostensibly hypothetical consideration of the legendary figure thus actually reflected his disparate history: 'A mi no me duda de que lo mismo se haría fascista en Roma que lord en Inglaterra o comunista en Moscú.'[123]

Many Don Juans demonstrated only the political opportunism typical of Machiavelli, with whom Don Juan was frequently compared. *Leonzio, ovvera la terribile vendetta di un morto* (1615), a play which possibly influenced Tirso de Molina's *burlador*, depicted its Count Leonzio, 'perverted by Machiavelli's doctrines', kicking a skull.[124] Both Machiavelli and Don Juan would argue that the end justifies the means, and scorn conventional moral values, although it would never occur to Machiavelli to suggest that unnecessary risks might add spice to an undertaking. Machiavelli's advocation of political mobility is reflected in the inconsistency between political poses which is typical of Byron's *Don Juan*. The nature, though not always the substance, of the arguments is fundamentally anarchic, fulfilling the assumed antagonism between the text and its readers by prohibiting complacency on their part. Political subversiveness swerving vertiginously into conservatism (as, for example, in Canto XV, stanzas 22–3) is part of this strategy.

Thus the relativism evident in the manner of the poem's utterances also characterizes its political stances. The opportunist Don Juan frequently exploited the ambiguity of 'libertà' for his own 'licence'. This distinction lies behind the narrator's ridicule of Don Juan's 'worthy' and 'impassioned' eulogy on the theme of freedom—in love (V, 126–8). The equation of Don

---

[122] Michelet, *Histoire de France* (XII), quoted in Molière, *Dom Juan*, 118.
[123] Ramiro de Maeztu, *Don Quijote, Don Juan y la Celestina* (Madrid: Colección Austral, Espasa-Calpe, 1938), 104.
[124] See also Gregorio Marañón, *Don Juan* (1940; repr. Madrid: Espasa-Calpe, 1967), 95: 'el amor donjuanisco ... no es otra cosa que la aplicación del maquiavelismo al amor humano'.

Juan with an anarchist dynamic might seem to suggest that the figure would be subversive of existing structures. However this subversion, like so much of the legend's 'radicalism', could also be seen as more apparent than real. Don Juan could in fact be exposed as perpetuating the very structures which his very presence seems to deny. A feminist politics, for example, might make such accusations—the democratic sympathies of Stendhal dictated that he did.

Because of his social position, as a member of the ruling class in decline, it would have been surprising for a French Don Juan to have survived the Revolution. This hypothesis has been considered in a recent essay by Beatrice Didier in which she asked: 'Did the Revolution kill Don Juan among other aristocrats?'[125] Stendhal's Don Juan was a figure of the *ancien régime*, and as such would undoubtedly have been guillotined. The associative link between the legend and the French Revolution was made by the reviewer of the Don Juan pantomime at the Lyceum when he included France among those nations brought low by the licentious behaviour of their citizens (*The Examiner*, 30 June, 1817). The two were also explicitly connected by Coleridge in his 'Critique of *Bertram*' (1816). Coleridge, however, could not allow Don Juan to become a 'victim' of the Revolution since his own political conservatism disapproved of the Revolution and his moral conservatism of Don Juan, although the two of course were not unrelated. Coleridge therefore compared Don Juan to Jean Baptiste Carrier, the French Revolutionist and Terrorist, chosen specifically as a 'contemporary' representative of atheism and materialism. Carrier established the Legion of Marat in order to kill as quickly as possible the prisoners who were crowded in the gaols. Many were shot *en masse* and others were sunk in the Loire. Carrier himself was guillotined during the Terror, on 16 November 1794. His career was invoked by Coleridge as evidence that the threat of Don Juan was no longer solely theatrical fiction:

[I]t is no less clear, nor, with the biography of Carrier and his fellow atheists before us, can it be denied without wilful blindness, that the (so called) *system of nature* (that is, materialism, with the utter rejection

---

[125] Beatrice Didier, 'Des Lumières au Romantisme. A-t-on guillotiné le commandeur?' *Don Juan* (Paris: Bibliothèque Nationale, 1991), 153–8, 153.

of moral responsibility, of a present Providence, and of both present and future retribution) may influence the characters and actions of individuals, and even of communities, to a degree that almost does away the distinction between men and devils, and will make the page of the future historian resemble the narration of a madman's dreams.[126]

Byron was doubtless recalling this passage when he proposed a final scene in the French Revolution as a suitable finale for his own poem. The existent poem permits a prophetic glimpse of this intention in the comic description of the 'completely *sans-culotte*' Don Juan (XVI, 111). Byron's own political leanings prevented his much-loved Juan from being either the antipathetic character of Carrier or one of the guillotined French nobility whose overthrow Byron, against his own status, supported. His choice was again a significantly specific one: writing to Murray in February 1821, he outlined his intentions for Don Juan, ultimately making 'him finish as *Anacharsis Cloots*—in the French Revolution'.[127] This anticipated denouement is highly significant of Byron's intentions for the poem's 'meaning'. And since Anacharsis Clootz has been neglected in recent criticism of the poem, it is important to recall the unique political configuration which he represented.[128]

ANACHARSIS CLOOTZ AS DON JUAN

Jean Baptiste, Baron de Clootz, was a Prussian baron best known as Anacharsis Clootz. A whimsical character, he notoriously described himself before the National Convention as 'l'orateur du genre humain', paraded ostentatiously around Paris in a scarlet Phrygian cap of liberty, and whipped up war fever among the foreign exile communities by proclaiming that the liberation of all Europe was at hand. Envisaging a world

[126] Coleridge, *Collected Works*, vii. *Biographia Literaria: II*, p. 214. The details about Carrier are taken from the footnotes of this edn.

[127] *Byron's Letters and Journals*, viii. 78 (letter to John Murray, 16 Feb. 1821). See also E. J. Lovell (ed.), *Medwin's Conversations with Lord Byron* (Princeton: Princeton University Press, 1969), 165: 'He shall get into all sorts of scrapes, and at length end his career in France. Poor Juan shall be guillotined in the French Revolution!'

[128] Exceptions are Elizabeth Boyd, *Byron's Don Juan* (New Brunswick, NJ: Rutgers University Press, 1945), 39–41, and Franklin, *Byron's Heroines*.

without barriers, he declared 'Il n'aura plus de desert; toute la terre sera un jardin'. Clootz was a well-known figure and as such is included among the narrator's initial list of 'heroes' in *Don Juan* (I, 3). The specific source for Byron's knowledge of Clootz was John Adolphus's *Biographical Memoirs of the French Revolution* (1799), a copy of which was included in the 1816 sale catalogues of the library at Newstead. Adolphus noted that Clootz collected a troop 'from the dregs of the people', consisting of Savoyards, pedlars, teachers of languages, and vagabonds, and that he dressed them in masquerade costumes, partly supplied from the wardrobe of the opera house, to represent all the nations of the world.[129] Clootz's renown was largely due to this significantly 'theatrical' behaviour.

Clootz was executed by Robespierre on 24 March 1794, ostensibly to substantiate the charge of a foreign plot. The real cause of dissent between Clootz and Robespierre displays a striking characteristic which Clootz shared with the traditional Don Juan—an audacious and rather impolitic disregard of religion. Clootz dropped his 'Christian' name Jean Baptiste for that of Anacharsis, borrowed from 'l'antiquite païenne'. Clootz joined the anti-Christian movement led by the extreme left-wing section of the Jacobins and proclaimed 'La seule vraie republique athée'. Commentators on Byron's poem have overlooked the irreligious dimension of Clootz's career. However it was detailed at length in the *Memoirs* of John Adolphus:

In his speeches to the legislative assembly, he mentioned the name of the Supreme Being with levity, but he afterwards professed himself an Atheist, and carried his profaneness to such an excess that he was called *the personal enemy of Jesus Christ.* He wrote a book proving the nothingness of religion, which he presented to the convention, with an assurance that it was the fruit of fifteen hours every day for four years.

It was at his instigation that Gobel (l'évêque de Paris) attended at the bar of the convention, and renounced his religion; and when the ceremony was over, Clootz's wife proposed that a statue should be erected to the bishop who had abjured the gospel.[130]

---

[129] John Adolphus, *Biographical Memoirs of the French Revolution* (London: J. Cadell, Jn. & W. Davies, 1799), 291.
[130] Ibid. 294–5.

Robespierre denounced the atheistic campaign as a counter-revolutionary manœuvre from abroad and began by personally attacking Clootz and expelling him from the club of Paris Jacobins. His speech exposes the suspicion that Clootz's aristocratic status automatically aroused: 'Atheism is aristocratic. Whereas the idea of a divine being—the supreme being . . . is very plebian! Can we think of a German baron as a patriot? Can we think a man who has more than 100,000 livres in investments as a sans-culotte?'[131]

John Adolphus described how Clootz appeared to harden in his atheism in the Luxembourg prison, 'he even reproached Pain [*sic*], who had just published the *Age of Reason*, and was there his fellow-prisoner, for retaining too many political and religious prejudices'. In a suitably blasphemous version of the Crucifixion, Clootz exhorted his fellow prisoners to die with resolution and endeavoured to confirm their atheist principles. Adolphus noted that, unlike the other prisoners, 'Clootz himself died with a firmness not to be expected from his principles'.[132] And Clootz, like the Catholic Don Juan, behaved thus despite, or because of, his Jesuit education.

Clootz was an appropriate figure for *Don Juan* because of his special configuration of inherited status with democratic principles. Clootz's attempt to disseminate atheism was specifically denounced by Robespierre as aristocratic free-thinking. This makes of Clootz a 'libertine', in its original sense of religious, rather than sexual, free-thinking. In England during the Napoleonic Wars the fear of republicanism was often disguised under condemnation of atheism or deism and the government proclamations against the writings of Hone and Carlile denounced them as 'treasonous' and 'blasphemous', convicting always however on the latter charge—the trial of William Hone in 1817 was one notable example of this political deception.[133]

Byron leaves his reader in little doubt as to the religion of his Don Juan (V, 102; XV, 50). His Catholicism is entirely in the

---

[131] Quoted in Alan Ruiz, 'Un regard sur le jacobinisme allemand' in *The French Revolution and the Creation of Modern Political Culture* (Oxford: Pergamon Press, 1989), iii. 256. See also Julia Kristeva, *Étrangers à nous-mêmes* (Paris: Fayard, 1988), 242.

[132] Adolphus, *Biographical Memoirs*, 295.

[133] See David V. Erdman, 'Byron and Revolt in England', *Science and Society*, 11 (1947), 235.

tradition of the Spanish legend. Indeed the anti-Catholicism of many reviews of theatrical Don Juans displays how the religious origin of the legend was never forgotten. The reviewer of the Don Juan pantomime at the Lyceum in *The Examiner* (30 June 1817) conjectured as to the background and motivation of Tirso de Molina, only to announce his defeat in the language of anti-Catholic satire:

Conjecture can come but little nearer to proof, where the truth is to be looked for in cells and sepulchres . . . Every one is now master of the history of the 'Libertine', its having found its original *nidus* in the brain of a Spanish Ecclesiastic, who, without the fear of the Inquisition before his eyes, dreamed over the dream of what probably were his own extravagances before he wrapped his vices and virtues equally in a cowl.

This religious censure of the legend was duly carried over into critical reviews of Byron's poem. The pamphlet, *Remarks Critical and Moral on the Talents of Lord Byron and the Tendencies of Don Juan*, published shortly after the publication of Cantos I–II in 1819, denounced the vices of the poem as evidence of the author's indoctrination by foreign, and specifically Catholic, influences:

it is not every one who has treated life as a masquerade, that has the hardihood to meet death in his *domino*. I cannot but suspect that his Lordship's views of Christianity are taken from a *bad* quarter; he has lived so much in Catholic countries, where the '*opus operatuum*', the *outward* forms and ceremonies of the *Church*, are every thing, and the *internal* obligations and spiritual efficacies of *religion* are nothing.[134]

Thus the poem's stressing of its hero's Catholicism was a further cause of provocation. Leila can only bear one 'Christian', and that, outrageously, is the Catholic Don Juan (X, 57); Aurora's specifically English Catholicism is made a virtue; and the Black Friar's history is celebrated in song as a heroic last stand for religious freedom (XVI, 40: 2). Indeed Aurora's Catholicism has a distinctly political dimension, for she is proud of her family's refusal to bend or bow to power and cherishes their religion because of its history of oppression (XV, 46).[135] In Regency England, a professed atheist was reviled, as indeed

---

[134] *Remarks Critical and Moral*, 30.   [135] See Franklin, *Byron's Heroines*, 159.

Shelley was, but he suffered fewer institutional penalties than a Catholic. When Lord Kinnaird suggested to Byron that future settings for his poem might include Rome, Byron replied that it was 'not impossible' that Don Juan might have visited there but that ' "these costermonger days" are unfavourable to all liberal extensions of Morality'.[136] Don Juan's faith is scarcely 'practising' but it continues to influence and explain certain decisions. He suggests to Adeline, for example, that Aurora would be the most suitable bride for him, given their shared Catholicism. Here the narrative and authorial motive is to taunt Adeline and her English readerly counterparts respectively (XV, 50). Adeline's prejudice against Aurora is described as 'a question far too nice | Since Adeline was liberal by nature' (XV, 52). While this refers to her sexual jealousy, it is compounded by the insinuation of religious prejudice.

Tirso's Don Juan Tenorio remained a superstitious believer; Molière's Don Juan and Goldoni's Don Giovanni are religious free-thinkers, yet both paradoxically 'keep their faith' in accepting the invitation to dinner with the Stone Guest. In the additional notes to his 1959 version of the Don Juan legend, *La Mort qui fait le trottoir*, Henry de Montherlant remarked that this bizarre 'faith' was a consequence of his gentlemanly codes of honour: 'Cet amoral est tellement homme d'honneur qu'il veut tenir les promesses qu'il faites à un "etre" (Dieu) dont il est convaincu de l'inexistence.'[137] Byron defends Catholicism because of its contemporary oppression. When the British sent aid to Catholics in the Iberian Peninsula, the refusal of full civil rights to their own subjects in Ireland took on an air of absurdity: 'Rebels in Cork are patriots at Madrid', as Thomas Moore pointed out.[138] The narrator's embrace of Catholicism thus reinforces the provocations of the poem, although Catholicism itself is not exempt as an object of satire: the painting described in Canto III, stanza 103, is not of the Annunciation, or the Assumption, but a rather eroticized depiction of the Immaculate Conception. Mary becomes a coy, but knowing participant:

[136] *Byron's Letters and Journals*, ix. 66 (20 Nov. 1821).
[137] Henry de Montherlant, *La Mort qui fait le trottoir* (1959; repr. Folio: Éditions Gallimard, 1972), notes, p. 163.
[138] *The Poetical Works of Thomas Moore* (Oxford: Oxford University Press, 1915), *The Sceptic: A Philosophical Satire* (1809), 142–5, 143, l. 58.

'Ave Maria! Oh that face so fair | Those downcast eyes beneath the almighty dove'. And while Don Juan's Catholicism is a provocation to many English Protestants, Don Juan himself is hardly a model for Catholic readers of the poem.

Byron's dismissal of conventional contemporary 'heroes' is a political and not a class decision. If these generals and military commanders perpetuate the hierarchy of an upper class, Byron chooses, despite appeals and arguments to the contrary, not an 'ordinary' hero in the mould of Fielding's Joseph Andrews or Tom Jones, but a distinctly aristocratic figure. More unusually, however, he is an aristocrat who is decidedly populist. Byron's allegiance to the Italian *carbonari* was undoubtedly as a result of their configuration of aristocratic social values with liberal political goals. His qualified republicanism was one conducted by gentlemanly or 'genteel' liberals. Don Juan and Anacharsis Clootz were both representatives of this special kind of configuration. They also shared a background of moral conservatism, a point made by Caroline Franklin in *Byron's Heroines* (1992):

> As the victim of the re-emergence of puritanical moral law in the purges of the Terror, the Don would thus become a comic martyr for sexual liberty, if his career was cut short on the block. The poet would thus neatly combine his hero's aristocracy with his potential for a subversion of society too radical even for the Revolution.[139]

Many burlesques, pantomimes, and other Regency versions were reclaiming Don Juan in the spirit of middle-class morality. To Byron, the reclamation of Don Juan would have represented a fate worse than death and he therefore intended his hero to become a martyr in the cause of sexual libertinism. Don Juan's possible execution was alluded to in his encounter with Gulbeyaz. Prophetically predicting his courage in the face of the guillotine, Don Juan, unlike his more conciliatory companion Johnson, courageously refuses circumcision: ' "Strike me dead | But they as soon shall circumcise my head! | Cut off a thousand heads, before—" ' (V, 71–2). The bawdy connection between beheading and castration is continued in the raging thoughts in which Gulbeyaz considers the most suitable punishment for Don Juan's sexual 'infidelity': 'Her first thought was to cut off Juan's head; | Her second, to cut only his—acquaint-

---

[139] Franklin, *Byron's Heroines*, 145.

ance' (V, 139). Because of his social position as a member of the ruling class in decay, Don Juan carried out Jacobinism in the only field open to him—that of sexuality.[140]

Don Juan's predilection for wives suggests that his behaviour was politically subversive of the capitalist structure. Montesquieu gave his Don Juan an awareness of this when he defined himself thus: 'the only function I have is to make husbands wild or fathers desperate'.[141] In appealing directly to the woman herself and most particularly to her sexual nature, Don Juan disrupted the ordinary process of the bargaining and exchange involved in bourgeois marriage. Indeed, he disrupted the very process of bargaining itself. In *De l'amour* (1822), Stendhal wrote of a Don Juan as an example of capitalism gone awry: 'In the great market-place of life, he is a dishonest merchant who takes all and pays nothing.'[142] The *burlador* always seeks the maximum profit for his investment: he buys on credit, offers his word, and attempts to escape making a final payment.[143] Many social historians, for example Lawrence Stone, Mary Poovey, and Keith Thomas, have claimed that the eighteenth-century middle classes defined themselves by the two 'qualities' of property and chastity. Keith Thomas quotes a source from 1804: 'The corrupting of a man's wife, enticing her to a strange bed, is by all acknowledged to be the worst sort of theft, infinitely beyond that of goods.'[144] Lawrence Stone noted that the two heroes of eighteenth-century working-class ballads were the highwayman (who preyed exclusively on the rich) and the sexual athlete.[145] Don Juan's disrespect of both property (his predilection for wives) and chastity might therefore explain his traditionally lower-class appeal.

---

[140] See Slavoj Zizek, *For They Know Not What They Do: Enjoyment as a Political Factor* (London: Verso, 1991), 116.

[141] Montesquieu, *Lettres persanes* (1721; repr. Paris: Garnier Frères, 1960), 103, letter 48: 'je n'ai d'autre emploi que de faire enrager un mari ou désespérer un père'.

[142] Stendhal, *Love*, 173.

[143] See Michel Serres, 'The Apparition of Hermes: *Dom Juan*', in *Hermes: Literature, Science, Philosophy* (Baltimore: Johns Hopkins University Press, 1982), 3–14, and Julia Kristeva, 'Don Juan ou aimer pouvoir', *Histoires d'amour* (Paris: Éditions Denoël, 1983), 243–63, 249.

[144] Thomas, 'The Double Standard', 210.

[145] Stone, *Family, Sex and Marriage*, 622.

However, this 'revolutionary' sexual behaviour is gendered. Women could hardly avail themselves of such revolutionary activity without incurring severe penalties and the degree to which they benefited from such activity is questionable. In 'Philosophy in the Bedroom', the Marquis de Sade argued the radical and anti-establishment force of his sexual libertinism: 'it is as unjust to possess a woman exclusively as it is to possess slaves . . . no man can be excluded from the possession of a woman, as soon as it shall be seen that women belong decidedly to all men'. Luce Irigaray rejected this sexual communism on the grounds that private property or public, woman is still property.[146] While the history of libertinism displays its origin in religious and political free-thinking, by the beginning of the nineteenth century, it was quickly, and exclusively, becoming representative of sexual permissiveness. Hobhouse, in praising Machiavelli as a 'libertine', regretted the changing definition of the epithet from one of 'patriotism' to that of 'debauch'.[147] The indistinction between liberty and licence was one which many writers and commentators of the Don Juan legend exploited. The following chapters question how revolutionary or radical such Don Juans, including Byron's own seducer, can appear from a feminist perspective.

[146] Quoted in Jane Gallop, *Feminism and Psychoanalysis: The Daughter's Seduction* (London: Macmillan, 1982), 90. See also Jane Miller, *Seductions: Studies in Reading and Culture* (London: Virago Press, 1990), 28.
[147] Quoted in *Complete Poetical Works*, ii (1980), 237 n. 486.

4
Don Juan and the Female Reader

On 6 April 1819, when the manuscript of the first two Cantos of
Don Juan was already circulating among his friends, Byron protested to John Murray: 'Neither will I make "Ladies books"—"*al
dilettar le femine e la plebe*"'.[1] This statement is ironic, for, in
adopting the theme of the Don Juan legend, Byron chose a
subject which was renowned for its popularity among exactly
those categories of audience, the working classes and women.
Both were 'classes' of readership which had been previously
derided by Byron. Chapter 3 has already considered the appeal
of the theme to 'la plebe', which the reviewers anticipated and
feared. The reviewers also attempted to prevent the dissemination of the text among female readers and the narration of
Laura, the serving girl in Flora Thompson's *Candleford Green*
(1943), illustrates the continuation of this prohibition within
the later Victorian period. Her employer, Miss Lane, forbids her
to read *Don Juan*, the one exception she makes from her father's library collection of *Scott's Poetical Works* and the Waverley
novels, Hume's *History of England*, the poetry of Cowper,
Campbell, and Gray, Thomson's *Seasons*, and the *Works of
William Shakespeare*. Laura is permitted to borrow all of these
books, proudly kept behind glass doors in the parlour. Byron's
Don Juan, however, she is told, is 'a terrible book . . . and most
unfit for her reading'.[2] Both as a servant, and as a girl, Laura was
doubly prohibited from reading *Don Juan*.

The fears of a pervasive female reading of the poem make the
sexual political issues raised by the legend and Byron's *Don Juan*
apparent, for the vehemence of the reviewers' fury cannot be
considered separately from the provocative context which the

---

[1] *Byron's Letters and Journals*, ed. Leslie A. Marchand (London: John Murray,
1973–82), vi. 106 (letter to John Murray, 6 Apr. 1819).
[2] Flora Thompson, *Lark Rise to Candleford* (Harmondsworth: Penguin, 1973),
Candleford Green (1943), 414–15.

Don Juan legend automatically effected. The reviewer of the Don Juan pantomime at Drury Lane for *The Theatrical Guardian* (1791), who criticized its 'licentious' acting, demonstrated the legend's tradition of incorporating the participation of the audience as part of its meaning and, in mocking those genteel spectators who sat in the pit, its contemporary reputation for political subversion. His review also raises the issue of gendered reception in its decorous reference to the pantomime's female spectators: if the galleries laugh at those in the pit, 'let it not be at the expense of the more delicate part of the audience'.[3] Although the constitutive nature of the reader's position within *Don Juan* has already been considered, the gendered distinctions which were continually made by reviewers and commentators remain as further demonstration of the poem's political nature. The participation of men and women in the legend of Don Juan was differentiated, since women who 'participated' risked the danger of their involvement being named seduction. The extent of the universal prohibition against women reading Byron's *Don Juan* therefore reveals most explicitly how political the poem was both intended to be and was in fact received as being.

The early history of the legend demonstrated a special relationship of intimacy between many of the versions and their implicitly male spectators. The appeal to a male audience is explicit in Giliberto's *Convitato di pietra* (1652), in which Arlequino displays a catalogue of his master's female conquests and openly taunts the male section of the audience: 'Take a look, gentlemen, and see whether someone of your family is on it.'[4] The epilogue of Shadwell's *The Libertine* (1675) directly addressed a male audience in asking: 'What will you be *Don Johns*? have you no remorse? | Farewell then, bloudy men, and take your course'.[5] The address to the male spectator was more frequently implicit. In Shadwell's play, for example, the Spanish heroines, Clara and Flavia, talk jealously of the liberty of Englishwomen on the eve of their own weddings. Women in

[3] *The Theatrical Guardian*, 11 (12 Mar. 1791), 14.
[4] Quoted in Leo Weinstein, *The Metamorphoses of Don Juan* (Stanford, Calif.: Stanford University Press, 1959), 25.
[5] *The Complete Works of Thomas Shadwell*, ed. Montague Summers (London: Benjamin Blom, 1968), i. 92.

England, they argue, are permitted a sexual licence denied to them in Spain:

CLARA: O that we were in England! there, they say a Lady may chuse a footman, and run away with him, if she likes him, and no dishonour to the Family . . . Though of late 'tis as unfashionable for a husband to love his wife there, as 'tis here, yet 'tis fashionable for her to love some body else, and that's something.[6]

England is also envied as a country where wives can spend their husband's estates and do exactly as they please without interference. This lengthy scene dramatizes a warning to the play's specifically English and male audience.

A similar cautionary tale may also be inferred from *Harlequin's Vision* (1817). This pantomime explained Don Juan's behaviour as being due to female desire: Proserpine, determined to enjoy him in hell, arranges to have Don Juan go through a succession of deeds wicked enough to deem him suitably qualified to inhabit her realm. And the suggestion of woman's culpability was further reinforced by the context in which the opening night of this pantomime was performed: it was programmed as the after-piece to Lillo's *George Barnwell* and would seem to be an oblique comment on that tragedy of an ingenuous young apprentice betrayed into sin and corruption through his love of a thoroughly debauched woman.[7]

The tendency of many Don Juan versions to sexual-political conservatism was frequently expressed in humour or invective against women. In Tirso de Molina's *El burlador* (1630), for example, Don Juan Tenorio and the Marqués de la Mota exchange misogynist banter, joking callously about the fates of prostitutes: Constanza's hair has fallen out, no doubt through venereal disease, Doña Inés has gone to 'Vejel', an obvious pun on 'vejez' (old age). Young prostitutes are called *trucha* ('trout') and old, *abadejo* ('cod').[8] The frequency of these jokes throughout the popular burlesques and pantomimes of the Regency Don Juan productions demonstrates the continuing vitality of this tradition within the legend, one which is also potentially

---

[6] Ibid. i. 59–60.

[7] This is noted by Frederich L. Beaty, 'Harlequin Don Juan', *Journal of English and Germanic Philology*, 67/3 (1968), 403.

[8] Tirso de Molina, *El burlador de Sevilla* (1630; repr. Madrid: Colección Austral, Espasa-Calpe, 1989), pp. 128–9, ll. 1212–32.

apparent in the depiction of the shrewish Done Elvira of
Molière's *Dom Juan* (1665) and the comically coloratura Donna
Elvira of Mozart's *Don Giovanni* (1787). W. T. Moncrieff's jibes
against wives in *Giovanni in London* (1817) provide a more
contemporary example of this tradition: Leporello joins in a
drinking song to 'Old England and Liberty!' but stops at celebrating personal liberty in altering the line to 'Old England!
you'll excuse the liberty; my wife's not dead, you know' (Act, I,
scene 3).[9] At the opening of the burlesque, the significantly
named Mrs Drainemdry has been sent to hell for being a shrew;
Mrs Porous because she was a scold; and Mrs Simpkins for a
(presumably sexual) '*faux pas*'. Jokes at wives and women could
of course be enjoyed by all sections of the audience but they
tend to address the male spectators directly. Women overhear,
and may laugh, but they are not included in the specific intimacy and recognition which such humour implies.

Byron's *Don Juan* is consonant with this tradition because the
masculine persona of the narrator almost continually addresses
a specifically male reader. And although the narrator does occasionally invoke the female reader, such occasions are always
clearly denoted. In comparison, the address of the poem to its
male readers is frequently implicit: for example, tears are described as a relief 'to them' and as torture 'to us' (V, 118); '*We*
tire of mistresses and parasites' (XIII, 100, my italics); Helen
chose Paris even though he was inferior to Menelaus, '(b)ut
thus it is some women will betray us' (XIV, 72). In Canto IX,
stanza 75, the narrator speaks of 'all bodies' but these bodies
are only those who long to 'mix with a goddess I For such all
women are at first no doubt'. '(Y)e youth of Europe', addressed
in Canto V, stanza 131, are those that need to learn from Don
Juan how to escape the sexual self-proffering of dowager ladies.
Canto IX, stanza 69, an explicit expression of Don Juanism,
includes its male readers in that 'delighted age' when women of
all ages may serve as the ocean in which 'we can our native sun
assuage'.[10] Moreover, the address is usually not only to a male

---

[9] Repr. in Oscar Mandel (ed.), *The Theatre of Don Juan* (Lincoln, Nebr.: University of Nebraska Press, 1963), 417.
[10] Other examples of this implicit address to male readers include: I, 123, 179; II,
118, 178; IV, 25; V, 130–1; VI, 10; XI, 34, 72; XII, 59–60; XIV, 64. Such references
often, but not always, concern sexual matters—see IV, 41; VIII, 125; X, 6.

reader, but to a specifically libertine one. The narrator claims, for example, that the pins in women's dresses were invented for 'our' sins (VI, 61); the things that make an English evening pass include a glass of claret and a single woman (V, 58); and 'Let us have wine and women . . .' is a paean to the pleasures of the *bon vivant* and, perhaps, the rake (II, 178). The narrator advises his fellow gallant not to waste time in determining whether his success with a lady is due to conquering her heart or her head: 'So they lead | In safety to the place for which you start' (XI, 34), and with an English lady, he urges patience: 'But though the soil may give you time and trouble, | Well cultivated, it will render double' (XII, 76); 'And your cold people are beyond all price, | When once you have broken their confounded ice' (XIII, 38). It is hardly surprising therefore that many contemporary reviewers censured the poem as a 'manual' for vice, a veritable guide for Don Juans.[11]

The implicit nature of these particularized addresses again illustrates the considerable degree of presumption contained within *Don Juan*. While the poem acknowledges its dependence upon female readers if it is to enjoy success—'Oh ye, who make the fortunes of all books, | Benign ceruleans of the second sex!' (IV, 108–9)—it continues to speak most frequently and implicitly to a circle of specifically male listeners. In the same way the poem continually addressed the 'gentle' reader, yet it owed its phenomenal success to the cheaper editions and to the lower-middle and lower classes who bought them. It was written from a specifically masculine perspective and addressed conspiratorially to masculine intimates, but was not unaware that women would overhear. Byron's *Don Juan* thus parallels many versions of the Don Juan legend which were obviously received by readers and spectators of both sexes—yet which implicitly addressed a male audience with female participants either deriding or welcoming their chance of inclusion, a position which was then equivalent to one of eavesdropping. The suggested exclusion was both prohibitive and all the more alluring for that.

Because of the absence of specifically female responses to early versions of the legend, it is difficult to quantify gendered

[11] See e.g. *The British Critic*, 2nd ser. 12 (1819), 202: 'a manual of profligacy'; and *New Bon Ton Magazine*, 3 (Aug. 1819), 234–9, 238.

realities of reception, rather than those female responses assumed, and hinted at, by the versions themselves. Queen
Christina of Sweden's remark—'Why, this is just the *Stone
Guest!*'—represents the bored dismissal of a popular and perhaps over-exposed tradition which is certainly not gender-
specific, although it does prefigure the kind of deflationary
rhetoric used by Jane Austen on her visit to the Don Juan
pantomime at the Lyceum Theatre in 1816. She carefully distinguished her own response from that of her young nieces who
accompanied her: 'I speak of *them*; *my* delight was very tranquil,
and the rest of us were sober-minded'. This response mirrors
her comment concerning Byron's *The Corsair* which enjoyed
otherwise sensational popularity among fashionable circles: 'I
have read the Corsair, mended my petticoat, & have nothing
else to do.'[12]

It is impossible to recover a 'typical' female response to the
legend, either because such a gendered response did not exist,
or because it is simply irretrievable. However, it is possible to
recreate the moral response which would have been expected
of, if not fulfilled by, women. Because women increasingly
became identified with piety and religiosity, it was expected
that moral censure of the legendary seducer and satisfaction
with his ultimate punishment represented the appropriate
female response. While the response of Louis XIV's mother
to Molière's *Dom Juan* is certainly insufficient to demonstrate
a gendered perspective, her condemnation of the play
reflects what the writers of conduct books and other prescriptive texts for female behaviour would have expected. In
Alfred de Musset's poetic version of the Don Juan legend—
'Namouna' (1832)—the female reader is directly addressed
when Hassan is described as naked, since the narrator expects
her disapproval.[13]

If the various female dramatis personae of the legend's forms
are seduced by Don Juan, what of the female spectator who also

[12] For Queen Christina's response see Nino Pirotta, 'The Tradition of Don Juan
Plays and Comic Operas', *Proceedings of the Musical Association*, 107 (1981), 60. *Jane
Austen's Letters to her Sister Cassandra and Others*, ed. R. W. Chapman (1932; repr.
Oxford University Press, 1952), 321 (15 Sept. 1813), 379 (5 Mar. 1814).
[13] For the condemnation of Louis XIV's mother see Shadwell, *Complete Works*, i, p.
cxxxii n. 3. Alfred de Musset, *Premières Poésies, Poésies nouvelles* (Paris: Gallimard,
1976), 'Namouna' (1832), iii–vii (pp. 157–8).

witnesses his charm and dashing behaviour? The representation of the stage Don Juan is observed by female dramatis personae and spectators alike. Since his appeal is blatantly directed towards women, his seducing tactics might effectively be seen to play upon women both on and off the stage. So although women, as exemplars of morality, were expected to reproduce the orthodox religious interpretation of the legend, they were also, paradoxically, suspected of vulnerability to Don Juan. If he was able to seduce the female characters on stage, the threat might also extend to those who similarly witnessed his dashing bravura and charisma within the audience.

This threat was not confined to stage versions of the Don Juan legend but reflected the pervasive unease concerning drama throughout its history. In *Clarissa* (1747–8), Lovelace takes the heroine to a performance of a play as the surest method of seduction, for, he believes, the performance will carry her attention out of herself and leave her more vulnerable to, because less conscious of, assault: 'Whenever I have been able to prevail upon a girl to permit me to attend her to a play, I have thought myself sure of her. The female heart, all gentleness and harmony when obliged, expands and forgets its forms when attention is carried out of itself at an agreeable or affecting entertainment.'[14] Although Clarissa's virtue resisted the design, her status as exceptional reinforces as much as it disproves Lovelace's theory. His scheming mirrors the fears of middle-class commentators concerning the moral effect of the theatre. And these fears increased throughout the eighteenth century as the venues of the theatres themselves became more disreputable.

The novel-reading habits of the female middle class might have appeared to enable a comparatively safe and private space, a position of chastity away from the public promiscuity of the theatres, literalized in the many prostitutes who traded around, or even within, the theatres, both minor and patent. However, reading also appeared to some to offer a dangerous subjectivity to groups whose use of such potential individualism threatened subversion—the working classes and women. And the interaction between women and the narrative imaginative text was

[14] Samuel Richardson, *Clarissa* (1747–8; repr. Harmondsworth: Penguin, 1985), 620 (letter 194).

increasingly viewed as not only gendered but sexualized. The imagination, far from being the moral faculty philosophers like Adam Smith described, was now viewed not only as the agent of vicarious gratification but also the very source of sexual feeling. In *A Vindication of the Rights of Men* (1790), Mary Wollstonecraft echoed eighteenth-century moralists in characterizing the imagination in explicitly sexual terms: it is a 'vigorous' principle, 'panting after' its object in 'eager pursuit'.[15] And, in *A Vindication of the Rights of Woman,* reading 'the unnatural and meretricious scenes sketched by the novel writers of the day' becomes an unnatural outlet for women's repressed sexuality.[16] In this ideology woman became 'the ultimately receptive reader, easily moved into immoral activity by the fictional representation of sexual intrigue'.[17] By 1798, some thought that even *Pamela* and *Clarissa* contained 'materials of such a dangerous complexion as rendered their performances improper for the eye of an innocent female'.[18]

It is the context of this ideological belief which explains why, despite the legend's considerable tradition of specifically masculine address, the popularity of the legend among women was always presumed. This was certainly the case in early nineteenth-century England: in *Letters from England: by Don Manuel Alvarez Espriella* (1807), Southey attributed the popularity of the legend directly to its female audience: 'but either the furies of Aeschylus were more terrible than European devils, or our Christian ladies are less easily frightened than the women of Greece, for this is a favourite spectacle everywhere.'[19] And this assumption has remained apparent within twentieth-century myth-criticism of the legend. For example, in his commentary on his anthology of Don Juan versions, *The Theatre of Don Juan* (1963), Oscar Mandel claimed that Don Juan did not become

---

[15] Quoted in Mary Poovey, *The Proper Lady and the Woman Writer* (Chicago: University of Chicago Press, 1984), 77.

[16] Wollstonecraft, *A Vindication of the Rights of Woman* (1792; repr. Harmondsworth: Penguin, 1992), 316. See also Patricia Meyer Spacks, 'Ev'ry Woman is at Heart a Rake', *Eighteenth-Century Studies*, 8/1 (Fall 1974), 38.

[17] Cora Kaplan, *Sea Changes: Culture and Feminism* (London: Verso, 1986), 160.

[18] *The Lady's Monthly Museum,* 1 (1798), 435. Quoted in Lawrence Stone, *The Family, Sex and Marriage in England, 1500–1800* (London: Weidenfeld & Nicolson, 1977), 675.

[19] Robert Southey, *Letters from England* (1807; repr. London: The Cresset Press, 1951), 101.

'irresistible' to women until the Romantic age, and offered the explanation that 'it is a trait of the female imagination to make him so'.[20] Because Don Juan's appeal was usually regarded as being sexual, the legend's popularity became linked with the favourable reactions of its female spectators. This ideology had significantly political consequences for the reception of Byron's *Don Juan.*

In *English Bards and Scotch Reviewers* (1809), Byron criticized Moore's poetry as being written expressly for a female audience, alleging that such a compromise would lead to an emasculation of the virile poetic tradition (ll. 283–8). Disquiet concerning the effeminization of literature is also evident in *Don Juan* (see, for example, VIII, 90 and XIV, 19, ll. 7–8). However, Byron's own early popularity had always been attributed to a devoted female, and predominantly upper-class, readership. Byron himself was aware of the cause of his popularity: he boasted of *The Corsair* (1814) as 'shining in boudoirs'. It was the memory of this popularity, and profitability, which made Murray write to Byron in Italy urging him to 'resume your old *Corsair* style, to please the ladies'.[21] Within *Don Juan* the narrator does acknowledge the dependence of the contemporary writer upon a female readership (IV, 108–12). Yet *Don Juan* did not represent a resumption of the old style of the Tales which had celebrated tragic and constant love. Instead Byron chose a theme which mirrored his own more recent reputation as a heartless seducer, for the rumours which prospered in England were of incestuous relationships (both that of the liaison with Augusta in England and with the Godwin 'sisters' in Switzerland) and of Venetian conquests of Don Juan-like proportions. The choice of Don Juan dictated that the categories of character (Don Juan), text (*Don Juan*), Don Juan-like author ('Byron'), and libertine style (the voice of the poem's Don Juan-like narrator) were not only blurred but mutually contaminating. Caroline Lamb illustrated the tendency to blur the distinctions of text-author/narrator-character in her imitative criticism of Byron's poem—*Gordon: A Tale* (1821):

[20] Mandel (ed.), *Theatre of Don Juan,* 28.
[21] E. J. Lovell (ed.), *Medwin's Conversations with Lord Byron* (Princeton: Princeton University Press, 1969), 206. For Murray's suggestion, see E. J. Lovell (ed.), *His Very Self and Voice* (New York: Macmillan, 1954), 267.

> Though Juan is so vicious, it will keep
> Its present eminence, and great promotion;
> So deep in glory has he dipped his pen,
> 'Twill always be preserved, and read by men.
>
> (I, 37)

These lines move without grammatical embarrassment from 'Juan' (the character) to 'it' (the poem) to 'he' (Byron) and in doing so they epitomize the synonymity with which each was received. And in each of these categories the relationship with the female reader was a special, because gendered, one—a consideration which is implied in Lamb's closing 'and read by men'.

THE FEMALE READER AND DON JUAN

In devoting four of the first stanzas (I, 2–5) to a studied rejection of military heroes, Byron opened the poem with an affront to his female readers, since it was largely their adulation which had made heroes of such commanders. Many of the stanzas recounting the Siege of Ismail specifically address a female readership: 'But oh, ye goddesses of war and glory! I How shall I spell the name of each Cossack' (VII, 14). And the poem suggests that Potemkin became a hero because he was adored by Catherine: 'This was Potemkin, a great thing in days I When homicide and harlotry made great' (VII, 37). Catherine's desire is lewdly portrayed as not only dependent on Potemkin's military statistics: 'This fellow, being six foot high, could raise I A kind of phantasy proportionate I In the then sovereign of the Russian people, I Who measured men as you would do a steeple.'

Despite the prevailing denial of female sexual desire, the enthusiasm of Englishwomen for military heroes such as Nelson and Wellington suggests how repressive the stipulation against the display or acknowledgement of such desire had to be. As a consequence, intensely romantic and often blatantly sexual fantasies gathered around these military heroes. The juvenilia of the Brontë sisters, for example, featured the Duke of Wellington as a centre of power and erotic desire.[22] The statue of Achilles in Hyde Park was London's first (almost) nude statue. It was commissioned by the women of Britain in honour of the Duke of Wellington and the idea for the statue was first suggested by Lavinia, Countess of Spencer, the staunchly Evangelical wife of the second Earl of Spencer. In 1814 she launched a public subscription—confined to women—and collected more than £10,000 in donations. The statue, originally entitled 'The Ladies' Trophy' was completed in 1822 and was quickly dubbed 'The Ladies' Fancy' by William Hone. Lady Holland wrote of the difficulty in determining the extent of the statue's nudity in such times: 'the artist had submitted to the female subscribers whether this colossal figure should preserve its antique nudity or should be garnished with a fig-leaf. It was carried for the leaf by the majority . . . The names of the *minority* have not transpired.' However it was widely rumoured that it was the gentlemen who headed the statue committee, not the lady subscribers, who insisted on the fig-leaf.[23]

Unlike the popular military heroes who aroused such speculation, the erotic appeal of Byron's subject could not be denied. It is this context which reveals the allusively sexual implications behind the opening words of *Don Juan*: 'I want a hero . . .', the lewd significance of which is reinforced by the suggestion of 'I'll . . . take . . .' (I, 1).[24] Throughout the poem, the narrator claims that it is the predisposition of women, or rather their imagination, which creates the character, Don Juan.[25] These references proliferate within the later Cantos as the responses towards the poem are incorporated into the self-consciousness of the text. By extension, it is not the female dramatis personae, or the insubstantial society ladies of Cantos XI–XVII, but the female readers of the poem who, in fantasizing about the hero, create him as a Don Juan. The references echo the ideological portrayal of the

[22] See Elizabeth Gaskell, *The Life of Charlotte Brontë* (1857; Harmondsworth: Penguin, 1975), 131.

[23] See Linda Colley, *Britons* (New Haven and London: Yale University Press, 1992), 257–8.

[24] See *Don Juan*, ed. T. G. Steffan, E. Steffan, and W. W. Pratt (Harmondsworth: Penguin, 1973), 669 n. 76: 1–2; *The Complete Poetical Works of Lord Byron*, ed. Jerome J. McGann (Oxford: Clarendon Press), v (1986), 734, l. 601.

[25] See e.g. XI, 33; XIV, 97; XV, 16 and 57.

imagination as sexual, an irrational force which totally disre-
gards moral restraint:

> And as romantic heads are pretty painters,
> And above all an Englishwoman's roves
> Into the excursive, breaking the indentures
> Of sober reason, wheresoe'er it moves,
> He found himself extremely in the fashion,
> Which serves our thinking people for a passion.
>
> (XI, 33)

For women to 'think' is then synonymous with their having
sexual ideas (see XI, 68, ll. 2–3)—a suggestion which Byron had
previously made in *The Waltz*.

Many modern readers of Byron's poem have criticized the
portrayal of his Don Juan as one-dimensional. The traditional
Don Juan frequently cultivated and exploited a sense of mystery. Tirso's *burlador*, for example, responds to Doña Ana's
questioning with the evasive reply: 'Quién soy? Un hombre sin
nombre'.[26] Modern criticism ignores the tendency of many versions to allow the other characters (and audiences) to complete
the fantasy which Don Juan represents. And this was thought to
be especially true of the female imagination.

The narrative defence mounted in Byron's *Don Juan* on behalf of the notorious seducer was one which attempted to make
Don Juan desirable, if not a hero, by countering potential moral
criticisms. Because women were prohibited from declaring
sexual desire openly, the adulation of military heroes was one
way in which they could circumvent the prohibition by declaring that their celebration was a response to martial glory, not
sexual allure. Byron declared that *Don Juan* was written in order
to counter the hypocrisy of English society, and this would
include the hypocrisy which dictated that women's sexual nature should be veiled, if not denied. He maintained that female
readers of *Don Juan* disliked the poem because it uncovered the
hypocrisy of 'sentiment' and demonstrated that such vaunted
fine feeling only disguised passions of a grosser nature.[27] We
should expect a review of the poem by the Hunts' own periodi-

---

[26] Tirso de Molina, *El burlador*, p. 78, l. 15.
[27] See Lovell (ed.), *His Very Self and Voice*, 452, and *Byron's Letters and Journals*, viii.
147–48 (6 July 1821) and vii. 202.

cal, *The Examiner,* to praise *Don Juan,* especially those Cantos which were published by John Hunt (Cantos VI–XVI). Indeed the review by 'Albany Fonblanque' of Cantos XV–XVI deals with these Cantos 'sympathetically' in that it echoes Byron's own comments upon the poem's female readers:

Lord Byron seems to take a particular delight in untwisting the delicate refinements of the female heart, as exhibited in that artificial state of society, where all its occupation is to refine; and we half suspect, that, in spite of CATO, many fair ladies have learned to understand themselves and their bosoms' proceedings much better, by a diligent perusal of his naughty and wayward Juan.[28]

The review by 'Fonblanque' notably stresses the class differential—it is upper-class ladies and their aspiring middle-class counterparts who are mocked for their artificial cultivation of refinement. This attitude is in itself a reflection of the argument of *Don Juan* and particularly the reasons for Adeline's studiously proper behaviour in concealing her adulterous passion for Don Juan: 'she was not apt . . . | To like too readily or too high bred | To show it (points we need not now discuss)' (XV, 10).

   The Monthly Review (August 1821), in its review of Cantos III–V, expressed the fear that female enthusiasm for the character would have dangerous implications, if not consequences: 'in particular the masters of families were very little inclined to recommend him to their wives and daughters, over whom the young man seemed qualified and disposed to exercise more influence than husbands and fathers could regard as desirable, when they contemplated the results of his fascination'.[29] The associative indistinction displayed recurrently by the reviewers is apparent in this excerpt's blurring of the distinction between the character, Don Juan, and the text, *Don Juan.* Because of the title of the poem, the recommendation of the book becomes a recommendation of 'him'. A fascination with the text of *Don Juan* is equivalent to a fascination with the character, Don Juan. And it was this last fascination which made the issue of 'consequences' most apparent. To be fascinated with such a character

---

[28] *The Examiner* (14 Mar. 1821), 163–4, 164. See also *Leigh Hunt's Literary Criticism,* ed. Lawrence Huston Houtchens and Carolyn Washburn Houtchens (New York: Columbia University Press, 1956), 158.
[29] *The Monthly Review,* 2nd ser. 95 (Aug. 1821), 418–24, 418.

seemed to presage a seduction which was already half-completed: within *Don Juan*, for example, Aurora's close observation of Don Juan is interpreted by the narrator as the 'most important outwork of the city' (XVI, 93).

That fascination was often judged to be equivalent to seduction is also evident in the following reaction by Byron to one of his female readers. Byron's account of a woman who had written and sent an illustration to him protesting at the erotic nature of his female portraits reveals that he outlandishly appropriated even this complaint as a kind of amorous self-gratification: 'The drawing represented Love and Modesty turning their backs on wicked Me,—and Sensibility, a fat, flushed, wingless Cupid, presenting me with a pen. Was not this a pretty conceit? At all events, it is some consolation to occupy the attention of women so much, though it is but by my faults; and I confess it gratifies me.'[30] This also reinforces the sense that Byron would have been disappointed if the reviewers had not replied in the way they did. *Don Juan* was intended to provoke and divide readers.

The fear of the reviewers was exacerbated by the apparent exoneration of the 'hero'. In *Remarks Critical and Moral on . . . Don Juan* (1819), the anonymous 'lady L.' humorously mimicked the moral response expected of her as a female reader:

The witty lady L. on being reproved by some one, for having Don Juan in her library, replied, 'Oh but you don't see in what good company I have placed him'; on looking again, it was found that her Ladyship had put the volume between Young and Cowper;—'As Don Juan,' continued she, 'is but a youth as yet, and vastly agreeable, I have put him there, in hopes of his reformation'.[31]

This riposte indicates the common expectation that Don Juan would be in need of reformation.

The Ladies' Monthly Museum (January–February 1822) doubted the propriety of the subject-matter ('the exploits of a libertine') for a female readership: 'but what are we to say of "Don Juan"? . . . The descriptions of the exploits of a libertine

[30] E. J. Lovell (ed.), *Lady Blessington's Conversations of Lord Byron* (Princeton: Princeton University Press, 1969), 122–3.
[31] *Remarks Critical and Moral*, 2.

are a bad friend for the display of extraordinary power, and that page should be for ever blotted from view, that cannot be perused by the female eye without diffusing a blush on the cheek.'[32] This citation suggests that the subject in itself was unsuitable for ladies: a compression of the passage would render the logic that: 'the exploits of a libertine cannot be perused by the female eye'. It had never been urged that women should stay away from the Don Juan theatrical productions and women, like men, had crowded to the popular Don Juan burlesques and parodies in the years 1817–24. The male fears aroused by the prospect of a huge female readership interpreting Byron's *Don Juan* therefore reveal the particular danger presented by this version of the legend. It is because Byron's *Don Juan* was widely perceived as constructing a defence of the notorious seducer that the poem's manifesto was deemed dangerous for female readers. If women exonerated the seducer, as indeed the poem both did and encouraged, then the threat offered by a reading of the poem was potentially one of female moral laxity.

THE FEMALE READER AND *DON JUAN*

In April 1823 Byron wrote to Douglas Kinnaird that Galignani, who published Byron's later works in Paris at competitive prices and largely for an expatriate readership, had reported to him that, of all his works, *Don Juan* was the most popular 'especially with the women—who send by hundreds slily—for copies', a boast which he repeated to John Hunt.[33] *The Literary Chronicle* (11 August 1821) admitted that *Don Juan* 'is universally read, much admired, often abused, expelled from reading rooms and book societies, proscribed at boarding-schools, abjured by married men, and read in secret by their wives throughout the whole kingdom'.[34] Secrecy was necessary when the censures against women reading *Don Juan* were so vehement. Reviews of the poem in the contemporary periodicals unanimously cautioned their predominantly male readers against permitting

---

[32] *The Ladies' Monthly Museum* (Jan.–Feb. 1822), 86–91, 90.
[33] *Byron's Letters and Journals*, x. 145 (to Douglas Kinnaird, 7 Apr. 1823).
[34] *The Literary Chronicle* (11 Aug. 1821), 495, review of Cantos III–V.

their wives and daughters to read the scandalous poem. *The New Bon Ton Magazine* (August 1819), for example, advised its readers not to buy the first Cantos of the poem. These readers are implicitly fathers of daughters: '[t]he author of Don Juan has proved that he can write a quarto which no modest woman can read, and which, consequently, no prudent parent can purchase'. The reviewer for the *Edinburgh Magazine and Literary Miscellany* (August 1821) made a similar distinction between male and female readers: 'poetry such as no man of pure taste can read a *second* time, and such as no woman of correct principles can read the *first*'.[35]

The suggested ban upon women reading *Don Juan* in these reviews displayed an extraordinary degree of consensus. However, the vehemence and frequency of the strictures themselves suggest that such exhortations were more prescriptive than descriptive. Male readers and reviewers of *Don Juan* did not so much expect as desire that the poem's morality would be censured by its female readers. Byron recognized the prescriptions encoded in the reviews when he referred to the 'eleventh commandment to the women not to read it', although he was certainly inaccurate in adding that they did not break it.[36] Examples of women readers who openly expressed their enjoyment of *Don Juan* include Mary Shelley and Lady Morgan.[37] Others, however, did keep the new literary commandment. Miss Jane Waldie wrote to Murray: 'Why will Lord Byron write what we may not read?'—although her complaint reveals that she is prevented by a socially dictated restraint rather than from personal choice.[38] And Augusta Leigh, despite her continuing affection for and intimate correspondence with Byron, exemplified the kind of (non-)reader encouraged by contemporary commentators. She combined a condemnation of the work itself, referring for example to the 'odious Don' and to the

[35] *New Bon Ton Magazine*, 3 (Aug. 1819), 234–9, 235. *Edinburgh Magazine and Literary Miscellany, or New Series of the Scots Magazine*, 80 (Aug. 1821), 181–5, 185, review of Cantos III–V.

[36] *Byron's Letters and Journals*, vi. 237 (letter to Richard Belgrave Hoppner, 29 Oct. 1819).

[37] *The Letters of Mary Shelley*, ed. Frederick L. Jones (Oklahoma: University of Oklahoma Press, 1947), 290 (March 1824) and *Lady Morgan's Memoirs: Autobiography, Diaries and Correspondence*, 2 vols. (London: Wm. H. Allen, 1912), ii. 102.

[38] Samuel Smiles, *A Publisher and his Friends* (London: John Murray, 1891), i. 405.

composition of the work in itself as 'execrable', with the illogical admission that she had not read it. Furthermore she added that she would not read it, because she had heard so much against it.[39]

Those magazines which addressed a specifically female audience attempted to counter the poem's dangerous reputation with a different strategy—they largely omitted *Don Juan* from any consideration of Byron's poetry. *The Belle Assemblée, The Lady's Magazine,* and *The Ladies' Monthly Museum* all reviewed most of Byron's work—but never *Don Juan*. The posthumous review of Byron's poetry in *The Ladies' Monthly Museum* (August 1824) attempted a comprehensive survey yet omitted any reference to *Don Juan*. *The Lady's Magazine* of January 1823 reviewed Byron's *Heaven and Earth* and pointed out a mistranslation of a verse from Genesis. Byron's status as a biblical authority was then mocked in referring to him as the author of *Don Juan*. This fleeting reference nevertheless demonstrates Byron's celebrity as the author of that work which is mentioned only as an index of his unorthodoxy.[40]

John Gibson Lockhart, who reviewed the poem for *Blackwood's Edinburgh Magazine* (August 1819), expressed the rather tentative hope that female readers might receive a moral lesson from *Don Juan*. However, that lesson was one which all would have recognized as contrary to the poem's own manifesto. After quoting five stanzas of Donna Julia's letter (I, 194–8) as displaying the consequences of illicit behaviour, the reviewer rather optimistically continued:

Perhaps there are not a few women who may profit from seeing in what a style of contemptuous coldness the sufferings to which licentious love exposes them are talked of by such people as the author of Don Juan. The many fine eyes that have wept dangerous tears over his descriptions of the Gulnares and Medoras cannot be the worse for seeing the true side of *his* picture.[41]

Once again the concern of the reviewer is that the female reader risks being seduced, although here it the seductive

[39] See Peter Gunn, *My Dearest Augusta* (London: Bodley Head, 1968), 213.

[40] *The Ladies' Monthly Museum* (Aug. 1824), 61–7. *The Lady's Magazine,* 2nd ser. 4 (Jan. 1823), 19–23, 19. See also *The Lady's Magazine,* 2nd ser. 3 (Oct. 1822), 566.

[41] *Blackwood's Edinburgh Magazine,* 5/29 (Aug. 1819), 512–18.

potential of the earlier Tales which is feared. The compassion aroused by their narratives is viewed as being 'dangerous'. The review continues with the highly qualified praise that *Don Juan* is at least comparatively open in design. This would ensure, the reviewer hoped, that its immorality could be more easily recognized and, consequently, resisted. The very title' of *Don Juan* provided this comparative openness of intent. The Byron who won the approval and favour of his female readers through the earlier Tales is now exposed as being the same Byron who writes as a Don Juan, for he speaks with contemptuous coldness of the sufferings caused by licentious love. The very title of *Don Juan* was sufficient to expose the earlier author of the romance tales as having composed such poetry as part of a more sinister scheme, the seduction of the female reader. *The New Bon Ton Magazine* (August 1819) also delivered a revisionist interpretation of Byron's poetic career, and again by appropriating the new evidence of his most recent publication. Here too the judgement is that the earlier poet had been deliberately deceitful in charming his considerable female readership under false pretences:

Fame has asserted that it is the production of a noble lord, who has taken no small pains to pamper public taste with many strange dishes, and who has sedulously striven to show a contempt of that taste and the public opinion, to which he was so largely administering, and courting, like an artful seducer with all his blandishments, in order to vitiate.[42]

The criticism is directed both at the dissimulation of the earlier poetry which had attracted and pleased, and at the comparative brazenness of the new publication which offends.

Both these reviews reflect the distinction between the passionate lover carried away by excessive emotion and the cold and calculating seducer-as-strategist. The writer of the earlier poetry masqueraded as the former, while *Don Juan* reveals Byron to have always been the latter. In the same review for *Blackwood's Edinburgh Magazine* (August 1819), Lockhart continued by making this distinction quite apparent. Byron's defence of his hero might have relied upon, and, in some cases,

---

[42] *The New Bon Ton Magazine*, 3 (Aug. 1819), 234–9, 234. See also *John Bull* (4 May 1823), 141–2.

benefited from, the indulgence which was given to the passionate youth—his own 'actions' (which in this case were authorial
decisions) were never rewarded with such leniency:

For impurities there might be some possibility of pardon, were they
supposed to spring only from the reckless buoyancy of young blood
and fiery passions,—for impiety there might at least be pity, were it
visible that the misery of the impious soul were as great as its dark-
ness;—but for offences such as this, which cannot proceed either from
the madness of sudden impulse, or the bewildered agonies of self-
perpetuating and self-despairing doubt—but which speak the wilful
and determined spite of an unrepenting, unsoftened, smiling, sarcas-
tic, joyous sinner—for such diabolical, such slavish vice, there can be
neither pity nor pardon.[43]

The title *Don Juan* was thus interpreted by many of the periodical reviewers as revealing the true 'nature' of Byron and his
ambitions as a poet. And Byron himself was judged to have
acted the part of Don Juan because he had deceived his previously adoring female readers.

THE FEMALE READER AND THE DON JUAN-LIKE AUTHOR

The excerpt from Lady Caroline's *Gordon: A Tale* (1821) has
already demonstrated an ease of modulation between the character of Don Juan, the text, and the author, exemplary of the
extensive contextual readings which were always allusively, and
often naïvely, biographical. This tendency to read *Don Juan*
biographically was directly attributed to the poem's female
readership by the author of *'Don John' or 'Don Juan' Unmasked*
(1819). Contemplating the sensational and enigmatic first announcements of the imminent publication of *Don Juan*—'In a
few days, DON JUAN'—the author expounds the conjectures
which female readers circulated, despite the advertisement's
seeming impenetrability: 'The curiosity of the town was raised
to the highest pitch to know the meaning of the enigmatical
line. The ladies, as was natural, supposed them to be used as a
signal for happiness, previously concerted between some fond

[43] *Blackwood's Edinburgh Magazine*, 5/29 (Aug. 1819), 512–18.

pair, whom time and space had separated.'[44] The swift publication by William Hone of this pamphlet itself punctured the
'mystery' of the poem's anonymous author. The author of this
pamphlet may thus have been mocking the absurdity of anticipating a romantic reconciliation between Lord and Lady Byron
when the title so plainly indicated otherwise. The traditional
theme of Don Juan would hardly warrant such a 'natural' sup-
position, for its plot of the compulsive seducer suggested that
the couple would remain estranged. An inherently female reading is thus ridiculed as wilful and moral fantasy. The ambivalence of the statement, however, is a reflection of the
contradictory impulses within versions of the legend current at
this time, for alternatively the author may have been mocking
those contemporary versions of the legend which did portray
the seducer as redeemed by a wife. Whichever of these contradictory readings may have been the intended one, they concur
in declaring a female interpretation to be thoroughly
biographical.

Of course, the tendency among the reviewers to confuse the
distinctions between *Don Juan* the text, Don Juan the character,
and the author of *Don Juan*, Byron, demonstrates that the currency of biographical readings was not exclusive to the poem's
female readers. The first readers of *Don Juan*, Byron's closest
friends, cautioned against publishing the poem because it so
overtly appeared to substantiate the sexual rumours which were
circulating about Byron's life abroad, immediately subsequent
to the scandal caused by his separation from his wife in 1816.
Hobhouse argued that he did not censure the deeds themselves, but the 'inexpediency of even appearing to make a boast
of them'. The risk was extreme because Hobhouse felt that
Byron had much to lose:

if you are mixed up, as you inevitably will be, with the character or
the adventurers or the turn of thinking and acting recommended
by the poem, it is certain that not only will you gain no credit by the
present reference, but will loose [sic] some portion of the fame at-
tached to the supposed former delineation of your own sublime and
pathetic feelings.[45]

---

[44] *'Don John' or 'Don Juan' Unmasked*, 5.
[45] Peter W. Graham, *Byron's Bulldog* (Columbus, Ohio: Ohio State University
Press, 1984), 259, 258 (5 Jan. 1819).

Hobhouse's opinions thus to a considerable extent predicted the revisionary judgements the reviewers would make upon Byron's earlier work in their responses to *Don Juan.*

Women were expected to be particularly susceptible to biographical readings, partly because they were characterized as notorious gossips, especially when such gossip was about amorous matters. This conventional view, evident in the excerpt from *'Don John' or 'Don Juan' Unmasked* quoted above, is also expressed in Canto IX, stanza 2, of *Don Juan,* where the narrator's allusion to the rumours of Wellington's womanizing are dismissed as originating from the 'tea hours of some tabby'. Such rumours of course are also deflected on to the figure of the old gossip, so that, having enjoyed the insinuation, the narrator evades the risk of being censured as prurient. Byron himself might have felt that he had been a victim of specifically female curiosity, for Mrs Thrale reported that '[a]ll the Misses in Bath were reading *Glenarvon*' and many female readers complained that Caroline Lamb's allusively biographical novel was always 'out' at the libraries.[46]

In addition, because the Don Juan legend explicitly addressed the issue of male–female relationships, it raised questions which women did not feel they could engage in with disinterest. A woman's stake in responding to a tale of a Don Juan was that she could not escape the element of personalization which that response was seen to imply. Hobhouse recognized the problematic nature of a female response when he wrote to Byron that the female readers of *Don Juan* were effectively caught within a double bind in their reactions to the character: 'Your Don is too much a joker to be a real favourite although the ladies like to be thought to appreciate his merits as they do those of substantial vice for fear of being taken for cold and passionless.'[47] Thus, to a certain extent, all female responses to the poem were judged to be 'autobiographical'. Feminist responses to the Don Juan legend still remain entrapped within this discourse of personalization for it is difficult to counter the notorious seducer without being accused of spoiling the fun.[48]

[46] George Paston and Peter Quennell, *'To Lord Byron'* (London: John Murray, 1939), 220.

[47] Graham (ed.), *Byron's Bulldog,* 314 (12 Aug. 1821).

[48] See Jane Miller, *Seductions* (London: Virago Press, 1990), 27.

In considering biographical readings, the most obvious category of readership is that of those women who did feel they
had a personal stake in a narration of Byron's *Don Juan*, that is,
those women who had been seduced by or had themselves
seduced Lord Byron. And this temptation to read biographically would have been increased by the poem's manifesto of
depicting Don Juan as the innocent seduced by women rather
than the initiating seducer. Responses of four of Byron's most
famous female partners—Annabella, Lady Byron; Claire
Clairmont; Lady Caroline Lamb; and Teresa Guiccioli—have
survived. These biographical responses might seem trivial:
Teresa Guiccioli's response to Byron's translating Canto I,
stanza 137, aloud as 'your husband is coming' was to rise in
panic, a response which might justify the appellation of an
example of 'the identificatory procedures of naive biographical
criticism'.[49] However, these responses do contribute to the examination of the illocutionary force of the text, in this case in
the sphere of sexual politics. They also demonstrate how
the performative and referential aspects of the text were
interrelated.

Lady Byron's response

Although all of these women might have felt that their personal
stake in any depiction of seduction written by Lord Byron was
considerable, this was especially the case for Lady Byron. The
satirical portrait of Donna Inez was widely perceived as being a
depiction of Byron's wife.[50] Beside the stanza which described
Donna Inez sending for physicians in an attempt to certify her
husband mad (I, 27), Hobhouse wrote in the margin: 'this is so
very pointed'. Byron's response was one which has already been
considered as typical of the poem's strategy as a whole: 'If
people make applications it is their own fault'.[51] Indeed,
Thomas Moore anticipated that the poem would prove unpopu-

---

[49] *Complete Poetical Works*, v (1986), 679. See also *Byron's Letters and Journals*, vi. 239
(to Murray, 8 Nov. 1819). For 'the identificatory procedures of naive biographical
criticism' see Jerome Christensen, *Lord Byron's Strength* (London and Baltimore:
Johns Hopkins University Press, 1993), 81.
[50] See V, 17: l. 3; VIII, 27: ll. 3–4; IX, 80; XV, 41, and the variant of XIV, 95: l. 8
(*Complete Poetical Works*, v (1986), 586).
[51] Ibid. v (1986), 675, I, st. 27 and I, l. 218 (st. 28, l. 2).

lar among ladies for this very reason, expecting that they would 'arm against' the 'unmanly' allusions in a demonstration of solidarity with Lady Byron.[52] Teresa Guiccioli fulfilled this prophecy to an extent in declaring to Byron: 'they are perfectly right to say that in *Donna Inez* you have presumed to depict your wife . . . If I were she, I would have forgiven all your failings of *1816*, but I would never forgive those of *1818*.'[53]

However, Lady Byron could, or would, not recognize her portrait in that of Donna Inez and she therefore declared herself unperturbed by the satire. She did not see how her 'sins' could be said to be 'pharisaical or pedantic' and brazened the criticisms out by professing that Byron did not think so either. He had, she argued, merely exploited the erroneous prejudices which some might have held in order to engage sympathy on his own behalf.[54] Hobhouse also read the first two Cantos in this way, interpreting them as an act of self-revelation which, he felt, would prove to be counter-productive. The poem's manifesto of a defence of the notorious seducer, Don Juan, would hardly help in the public (opinion) trial of Byron, who was accused of Don Juan-like behaviour, versus his wife:

The fact of the other party having no charge to make is rapidly though silently establishing itself: and nothing but an assault from you can possibly impede the progress of this truth. This hostility is in a manner mixed up with the *whole poem* and her ladyship must see it and will point it out to those who do not see it before . . . Let me also remark that if the case should ever be made public your story will lose half its weight by having been before half frittered away by hints and innuendos.[55]

The adoption of the theme of Don Juan was a risky one; to have defended the notorious libertine was even more dangerous; and to have expressed this in sexual innuendo and banter was to conform to the prejudices of his moral accusers.

Lady Byron further added that she had enjoyed the 'quizzing' of many stanzas and would not therefore prevent others from

[52] *Memoirs, Journal and Correspondence of Thomas Moore* (2nd edn.; London: Longman, Green, Longman & Roberts, 1860), 210 (13 June 1819).

[53] Quoted in *Shelley and his Circle: 1773–1822*, ed. Donald Reiman (Cambridge, Mass.: Harvard University Press, 1986), vii. 419.

[54] Ethel Colburn Mayne, *The Life and Letters of Anne Isabella, Lady Noel Byron* (London: Constable, 1929), 283.

[55] Graham (ed.), *Byron's Bulldog*, 258 (5 Jan. 1819); my italics.

enjoying the humour of the poem, though this magnanimity might suggest only that she wished to be perceived as behaving thus rather than that she had genuinely enjoyed it.[56] She might also have enjoyed the spectacle of Byron scoring an 'own goal' in their contest for public favour by writing so allusively, provocatively, and even offensively, of Don Juan.

Claire Clairmont's response

In the cases of Claire Clairmont and Lady Caroline Lamb, their readings of *Don Juan* inspired literary replies. Claire Clairmont considered writing her own 'Don Juan', of which fragments remain in the jottings she made in her diary between 1 February 1820 and 29 June 1821 under the heading 'Hints for Don Juan'. Although these lines remain only as brief notes, they are sufficient to demonstrate that Claire Clairmont intended the work to be a critique, or perhaps a parody, of Byron's *Don Juan*. In these notes, Byron's poetry is criticized for being too corporeal and lacking soul, and ultimately, for being immoral. The character of Don Juan is associated with Byron, signified for example by the recurrent references to physical deformity, and the bombast of many of the lines marks the character as mimicking the Byronic hero, a recognizable literary commodity.[57] In the sketches of caricatures for 'Albè' (Byron) which she wrote on 8 November 1820, the figure Byron is given lines which Clairmont had previously ascribed to her Don Juan. The compression of these lines makes Don Juan's relation to men and women a violent one: 'The maid I love, the man I hate— I I'll kiss her lips and break his Pate'—the first line of which is taken from *The Giaour*.[58] There is a deliberate indistinctness between the character, Don Juan, and author of *Don Juan*: 'he looks upon her [Nature's] fair adorned breast, not as if it were the bosom of beauty, the pillow upon which the golden locks of poetry should repose, but as so much space allotted for the completion of his desires'.[59]

---

[56] Mayne, *Lady Byron*, 283.

[57] See e.g. *The Journals of Claire Clairmont*, ed. Marion Kington Stocking (Cambridge, Mass.: Harvard University Press, 1968), 197 (18 Dec. 1820).

[58] Ibid. 182–3 (Wednesday 8 Nov. 1820); see also 173 (3 Sept. 1820). The line is taken from *The Giaour* (l. 1018).

[59] Ibid. 226 (15 Apr. 1821).

Claire Clairmont regarded *Don Juan* as an apologia. On 1 February 1820, at Pisa, she wrote in her journal that the poem: 'appears to me a soliloquy upon his own ill-luck—ungraceful and selfish—like a beggar hawking his own sores about and which create disgust instead of Pity'.[60] But her own response did not escape personalization. Her hints for a new 'Don Juan' reveal that it itself was motivated by her own feelings of betrayal and possible revenge. In the jotting for 26 December 1820, for example, Hunt and 'Albè' are suggested as illustrative examples of pride, a sin which is characterized as disguised vanity. The caricature of Byron includes an Italian mistress, Fornara, who is rather cruelly depicted with fumes inscribed 'garlic' curling from her mouth, the force of which knocks the footman backwards. Byron himself is afflicted with venereal disease, and this, it is claimed, is the inspiration for his poetry in literary outpourings of discontent and remorse.

Lady Caroline Lamb's response

Lady Caroline Lamb wrote to Murray: 'You cannot think how clever I think "Don Juan" is, in my heart', an acknowledgement which itself includes the difficulty of women admitting such enjoyment.[61] Her novel *Glenarvon* (1816) having previously influenced the writing of *Don Juan* itself, Caroline Lamb responded to the publication of Byron's poem with two poetical publications of her own—*A New Canto* (1819) and *Gordon: A Tale. A Poetical Review of 'Don Juan'* (1821). Both poems identify themselves strongly with Byron's poem in adopting the conversational facility of its *ottava rima*. *A New Canto* narrates an apocalyptic fire in London and beyond, in which Drury Lane and Covent-Garden, among other buildings, are engulfed in flames (stanza 20). The identification between the two voices, that of Byron's *Don Juan* and Lamb's *A New Canto*, is intense: the final stanza (27) modulates into a reference to 'our flights poetic' and the verses punish, through the impersonated voice of Byron's narrator, the canting English public who had condemned the 'immorality' of both *Glenarvon* and *Don Juan*.

[60] Ibid. 121 (Pisa, Tuesday 1 Feb. 1820).
[61] Smiles, *Publisher and Friends*, i. 405.

Gordon discusses *Don Juan* itself. In the first Canto the poem celebrates the genius of *Don Juan* but condemns its immoral principles. In the second Canto an argument develops between the poem's narrator and a ghostly visitor concerning the merits of *Don Juan*. The narrator's voice parallels that of *Don Juan*, but this time the distinction between the two is clearly marked to allow an ironic mocking of Byron's poem. This tactic is most explicit in the parallel stanza to *Don Juan* (I, 222). Caroline Lamb quotes the first four lines of Canto I, stanza 199, and mockingly adds:

> To see what people say is awkward rather,
> At least in my view, if not so in his,
> 'The first four rhymes are' Byron's 'every line,
> For God's sake, reader! take them not for mine.'
>
> (stanza 71)

Both works consider the poetic voice of Don Juan as a seducer. The narrative voice of *A New Canto* mimics that of *Don Juan*—whom it is hinted is equivalent to Byron ('And I in Italy . . .'; stanza 18). The only person who is shown to profit from the apocalyptic fire is the rake, the voice of whom the narrator adopts:

> Mark yon bright beauty, in her tragic airs,
> How her clear white the mighty smother tinges!
> Delicious chaos! that such beauty bares!—
> And now those eyes outstretch their silken fringes,
> Staring bewildered—and anon she tears
> Her raven tresses ere the wide flame singes—
> Oh! would she feel as I could do, and cherish
> One wild forgetful rapture, ere all perish!
>
> (stanza 7)

Since *Gordon* is more explicitly concerned with the text *Don Juan* than with its hero, it is the poetic style of Byron's poem which becomes the seducer. Like Circe's draught, its influence is 'pernicious' (II, 19) because it is so difficult to resist. Many stanzas relate how impossible it is for the (female) reader to preserve an independence from the seducing power of the poem: 'Who can like him set all your soul on fire | With all the violence of strong desire?' (I, 10). Here the 'him' is both poem and author, explicitly continued in the following stanza's: 'Who can . . . [l]ike him be read without a full satiety?' and in stanza 17 in which the narrator sits down '(t)hinking to read this hero of the town', an indistinction between the poem, the character, or Lord Byron (see also I, 37 quoted above). Their—and its—seductions are portrayed as impossible to resist, since sins are portrayed in such a light, 'that even piety | Can scarce preserve us from the dreadful thirst | To sin *just so* ourselves' (I, 11). *Don Juan* is thus portrayed as an invitation to immorality, a manual of vice. And the language of Lamb's own stanzas is sexualized in the same way as the text upon which they comment:

> He, by the power of his persuasive song
> Can make you fancy you his heroes see;
> His magic numbers drag your soul along
> With such resistless force, you're no more free;
> No matter if the thing be right, or wrong,
> He has your heart, and you must go where he
> Points out the way; he is your only lord,
> He speaks, you listen, then obey his word.
>
> (I, 12)

Despite the anonymity of Lamb's publication, this reader is implicitly gendered female, for the description of lordship would be an inappropriate one to a male reader (although it does continue the synonymity between the text and author, 'Lord' Byron). The activity of reading becomes one of sexual predation and ultimate conquest for Byron's text, capitulation for the reader:

> How suitable the language to the sense!
> And then its purity is quite enchanting:
> The o'erwhelming force of his bold eloquence,
> So ravishes the soul, that while 'tis planting,
> With all the power of its omnipotence,
> The ideas in your mind which he is chanting,
> Resistance all is gone, you are no longer
> What once you were: the strong yields to the stronger.
>
> (I, 27)

This conquest however is effected by the rather nefarious method of the traditional seducer—hypocrisy—for this text works by screening its true nature until it has ensnared the reader whose soul has been effectively 'ravished'.

While the text of *Gordon* talks of the corruption which this portrayal of Don Juan extends, it identifies with a reader who cannot refuse its blandishments: 'For Juan's fate I could not but condole, | Nor keep myself from following as he run' (I, 24). The language is that of involuntary seduction, an attraction which cannot be resisted. However, the additional notes to *Gordon* echo the condemnation of the reviewers as the author of *Don Juan* is explicitly identified with Don Juan. He is depicted as exerting the same force over his readers as the notorious seducer over his female conquests: 'It was my intention to have made some remarks on the facility with which this assassin of morality obtains access to our wives and our daughters; how the poison of his sentiments, more deadly than the asp of Cleopatra, is, like that, carried in a basket of sweets to their bosoms.'[62] It is significant that Lady Caroline Lamb throughout both these works never dropped the pose of masculine authorship. It certainly allowed her to mimic the rakish narrator of *Don Juan*. In addition, *A New Canto* and *Gordon* were published anonymously. Both decisions would have aided her attempt to escape the biographical interpretations which would otherwise have greeted her own publications.

Teresa Guiccioli's response

Some months after reading Cantos I–II of *Don Juan* in a French translation, Teresa Guiccioli urged Byron not to continue with its composition. In several letters in 1821 Byron told Murray, Hobhouse, and Augusta that Teresa Guiccioli had made him promise not to continue with his poem after the publication of Cantos III–V.[63] Her insistence was largely as a result of reading, not the poem itself, but an article in the Milan *Gazzetta* which quoted attacks on Byron's morals from various English papers and reviews.[64] Byron's narration of Teresa's interdiction was much publicized and has been ranked with the poem's own strategies of digressions and interruptions by Jerome Christensen in *Lord Byron's Strength* (1993) as 'elaborations on

---

[62] *Gordon: A Tale*, 77.
[63] *Byron's Letters and Journals*, viii. 145–6; 147–8, 198, 235.
[64] See Marchand, *Byron: A Biography*, ii. 912–13.

the text they ostensibly interrupt'.[65] Certainly Byron deliberately and conspicuously tried to conceal the dates of composition of Cantos VI and VII, the resumption of the poem, which
he claimed had been given a new dispensation from Teresa
provided it was 'more guarded and decorous and sentimental in
the continuation than in the commencement'.[66] Byron, however, never attempted to discourage the degree of scandal with
which the poem had consistently been associated—the choice
of title was only the first of many such examples, and his acknowledgement of Teresa's displeasure was just such another.
Teresa Guiccioli's objections to the poem were themselves due
to the notoriety of other Don Juan versions.

In her memoirs of Lord Byron's life, Teresa Guiccioli relates
an anecdote which illustrates how she was unable to resist the
personalization which an attitude to the Don Juan legend was
seen to imply. During a general conversation upon the subjects
of women and of love, Mr Medwin eulogized the devotedness,
constancy, and truth of women. Byron, in a characteristic spirit
of opposition contradicted his arguments, 'as Don Juan or
Childe Harold might'. The speaker of the memoirs (which
Guiccioli wrote in the third person) claims that it was evident
that Byron was merely adopting a contrary stance which did not
represent genuine principle. Later she confides her disquiet to
Byron, fearing that others will not understand that his profession of such unchivalrous opinions was a deliberately adopted
pose: 'M– will not fail to repeat your words as if they were your
real opinions; and the world, knowing neither him nor you, will
remain convinced that he is a man full of noble sentiments, and
you a real Don Juan, not indeed your own charming youth, but
Molière's Don Juan!'[67] This distinction echoes Teresa
Guiccioli's alleged reason for her dislike of *Don Juan*—that it
was too like Mozart's *Don Giovanni* (quoted in Chapter 1).[68] In
referring to her desire that Don Juan should 'remain in Hell (or

---

[65] Christensen, *Lord Byron's Strength*, 263.
[66] *Byron's Letters and Journals*, ix. 182. For the dating of the composition of Cantos
VI and VII, see Truman Guy Steffan, *The Making of a Masterpiece* (Austin, Tex.:
The University of Texas Press, 1959), 384, and Byron, *Complete Poetical Works*,
v (1986), 714–15.
[67] Teresa Guiccioli, *Lord Byron, jugé par les témoins de sa vie* (London: Richard
Bentley, 1869), i. 441–2, 442.
[68] Lovell (ed.), *Medwin's Conversations*, 164.

go there)', Byron recognized that his poem was consciously being measured against the traditional stereotype of the villainous seducer.[69] However, he could always, and possibly did, reassure Teresa's fears about the moral propriety of the poem by arguing that his Don Juan was innocent and totally unlike the legendary seducer—exactly the kind of arguments that recent criticism has made concerning the poem and its (lack of) relation to the legend. Most contemporary readers, it would seem, did not concur and Byron's argument can be interpreted as a manœuvre to conciliate his mistress. Byron was able to deploy such an argument because of the ambivalence with which Don Juan is portrayed. Shrouded in innuendo and doubting allusions, Byron can always claim the corruption as the reader's own. These rhetorical manœuvres have already been considered in Chapter 2 as a provocation to the most moral of readers. This strategy can now be seen as inspired by gendered considerations, for the most moral of readers, it would have been presumed, were female.

THE FEMALE READER AND THE LIBERTINE STYLE OF *DON JUAN*

Byron boasted to Augusta that a lady from Pimlico had fallen in love with him as a consequence of reading *Don Juan*. This passage also reinforces the portrayal of the contemporary constraints upon a female reception of the work, for in speaking of her liking for the poem he adds: 'I suppose that she is either mad or *nau*[ghty]'.[70] It is in this context of 'naughty' women that the response of Harriette Wilson to *Don Juan* ought to be considered. Harriette Wilson frankly wrote to Byron of her enjoyment of *Don Juan*, and, even more daringly, in an imitative style of sexual innuendo. Her letter was written from Paris at 'exactly 20 minutes past 12 o'clock at night' and was signed 'good night', since reading and writing about *Don Juan* are suitably nocturnal activities:

Don Juan kept me up, the whole of last night. I will not attempt to describe its beauties, as they struck, and delighted me; because that

---

[69] *Byron's Letters and Journals*, viii. 145–6 (to John Murray, 4 July 1821).
[70] Ibid. x. 29 (to Augusta Leigh, 7 Nov. 1822).

would be at the expense of another night's rest . . . Strange to tell, I
never heard of *Don Juan* till I found it on Galignani's table yesterday
and took it to bed with me, where I contrived to keep my large *quiet*
good-looking brown eyes open (now, you *know*, they are very handsome) till I had finished it . . . Reading *Don Juan* made me think of you
all day; and so I could not go to bed without presuming to write to you
again.[71]

Harriette Wilson may be said to have countered the challenge
of *Don Juan*'s narrative style in appropriating her response to it
as an opportunity for flirtation with its author. She too conflates
the poem with Byron, since reading the poem makes her think
of the author 'all day'. Her frank enjoyment of the poem would
not have surprised the conservative reviewers since, as a notorious courtesan, she would be expected not only to understand,
but also to enjoy the poem's bawdy humour. *The Gentleman's
Magazine*, for example, explicitly condemned the poem as 'almost throughout scandalously licentious and obscene, fit only
for the shelves of a brothel' (September 1823).[72]

Women in late eighteenth-century society were expected to
speak as properly as they were to behave. In 1782, for example,
Hester Thrale shocked her female companions by reading
aloud a passage from the *Spectator* and reported that: 'even the
Maid who was dressing my Hair, burst out a' laughing at the
Idea of *a Lady* saying her Stomach ach'd, or that something
stuck between her Teeth'.[73] The delicacy of 'lady-like' speech
was to become even more acutely prescribed in the increasing
moral hegemony of the Napoleonic era, exemplified by the
proliferation of Dr Bowdler's adaptations of texts. Extreme
prudishness was deemed appropriate for genteel female
speech. Within this context the language of sexuality was entirely prohibited to women. Anna Clark, in *Women's Silence,
Men's Violence* (1987), discussed how female exclusion from
'immoral' diction prevented them from testifying against sexual
assailants. If the victim of rape could testify that emission had
occurred, her frankness branded her as immodest and her

---

[71] *Memoirs of Harriette Wilson*, iv. 217. Paston and Quennell, *'To Lord Byron'*, 159
and 161.
[72] *The Gentleman's Magazine*, 93/2 (Sept. 1823), 250–3, 251, review of Cantos VI–
VIII. See also *The Eclectic Review*, 12 (Aug. 1819), 150, review of Cantos I–II.
[73] Poovey, *Proper Lady*, 14.

attacker would be less likely to be prosecuted. If women used colloquial terms, the only terms they knew, to describe what happened to them, upper-class judges would brand them as immoral. *The Morning Chronicle* (3 August 1826) made this difficulty apparent in appealing to the shame which fathers would feel if their daughters were heard to utter such indecorous language. The commentator declared that:

no female not uninitiated into vice, or neglected in education, can possibly go through the ordeal of a public trial; and the father is not to be envied who would not rather allow the injury to his daughter to escape punishment, than hear the daughter answer those questions, which . . . must be put to her, before a conviction can be obtained.[74]

Wollstonecraft recognized and exposed the double bind. When the heroine of *The Wrongs of Woman* (1798) pleads her own case in court, the judge attacks the 'fallacy of letting women plead their feelings . . . What virtuous woman thought of her feelings?'[75]

Any narration of the Don Juan legend entailed the same difficulties for a female readership, since, like the rape trial, no telling of the legend could be innocent of sexual knowledge. The language of sexuality, however allusive or disguised, was inseparable from the telling. Although the very subject of Byron's *Don Juan* in itself threatened dangerous consequences for the female reader, the majority of reviewers cited its frank expression of the subject as the predominant bar to a female reading. For example, Hobhouse anticipated the strictures of the reviewers in warning Byron that the poem would be unfit reading for ladies, because of the indecency of its language:

You are aware, of course, that the poems cannot get into my lady's chamber—were there only the *urine* rhyme I presume that would be sufficiently excluding. . . . I need only remind you that you used to pride yourself and with great reason upon your delicacy—now it will be impossible for any lady to know Don Juan to be seen on her table, and you would not wish to be crammed like 'the man of feeling' into her pocket.[76]

---

[74] Clark, *Women's Silence*, 63.
[75] Wollstonecraft, *Mary and The Wrongs of Woman* (1976; repr. Oxford: Oxford University Press, 1991), 198–9, vol. ii, ch. 17.
[76] Graham (ed.), *Byron's Bulldog*, 272 (on receiving Canto II, 16 June 1819); 259 (5 Jan. 1819).

The prurient allusions to the book's entering 'my lady's chamber', or being crammed surreptitiously into a pocket, illustrate the allusively erotic implication of female reading, here suggestively linked to corrupt readings of such apparently 'innocent' texts as MacKenzie's sentimental novel. Byron did concede in omitting the offending 'urine' rhyme (variant II, 10, ll. 7–8). Other lines removed from Canto I were the stanzas on venereal disease (I, 131, and the final couplets of 129 and 130) and Canto I, stanza 15, which was interpreted as alluding too openly to Lady Byron. These omissions were approved by Murray and Hobhouse but they were unauthorized by Byron. Murray suggested the removal of certain offensive words from Canto II specifically because '(t)hese ladies may not read'.[77] However, these attempts proved insufficient to satisfy the moral strictures of the reviewers. *The European Magazine* (August 1821) sardonically anticipated that Byron might eventually render his verse respectable—but it was a recognizably tenuous hope: 'So finishes Canto Five; and if the right honourable author continues to purify his verses as he proceeds, perhaps Canto Twenty-Five may possibly be written in a style sufficiently devoid of objectionable language, and improper allusions, to allow of its being read aloud, and introduced to the ladies.'[78]

The omissions in the manuscripts of Cantos VI–XVI which Mary Shelley copied testify to her own dislike of the frankness of many lines. For example, she omitted the manuscript lines 1–2 of Canto VIII, stanza 76: 'taken by the tail—a taking | Fatal to warriors as to women' (which were subsequently changed by Byron to end 'bishops as to soldiers') and lines 7–8 of Canto VIII, stanza 130: 'But six old damsels, each of seventy years, | Were all deflowered by different grenadiers'. Where she could, she dephysicalized the language, changing, for example, the use of 'breast' in Canto VI, stanza 67, line 5, to 'heart'. In her letter to Edward John Trelawny of 27 December 1830, referring to *The Adventures of a Younger Son*, she asked his permission to deal with the text as she had done when copying out the manuscripts of *Don Juan*, Cantos VI–XVI, that is, to omit those passages which offended her taste. In the same letter she also explicitly linked the use of frank and indelicate expression with a betrayal of female readers: 'I strongly object to coarseness,

---

[77] Smiles, *Publisher and Friends*, i. 402.
[78] *The European Magazine* (Aug. 1821), 181–5, 185, review of Cantos III–V.

now wholly out of date, and beg you for my sake to make the
omissions necessary for your obtaining female readers . . . Certain words and phrases, pardoned in the days of Fielding, are
now justly interdicted.'[79] Byron frequently compared his poem
to the writing of Fielding, among a list which included Ariosto,
Boiardo, Voltaire, Pulci, and Smollett, as evidence of its comparative innocence.[80] This argument was unlikely to have persuaded Mary Shelley. When William Hone read aloud a list of
writers who had written political parodies, the judges at his trial
only countered that they would happily have prosecuted
Luther, Milton, and all the others had they had the opportunity.[81] In the same way, Byron's argument was irrelevant to Mary
Shelley's declaration because, she argued, the standards by
which immorality and indecorousness were measured had
changed.

The reviewers recognized the literary techniques of pun, innuendo, and allusion as representing the deployment of authorial, rather than narrative, tactics, and they hoped that in this
recognition they might counteract the insidious strength and
appeal of the devices. One attempt to render the poem safe for
female reading was to quote only acceptable and previously
selected excerpts from the poem:

Don Juan is a sealed book to the ladies of our time (to say no more)
and you will be doing them a great favour in thus affording a few
extracts, upon the 'Family Bowdler' principle, from a work, which, as
a whole, they have no chance of seeing; or, if they did see it, of reading
three pages in it without blushing to the back-bone.[82]

This was frequently an impossible task, for it was exceedingly
difficult to censor what the most moralistic of its readers would
object to, so indissolubly was the offensive writing threaded
throughout the narrative. Subject-matter and expression were
inextricable because the corrupt understanding of the phrasing
was fed by the subject-matter of libertinism. The possibility of a
woman maintaining an innocent reading of Don Juan was prevented by the apparent pointing of the text itself. The change in

---

[79] *The Letters of Mary Wollstonecraft Shelley* (Baltimore and London: Johns Hopkins
University Press, 1980), ii. 36.
[80] See e.g. *Byron's Letters and Journals*, vi. 77, x. 68, 98.
[81] See Christensen, *Lord Byron's Strength*, 95.
[82] *Blackwood's Edinburgh Magazine*, 14 (Sept. 1823), 292, review of Cantos IX–XI.

Byron's diction—from the decorous elevation of chivalric language in the Tales to the sexually suggestive language of *Don Juan*—was to a great extent dictated by the choice of the Don Juan theme itself. Hobhouse recognized, although he did not condone, the constraint imposed upon the style by the content of sensuality: 'I recollect you used to object to Tom Moore his luxuriousness, and to me my use of gross words, yet your scenes are one continued painting of what is most sensual.'[83]

The young Byron did not question the propriety of gendered readings: in a letter to John M. B. Pigot (10 August 1806) he had ordered such erotic poems as 'To Mary' to be printed separately from the other stanzas of *Fugitive Pieces* as they were '*improper* for the perusal of ladies'.[84] Within *Don Juan*, he questioned such an attitude. This is evident in his oblique manner of portraying the shipwreck. In *Byron: A Poet before his Public* (1982), Philip Martin discussed the careful avoidance in Canto II of any direct reference to the notorious shipwreck of the French frigate, the *Medusa*, in 1816 in which its passengers survived only by consuming human flesh. Martin argues that this omission ironically mocks the commentator of *The Quarterly Review* (17 October 1817) who appropriated the story as a patriotic moral lesson on the anarchy of the French political system. It also represents a disingenuous deference to lady readers. While Byron would have known that many ladies had in fact been reading of the wreck of the *Medusa*, its apparent absence from his account shows him 'sardonically participating in the decorous game of unmentionables'.[85] This reading is certainly supported by Byron's advice to Augusta: he suggested that Murray should point out the stanzas on Donna Inez for her, '(for fear yr. delicate feelings should be shocked by stumbling on a Shipwrecke)'.[86]

There are also many explicit examples of the narrator's ridicule of gendered speech and reading within the narrative of *Don Juan*. For example, even Donna Inez, whose behaviour is guided by the conduct books, is described as speaking in a

[83] Graham (ed.), *Byron's Bulldog*, 258 (5 Jan. 1819).
[84] *Byron's Letters and Journals*, i. 97.
[85] Philip W. Martin, *Byron: A Poet Before his Public* (Cambridge: Cambridge University Press, 1982), 213.
[86] *Byron's Letters and Journals*, vii. 239 (30 Nov. 1820).

mode which is 'not pure' (I, 13). Canto V, stanza 55, mischievously implies that the speaker of the ensuing curse is female: 'Some female head most curiously presumes | To thrust its black eyes through the door or lattice | As wondering what the devil noise that is'. Indeed, the poem implies throughout that women would be more than capable of understanding *double entendres* and allusions, accustomed as they are to dissembling and speaking in codes: many females are of 'perspicuous comprehension' (XV, 80). The description of the female missal of Canto XIII, stanza 105—'Which like a creed ne'er says all it intends'—is paradigmatic of the text of *Don Juan* in its deliberately cunning use of mystery, and recollects the specifically sexual innuendo of Donna Inez's family missal with its amorous figures sketched in the margins (I, 46). The narrator's ridicule of a theory of gendered interpretations is also evident in his disquisition upon riddles and allusions in Canto IX, stanzas 48–52. Don Juan's position in Russia is described as being of 'high official station' (IX, 48), a recognizable and popular example of sexual innuendo, made especially so by its inclusion within quotation marks and by its allusive echo of the lover's 'Highland welcome' in Canto VI, stanza 13. The corrupt reading is further encouraged by the subsequent ostentation of a direct address to the female reader: 'Oh gentle ladies, should you seek to know | The import of this diplomatic phrase, | Bid Ireland's Londonderry's Marquess show | His parts of speech . . .'. The image of Castlereagh showing his 'parts' in itself constitutes obvious bawdiness (IX, 49). The narrator continues by mocking the claim that a female reader would naïvely miss the sexual allusion. He tells of a conversation between an English and an Italian lady, with the English lady inquiring about the function and duties of a *cavalier servente*, and her Italian friend replying only: 'Lady, I beseech you to suppose them' (IX, 51). The narrator appeals to his female reader to exercise the same fastidiousness regarding the role of Don Juan in Russia:

> And thus I supplicate your supposition
> And mildest, matron-like interpretation
> Of the imperial favourite's condition.
> 'Twas a high place, the highest in the nation . . .
>
> (IX, 52)

The narrator's appeal to the most modest interpretation concerning Don Juan's position in Russia is a deliberately ironic suggestion because the narrative continues with a repetition of the sexual innuendo in the preceding stanza 48, just four stanzas previously: ' 'Twas a high place, the highest in the nation'.[87] The most naïve of readers is given several opportunities to pick up the suggestiveness.

In *A Vindication of the Rights of Woman* (1792), Mary Wollstonecraft both admitted a female talent for suggestive understanding and condemned it as demeaning: women's 'sexual tricks' are associated with *double entendre*, a development of what she calls 'bodily wit' which evolves from the 'jokes and hoyden tricks' which women learn if they are 'shut up together in nurseries, schools, or convents' and which resemble 'the double meanings which shake the convivial table when the glass has circulated freely'.[88] Society's division of reading according to gender was also becoming more difficult to sustain with the increase in number of publications and more widespread female education and literacy. The absurdly 'chivalrous' protection of the female reader was ultimately overcome by historical events. Copyright, libel laws, and quarto volumes might attempt to preserve female immunity from moral subversion, but the events of 1807–20 culminated in detailed tales of adultery and lust for the consumption of newspaper readers. These years cover the extended marital bickering of the Prince Regent and his wife Caroline. In 1807 she was accused by Parliament, with George's encouragement, of bearing a bastard child. The 'Delicate Investigation' ultimately found her innocent of this charge, although her fight for recognition and access to her daughter provoked considerable Whig activity in her favour, especially between February–April 1813 and June–July 1814. The affair then ended anti-climactically with the Princess accepting the government's bribe and departing for the Continent. Her predicament came to attention again in 1817 when she was not invited to the funeral of her daughter, Princess Charlotte. On George's succession to the throne in 1820, the estranged Caroline returned from Italy and demanded inclusion by name in the Anglican prayers for the Royal Family. The moral issue of

[87] *Complete Poetical Works* (1986), 740, Canto IX, l. 412 p. 740.
[88] Wollstonecraft, *A Vindication*, ch. 7, p. 240.

the Queen's fidelity then became a political crisis as opposition Whigs and radicals alike rallied around her cause. There was little doubt as to Caroline's 'guilt', but the people chose to believe she was innocent because George's own philanderings had long been notorious. The newspapers carried the lurid details of the trials: 'Did Barbara Kress, the Karlsruhe chambermaid, really find evidence of sexual intercourse in the bed she made in Bergami's room? Did she see the queen half naked in his arms? Was it true that Bergami helped Caroline undress for a costume ball in Naples?'[89] During the trials of William Hone in 1817, the very pamphlets which the government was trying to suppress were reproduced in the transcripts and newspaper accounts of the proceedings. They thus enjoyed a more extensive circulation than would have otherwise been possible through Hone's own efforts. In the same way, when *Don Juan* was denied copyright as an immoral and blasphemous publication, the piracies which succeeded only strengthened the activity which the act was intended to prevent—again a wider dissemination. Such were the anomalies of the English legal system. In the case of the Queen Caroline affair, the newspaper accounts allowed the public's examination of the Royals' sexual behaviour. For three months, while the Upper House debated the measure and successive indecorous details were gossiped about, the English public, including wives and daughters, 'talked almost incessant bawdy'.[90] If Byron's argument of literary precedents for his 'voluptuous' writing was ineffectual as a refutation of prevailing standards, his citing of the Caroline case could not have been so dismissed. Indeed, Byron himself wrote of his own work's comparative innocence: 'The Queen has made a pretty theme for the journals. Was there ever such evidence published? Why it is worse than "Little's Poems" or "Don Juan"'.[91]

Byron was not alone in thus comparing his poem to the Queen Caroline case. *Blackwood's Edinburgh Magazine* (August

[89] Quoted in Thomas W. Lacqueur, 'The Queen Caroline Affair: Politics as Art in the Reign of George IV', *Journal of Modern History*, 54 (1982), 417–44, 448.

[90] Arthur Bryant, *The Age of Elegance 1812–1822* (1950; repr. Glasgow: William Collins, 1975), 393.

[91] *Byron's Letters and Journals*, x. 68 ('voluptuous') and vii. 207 (to Thomas Moore, 17 Oct. 1820).

1821) reviewed *Don Juan*, Cantos III–V, with an obvious allusion
to the trial of Caroline:

> He shows his knowledge of the world too openly; and it is no extenu-
> ation of this freedom that he does it playfully. Only infants can be
> shown naked in company, but his Lordship pulls the very robe de
> chambre from both men and women, and goes on with his exposures
> as smirkingly as a barrister cross-questioning a chamber maid in a case
> of crim. con.[92]

The reviewer's complaint is that the innuendoes are so very
obvious. The narrator of *Don Juan* is certainly not coy about the
innuendoes which he makes. Instead his double-talk is flaunted.
The narrator of Robert Bage's novel, *Hermsprong* (1796), acknowledged that in describing his mother as 'chaste', he would
arouse the antagonism of his most moral, that is female, readers, because he was born illegitimately: 'There may be, especially among my fair readers, some who may object to the
epithet which I have given my mother . . .'. This sally against the
moral tenets and preconceptions of the female reader in
particular is similar to that later employed by the narrator of
Don Juan: Bage's narrator claims that he is 'a person infinitely
nice in matters of epithet'. However, he continues by invoking
those occasions when he would permit himself indelicate expression: 'I never permit an improper [epithet] to descend
from my pen, or my tongue, unless I am writing a dedication, or
addressing a lord or a lady, or unless I am making love'.[93] This
last occasion is of particular interest because, in giving so many
Don Juan-like lines to the narrator, Byron effectively made this
persona a seducer. It is in this context that the narrator's mode
of address becomes one of seduction. Camille Paglia, in *Sexual
Personae* (1990), considers the narrator's overstatement of
apology towards the reader for calling his hero Juanna: 'I say
her because | The gender still was epicene' (VI, 58). In this
example, Paglia claims Byron 'wantonly stresses the sexual
equivocal . . . Even at his most perverse, Spenser is never this
coy. Byron is flirting with the reader, something new in

---

[92] *Blackwood's Edinburgh Magazine*, 10 (Aug. 1821), 107–15, 115.
[93] Robert Bage, *Hermsprong* (1796; repr. Oxford and New York: Oxford University
Press, 1985), 1–2.

literature.'[94] It is the narrator's parade of a knowing coyness
which exposes the ironic spirit, although this very self-awareness
only reinforced the moral reader's sense of its offensiveness.

Byron's own stance in the argument that poetry could be
seducing was typically contradictory. He is alleged to have told
Madame de Staël that her novels *Delphine* and *Corinne* were 'very
dangerous productions to be put into the hands of young
women' and in November 1820 he wrote to Moore that the
sordid details concerning the adultery trial of Queen Caroline
would result in the Miss Moores and Miss Byrons presenting
them with 'a great variety of grandchildren by different fathers'.[95] Yet in October 1819 Byron wrote concerning his own
poem, *Don Juan*, that 'the reading or non-reading a book—will
never keep down a single petticoat'.[96] He also mocked the
prevailing belief in Canto III of his poem. Because Haidée and
Don Juan are unmarried lovers, the narrator addresses the
implicitly female (because 'chaste') reader:

> Then if you'd have them wedded, please to shut
> The book which treats of this erroneous pair,
> Before the consequences grow too awful;
> 'Tis dangerous to read of loves unlawful.

> (III, 12)

Such advice is guaranteed to attract all the more, in the same
way that the vehemence of the reviewers' pronouncements
against *Don Juan* encouraged the very reading which they were
attempting to prevent. Tantalizingly selective excerpts which
were quoted in the reviews only increased the allure of the text.
In fact, such reviews often chose as excerpts those passages
which were most offensive because they vindicated their horror
and moral outrage. For example, *Blackwood's Edinburgh Magazine* (July 1823) quoted several stanzas from *Don Juan* with the
following proviso: 'It is a pity to reprint such things, but a single
specimen here may do good, by the disgust for the whole which

---

[94] Camille Paglia, *Sexual Personae* (London: Penguin, 1991), 353. See also Marlon
B. Ross, in Anne Mellor (ed.), *Romanticism and Feminism* (Bloomington, Ill.:
Indianapolis University Press, 1988), 31.
[95] Michael Foot, *The Politics of Paradise* (London: William Collins, 1988), 186;
Byron's Letters and Journals, vii. 220 (to Thomas Moore, 5 Nov. 1820).
[96] *Byron's Letters and Journals*, vi. 237 (to Richard Belgrave Hoppner, 29 Oct.
1819).

it must create'. The stanzas reprinted described the disappointment of the Ismail widows at the continence of the Russian soldiers in not raping as extensively as the French army (VIII, 128–34). *The Literary Gazette* (19 July 1823) also quoted these stanzas, and with the same justification.[97] In this way the reviews circulated those passages which they most feared and thus ministered to the very immorality which they condemned. They declared their intention to shield the female reader from at best, offence, or at worst, corruption. Yet in attempting to refute the power of such passages they perpetuated it. *Don Juan* itself displays a more self-conscious awareness of how what is prohibited might attract all the more—the occasional coyness about phrases which are not for 'ears polite' is one example of this, as is the audacious advice to the reader to close the book (III, 12). In 1823 Byron wrote to John Hunt: 'of all my works D[on] Juan is the most popular—and sells doubly in proportion—especially amongst the women who send for it the more that it is abused'.[98] In *Candleford Green*, Miss Lane's prohibition and threat to destroy *Don Juan* in the next garden bonfire predictably rouse Laura's curiosity all the more. It certainly makes her transgression exciting: 'Laura knew she ought to be, and was, ashamed of herself, guiltily devouring *Don Juan* with glances at the door'.[99] The imagery of the attraction of the forbidden is a significant one for a text about, and named, *Don Juan* since the legendary seducer frequently seduced wives and nuns for the pleasure of the transgression.

In October 1822 Byron again attempted to placate Murray's fears, arguing that 'No Girl will ever be seduced by reading D[on] J[uan]'.[100] However, he did add that if she wished to be seduced she might find other reading suitable: 'she will go to Little's poems & Rousseau's romans—for that—or even to the immaculate De Staël', the active desire of the female reader implicit in the phrasing 'she will go to . . . for that'. Byron's contradictory statements might thus be resolved as an attempt to save his own poem from a censure which he himself ex-

---

[97] *Blackwood's Edinburgh Magazine*, 14 (July 1823), 88–92, 89, review of Cantos VI–VIII. See also *The Literary Gazette* (19 July, 1823), 451–3, 453, review of Cantos VI–VIII.

[98] *Byron's Letters and Journals*, x. 146 (letter to John Hunt, 9 Apr. 1823).

[99] Thompson, *Lark Rise to Candleford*, 414–15.

[100] *Byron's Letters and Journals*, x. 68 (to John Murray, 25 Oct. 1822).

tended to others. This is exactly the argument levelled against amorous verse in *Don Juan*, Canto V, stanzas 1–2, in which the narrator claims for his own poem a comparatively chaste style which is '(p)lain, simple, short, and by no means inviting'. The deliberate hypocrisy of this claim is, however, quickly discovered. All passions in *Don Juan* are certainly not 'in their turn attacked', and the poem itself is an invitation to the widest spectrum of readers to read allusively, that is suggestively. When Byron claimed that he had gained an adoring admirer in the lady-reader from Pimlico, he also contradicted his claim that the poem was chaste and 'by no means inviting'. Moreover, the language of this boasting letter to Augusta, motivated in part by her own chilly rejection of the poem, was blatantly that of seduction.

The reviewers of *Don Juan* specifically cautioned, not just against the frank indelicacy of many of the poem's expressions, but, more fearfully, against the contamination which the mode of reading encouraged by the poem implied. Sexual innuendo, pun, and allusion were deliberately deployed by the narrator to shield himself from censure. The reviewers were aware of and feared the implication for a female reader: 'yet I marvel how any modest maiden or virtuous matron can allow herself to read it, and not impugn her own innocence: such a cage of unclean birds it is impossible to turn into the imagination, but they must leave a trace or a taint on the heart'.[101] This review by *The Imperial Magazine* (October 1821) implicitly refers to the narrative tactics of innuendo and allusion, for the understanding of these devices requires participation in the production of their, frequently bawdy, meaning. Both the narrator and the hero, Don Juan, are enabled to retain a certain innocence which the reader, as reader, never possessed. Although this strategy operated upon all readings of the poem, the consequences were perceived to differ according to class and gender. As the act of seduction was concomitant with the woman's loss of innocence, so too the female reader's participation in the text betrayed her already, or simultaneous, corruption.

Despite the obvious disparity in dates, Freud's case-study of 'Dora' in 1905 is relevant here. This was an analysis of an 18-

---

[101] *The Imperial Magazine*, 3 (Oct. 1821), cols. 945–8, review of Cantos III–V.

year-old girl whom Freud 'diagnosed' as possessing a repudi-
ated heterosexual desire for her father and a homosexual at-
tachment to her father's mistress. In this case-study, Freud
expressed his awareness of the difficulty in talking to Dora
about her 'illness' in a language which would not pervert. Mary
Jacobus, in her consideration of his analysis ('Dora and the
Pregnant Madonna', 1986), writes that Freud insists 'that he
never imparted his own sexual meanings to her until it became
clear that (as always proves the case) she already knew'.[102] This
double bind reflects that of the rape victim who cannot speak of
the crime without appearing to be complicit with it, evident in
the passage from *The Morning Chronicle* (3 August 1826) quoted
above, and still existing in those rape trials in which consent is
the principal issue.[103] The inevitable contamination of understanding was also considered by Rousseau in *Emile* (1762) in
which the 'chasteness of language' was stated to reside in the
absence rather than the careful avoidance of indecent meanings, since 'if we are to avoid them, they must be in our
thoughts'.[104] So too the periodical reviewers feared that any
reading of *Don Juan* would either effect or consolidate a loss of
innocence. No reading of the text could be 'virtuous'—and
they were tainted within their own complaints.

When Murray cautioned Byron against publishing the first
Cantos of *Don Juan*, he advised 'if you do anything it must be
done with extreme caution; think of the effects of such seductive poetry!'[105] The reviews of *Don Juan* display an extraordinary
degree of consensus in branding the author of *Don Juan* as
libertine, an accusation which they supported by citing the
evidence of the corrupting influence of the style itself.[106]
Caroline Lamb in *Gordon* also acknowledged the extent of the
manipulation which the text was portrayed as exercising. It was
an effect which she proclaimed herself unable to resist, although she more prudently adopted the persona of a seduced

---

[102] Mary Jacobus, *Reading Woman* (London: Methuen, 1986), 185.
[103] See John Forrester, *The Seductions of Psychoanalysis* (Cambridge: Cambridge
University Press, 1990), 333.
[104] Rousseau, *Emile*, 288–9.
[105] Smiles, *Publisher and Friends*, i. 402.
[106] See e.g. *The Eclectic Review* (Aug. 1819); *The Investigator* (1822), 315–71, 340,
review of Cantos I–II, III–V, and *Edinburgh (Scots) Magazine*, 2nd ser. 9 (Aug. 1821),
105–8, 105–6, review of Cantos I–II, III–V.

'male' reader. And in Flora Thompson's account Laura's enjoyment of reading *Don Juan* is allusively corrupt, since this 'education' is an adoption of 'knowingness':

> How fascinating the book was! She felt she simply had to know what
> came next, and the blue skies and seas of those foreign shores and the
> seaside loves and golden sands and the wit of the author and the
> felicity of his language and the dexterity of his rhymes enchanted her.
> She was shocked by some of the hero's adventures, but more often
> thrilled. *Laura learnt quite a lot by reading Don Juan.*[107]

In all these considerations of the poem's female readership,
the emphasis was always upon the 'effect'. The debate concerning the moral 'consequences' of the poem *Don Juan* illustrates
how political the contemporary readings of the poem were: the
text of *Don Juan* was viewed as inheriting the seducing tactics
and disposition of the theatrical character. In Canto XVII,
stanza 12, the narrator coyly professes a reluctance to elucidate
the 'tender moonlight situation' of Don Juan and the Duchess
of Fitz-Fulke—'Unless some beauty with a kiss should bribe'.
This incomplete Canto was not published until 1903, an ironic
gesture for a stanza which literalizes the fear of the Regency
reviewers that the relationship between the author and his female reader was a sexual one.

---

[107] Thompson, *Lark Rise to Candleford*, 414–15; my italics.

5

The Seduction of Don Juan

In *Don Juan*, Canto VII, stanza 19, there is a brief reference to
Captain Smith who is from 'country quarters | At Halifax', an
allusion to a song from George Colman's popular play *Love
Laughs at Locksmiths* (1818). Jerome McGann, who cites the
reference in his commentary to the poem, notes only that the
character was 'renowned for his seductions'. Contemporary
readers however would have recalled the song's more sinister
ending:

> A captain bold in Halifax,
> Who dwelt in country quarters,
> Seduc'd a maid who hang'd herself
> One Monday in her garters.[1]

This example is a small one, yet it concisely illustrates the
argument of this book concerning the importance of the Don
Juan legend to a reading of Byron's *Don Juan*. Here, as in the
poem as a whole, we are made aware of the presence of the
unspoken, the constitutive influence of the reader's assumptions and knowledge, and the sexual-political implication of this
knowledge. We are also reminded of what is forgotten if we
ignore such a context.

The current critical consensus which regards Byron's Don
Juan as a passive innocent is usually justified by the argument
that he is not the seducer, but the seduced.[2] The interpretation
that Byron's Don Juan is the object of seduction has been
influential, not least within the history of the Don Juan legend

---

[1] The song is printed in *Don Juan*, ed. T. G. Steffan, E. Steffan, and W. W. Pratt
(Harmondsworth: Penguin, 1973), 659. For McGann's comment, see *The Complete
Poetical Works of Lord Byron*, ed. Jerome J. McGann, 7 vols. (Oxford: Clarendon
Press), v (1986), 724.

[2] See e.g. Peter W. Graham, Don Juan *and Regency England* (Charlottesville, Va.:
University Press of Virginia, 1990), 9, and Caroline Franklin, *Byron's Heroines* (Oxford: Clarendon Press, 1992), 148–9.

itself, since Byron's poem undoubtedly influenced many later versions which made the figure's passivity explicit.[3] Shaw's story 'Don Giovanni Explains' (1887) relates how the attractiveness of the seducer compels a young girl to make advances even to his ghost—while in *Man and Superman* (1903), John Tanner fails to escape from Ann's 'pursuit' of a husband, even if that pursuit adopts the stationary entrapment of a spider's web.[4] In Edmond Rostand's *La Dernière Nuit de Don Juan* (1921), the dead Don Juan encounters the spirits of the women whom he has 'seduced' (Act II, scene 1):

GHOST OF WOMAN: You looked at me when I had chosen you . . .
DON JUAN: But I seduced you!
GHOST: When we decided it for you!
DEVIL: 'Oh, how I seduced the magnet', the iron said
                 to itself.[5]

Many of the most famous twentieth-century interpretations of the legend have also claimed that Don Juan is seduced by his 'conquests'. Gregorio Marañón and Ortega y Gasset respectively argued that Don Juan was emblematic of effeminacy and virility. Both, however, agreed that he was seduced rather than seducing.

Yet it is this interpretation—of Don Juan as seducee—which has most frequently determined the exclusion of Byron's poem from the history of the Don Juan legend. This chapter will question the portrayal of Byron's Don Juan as the victim of seduction in considering the poem from an explicitly feminist perspective, a sceptical reading which has much in common with the suspicious interpretations typical of the poem's initial reception. This feminist reading of *Don Juan* needs to remember the context of the Don Juan legend, as one which implicated the poem within Regency debates concerning seduction.

---

[3] See *La Passion selon Don Juan* (Bibliothèque Nationale: 25 Apr.–5 July 1991), 162, annotation to the lithograph by Achille Deveria 'Lord Byron et la Comtesse Guiccioli' (1842).
[4] George Bernard Shaw, 'Don Giovanni Explains' (1887), in *Short Stories, Scraps and Shavings* (London: Constable, 1932), 95–116, 115; *Man and Superman* (1903; repr. Harmondsworth: Penguin, 1973), e.g. p. 129, Act III, and, for the image of the spider, Shaw's letter to Arthur Bingham Walkley, p. 20.
[5] Translated in Oscar Mandel (ed.), *The Theatre of Don Juan* (Lincoln, Nebr.: University of Nebraska Press, 1963), 603.

It attempts to counter the univocality of the 'traditional' legend by extending the definition of the Don Juan legend so that it includes female, if not feminist, voices—Wollstonecraft's *A Vindication of the Rights of Woman* (1792), George Sand's *Lélia* (1833), and the career of Madame Vestris, the most notorious Regency stage Don Giovanni. And it allows these alternative perspectives to comment on the commonplace assumption that Don Juan is not the seducer, but the seduced.

SEDUCTION IN *DON JUAN*

In Byron's *Don Juan* the hero's affairs are always initiated by the woman, regardless of whether she is extrovert, as her Grace Fitz-Fulke so evidently is, seemingly retiring, like Haidée, or a chance acquaintance like the Romagnole opera singer. The conventions of seduction are themselves reversed. In Richardson's infamous tale of seduction, the rakish Mr B hides in a closet while Mrs Jervis tells Pamela she hears only a cat.[6] When Don Juan is approached by Fitz-Fulke disguised as a ghostly Friar, he stumbles over the cat whose tread is '[s]o like a spiritual pit-a-pat | Or tiptoe of an amatory Miss, | Gliding the first time to a rendezvous' (XVI, 112). And Fitz-Fulke appropriates the games of the Rakehell club in dressing as a monk in order to seduce Don Juan. To dress as a woman was a trick frequently used by a libertine to deceive (as, for example, in Louvet's *Chevalier de Faublas*, 1787–90). In Byron's poem it is the desire of the woman (Gulbeyaz) which causes the hero to cross-dress. And the echoes within *Don Juan* of Henry Fielding's *Joseph Andrews* (1742) suggest that Byron was attempting to rewrite the traditional legend, just as Fielding had reversed the traditional genders of the guilty male/innocent female scenario in his parody of Richardson's *Pamela* (1740).[7]

---

[6] Samuel Richardson, *Pamela* (1740; Harmondsworth: Penguin, 1985), 95.

[7] Henry Fielding, *Joseph Andrews* (1742; Harmondsworth: Penguin, 1977). Compare Gulbeyaz's questioning of Don Juan (V, 116) with Lady Booby's of Joseph: 'she asked him, *if he had never been in Love?*' (bk i, ch. 5, p. 48) and Gulbeyaz's swift conjectures as to a suitable punishment for his refusal of her (V, 139) with Betty's deliberations concerning Joseph (bk i, ch. 18, p. 98). A comparison between Gulbeyaz and Lady Booby was made by *The Examiner* (26 Aug. 1821), 538.

Thus the pattern for seduction which the poem appears to offer is one of assertive woman and submitting and compliant Don Juan. It would certainly seem that Byron intended to demonstrate how in 'reality' the Don Juan of Regency England was likely to be female. In a letter to Hoppner (29 October 1819) in which he spoke of the early reception of *Don Juan* in England, he also referred to the rumours of his own Venetian 'conquests': 'I should like to know *who* has been carried off—except poor dear *me*. I have been more ravished myself than anybody since the Trojan War.'[8] In a later conversation with Medwin, referring specifically to *Don Juan* itself, Byron claimed he was being 'true to Nature in making the advances come from the females'.[9] Among the narrator's expressed 'intentions' is to educate the (male) reader who might share the popular misconception that women are always the victims of seduction and never its perpetrators. In Canto V, stanzas 130–1, for example, he openly cautions the naïve youths of Europe against the sexual predations of dowager ladies. And the reference to Potiphar's wife allusively connects Don Juan with the victimized Joseph, here and in his relationship with Donna Julia (I, 186).

Despite these obvious reversals, however, Byron's version demonstrates more similarity to than difference from the earliest traditions of the Don Juan legend. To a considerable extent, this was a result of the poem's conscious opposition, if not to the versions of the legend current in the Regency era, at least to the moral conservatism which influenced these new versions. Many of the versions of the Don Juan legend reflect the sexual politics current at their time of writing, a history of which is briefly outlined below. Byron's *Don Juan* is both a response to, and occasionally—if inadvertently—a reflection of, such questions.

Chapter 3 considered how the belief in the insatiable female sexual appetite aided the pervasive dissemination of the legend in the seventeenth century. Don Juan's 'egalitarianism'—for his

---

[8] *Byron's Letters and Journals*, ed. Leslie A. Marchand (London: John Murray, 1973–82), vi. 237. See also vi. 257 (to Murray, 10 Dec. 1819) and x. 178 (to Douglas Kinnaird, 21 May 1823).

[9] E. J. Lovell (ed.), *Medwin's Conversations with Lord Byron* (Princeton: Princeton University Press, 1969), 165.

conquests were made irrespective of class or status—served only to reinforce a more reactionary manifesto: all women were judged to be equal, but only in so far as they were equally inferior. And this inferiority was largely ascribed to their insatiable and uncontrollable sexual nature and its threat to the social order. This logic is neatly encapsulated in the progression of Byron's catalogue of Venetian conquests to Hobhouse and Kinnaird: 'some of them are Countesses—& some of them Cobblers wives—some noble—some middling—some low—& all whores'.[10] Moreover, the tradition of many of the Don Juan versions of warning their male spectators, evident in, for example, Clara and Flavia's jealousy of the sexual licence enjoyed by their 'English' counterparts, and continued in the address of Byron's *Don Juan* to men and about women, demonstrates how the apparently subversive nature of the Don Juan legend and its accompanying social satire often served instead to legitimize patriarchy. The uniformity of sexual appetite assumed among all classes of women highlights the way in which early versions of the legend not only admitted that women had a sexual nature, but perpetuated the belief that it was this characteristic which was shared universally and essentially—that it was in fact what made them women. They were thus rendered simultaneously attractive, available, and susceptible to Don Juan.

However, the perceived uniformity of female sexual insatiability gradually became outmoded with the new stratification of class sexualities and the emergence of middle-class hegemony. Throughout the eighteenth century, the emerging middle classes consolidated their position by distinguishing themselves from the promiscuity of the upper and working classes. Marriage alone could secure the structure of their emerging society. Because male desire required an object, and women were that infinitely provocative object, the social subordination of women to the will of men would ensure the containment of passion. The possibility of woman's civil, economic, and psychological independence was rejected because it would also evoke the independent and licentious exercise of her supposedly libidinous nature. The licentious cause of the downfall of

[10] *Byron's Letters and Journals*, vi. 92 (19 Jan. 1819).

empires (considered in Chapter 3) was also gendered, for it was effeminate luxury which would destroy civic virility.[11] In this way, Rousseau linked the potential of the new middle class to the simultaneous suppression and exploitation of woman's nature. The method advocated was to harness female sexual desire to the family unit and married chasteness. The prescriptive feminine ideal, of chastity, propriety, and correctness, quickly became descriptive proof of her moral superiority.

Although this ideal gathered ideological force throughout the eighteenth century as a quality proudly considered by the middle classes to be their own, in the post-Revolutionary years of the 1790s it was urged upon all classes as a cultivated reaction against the threat of perceived French excess. Pre-existing anxieties about the position of woman thus became still more intense after war with France broke out in 1793. Women were deluged with conduct books, sermons, homilies, novels, and magazine articles insisting that good order and political stability necessitated the maintenance of separate spheres. Richard Polwhele's *The Unsex'd Females* (1798), Bishop George Horne's tract, *Picture of the Female Character as it ought to appear when formed* (1799), and John Bowles's *Remarks on Modern Female Manners, as Distinguished by Indifference to Character, and Indecency of Dress* (1802) indicate even within their titles an adherence to this conservatism.

The ideal of the chaste and correct woman was also one which women themselves helped to perpetuate and this is reflected within *Don Juan* in Donna Inez's conscious adoption of proper behaviour (I, 16). Donna Inez attempts to emulate the feminine qualities urged upon women by the novels of Maria Edgeworth, the books on education by Sarah Trimmer, and Hannah More's popular *Coelebs in Search of a Wife, comprehending Observations on Domestic Habits and Manners, Religion and Morals* (1809). This last celebrated the ideal woman of Lucilla Stanley as being devoted to domestic duties, religious, modest in dress, silent unless spoken to, deferential to men, and devoted to good works. The work ran into eleven editions within nine months. Mary Poovey, in *The Proper Lady and the Woman Writer* (1984), described woman's relation to sexual desire at this time as

---

[11] See Franklin, *Byron's Heroines*, 107.

'mediate'. Desire might centre on and return to a woman, but it could not originate in her emotions, her imagination, or her body:

as the immediate social turmoil of the revolutionary decades subsided, women were again more frequently applauded for their moral virtues than reprimanded for their wayward appetites. Rapidly, women's position was consolidated. As embodiments of the pure ideals of the middle classes, they were celebrated during the nineteenth century for their superiority to all earthly desires.[12]

Chapter 3 considered how even radical circles of the first decades of the nineteenth century became morally conservative, supporting marriage and strict, though especially female, chastity. This was evident in the 'chivalrous' defence of Queen Caroline's honour by radical writers and the image which they perpetuated of the 'unprotected female' assailed by the might of the crown.[13] The notion that women had a unique moral mission to perform was thus popular among all kinds of groups, anti-feminist as well as feminist. Its ideological function was highly ambiguous. In anti-feminist discourse, it usually served to buttress sentimental dogmas of domestic womanhood which allowed women to rule the private sphere of the home. And among feminist writers it led to a celebration of female specialness and moral superiority which jostled uneasily with arguments against the concept of an innate femininity. This latter perspective has been seen as exemplified in the writing of Mary Wollstonecraft and especially in *A Vindication of the Rights of Woman* (1792). While accepting Rousseau's description of women as suffused in sensuality, Wollstonecraft ascribed the cause to culture rather than nature and exhorted middle-class women to moral rectitude and reason. Woman's pleasure was rejected as a temporary expedient while it remained inextricably bound to her dependent and deferential status: 'Supposing, however, for a moment, that women were, in some future revolution of time, to become, what I sincerely wish them to be,

---

[12] Mary Poovey, *The Proper Lady and the Woman Writer* (Chicago: University of Chicago Press, 1984), 34.

[13] See Leonore Davidoff and Catherine Hall, *Family Fortunes: Men and Women of the English Middle Class, 1780–1850* (London: Century Hutchinson, 1987), 152.

even love would acquire more serious dignity, and be purified in its own fires . . .'.[14]

Wollstonecraft's moral puritanism has been regarded as illustrative of the limited appeal of *A Vindication*—that it is an appeal on behalf of, and voiced by, middle-class woman.[15] However, her own repression of passion was culturally determined. Convention, either idealizing women as sexually passive or condemning them as wantons, predetermined the limits of articulation within which Wollstonecraft could make her argument. Indeed, the dissemination and reception of *A Vindication* was considerably curtailed after the sexual scandal caused by Godwin's publication of his biographical memoirs of his wife. A life which had included a public male lover, an illegitimate child, and a second conceived out of wedlock, obviously did not represent the kind of moral conduct urged as proper for a woman.[16]

It is an historical irony that Wollstonecraft, who was censured as sexually irresponsible and wanton, is today considered by many feminists to present a problematical puritanism, a negative construction of female sexuality with which the present conflict over sexual politics is still partly preoccupied.[17] However, if *A Vindication* is reconsidered as a response to libertine thinking, among which Wollstonecraft would have included Rousseau, then its full polemical address must be understood as part of a wider debate, including what Wollstonecraft was arguing against. This would 'vindicate' her vehemence and apparent extremity. *A Vindication* might thus be interpreted as a response to the Don Juan legend, though it is never explicitly addressed (or 'intended') as such. That Wollstonecraft's target was a specifically libertine discourse is apparent in her comments on relationships between the sexes: 'I only exclaim against the sexual desire of conquest when the heart is out of the question . . .'. The 'voluptuary', who puts the 'refinements

[14] Mary Wollstonecraft, *A Vindication of the Rights of Women* (1792; repr. Harmondsworth: Penguin, 1992), ch. 6, p. 227.

[15] See Mike Gane, *Harmless Lovers? Gender, Theory and Personal Relationships* (London: Routledge, 1993), 63–74.

[16] See Regina M. Jones, 'On the Reception of Mary Wollstonecraft's *A Vindication of the Rights of Woman*', *Journal of the History of Ideas*, 39 (1978), 293–302.

[17] See Cora Kaplan, *Sea Changes* (London: Verso, 1986), ch. 2, 'Wild Nights: Pleasure/Sexuality/Feminism', pp. 31–56.

of love out of the question', makes women the slaves of 'casual lust', if not 'literally speaking, standing dishes to which every glutton may have access'.[18] It is an error to claim that Wollstonecraft rejects female desire as degrading because throughout *A Vindication* a careful distinction is maintained between the heartless seducer and the genuine lover, who loves 'the individual, not the sex'. Her advice to women is therefore to refuse the rake, not the sincerely passionate lover. Dr Gregory in *Legacy to his Daughters* advises that a proper 'womanly' behaviour is to be reserved, to admit of no frankness. Wollstonecraft adds: 'This desire of being always women, is the very consciousness that degrades the sex—excepting with a lover, I must repeat with emphasis, a former observation . . .'.[19]

George Sand's version of the Don Juan legend, *Lélia* (1839), follows the feminism of Mary Wollstonecraft's *A Vindication* in that it also urges women to refuse the seduction offered by the libertine. In this novel Sand was consciously rewriting not just the Don Juan legend but a particular, and new, version of it. The ideology of the virtuous and morally impeccable woman was reflected in many of the versions of the Don Juan legend written during the Romantic period. Although earlier versions often included women who attempted to redeem Don Juan through virtuous love (for example, Molière's Done Elvira and Shadwell's Leonora), their attempts were always ineffectual. Alonso de Córdoba y Maldonado's version, *La venganza en el sepulchro* (1690s), was the only exception in portraying its Don Juan as faithfully in love with Doña Ana. It anticipated a direction which became prevalent in the Romantic period. In E. T. A. Hoffmann's *Don Juan* (1813), Mozart's Don Giovanni and Donna Anna are portrayed as genuinely in love with one another and the contemporary idealization of woman is reflected in Hoffmann's portrayal of Donna Anna as an embodiment of purity and incorruptibility. Hoffmann's story is frequently cited as having 'romanticized' the legend. However the Regency Don Giovanni burlesques also shared this pattern. In the Drury Lane pantomime of the legend, *Harlequin's Vision* (1817), Don Juan repents of his former follies and begs forgiveness of his wife,

[18] Wollstonecraft, *A Vindication*, ch. 4, p. 148; p. 254.
[19] Ibid., ch. 5, pp. 197, 202.

Donna Elvira, for abandoning her. Moncrieff's burlesque, *Giovanni in London* (1817), was subtitled *The Libertine Reclaimed*, as Don Giovanni was reformed by marriage to the obviously named Constantia.

That these changes to the legend were effected as a consequence of the prevailing ideology of correct womanhood is demonstrated by a version of the legend which also participated in the prescriptive discourse concerning female conduct: 'The Libertine Reclaimed, a Tale', printed in *The Lady's Magazine* of April 1795. In this story the profligate Mr Fairfax, who has accumulated debts and risks losing his estate, chooses marriage to a wealthy heiress as the solution to his obvious financial difficulties. When he predictably returns to his dissolute life, the couple separate, and the wife endeavours to forget her faithless husband, 'in her admiration of the beauties of nature and her attention to the education of her child'. Later, roused by an insult to his mistress, Fairfax challenges the offender and is wounded in the subsequent duel near the country retreat of his wife. She compassionately goes to his assistance and her subsequent care of her estranged husband ensures his recovery. Meanwhile, his mistress, on hearing that Fairfax has been taken to his wife's house, swiftly exchanges him for another man. The exceptional fidelity and tenderness of Fairfax's wife immediately convert him to a love of virtue: 'Most amiable and best of women, whom Providence seems to have bestowed on me to be my guardian angel . . .'. The moral is not reserved for the ending of the tale but, evading any risk of misinterpretation (often a hazard in versions of the Don Juan legend), pre-empts its telling. In the first paragraph the female reader is told that: 'To suffer with patience, to rise superior to misfortune, and to repay unmerited ill-treatment with benevolence, are virtues which not only promote the happiness of those who can exercise them, but frequently recall the licentious to the pains of their duty.'[20] The reformation of Don Juan was ideologically necessary to the writers and readers of the ladies' magazines, since it was the only way (barring refusal) in which woman could be seen to triumph morally. The heroine of this version had, of course, first married the rake.

[20] *The Lady's Magazine*, 26 (Apr. 1795), 159–60.

These tales of the reclaimed Don Juan continued in many nineteenth-century versions. In Pushkin's *The Stone Guest* (first written in 1830 and published in 1839), Don Juan is an amiable young man converted to true love by Anna. In Alfred de Musset's 'Namouna' (1832), Théophile Gautier's *La Comédie de la Mort* (1838), and Nikolaus Lenau's *Don Juan* (1844), Don Juan is searching for an ideal woman, one who might combine erotic and sacred qualities or incarnate all the pleasures of collective womanhood.[21] Zorrilla's *Don Juan Tenorio* (1844) depicts Don Juan redeemed through his love for Doña Inés. The spirit of these versions is succinctly expressed by Sténio in George Sand's *Lélia* (1839): 'And do you know, my sisters, what this angel did when it was transformed into a woman? It loved Don Juan and made him fall in love too, before purifying and converting him.'[22]

It is curious that myth-criticism of the legend has frequently aligned Byron's poem with the tradition of Romanticism which is typical of the early nineteenth-century versions.[23] The modern editor of *Lélia* annotated Sténio's speech as referring specifically to Byron's *Don Juan*.[24] The earliest translations of Byron's poem into Spanish were retitled *Don Juan, o El hijo de Doña Inés*, and this filial emphasis was reinforced by being deliberately added to the first stanza: 'Quiero celebrar a nuestro antiguo amigo don Juan, *el hijo de Doña Inés*, todos le hemos visto . . .' and 'Prefiero celebrar las hazañas de nuestro comun y antiguo amigo don Juan, *el hijo de Doña Inés*, a quien todos hemos visto que . . .' (my italics).[25] Such adjustments would have attracted the Spanish reader's attention to an allusion to the more celebrated and topical work of Zorrilla, whose Don Juan was loved and reclaimed by Doña Inés. First performed in

---

[21] Alfred de Musset, 'Namouna' (1832); see also J. W. Smeed, *Don Juan* (London: Routledge, 1990), 56 (Gautier) and Henry T. Finck, *Richard Strauss: The Man and his Work* (Boston: Little Brown, 1917), 166 (Lenau).

[22] George Sand, *Lélia*, ed. Pierre Reboul (Paris: Garnières Frères, 1960), *La Lélia de 1839*, ch. 62, p. 513: 'Et savez-vous, mes sœurs, ce que fit l'ange, quand il fut métamorphosé en femme? Il aima don Juan et s'en fit aimer, afin de le purifier et de le convertir.'

[23] See e.g. Jean Massin, *Don Juan: Mythe littéraire et musical* (Paris: Éditions Stock, 1979), 91–2.

[24] Sand, *Lélia*, 290.

[25] *Don Juan, o El hijo de Doña Inés* (Madrid, 1843–4), 7. *Don Juan: El hijo de Doña Inés*, 2 vols. (Madrid, 1876), i. 9.

1844, this play was therefore associated with the Spanish translations of Byron's poem of 1844 and 1876, despite its strictly anachronistic allusion.

More recent commentators have highlighted the idyll with Haidée to support their comparison of Byron's and Zorrilla's variations.[26] It was this episode which, more than any other, was chosen as a subject by painters of scenes from Byron's *Don Juan*: four lithographs by the French artist Nicholas Eustache Maurin (1799–1850), painted in 1837; a crayon sketch by Delacroix (1798–1863); a small oil-painting by Alfred Johannot (1800–37); an oil-painting by Ford Madox Brown (1821–93); in 1874 by the French artist Alfred-Philippe Roll (1846–1919); in 1839 by Claude-Marie Dubufe (1790–1864); and by Claude-Louis Muller (1819–92).[27] That of Ford Madox Brown is especially interesting—the one English painter to adopt the subject of Don Juan's rescue by Haidée, his tableau is that of a pietà, as a supine Don Juan encircles the cross of an oar with one leg, and Haidée stands over him as *mater dolorosa*. Byron's 'idyll', however, is structured ironically by its belated appearance in the poem, and by its subsequent disappearance from the narrative, a mere interlude in the continuing serialization of the hero's love affairs. The positioning and hasty termination of the Don Juan–Haidée idyll parallels the doubts which many spectators felt concerning the moral ending of traditional treatments of the Don Juan legend in which the abruptness and brevity of the ending seemed to ironize the gesture of morality itself—although it probably contributed to the very poignancy which inspired painters and later writers.

The consideration of the 'romanticism' of Byron's version of the legend returns to the question of the interpretation of Don Juan himself. To argue that the episode with Haidée represents the 'reclamation' of the seducer is to interpret his character benevolently—a reading which was not effected by many of the poem's contemporary readers. However, if Don Juan is interpreted as a traditional seducer, many of the poem's heroines then appear as abandoned females. If *Don Juan* attempted to portray its female characters as more worthy of the appellation

---

[26] See e.g. José Luis Blanco y Quiñones, *Lord Byron* (Madrid: EPESA, 1971), 155.
[27] *La Passion selon Don Juan*, 128–33.

of seducers, the attempt was frustrated by the narrative focus upon Don Juan. The poem dictates that he move on, without considering how the very expendability of its heroines might ensure them a sympathetic reading, or at any rate frustrate the attempt to portray them as female rakes. This consequence can be interpreted interstitially from Byron's discussion of his intentions for the poem with Medwin in 1822:

I left him in the seraglio. There I shall make one of the favourites, a Sultana . . . fall in love with him, and carry him off from Constantinople . . . Well, they make good their escape to Russia; where, if Juan's passion cools, and I don't know what to do with the lady, I shall make her die of the plague. England . . . In his suite he shall have a girl whom he rescued during one of his northern campaigns, who shall be in love with him, and he not with her.[28]

If Byron's female characters are the true Don Juans of the poem, as modern criticism would imply, they never exhibit the 'cooling passion' so typical of the restless seducer and here significantly linked to the poem's eponymous hero. Don Juan is separated from each relationship and the females are left to pine his absence in conventionally feminine fashion. Donna Julia's letter to Don Juan expresses the conventional lament of the 'abandoned' woman: 'You will proceed in beauty and in pride, | Beloved and loving many. All is o'er | For me on earth . . .' (I, 195). Her destiny is envisaged as an apparently contradictory future life: woman's fate may be 'to love again, and be again undone', but Donna Julia's resides in the convent. Similarly the prediction that Don Juan and Haidée would wither apart (IV, 10 and 27) proves true only for her and her unborn child. Haidée's dream (IV, 31–5), like that of Dudù (VI, 75–7), is prophetically one of abandonment and betrayal (both Haidée and Dudù may be said to be 'betrayed' in that Don Juan fails to remember them). The complaint of Donna Julia's letter is replicated quite literally in Haidée's case. Bereft of Don Juan, she becomes empty (IV, 58–73), with no memory, no response or recognition, no appetite, no pulse, no voice, and no memorial of a grave. Her only commemoration is in song as an example to other love-lorn women: 'many a Greek maid in a loving song | Sighs o'er her name' (IV, 73). Indeed, because the

---

[28] Lovell (ed.), *Medwin's Conversations*, 164–5.

poem is compelled to follow the fate of its hero, Don Juan's catalogue of lovers is foregrounded, despite the poem's manifesto of his innocence. The experience of female promiscuity is therefore outside the poem's control because the narrative itself chooses not to enact it. The vaunted immorality of women remains within the rhetoric of the narrator, himself an embodiment of specifically masculine libertinism. While the frankly libidinous heroines—Gulbeyaz, Catherine, and Fitz-Fulke—will certainly have other lovers, these future lovers lie beyond the limits of the narrative and consequently carry little or no imaginative conviction. Thus despite the narrator's repeated claims that woman's constancy is a 'myth', the structural monogamy of Byron's heroines within the frame of the poem reveals more similarity than difference from traditional treatments of the Don Juan legend.

Considerations of the seducer/seduced debate have been complicated by the conflation between seduction and betrayal which is usually assumed. If Byron's heroines 'seduce' Don Juan, they do not desert him but rather are abandoned by him. And while Byron's heroines might be categorized as 'seducers' of the vulnerable Don Juan, this is true only in so far as they initiate the sexual relationship. After this initial step, they relinquish much of the 'power' which this gesture is seen to represent. In the Russian court the traditional attributes of the sexes are certainly reversed—the women ogle Don Juan, the male courtiers tremble with jealousy (IX, 78), and the imperious position of Catherine demonstrates that acts of tyranny are not gender-specific. However, Catherine resumes a conventionally feminine adoration of her lover in her private affairs: 'each lover looked a sort of king . . . I A royal husband in all save the ring' (IX, 70). Moreover, her unselfish relinquishing of the ailing Don Juan displays a disinterest and unpossessiveness which is not entirely consonant with a character who is otherwise portrayed as tyrannous, and whose sexuality is consistently portrayed as obscenely rampant. Those critics who have interpreted the scene of Lambro's court in his absence as a portrait of an effeminate society have metonymously assumed that the new ruler is Haidée. However they forget that, as reported in the servants' account of life since Lambro's 'death', Haidée has yielded power to Don Juan: ' "Our mistress!" quoth a third,

"Our mistress—pooh— | You mean our master—not the old but new"' (III, 43).

The relationship between Byron's version and the traditional Don Juan legend is therefore more intricate than a straightforward inversion would imply. In George Sand's version, for example, the legend is more accurately 'reversed', in that Lélia urges the novitiates to refuse the seduction which Don Juan—and Sténio in his telling of Don Juan—extend. Sténio portrays Don Juan as rescued by an angel in the incarnation of woman because he himself is attempting to woo Lélia. And since he delivers his speech as a kind of moral lesson for the edification of an assembled audience of nuns and novitiates, an audience for which the story of Don Juan is, unusually, new, Lélia feels compelled to refute his 'mythological' tale:

Learn, my children, that in this time of strange despairs and inexplicable fantasies, Don Juan has become a type, a symbol, a glory, almost a divinity. Women like men who resemble Don Juan. Women imagine themselves to be angels who have received from heaven the mission and the power to save all these Don Juans. Friends, like the legendary angel the women do not save the men and are instead damned with them.[29]

The depiction of libidinous women in *Don Juan* is the poem's most confrontational policy towards the prevailing tradition of virtuous heroines and a deliberate rejection of the incarnated angels of Romantic versions of the legend. It also remains entirely consonant with the earlier traditions of the Don Juan legend, for Byron's poem spoke of female passion in a way which was quite unprecedented in the reactionary years after Waterloo, and in a way which was certainly inadmissible to contemporary women writers. Thus, despite the reviewers' censures of *Don Juan*'s subject and style, its price and consequent readership, their greatest fury was reserved for its portrayal of women. The review of the Don Juan–Gulbeyaz episode by *The Literary Gazette* (11 August 1821) is typical of the outrage at the

---

[29] Sand, *Lélia, La Lélia de 1839*, ch. 62, p. 513: 'Apprenez, mes enfants, que, dans ce temps d'étranges désespoirs et d'inexplicables fantasies, don Juan est devenu un type, un symbole, une gloire, presque une divinité. Les hommes plaisent aux femmes en ressemblant à don Juan. Les femmes s'imaginent être des anges et avoir reçu du ciel la mission et la puissance de sauver tous ces don Juans; amis, comme l'ange de la légende, elles ne les convertissent pas, et elles se perdent avec eux.'

poem's depiction of openly licentious women. It attacked the episode as describing: 'the abominations of Oriental customs, or the hardly less disgusting picture of female passion seeking gratification in the most direct and coarsest way'.[30] Female flirtation is so invariable that even the apparently chaste Donna Inez is revealed to be only hypocritically chaste. She too has a scandalous past in her affair with Alfonso and it is this affair which determines subsequent events, since it explains Donna Inez's deliberate myopia concerning Don Juan and Donna Julia (I, 101, ll. 7–8).

The narrator's stressing of female libidinousness at times overrides narrative and psychological plausibility. Donna Julia's indignant protestation of innocence includes an indiscreet allusion to the certainty of a 'future' lover: 'Was it for this that no *cortejo* ere | I yet have chosen from out the youth of Seville?' (I, 148). Her letter of female tragedy, often cited as a sympathetic depiction of the narrow and thus necessarily obsessive lives of women, is not entirely traditional in its trope of female abandonment. The overlooked subversion of Donna Julia's lament that woman's destiny is 'to love again, and be again undone' (I, 194) is that woman is ultimately consolable. The more unorthodox implication is indirectly betrayed by Mary Shelley's quotation of and comment upon this passage in a letter to Teresa Guiccioli after Byron's death (May 1824):

Didn't dear Byron himself say (he who knew so thoroughly the female heart) that the whole of woman's existence depends on love, and therefore losing a love there is no other refuge than

> To love again and be again undone

But we, dear Guiccioli, are deprived of this refuge. Destiny gave to both of us the first spirits of the age, loving them, there is no second love.[31]

Mary Shelley attempts to commend the sentiments of the line for its accuracy in the delineation of woman: Byron 'knew so thoroughly the female heart'. Yet she quotes the one line which is not applicable to her, or to Teresa Guiccioli's, case. Their

---

[30] *The Literary Gazette* (11 Aug. 1821), 497–500, 497, review of Cantos III–V.
[31] *The Letters of Mary Wollstonecraft Shelley*, i. 420–1 (May 1824). Teresa, however, did remarry.

experience instead conforms with and reinforces the ideology of the virtuously faithful woman, whose constancy to her lover continues even beyond his death. The very choice of Don Juan was intended as a rebuke to this convention, for in selecting the legendary seducer after dismissing more traditional military heroes (I, 2–5) Byron exposed the erotic desire with which Regency women invested their heroes (see Chapter 4).

The promiscuity of women is assumed, sometimes casually, by the narrator throughout the poem. The venereal disease which infects the master's mate of the longboat was presented '[b]y general subscription of the ladies' (II, 81). The Sultan maintains the 'virginity' (more correctly the chastity) of his concubines only with the aid of guards, sentries, an imperious 'Mother of the Maids', bolts, a wall, and, most sinisterly, now and then an 'example' (VI, 32). His eunuch slave, Baba, grumbles against the immorality of 'all women of whate'er condition' (VI, 117), an echo of the sexual 'egalitarianism' espoused by many Don Juans. In Canto VI, stanza 94, the narrator describes all pedigrees as being tainted by the infidelity of some distant and specifically female relative whose promiscuity is circuitously expressed in the description of her as 'the antipodes of Timon | That hater of mankind'. Supposedly 'chaste' matrons are fond of adulterous 'marriage in disguise' (IX, 76; see also VI, 24 and VIII, 27). And while the description of a wife—'[w]hose husband only knows her not a whore' (IV, 17)—appears to balance between the motif of deceptive appearances (only the husband can validate her chastity) and that of insatiable woman (the cuckolded husband alone is blind to his wife's infidelities), the previous line makes only the second reading possible: 'Where Hymen's torch but brands one strumpet more'. Even Eve's action in Eden becomes libidinized, for it is a fond search which has Eve literally groping for the apple (IX, 19).

The consistency of female response to Don Juan is therefore absolute. In the chance encounter with the Romagnole singer, she displays obvious willingness; on his entrance at Catherine's court, the Russian ladies leer lustily at him; in England he is quickly evaluated as a potential husband. Adeline, who was professedly 'a pitch beyond a coxcomb's flight' (XIV, 57), succumbs. Aurora shows signs of softening towards Juan (XVI, 92–

3) and inspires a digression on the sexual fantasies of 16-year-old girls (XV, 86). Like the delineation of Don Juan, the portrayal of Aurora in this section (XV, 80–6) deliberately encourages uncertainty with a haze of contaminating insinuations and juxtapositions, defensive prepositions and doubting qualifications. The narrator openly declares the provisionality of his report—Aurora's smile contemplating Don Juan might not be historical fact but only a guess, presumably a guessing of the behaviour expected of a young girl facing Don Juan (XV, 80). Although Adeline's fears that her rival might 'thaw to a coquette' are dismissed (XV, 81, l. 8), the subsequent line insinuates otherwise in the use of its connecting preposition: '*But* Juan had a sort of winning way' (XV, 82, l. 1, my emphasis). Aurora is flattered by Don Juan's attentions: 'from such slight things will great commence' is added as an aside (XV, 83, l. 5). '*And then* he had good looks . . .' seems to presume that such an explanation is necessary (XV, 84, my italics). The returning insistence in stanza 85 that Aurora is uninterested is quickly undermined by the narrator's disquisition upon how no one—including such august figures as Virtue and Socrates—can be exempt from possible lapses. If such seemingly irrelevant digressions do not presume an association, they nevertheless create it:

> Aurora, who looked more on books than faces,
> Was very young, although so very sage,
> Admiring more Minerva than the Graces,
> Especially upon a printed page.
> But Virtue's self with all her tightest laces
> Has not the natural stays of strict old age,
> And Socrates, that model of all duty,
> Owned to a penchant, though discreet, for beauty.
>
> And girls of sixteen are thus far Socratic,
> But innocently so, as Socrates.
> And really if the sage sublime and Attic
> At seventy years had phantasies like these,
> Which Plato in his dialogues dramatic
> Has shown, I know not why they should displease
> In virgins; always in a modest way,
> Observe, for that with me's a *sine quâ*.
>
>   (XV, 85–6)

These stanzas seem to argue Aurora's reserve and susceptibility in turn. But ultimately Aurora is implicated in the innuendoes on Socratic 'phantasies' and the impression that remains is that she may yield to Don Juan.

Byron's 'revision' of the Don Juan legend is a critical commonplace. However, this did not include the portrayal of a woman who might resist his seducer, perhaps because it would have concurred with the prevailing ideology of the virtuous woman against which he was reacting, or perhaps because of his own attraction to the Don Juan 'myth' in which all women invariably fall in love with the seducer. Byron's version of the legend was thus to depict women who would both irresistibly succumb to passion for Don Juan and would frequently initiate the sexual relationship in order to satisfy this desire. It was a portrayal which was impossible for contemporary women writers: seduction by a genuine lover could only be 'passively' accepted and never initiated. In her novel *Patronage* (1814), Maria Edgeworth portrayed the ideal of female behaviour in the character of Caroline Percy. She carefully represses any incipient passion she might feel for an undeclared lover, Colonel Hungerford: 'I cannot forget, that the delicacy, honor, pride, prudence of our sex, forbid a woman to think of any man, as a lover, till he gives her reason to believe, that he feels love for her'. Edgeworth vindicates this restraint by making Colonel Hungerford choose another. In *Memoirs of Emma Courtney* (1796), Mary Hays created a passionate heroine who does not follow convention by waiting for a male declaration of love. Her readers were duly scandalized, although the novel ultimately cautioned against such improper behaviour: Emma Courtney's frankness in her letters to Augustus Harley proved ill-advised since he was already married.[32]

Don Juan denies the 'propriety' of the conventional prescription and the prevailing ideology which determines it. Nevertheless, the pressure which the ideology exerted upon the text is evident interstitially, for, in order to portray female sexuality in a frank and approbatory manner, the poem was forced to envisage circumstances in which such a portrayal would be possible.

---

[32] Maria Edgeworth, *Patronage*, vol. ii, ch. 18, p. 211. See also Elinor's similarly unfortunate declaration of love to Harleigh in Fanny Burney, *The Wanderer; or Female Difficulties* (1814; repr. London: Pandora Press, 1988), p. 160 (ch. 18).

Although the female characters of *Don Juan* take the sexual initiative, their behaviour is possible only when circumscribed within strictly limited configurations. These special circumstances undermine the attempted naturalization of the female seducer and reveal the element of conscious polemic within Byron's rewriting of the legend. If his Don Juan is an inauthentic libertine, allowing himself to be ('passively') seduced, the poem manipulates scenes to a considerable extent in order to create the circumstances under which this might apply, a process of 'build[ing] up common things with commonplaces' (XIV, 7).

The 'strength' of the female characters, for example, occurs, and is only possible, because Don Juan is 'weak'. Donna Julia is forced to take the initiative in the relationship with Don Juan, who, however precocious in his mother's eyes, is a naïve and timid 16. She has all the 'natural' advantages over him of seven years' seniority and of marriage. After this initiation Don Juan can never again plead the cause of sexual inexperience which was his defence from moral accusation in Canto I. However, the Don Juan who is nurtured by Haidée is as little able to precipitate an affair, washed up half-senseless after near-death by shipwreck and starvation. His illness and exhaustion make him doubly vulnerable and in need of care, which the rather timid Haidée is then emboldened to effect. Later exiled and beaten by Lambro and his servants, his wounds prevent a response to the proffered charms of the Romagnole singer. Gulbeyaz and Catherine both dominate in their relationships with Don Juan due to their considerable superiority in age and status: Gulbeyaz is a favourite of the Sultan and is 'ripe' in age (it is suggested in Canto V, stanza 98, that she is 26), Catherine is Empress of Russia and is menopausal (X, 24 and 47). They respectively own and employ Don Juan. Of the dynamics between Don Juan and Dudù, little is revealed—an omission of the one liaison where the woman epitomizes languishing sensuality (although Dudù does possess some kind of authority over Don Juan in introducing him to harem procedure). In England, Don Juan regains his position of submission in the pattern of his relationships with Lady Adeline and her Grace Fitz-Fulke, this time due to his status as a foreigner, as someone who is unfamiliar with the codes of English society life and needs guidance as to correct etiquette. Fitz-Fulke's proficiency in courting sexual scandal obviously makes her an experienced player. Adeline's labouring of her forty days' superiority in 'age' is mocked (XIV, 52) but it does allow her to justify her domineering role of moral counsellor towards Don Juan. Aurora alone manages to surpass Don Juan in timidity, although her most 'encouraging' smile (XVI, 93) is significantly a consequence of his abstraction. The continually changing circumstances therefore allow Don Juan to retain his position of inferiority throughout the poem. These female 'seducers' could, and sometimes do, justify their behaviour as Fielding's Slipslop rationalized the necessity of taking the initiative when making love to Joseph Andrews: 'If we like a man, the lightest hint *sophisticates*. Whereas a boy *proposes* upon us to break through all the *regulations* of modesty, before we can make any *oppression* upon him.' Since Byron borrowed Fielding's ensuing image of the pike and the roach to describe the female sexual appetite (see XIV, 26), it is likely that he knew this passage and perhaps would have enjoyed such malapropisms as the confusion between 'impression' and 'oppression'.[33]

In addition, it is also suggested that the dynamics of these relationships are unusual, for these 'strong' female characters are otherwise in positions of submission. Donna Julia has hitherto been faithful to a considerably older and busier Don Alfonso. Indeed, it is largely because she has been a faithful wife that her indignant display of innocence proves convincing. Haidée has always yielded filially to the indulgence of Lambro. Gulbeyaz abhors the Sultan (VI, 90) and errs from inanition (VI, 9), sharing her husband with 1,500 concubines and three wives. Lady Adeline compromises her integrity in order to further her husband's political career: the guests with whom she ingratiates herself are secretly despised, whatever the narrator's spirited defence of 'mobilité'. Even her Grace Fitz-Fulke hints at previous grounds for complaint in her marriage, though any sympathy is dissipated by the narrator's irony:

> And Hayley's *Triumphs*, which she deemed pathetic,
> Because, she said, her temper had been tried

---

[33] Fielding, *Joseph Andrews*, bk i, ch. 6, p. 52.

So much. The bard had really been prophetic
Of what she had gone through with, since a bride.

(XVI, 50)

The dazzling power of the women's uncharacteristic domi-
nance in their relationships with Don Juan disguises the special
circumstances which have produced it in the first place.

Don Juan's notable effeminacy also entails that traditional
gendered ascriptions of masculine/strength and feminine/
weakness do not apply and the characteristically maternal nature of the relationships reinforces this sense of the 'passivity' of
the seduced Don Juan. Both traits are significant to the project
of this book as a whole and its argument for a more inclusive
definition of the legend, because both Don Juan's effeminacy
and filiality anticipate many twentieth-century psychoanalytical
interpretations of the 'myth'. These concurrences of Byron's
Don Juan with modern psychoanalytical theories are not intended as indexes of the 'truth' of the legend. To argue that
Byron's version is consonant with such thinking is not to claim
that his Don Juan must therefore be authentic. Modern
feminisms have questioned the truth-claims of psychoanalysis
while accepting it as a discourse which is descriptive of socio-
historical reality rather than essentially 'true'. It is because these
cultural and ideological readings have been shared so extensively—by literature and its interpretation—that they appear as
truth.[34] The psychoanalytical 'versions' are considered here because their similarity to Byron's *Don Juan* argues for, or at least
supports, the inclusion of Byron's poem within the legend. It is
certainly paradoxical that Byron's version, which shares many
characteristics with later theoretical discourse on the legend,
has been neglected by literary and traditional myth-critics.[35]

In 1924 Otto Rank published *The Don Juan Legend*, the first
full-length psychoanalytical reading of the legend. He argued
that the legend's power resided in its telling of the male's

[34] See James Bennet Mandrell, *Don Juan and the Point of Honour* (Philadelphia:
Pennsylvania State University Press, 1992), 45.

[35] One recent exception is David Punter, who addresses the psychology of Byron
and *Don Juan* through psychoanalytical approaches to the Don Juan legend, including that of Otto Rank. '*Don Juan*, or, the Deferral of Decapitation', in Nigel Wood
(ed.), *Don Juan: Theory in Practice* (Buckingham: Open University Press, 1993),
122–53.

doomed pursuit of the mother, rooted in the biological wish for exclusive possession of her: 'the characteristic male fantasy of conquering countless women, which has made the hero into a masculine ideal, is ultimately based on the unattainability of the mother and the compensatory substitute for her'.[36] Don Juan ultimately fulfils this primal desire by being 'swallowed' by the grave, an obvious womb symbol according to Rank's theory. In early versions of the legend Don Juan's mother was always absent. The Don Juans of, for example, Tirso de Molina and Molière, have dramatic arguments with their fathers who subsequently disown their sons. In Byron's *Don Juan*, however, Don Jóse is a relatively, and given his habit of philandering a provocatively, insignificant influence upon his son's life. Byron's version was instead the first to include a portrayal of the seducer's mother, and it was for this reason that Otto Rank referred to Byron's poem within his consideration of the Don Juan legend. Claiming that the heroines of the versions represented mother-figures, Rank catalogued examples of the faithless or 'untrue' mother as being typical of the later versions of the legend: 'as in Holtie (1834) and Byron (1819–1824), who gave the hero a fickle mother, or in Pushkin (1830), where Laura is as faithless and wanton as the hero himself'.[37]

In 'The Legend over Time' (chapter 9), in which he considered the historical adaptations made by the legend's successive authors, Rank again cited Byron's version as paradigmatic of his argument:

As a prototype of the etiological motivation, one would cite the poem of Byron (1819–24), who had the hero grow up under the influence of an overly affectionate mother and an unfaithful, plainly 'donjuanesque' father, about whose escapades the mother kept a 'catalogue'. The identification with the father then finds poetic expression in the first romantic adventure of the sexually unenlightened hero with an obviously unfaithful 'mother figure'. It continues in the heroically-tinged rescue of the principal character by a tender loving woman.[38]

---

[36] Otto D. Rank, *The Don Juan Legend*, tr. David G. Winter (1924; repr. Princeton: Princeton University Press, 1975), 95.
[37] Ibid., ch. 8, p. 101.
[38] Ibid., pp. 109–10.

Rank's analysis of Don Juan's ultimate fate as symbolic of his return to the womb/grave might also be perceived in the Don Juan–Haidée scenario: she becomes the vampiric figure who 'o'er him still as death | Bent, with hushed lips, that drank his scarce drawn breath' (II, 143).

Oedipal configurations are apparent throughout Byron's *Don Juan*—as in the triangular relationships of Don Juan with Donna Julia and Don Alfonso; with Haidée and Lambro; with Gulbeyaz and the Sultan; with Lady Adeline and Lord Henry Amundeville; and with her Grace Fitz-Fulke and Fitz-Fulke himself—in which the third party always represents a cultural obstacle to the sexual liaison of the first two, whether as husband or as father. This is also usually the case in variations of the Don Juan legend, in which the obstacle is not always the father of more frequently canonized versions (Tirso's Don Gonzalo de Ulloa; da Ponte's Commendatore), but sometimes an unspecified figure of authority (Molière's Commandeur) or a brother (Shadwell's Don Octavio). In addition, Don Juan's attraction to a woman is often a consequence of her married status and, as we have seen, it is this which makes so many of the Don Juan versions seem politically subversive.

In Byron's poem the Oedipal structure is most overt in the first of Don Juan's sexual encounters where the obstacle, Don Alfonso, is, or at any rate has been, the lover of his mother— whereas the potential Oedipal dramas of the final two triangles are diffused as Lord Henry and Fitz-Fulke fail to 'materialize' as true obstacles.[39] Most crucially for a feminist consideration of Byron's poem, there is also an implied maternity in the attitudes of the female characters towards Don Juan. Haidée, although she is of a similar age (17: II, 112), nurtures and cares for the abject Don Juan, explicitly as a mother would: Don Juan is described as '[h]ushed as a babe upon its mother's breast' (II, 148), Haidée 'watched him like a mother' (II, 158), and taught him his 'alpha beta' (II, 163).[40] The difference in age between Catherine and Don Juan is so great that instead of stirring

---

[39] See Jerome Christensen, *Lord Byron's Strength* (London and Baltimore: Johns Hopkins University Press, 1993), 329.

[40] See Peter J. Manning, *Reading Romantics* (New York and Oxford: Oxford University Press, 1990), ch. 6, '*Don Juan* and Byron's Imperceptiveness to the Spoken Word', pp. 115–44.

scandal, their relationship attains respectability. Even the morally demanding Donna Inez commends the 'maternal' love of the Empress for her son (X, 32–3), exploiting the apparent Platonism to disguise her real enthusiasm for the financial profits of the match. The ostensible innocence of age difference could thus legitimize a relationship—an argument deployed less convincingly by Lady Adeline who cites her forty days' seniority as evidence that any solicitude for Don Juan is the proper expression of 'maternal fears' (XIV, 52). She plans to 'wean' him from sexual danger (XIV, 65), while Lord Henry cautions her against attempting to hold him in 'leading strings' (XIV, 66). These maternal references reinforce the ostensible 'innocence' of these relationships.

Despite its imaginative enfoldment over a period of years, references to Don Juan's weaning occur in disparate Cantos of the poem (II, 8 and XIV, 65). He certainly retains his conspicuous youth throughout, a youthfulness which manifests itself as an adolescent androgyny: he is described as having a 'half-girlish face' (I, 171), is 'feminine in feature' (VIII, 52), 'beardless' (VII, 62), and frequently 'blushing' (V, 124; IX, 47); he weeps on leaving Spain (II, 16), at the slave-market (V, 8), and when recalling Haidée (V, 18 and 117); and his 'chaste' dancing is compared to the Camilla of poetic convention (XIV, 39). It is these attributes which allow his convincing transformation as a concubine in Canto V. The sexual ambivalence of the beau had long been commonplace. In Fielding's *Love in Several Masques* (1728), Wisemore mistakes two beaux in 'paduasoy coats, and breeches' as two women in male dress and, being told of their true sex, exclaims: 'perhaps by them this amphibious dress may be a significant calculation; for I have known a beau with every thing of a woman but the sex, and nothing of a man besides it'.[41] Mozart's scoring of the part of Cherubino in *Le nozze di Figaro* for female voice might also be cited as a representation of the beau's sexual ambivalence, as it is of the androgyny of the youth.

Mary Wollstonecraft's vehemence against the rake was directed against his incipient homosexuality—a 'perversion'

---

[41] *The Complete Works of Henry Fielding* (London: George Bell, 1889), *Love in Several Masques* (1728), Act I, scene 2, p. 797.

which would be guaranteed to stir her (middle-class) reader's disgust (and class opposition): 'So voluptuous, indeed, often grows the lustful prowler, that he refines on female softness. Something more soft than woman is then sought for; till, in Italy and Portugal, men attend the levees equivocal beings, to sigh for more than female languor.'[42] The sexual innuendo of the comparison of Don Juan with Alcibiades in *Don Juan* (XV, 11) hints at the hero's homosexuality rather than effeminacy. Although Alcibiades' speech in *The Symposium*, in which he tells of his failure to seduce Socrates, was deliberately omitted in early translations (for example, that of Sydenham in 1767), it was added in the first complete edition of Plato, prepared by Thomas Taylor in 1804.[43] Byron probably knew of Alcibiades' speech (see *Don Juan*, XV, 86) and therefore compares his hero with the sexual as much as the athletic Alcibiades. The brief insinuation of homosexuality also links Byron's Don Juan with twentieth-century psychoanalytical considerations of the legend—this time with that of Gregorio Marañón who argued that Don Juan's nature was essentially homosexual, sexually immature, weak, and only indecisively 'masculine'. The two interpretations—that of Don Juan's confrontation with the Oedipal situation after the event, and that of his homosexuality—are of course not unrelated in psychoanalytical discourse.[44]

Byron's effeminization of his hero is not an idiosyncratic element within the history of the legend, awaiting twentieth-century psychoanalysis for vindication. It is a trait which the poem also shares with many contemporary representations of Don Juan. In his review of *The Libertine* at Covent-Garden (*The Examiner*, 25 May 1817), Hazlitt explicitly interpreted Kemble's performance of the seducer as being feminine:

[42] Wollstonecraft, *A Vindication*, 254. Compare Thomas Paine's notorious ridicule of the aristocracy as a 'seraglio' in which gentlemen were 'drones'. *The Rights of Man*, part ii (1792), ch. 5, p. 249.

[43] Louis Crompton, *Byron and Greek Love* (Berkeley, Calif.: University of California Press), 90.

[44] Gregorio Marañón, 'Notas para la biología de Don Juan', see Mandrell, *Don Juan and Point of Honour*, 239. See also Jane Gallop on the 'ladies' man' in *Feminism and Psychoanalysis* (London: Macmillan, 1982), 35 and 38. That the Oedipal situation causes both homosexuality and Don Juanism, see C. G. Jung, 'Pscyhological Aspects of the Mother Archetype' (1954), in *Collected Works of C. G. Jung* (2nd edn.; Princeton: Princeton University Press, 1969). ix/1, para. 162.

Mr Charles Kemble did not play the Libertine well. Instead of the untractable fiery spirit, the unreclaimable licentiousness of Don Giovanni, he was as tame as any saint:

> And of his port as meek as is a maid.

He went through the different exploits of wickedness assigned him with evident marks of reluctance and contrition; and it seemed the height of injustice that so well meaning a young man, forced into acts of villainy against his will, should at last be seized upon as their lawful prize by fiends come hot from hell with flaming torches.[45]

This judgement was repeated in Henry Crabb Robinson's diary entry concerning Kemble's performance: 'Charles Kemble played the highly spirited reprobate very tamely indeed' (20 May 1817).[46] Hazlitt also commented upon the 'softness approaching effeminacy' in the expression of Ambrogetti's face when he played the part of Don Giovanni in Mozart's opera at the King's Theatre in May 1817. And Hazlitt added that this enactment lessened 'the violent effect of his action'.[47] The reception which these effeminate Don Juans encouraged was thus one of increased sympathy. Julia Kristeva combined the two discourses—psychoanalytical and political—in describing the androgynous adolescent as 'the innocent and justified pervert'.[48]

A justified and sympathetic Don Juan was also the consequence of another significant feature of many performances of Don Juan versions on the Regency stage: that of the impersonation of the infamous seducer by actresses. Madame Vestris was by far the most notorious and popular of these cross-dressing Don Giovannis, although the fact that many actresses performed the 'breeches' role demonstrates the pervasiveness and popularity of the practice.[49] These cross-dressing performances

---

[45] *The Complete Works of William Hazlitt*, ed. P. P. Howe (London: J. M. Dent, 1930–4), v. 370. Caroline Franklin considers this review in *Byron's Heroines*, 628.

[46] Henry Crabb Robinson, *The London Theatre, 1811–1866*, ed. Eluned Brown (London: The Society for Theatre Research, 1966), 76.

[47] Hazlitt, *Complete Works*, viii. 224–5 (*The Examiner*, 18 May 1817).

[48] Julia Kristeva, 'The Adolescent Novel', in John Fletcher and Andrew Benjamin (eds.), *Abjection, Melancholia and Love: The Work of Julia Kristeva* (London: Routledge, 1990), 8–23, 14. See also Marañón, *Don Juan*, 73–4.

[49] Mrs Gould, Mrs Brooks, Mrs Jordan, Miss Stevenson, Mrs Waylett, Miss Copeland (Mrs Fitzwilliam), Miss Cubitt, Miss Healy, Mrs Baker, and Madame Vestris all played Don Juan roles.

also increased the degrees of sympathy and indulgence offered to the once heinous seducer. Charles Lamb applauded Mrs Jordan's playing of the role of the seducer in *Giovanni in London* in 1818: 'You have taken out the sting from the evil thing.' Her performance turned 'all the mischief into fun as harmless as toys, or children's make-believe'.[50] Robinson's account of Madame Vestris's playing of the Don repeated this judgement and in language which is almost identical to that of Lamb's review, particularly in the repetition of 'harmless'. He claimed that she rendered the character 'as entertaining as possible' and added that at the same time 'there is an air of irony and mere wanton and assumed wickedness which renders the piece harmless enough'.[51] Within this context therefore—the effeminate or cross-dressing performances of Don Giovannis and the benevolent responses which they encouraged—the 'vulnerabililty' of Byron's Don Juan might be interpreted as a political manœuvre to ensure further sympathy for the hero.

Many critics have commented upon the instances of sexual role-reversal which occur throughout the poem. Local instances include the Islamic houris who desire men in their virginal state (VIII, 113); the 'wicked wives' who sigh beside their husbands for 'some bachelor' (VI, 24); and the personification of polygamy as female (VIII, 105). Central events present Don Juan himself 'reversed' as the cross-dressing Juanna, bought by the Sultana, and as a male prostitute, employed by the Empress of Russia and first 'tested' by her *éprouveuse*. Many commentators have argued that these reversals portray the reality of women's sexual oppression by inverting the acceptable forms which that oppression assumes—the barter and exchange of women, in markets or in marriage, and their prostitution within such relationships. Such reversals, however, which would also include the rampant libidinousness of the varied women portrayed by the narrator, are considerably more problematic when they are reconsidered within the political dimension of the Don Juan legend. Perhaps contemporary readers of *Don Juan* could be

[50] *The Works of Charles and Mary Lamb*, i. 373, *The Examiner* (22 Nov. 1818).
[51] Quoted in Clifford John Williams, *Madame Vestris; A Theatrical Biography* (London: Sidgwick & Jackson, 1973), Apr. 1822, p. 58. See also *Memoirs, Journal and Correspondence of Thomas Moore* (London: Longman, Green, Longman & Roberts, 1860), 313 (18 Mar. 1822, Drury Lane).

accused of a too literal reading—something like Annabella Milbanke's 'naive biographical criticism' reproved by Jerome Christensen—but this was because they read the poem as implicated within the political debate which the legend automatically presumed. For example, the claim that the terms 'mistress' and 'mutability' are 'synonymous' (XVI, 20) might be said to be merely typical of the narrator's sated cynicism. But it becomes an audacious and provocative gesture when the frame of *Don Juan* is recalled. In the same way, the interpretation of a rakish Don Juan created a figure who would enjoy and benefit from the opportunity which the *éprouveuse* offered. The portrait of a suffering Don Juan, subjected to female lust which he could not reciprocate, would have been an entirely absurd interpretation to the poem's contemporary readers. Within the premiss of a defence of Don Juan, the sexual role-reversals appear as so many more extenuations of his conduct. But they also reveal the asymmetry of perceptions of sexual behaviour in the Regency period.

IRREVERSIBILITIES

Byron's *Don Juan* claims that both sexes are equally likely to be faithless. Johnson's break of pattern in describing the courses of his various marriages is one expression of this theme:

> 'Well then your third,' said Juan, 'What did she?
> She did not run away too, did she, sir?'
> 'No faith'—'What then?'—'I ran away from her.'
>
> (V, 20)

Such lines aim to frustrate the preconceptions and categorizations of perpetrator and innocent, the language of responsibility. However they also disguise the very real difficulties which a woman would face in an attempt to flee from her husband and the excess penalties which she would incur as a result of legally entrenched inequalities. The opinion of Parliament was that the virtuous wife ought to forgive the guilty husband but that it would be degrading for the husband to forgive the guilty wife.[52]

---

[52] See Keith Thomas, 'The Double Standard', *Journal of the History of Ideas*, 20 (Apr. 1959), 202.

The notorious case of Georgiana Cavendish, Duchess of Devon-
shire, illustrates the gender disparity. She was forced into a two-
year continental exile in 1791 for her sexual indiscretion with
Charles Grey which culminated, and revealed itself, in pregnancy; Charles Grey later became Prime Minister. These disparate fortunes reflect the unequal treatment of the Duchess's
affair and the Duke's many and notorious sexual liaisons.[53] The
trial of Queen Caroline was a very public example of the sexual
double standard, and although the popular and political support for her seemed to demonstrate a growing intolerance with
this inequality, potential revolutionary impulses were recuperated within the conventional expressions of chivalry on her
behalf. Sexual inequality continued far beyond Byron's lifetime.
The Divorce Act of 1857, for example, permitted a wife to be
divorced for simple adultery, whereas a husband could be divorced only if the act were accompanied by aggravating circumstances such as cruelty, desertion, bigamy, rape, sodomy, or
bestiality. It was not until 1923 that the grounds for divorce
were made the same for both sexes.[54]

Some of these material inequalities can be glimpsed within
Don Juan and make the ostensible 'role-reversals' asymmetrical.
Juanna's tears, for example, may be a consequence of being
'forced to feel feminine and reduced to behaving (or freed to
behave, depending on how one chooses to look at it) in accordance with his disguise'—as Peter Graham argues. However,
Juanna's tears are a womanly act with a difference—for
Gulbeyaz is shocked that a man should cry (V, 118)—a point
which Graham also notes.[55] While the poem's narrator explicitly
differentiates the significance of the act of weeping for both
sexes—'To them 'tis a relief, to us a torture' (V, 118)—he does
not concede the obvious advantage which Don Juan enjoyed as
a result of his display of tears.

It is significant that *The Investigator* (1823) singled out the
episode of the cross-dressing Juanna as portraying Don Juan 'in

[53] See Roger Lonsdale (ed.), *Eighteenth-Century Women Poets* (Oxford, New York:
Oxford University Press, 1990), 510.

[54] Lawrence Stone, *The Family, Sex and Marriage in England, 1500–1800* (London:
Weidenfeld & Nicolson, 1977), 503.

[55] Graham, Don Juan, 84. Compare Conrad's fluctuating reactions towards
Gulnare in *The Corsair* (1814), Canto III, stanza 17.

disguise . . . in strange metamorphoses from a seducer to an object to be seduced'.[56] This interpretation differs from modern criticism in that only the Turkish adventure is seen as exemplifying the pattern of a seducer/seduced reversal. Since 'she' is mistaken for a woman, not a womanly man, the reversal is more nearly equivalent, and this is demonstrated in the threat which Juanna most materially faces—that of potential sexual assault:

> 'You fool! I tell you no one means you harm.'
> 'So much the better,' Juan said, 'for them;
> Else they shall feel the weight of this my arm,
> Which is not quite so light as you may deem.
> I yield thus far, but soon will break the charm
> If any take me for that which I seem,
> So that I trust for everybody's sake
> That this disguise may lead to no mistake.'
>
> (V, 82)

This stanza also literalizes how male 'weakness' can be recuperated as power. Don Juan's fear of rape is countered by his bluster of physical threat against any potential male assailant. His position of 'victim' is therefore already differentiated from that of woman. The absurdity, if not impossibility, of rigid inversion was inadvertently demonstrated by *The Monthly Magazine*'s spoof of forthcoming publications listed in 'Literary Prophecies for 1797' by 'Tiresias, Jn.': 'A novel, by a lady, will make some noise, in which the heroine begins by committing a rape, and ends with killing her man in a duel'.[57] Although this humorous article was designed to express the fear of women's 'muscular power' and influence in the cultural sphere, its irony collapses into absurdity.

The Juanna episode thus reveals the asymmetry and non-equivalence between gendered situations. Male surrender and yielding to traditionally 'feminine' feeling and emotion can always be recuperated later as power. Susan J. Wolfson, in her consideration of 'effeminate character' in *Sardanapalus*, emphasized the importance of the King's emphatically heterosexual nature: 'by designing an effeminate character which retains

---

[56] *The Investigator* (1822), 315–71, 343, review of Cantos I–II and III–V.
[57] *The Monthly Magazine* (Feb. 1797). Quoted in Lonsdale (ed.), *Eighteenth-Century Women Poets*, p. xl.

heterosexual masculinity, Byron can at once imply a power in reserve and set effeminacy into play as a sign of something other than mere decadence or incapacity'.[58] The already constituted political power of the sexes prevents the possibility of mutual metamorphosis.

While the different perceptions of male and female sexual behaviour dictated that a woman would be more severely punished for misdemeanours, the strict morality expected of her also allowed her to adopt the position of innocent or victim if there were any degree of doubt. In Robert Bage's novel, *Hermsprong*, Lord Grondale and Miss Fluart discuss the partiality of social opinion:

Miss Fluart: '. . . when a man and a woman go quietly into a post-chaise together, it may puzzle the judge and jury to determine whether the He carries away the She, or the She the He!'
   'The law, madam, respecting the delicacy of the sex, always supposes the man the seducer, and treats him accordingly'.[59]

Even the contemporary designation of an 'improper' lady (an unmarried woman who is not a virgin, for example) accords a denial of responsibility by calling her 'abandoned'. She may actively have abandoned all scruples, but the inference remains that she has *been* abandoned.

Don Juan repeatedly suggests that convention allows the woman the possibility of being 'immoral' while retaining a reputation for morality: 'oh shame, | Oh sin, oh sorrow, and oh womankind! | How can you do such things and keep your fame?' (I, 165). The tiptoe which Don Juan thinks he hears is compared to that of 'an amatory Miss' gliding to a rendezvous, a description which ironizes the expression of 'chasteness' which is applied to the echo of her footsteps (XVI, 112). And, within the suspicion generated by the narrative voice, the definition of female virtue as '[t]hat lady who should be at home to all' (XII, 79) is open to ambiguity, or rather, to innuendo. It is because of this loading in her favour, the poem argues, that woman can be the better dissembler. She can manipulate appearances, being all things to all men, and never herself. All the

    [58] Susan J. Wolfson, ' "A Problem Few Dare Imitate": *Sardanapalus* and "Effeminate Character" ', *ELH* 58 (1991), 867–902, 872.
    [59] Bage, *Hermsprong*, ch. 68, p. 213.

heroines of *Don Juan* 'naturally' dissemble well: for example, Donna Julia's indignant protestation of innocence; Haidée's serpent-like eyes which hide their real power (II, 117); Gulbeyaz's elaborate scheme of passing Don Juan off as a concubine; Dudù's feigned innocence explaining her 'dream'; Adeline's hypocritical sycophancy to her guests; her Grace Fitz-Fulke's obvious proficiency in disguise. Aurora remains an exception, as does the country servant girl whose conspicuous pregnancy it would be impossible to disguise.[60] Dissimulation (XV, 3) and Christianity (VII, 57) are both gendered as feminine, the latter because of its contrasting inward and outward show. And Susan J. Wolfson has noted how the language which Byron uses to describe 'mobility' is taken from Madame de Staël's description of feminine consciousness in *Corinne*.[61] Within a poem which deploys a deliberately hypocritical style, and whose hero is the most notorious sexual hypocrite, Byron provocatively reveals women as the consummate practitioners of hypocrisy.

Thus while the narrator of *Don Juan* recognizes differences between the sexes, he does not accept that these represent inequalities for women. *Don Juan* appears to valorize and even envy women this kind of 'power' in a way which is reminiscent of Rousseau's prescriptions for womanhood as embodied in Sophie of *Emile* (1780):

[a woman's] strength is in her charms, by their means she should compel him to discover and use his strength. The surest way to arouse this strength is to make it necessary by resistance. Thus pride comes to the help of desire and each exults in the other's victory. This is the origin of attack and defence, of the boldness of one sex and the timidity of the other, and even of the shame and modesty with which nature has armed the weak for the conquest of the strong.[62]

Wollstonecraft recognized the kind of influence which such writers as Rousseau and Byron would offer women but she urged them to refuse it as being 'the arbitrary power of beauty'. She indicted the 'Mohammedan' view of woman as catering to

---

[60] For additional examples of feminine hypocrisy, see I, 178; III, 41; VI, 14; XI, 36; XII, 66, 73.
[61] Wolfson, ' "Their She-Condition"', *ELH* 54 (1987), 599 and 614 n. 26.
[62] Rousseau, *Emile*, 322.

masculine appetite and denied the benefits earned by the coquette as a form of alienated empowerment, illicit privileges
comparable to the illegitimate power enjoyed by the aristocracy.[63] Her reply to Rousseau is explicit within *A Vindication:*
' "Educate women like men", says Rousseau, "and the more they
resemble our sex the less power they will have over us." This is
the very point I aim at. I do not wish them to have power over
men; but over themselves.'[64] And it is Wollstonecraft's argument
for women's self-valorization which links her ('radical') writing
with the ('conservative') writing of contemporary writers such
as Hannah More and which distinguishes them both from male
conduct writers such as Richard Polwhele and from 'libertine'
writers such as Rousseau.[65]

The consistency of response between these women writers,
who are more usually portrayed as adversaries, is an important
context for *Don Juan.* Byron's poem frankly portrayed female
desire in a way which was inadmissible to contemporary women
writers, both 'feminist' and 'anti-feminist', 'jacobin' and 'anti-
jacobin'. However one female Regency figure did dare to portray a frank sexuality—the cross-dressing actress Madame
Vestris. And because her most notorious role was as Don
Giovanni, she also plays a significant role within the history of
the Don Juan legend. Her career demonstrates the kind of
sexual-political bind of which Wollstonecraft and More spoke
and which Wollstonecraft herself did not escape, especially in
the posthumous reception of *A Vindication.* The case of Madame Vestris also demonstrates the asymmetry of the sexes and
the reception of her performances, like the reception of
Byron's poem, exposes the political significance and consequences of the Don Juan legend.

MADAME VESTRIS

Although she was ostensibly representing the notorious and
distinctly male seducer, Vestris's performances were popular

---

[63] Wollstonecraft, *A Vindication*, 103 and *passim.*
[64] Ibid. 156.
[65] See Mitzi Myers, 'Reform or Ruin: "A Revolution in Female Manners"', *Studies in the Eighteenth-Century*, 2 (1982), 199–216.

because they were not incommensurate with a displayed 'femininity'. One contemporary response commented that 'she refined and threw grace into the character which a coarse masculine woman, generally known in green-rooms as "Joe Gould", had previously rendered quite unfit to be seen'.[66] Even though the actresses who played Don Giovannis were enacting men, the audiences did not forget their biological sex and would not forgive gender transgressions of manner. Thus audiences preferred their actresses to be feminine, even when portraying men. This preference reflected the anxiety concerning the status and deportment of women, literalized in the protests against their adoption of trousers and other emblems of masculine dress.[67]

The popular ballad composed about Vestris after her 'breeches' role as Don Giovanni provides a glimpse of why her adoption of the part became such a hit:

What a breast—what an eye! What a foot, leg, and thigh,
What wonderful things she has shown us,
Round hips, swelling sides, and masculine strides—
Proclaim her an English Adonis!

In *Macheath* how she leers, and unprincipled appears,
And tips off the bumpers so jolly.
And then, oh, so blest, on two bosoms to rest,
And change from a *Lucy* to *Polly*.

Then in *Don Giovanni*, she puts life into many,
And delights with her glees and her catches;
Her best friend at will, she can gracefully kill,
And the wife of his bosom debauches.

The profligate youth she depicts with much truth,
All admire the villain and liar.
In bed-chamber scenes, where you see through the screens,
No rake on the town can come nigh her.

Her example so gay leads all the young astray,
And the old lick their lips as they grin;

[66] Quoted in Leo Waitzkin, *The Witch of Wych Street* (Cambridge, Mass.: Harvard University Press, 1933), 51 n. 5. See also M. Willson Disher, *Clowns and Pantomimes* (New York: Benjamin Blom, 1968), 291.
[67] See L. Colley, *Britons* (New Haven and London: Yale University Press, 1992), 242.

And think, *if she would*, why, mayhap they *still could*
Have the pleasure and the power still to win.

How alarming is beauty when ankle and shoe-tie
Peep out like a bird from the nest,
They are like heralds of delight, and morn, noon, and night,
Fond fancy can point out the rest.

Then, be breeches on the go,
Which appears with such grace upon many;
But VESTRIS to please, must her lovely limbs squeeze,
In the pantaloons of DON GIOVANNI.

Her very hair and style would corrupt with a smile—
Let a virgin resist if she can;
Her ambrosial kisses seem heavenly blisses—
What a pity she is not a man.[68]

This rollicking song illustrates many features of the contextual representations of Don Juan—the 'gracefulness' (with its connotations of aristocratic behaviour) of the murderer Don Giovanni; his reputation as an encouragement of, rather than palliative against, vice; the admiration which he attracts, despite being a 'villain and liar'; and his corruption of the virgin. It also demonstrates that Vestris's success was a consequence of the pleasure she provided as a specular image of erotic woman. The audience envisaged in the song is exclusively male—'the old' of stanza 5, for example, lick their lips in sexual 'anticipation', which is also a consequent and simultaneous gratification. The role of Don Giovanni allowed a greater degree of eroticism to be displayed in an otherwise repressive society. A female character would not have allowed a peek through the screens, a glimpse of more than an ankle, or of legs squeezed into tight elastic pantaloons. In Byron's own note concerning Madame Catalani in *English Bards and Scotch Reviewers* (1809), he noted: 'we are still black and blue from the squeeze on the first night of the lady's appearance in trousers'.[69] The role of Don Giovanni thus allowed the male spectators a scopophilic pleasure without the moral censure which would have entirely prohibited a display of 'female' nudity.

---

[68] Quoted in *Memoirs of . . . Madame Vestris* (London, 1939), 54.
[69] *Complete Poetical Works*, i (1980), 411, Note to *English Bards and Scotch Reviewers*, l. 615.

Hazlitt's review of Vestris's performance for *The London Magazine* (July 1820) differs from popular opinion in his preference of the 'masculinity' of Mrs Gould in the same role:

but, we confess, we had rather see her petticoated than in a Spanish doublet and hose, hat and feather . . . we like her best in petticoats. It cannot be denied that Mrs Gould (late Miss Burrell) of the Olympic, who played it first, was the girl to play Giovanni in London. She had a hooked nose, large staring eyes, a manlike voice, a tall person, a strut that became a rake.[70]

Hazlitt remained unconvinced by Vestris's performance because she 'shrinks back into feminine softness and delicacy'. However, his florid descriptions of her appeal betray that this may have been a consequence of his interpretation rather than any faulty theatrical realism on her part, already apparent in 'we like her best in petticoats': 'There is a pulpy softness and ripeness in her lips, a roseate hue, like the leaves of the damask rose, a luscious honeyed sound in her voice, a depth and fulness too, as if it were clogged with its own secrets, a languid archness, an Italian lustre in her eye, an enchanting smile, a mouth—shall we go on?'[71] Hazlitt's coyly abrupt termination of the cataloguing of her physical charms betrays the tendency of the entire review. Hazlitt's review of the 'piece' returns the actress firmly to sexual objectification and appraisal. Despite her enacting of a strongly sexual subjectivity, the character of Madame Vestris was inescapably imprisoned and recontained within the cultural sphere as sexual object.

It is thus unsurprising that the part of Don Giovanni was to taint the reputation of Madame Vestris. Reviewers recognized that many spectators came merely to ogle—'every buck and blood in London crowded to the theatre to see her'[72]—and muttered against the propriety of the venture, a 'breach' of modesty:

We pity Madame Vestris, from every consideration from which her performance of Don Giovanni has been attended . . . We feel bound to treat it as a part which no female should assume till she has discarded every delicate scruple by which her mind or her person can be

---

[70] Hazlitt, *Complete Works*, xviii. 351–2.
[71] Ibid.
[72] *Memoirs of Mme Vestris*, 55.

distinguished. We counsel her to solicit the exemption she cannot command, and rather do anything than adhere to a task that is fraught with viler consequences than we shall venture to describe.[73]

The subsequent apocrypha which surrounded Madame Vestris's life resulted in such publications as *The Memoirs of the Public and Private Life, Adventures and Wonderful Exploits of Madame Vestris, the Don Juan of the Present Day* and *Memoirs of the Life, Public and Private Adventures of Madame Vestris, to which is added, the Amorous Confessions of Madame Vestris . . . in which will be found most curious anecdotes of many eminent roués and debauchees of the day; with various others of public notoriety.*[74] Any actress who tried to emulate Vestris's phenomenal success did so at the risk of her reputation and exposed herself to innuendo—the kind of 'material' disadvantages which most women would have found intolerable. Such were the consequences of being recognized as 'the [female] Don Juan of the Present Day'.

That Madame Vestris's adoption of the dominant, sexually assertive role of Don Giovanni was only to lead to her sexual objectification is indicative of the difficulties of any attempt to create a reversal of roles in the Regency sexual scenario because of existing inequalities. Although the case of Madame Vestris belongs most clearly to the public sphere of the theatre, it remains emblematic for the question of the depiction of female sexuality. It also parallels the attempt in *Don Juan* to portray Don Juan as a victim of female sexual predation, since these female portraits were reinscribed within a libertine discourse which reappropriated any 'power' they might have possessed. The overt sexuality of Gulbeyaz, for example, is associatively linked with the street prostitutes of London (compare the use of 'Paphian' in V, 96 and XI, 30). The frankly erotic portraits of a dishevelled and breathless Donna Julia (I, 158), Haidée's heaving breast (III, 70), Dudù who looks 'adapted to be put to bed' (VI, 41), and the sleeping harem concubines (VI, 65–9), may have been intended as illustrations of the power which women could effect over Don Juan—but within the frame of *Don Juan* these descriptions become implicated in its libertine discourse. Indeed Haidée's attraction is explicitly connected

[73] *Theatrical Inquisitor* (June 1820). See also *Memoirs of Mme Vestris*, 55.
[74] Quoted in Waitzkin, *Witch of Wych Street*, 9.

with the desires of the male reader: 'Short upper lip—sweet lips! that make us sigh' (II, 118). The depiction of Catherine confirms the suspicion that the sexual nature of young and pretty women only would be approved. She is consistently described in coarse and frequently obscene terms.[75]

It is not surprising therefore that the Don Juan–Haidée episode, so idealized by subsequent painters, myth-, and literary critics, infuriated the poem's contemporary reviewers. Thomas Moore warned Byron: 'Young Haidée is the very concentrated essence of voluptuousness, and will set all the women wild.'[76] His fears about the reception of the depiction of Haidée were certainly fulfilled by the reviewers' outrage at this and other female portrayals. The reaction of the conservative newspaper, *The Champion* (1 August 1819) is typical: 'Haidée is described . . . with all the seductive voluptuousness in which he so unscrupulously delights to luxuriate.'[77] The most severe censure however was reserved for the portrayal of Gulbeyaz: 'the licentious poet revels in a sensuality so consonant to his taste, as is afforded by a warm description of the degradation of a female, adorned with all that can be conceived of personal loveliness in women, to a pitch of wantonness, from which even the libertine of his own depraved imagination turns in disgust'.[78] This reviewer accords a degree of libertinism to the figure of Don Juan, only to argue that it is surpassed by that of the author. The erotic possibilities of the poem were fully 'realized' in the cheap piracies of the text which, as reported by *The Quarterly Review* (April 1822), were illustrated with 'obscene' engravings.[79] In addition, the outlets for the selling of these piracies were shops which were centres of radical culture, regularly raided because they specialized in uneasy alliances of politically subversive literature, anti-religious propaganda, advice on birth-control, and pornography.[80]

---

[75] See e.g. VI, 92, 96; VII, 37; VIII, 68; IX, 54, 58, 67; X, 26, 29, 48.

[76] *Memoirs . . . of Moore*, 210 (13 June 1819).

[77] *The Champion* (1 Aug. 1819), 488–90, 490.

[78] *The Theatrical Inquisitor* (1822), 343, review of Cantos I–II and III–V.

[79] Quoted in Hugh J. Luke, 'The Publishing of Byron's *Don Juan*', PMLA 80/2 (June 1965), 202.

[80] See William St Clair, 'The Impact of Byron's Writings', in Andrew Rutherford (ed.), *Byron: Augustan and Romantic* (London: Macmillan, 1990), 18.

Among the links which bind Mary Wollstonecraft's *A Vindica-tion*, Madame Vestris's career, and Byron's *Don Juan* is the importance of contemporary reception in determining their meaning and political import. And this reception is linked to prevailing sexual-political convention. Although I have argued that each of these examples participates within the Don Juan legend, the context of the legend is most significant for Byron's poem. Without recognizing *Don Juan*'s inscription within the debates which the legend automatically effected, the responses of its contemporary readers can only be misunderstood. It is the context of the legend which explains the preconceptions and automatic suspicions of the poem's contemporary readers (considered in Chapter 2); its appeal to lower- and provocation to middle-class readers (Chapter 3); and its apparently seductive and corrupting invitation to the female reader (Chapter 4). To interpret *Don Juan* as a version of the legend is to recognize the poem's participation within the ideology which the legend extends. This chapter has therefore emphasized the similarity of Byron's poem to other versions of the legend in deliberate opposition to the pervasive claim that the legend is 'reversed' and that Don Juan is seduced. It has explored a variety of ways in which he can be re-recognized as a seducer—in that the heroines are conventionally and femininely faithful and heartbroken; in that the hero himself anticipates the twentieth-century Don Juans of psychoanalytical theory; in that the 're-versal' of roles which the critics propose is impossible within a society in which inequalities between the sexes exist. The aim of this chapter has been to consider the implications of *Don Juan*'s representation of seduction from a feminist perspective. Jane Miller urges feminism to be aware of the risks of seduction: 'it is possible to construe women's inclusion as willing participants in their own seduction as a sleight of hand disguising their exclusion from the language which performs it'.[81] Only the response of feminism will prevent such discourse from maintaining its status as monologue—whether it is that of Byron's *Don Juan* or the Don Juan legend. As readers of Byron's poem, we ought to remember that the traditional Don Juan 'myth' is in fact many versions of a legend, and that it includes such influential, al-

[81] Jane Miller, *Seductions* (London: Virago Press, 1990), 27.

though frequently neglected, versions as Byron's *Don Juan*. As feminists, we need to realize that, despite the considerable variety of its versions and interpretations, the legend represents a masculinist ideology which has been remarkably uniform. Thus, as feminist readers of Byron's *Don Juan*, we should recognize that it represents as much a version as a 're-version' of the legend, with the political position which that entails. Lévi-Strauss's inclusive definition of a 'myth' is especially necessary from a feminist perspective, for its generosity of scope allows feminism's own spokes(wo)men to be heard. These would include, not only less frequently canonized versions such as George Sand's *Lélia*, or the forgotten career of Madame Vestris, but also the responses to sexual libertinism throughout history—those of Mary Wollstonecraft's *A Vindication of the Rights of Woman* and the many other women authors who wrote of seduction, if only to disapprove of it. And these responses would also include the contemporary readers and reviewers of Byron's *Don Juan* who both resisted and affirmed their own conception of the Don Juan legend. Only then can the legend, or indeed Byron's particular version of it, be denied its incipient univocality.

Epilogue: Contemporary Seductions

On 23 March 1823 Mary Shelley wrote to Byron: 'Is Aurora a portrait? ⟨She is⟩ Poor Juan. I long to know how he gets out of or rather into the net.'[1] This response demonstrates the contamination of even the 'virginal' Aurora within the sexualized sphere of *Don Juan*, but it is also exemplary of the way in which the poem encouraged its readers to sympathize and identify with the hitherto morally beleaguered libertine and attempted to portray him as the victim rather than the perpetrator of seduction. While the attempt to defend Don Juan may be said to have failed with the poem's most vocal contemporary readers, it has enjoyed considerable, if belated, success with many later nineteenth- and twentieth-century critics. This does not make these later readings invalid, but it does make them historical. This book is intended as a cautionary account of what narrow understandings of 'myth' neglect, how our definitions of myth must consider not just the point of 'origin' and those versions which appear to adhere to this origin in a more or less explicit way. Myths are characterized as much by the cultural authority which they wield as by their pedigrees. Myths are stories which are told in public. Thus they include such examples as our continuing use of the word 'narcissistic', contemporary cinematic narratives, video games, tabloid head-lines, and the urban myths circulated in gossip as much as adaptations of ancient Greek or Roman myths.[2] Similarly, the myth of Don Juan in the Regency period was as much a product of the debate about his character—discussed in theatrical re-views and among audiences—as of any one or more 'versions'.

Clearly this level of intense debate about Don Juan no longer applies in quite the same way—despite the recent Hollywood

---

[1] *The Letters of Mary Wollstonecraft Shelley* (Baltimore and London: Johns Hopkins University Press, 1980), i. 324 (30 Mar. 1823).

[2] See Marina Warner, *Managing Monsters: Six Myths of Our Time* (London: Vintage, 1994), 13 and *passim.* Warner's most obvious debt is to Roland Barthes, *Mythologies*, tr. Annette Lavers (London: Paladin, 1973) and his theory that myth is a motivated message, 'a type of speech chosen by history' (p. 110).

film *Don Juan de Marco* (1995) which significantly is based in part on Byron's *Don Juan*.[3] However, public debate about the issue of seduction continues, especially in recent controversies over 'date rape' and codes of practice for American students on verbal consent before sex. In her consideration of Stephen Frears's film *Dangerous Liaisons* (1988), Marina Warner argues that the renascence in interest in Laclos's novel is due to the contemporary fantasy about women's sexual domination and responsibility for men's desire.[4] Her argument is certainly supported by Roger Vadim's, comparatively recent, film version of the Don Juan legend. This was entitled *Don Juan, ou et si Don Juan était une femme* (1973) and starred Brigitte Bardot as the manipulative seductress. Reading Byron's poem today therefore still involves participation in such debates. Paul Johnson regretted the contamination which a literary classic such as *Don Juan* might suffer in this climate. In an editorial in the *Sunday Telegraph* before the 1992 general election he alleged that Labour planned to destroy English culture with political correctness: 'PC lays down that a student mob can scream four-letter words at the authorities with impunity but that a lecturer who quotes Byron's line, "But saying she would ne'er consent, consented", must be banned from campus, as an insult to feminists and an invitation to date-rape.'[5]

Don Juan participates in rather than precludes debate. It certainly anticipates perspectives on seduction which strike many readers as 'modern'—the frank avowal of female desire; the possibility of woman's sexual initiative and of role-reversal such as the often effeminate Don Juan 'mothered' by assertive women. Yet Chapter 5 illustrated how these positions of female 'power' were often recuperated, and not just by the prevailing codes of Regency society. Women's power was also often relinquished by themselves. The Empress of Russia, for example, looks on her lover as on a king (IX, 70)

[3] Directed and written by Jeremy Leven. When psychiatrist Dr Jack Mickler (Marlon Brando) visits the grandmother of Don Juan de Marco (Johnny Depp), he discovers in his bedroom copies of Tirso de Molina's *El burlador de Sevilla* and Byron's *Don Juan*.

[4] Marina Warner, 'Valmont—or the Marquise Unmasked', in Jonathan Miller (ed.), *The* Don Giovanni *Book* (London: Faber & Faber, 1990), 93–107.

[5] Paul Johnson, 'The Labour Plot to Destroy England', *Sunday Telegraph* (29 Mar. 1992).

and in Lambro's absence Haidée relinquishes her power to Don
Juan (III, 43).

This relinquishing of power is not so much an 'active' or
conscious gesture, as it is an automatic and unavoidable consequence of their desire and the reversibility of power to which it
exposes them. Byron was not unaware of this argument—Lady
Blessington recounted her debates with him on this subject:

Byron has a false notion on the subject of women; he fancies that they
are all disposed to be tyrants, and that the moment they know their
power they abuse it. We have had many arguments on this point—I
maintaining that the more disposed men were to yield to the empire
of women, the less were they inclined to exact, as submission disarmed,
and attention and affection enslaved them.[6]

Such reversibility makes the determination of power within the
seduction scenario irrelevant since any 'power' is immediately
and automatically relinquished. *Don Juan* itself displays the
reversibility of seduction and in ways which prefigure a post-
modernist discourse which can also be considered as participating within, and indeed as constituting a version of, the Don
Juan legend. This discourse is that of the French theorist,
Jean Baudrillard.

BAUDRILLARD'S SEDUCTION

Baudrillard opens *De la séduction* (1979) with a consideration
of the turn of the nineteenth century as the crucial episteme
in the history of seduction: 'The eighteenth century still
spoke of seduction. It was, with valour and honour, a central
preoccupation of the aristocratic spheres. The bourgeois Revolution put an end to this preoccupation. . . . The bourgeois era
dedicated itself to nature and to production, things quite
foreign and even expressly fatal to seduction.'[7] Baudrillard's
return to this period is significant, since much of his writing
can be seen to have been anticipated by Byron's *Don Juan*.
Here, Baudrillard's nostalgia for the seduction of the

---

[6] E. J. Lovell (ed.), *Lady Blessington's Conversations of Lord Byron* (Princeton:
Princeton University Press, 1969), 123.

[7] Jean Baudrillard, *Seduction*, tr. Brian Singer (London: Macmillan, 1990), 1. All
future references to *Seduction* are from this edn. and will be cited in the text.

eighteenth century—ceremonial, ritualistic, strategic, and aristocratic—echoes *Don Juan*'s return to earlier traditions of the Don Juan legend and its defence of a sexual libertinism which was increasingly identified with anachronistic aristocratic privileges.[8]

Although seduction is often reduced to sexuality, in Baudrillard's definition it is not the same thing at all, for he argues that desire and sexuality belong to the sphere of production, in that they *pro-duce(re)* or make appear. The concepts of psychoanalysis, for example, belong to this sphere in creating the unconscious and its effects.[9] In distinguishing seduction from sexuality, Baudrillard returns to the end of the eighteenth century in order to explain that seduction is that which utilizes desire, and only as a tactic: 'This is the central theme of the libertine sexuality of the eighteenth century, from Laclos to Casanova and Sade (including Kierkegaard in *Diary of a Seducer*), for whom sexuality still retains its ceremonial, ritual and strategic character, before sinking, with the Rights of Man and psychology, into the revealed truth of sex' (p. 18). For Baudrillard, the Romantic period marked the beginning of the modern fixation with 'psychic interiority', a creation which Julia Kristeva claims is affirmed in and by the nineteenth-century psychological novel and which decrees that 'the baroque game (Don Juan, Casanova) can—and must—cease'.[10] Kierkegaard argued that Byron's version of the Don Juan legend failed, because in transferring the representation of the erotic from music to language, Byron ought to have made the seducer a reflective personality. An ideality which might correspond to that of the musical-erotic could only be recaptured in the psychological realm: 'the counterpart to Don Giovanni must be

---

[8] See also *Seduction*, 39: sexuality, desire, and *jouissance* are described as the ideal of 'inferior classes, the bourgeoisie, then the petty-bourgeoisie—relative to the aristocratic values of birth and blood, valour and seduction'. Baudrillard returns to the 18th-cent. tradition of libertinism in contrasting that 'warm' form of seduction with the contemporary 'cold' seduction through the mediums of the masses and of the image: 'To be sure, seduction in the age of the masses is no longer like that of *The Princess of Clèves, Les Liaisons dangereuses* or *Diary of a Seducer*' (p. 95).

[9] Compare J. B. Mandrell's critique of the intervention of psychoanalysis within the 'myth' of Don Juan as perpetuation rather than explication in *Don Juan and the Point of Honour* (Philadelphia: Pennsylvania State University Press, 1992).

[10] Julia Kristeva, 'The Adolescent Novel', in John Fletcher and Andrew Benjamin (eds.), *Abjection, Melancholia and Love* (London: Routledge, 1990), 18.

a reflective seducer in the category of the interesting, where the issue therefore is not how many he seduces but how'.[11] Kierkegaard himself attempted to create such a personality in Johannes of 'The Seducer's Diary'. Byron's Don Juan, however, returns to the baroque tradition of the legend—even its dating (in the 1790s) is deliberately anachronistic and nostalgic. Byron's Don Juan, unlike Johannes, never discusses strategy, never even claims to be a seducer.

For all that—indeed because of that—Byron's Don Juan exemplifies Baudrillard's definition of the consummate seducer. In *L'Autre par lui-même* (1987), Baudrillard describes seduction as operating according to rules which are similar to those of martial arts—view the opponent from the side, never attack him/her from the front, in fact, never 'attack'.[12] Taking the initiative is equivalent only to a clumsy gesture in a vulgar seduction. The 'true' seduction is that of the object: 'Let's imagine the Object as a passionate form. For the subject does not have a monopoly upon passion—its exclusive domain would instead be that of action. The Object is passive in the sense that it is the site of a passion, objective, seducing and vengeful.'[13] The object can be both seducing and passive, indeed it is seducing in its passivity. Whereas the passions of the subject are differential, energetic, ethical, and heroic, those of the object are the ironic passions of ruse, conformity, silence, and voluntary servitude (*L'Autre par lui-même*, 80). All of these 'objective' passions are adopted by Byron's Don Juan: ruse ('And smiling but in secret—cunning rogue', XIV, 37, and 'He had the art of drawing people out | Without their seeing what he was about', XV, 82); conformity (he '[w]as all things unto people of all sorts', XIV, 31, and 'had, like Alcibiades, | The art of living in all climes with ease', XV, 11); noticeable silence

---

[11] Kierkegaard, *Either/Or: I* (1843), ed. and tr. Howard V. Hong and Edna H. Hong (Princeton: Princeton University Press, 1987), 9; see pp. 106–8.

[12] Jean Baudrillard, *L'Autre par lui-même* (Paris: Éditions Galilée, 1987), 60: '[a]insi du désir dans la séduction: ne jamais prendre l'initiative du désir, pas plus que de l'attaque'. All future references from *L'Autre par lui-même* are from this edn. and will be cited in the text. Translations are my own.

[13] *L'Autre par lui-même*, 79: 'Imaginons l'Objet sous forme passionnelle. Car le sujet n'a pas le monopole de la passion—son domaine réservé serait même plutôt celui de l'action. L'Objet, lui, est passif au sens où il est le lieu d'une passion, objective, séduisante et vengeresse.'

throughout the narrative; and voluntary servitude, literalized in his compliant employment by Catherine.

Baudrillard distinguishes between the vulgar, impure seducer and the accomplished seducer. The impure seducer—and Baudrillard cites the traditional Don Juan and Casanova as examples—exercises a cynical deception for sexual ends, dedicating himself to the accumulation of sexuality, which, Baudrillard argues, is only the economic residue of seduction. This vulgar seducer wears a mask in order to deceive (instead of being oblique), proceeds by persistence (whereas he ought to proceed by absence), and betrays the secret in openly saying: 'I know you want to be seduced and I'm going to seduce you.'[14] The vulgar seducer wants to become a subject and envisages the other as the victim of his strategy—a naïve theory which underestimates the power of the object:

Traditionally the seducer was an impostor who employed subterfuge and villainy to achieve his ends—or at least who *believed* he was employing them. For the other, by allowing herself to be seduced, by succumbing to the imposture, often voided it, stripped the seducer of his control. In effect, he falls into his own trap for having failed to consider seduction's reversible power. The following always holds: the one who seeks to please the other has already succumbed to the other's charms.[15]

Yet, despite Baudrillard's dismissal of such seducers as Don Juan and Casanova as vulgar, his theories of seduction echo arguments which have been made by countless Don Juans. His claim, for example, that 'the challenge, not desire, is at the heart of seduction' is reminiscent of the seducer's traditional pleasure in the chase (*L'Autre par lui-même*, 51). And Don Juans, among other seducers, have traditionally pleaded in their own defence that their conduct was involuntary, given the *seducing* beauty of the woman (and it usually has been *she*). She need not act or behave in any particular manner. Her existence alone, and more particularly her beauty, is cited as explanation and cause of the seduction. Molière's Dom Juan, for example,

[14] See *De la séduction*, 'La Stratégie Ironique du Séducteur', 135–63, (*Seduction*, 98–118); and *L'Autre par lui-même*, 59.

[15] *Seduction*, 176–7. Singer's translation does not illustrate the gender ambiguity of Baudrillard's original. 'Le séducteur' is masculine; the other might be masculine or feminine 'se'. (See *De la séduction*, p. 242.)

claimed: 'beauty delights me wherever I find it, and I easily yield
to the gentle violence with which it carries me away'.[16] However,
traditional Don Juans who argued the seducing power of the
woman in defence of their behaviour are, in Baudrillard's account, naïvely unaware that the logic was more than tactical
rhetoric. The real seducer is thus paradoxically the one who
knows that (s)he has already been seduced.

More traditional Don Juans may be subjects who stimulate
desire; Baudrillard's 'true' seducer initiates a seduction in
which distinctions dissolve and responsibility is a meaningless
concept. Within this logic, Byron's Don Juan is the most sophisticated of seducers—in being seduced (*Seduction*, 81):

Is it to seduce, or to be seduced, that is seductive? But to be seduced is
the best way to seduce. It is an endless refrain. There is no active or
passive mode in seduction, no subject or object, no interior or exte-
rior: seduction plays on both sides, and there is no frontier separating
them. One cannot seduce others, if one has not oneself been seduced.

Baudrillard's vision is a utopian one, in which seduction would
eradicate binary oppositions, would eradicate opposition itself.
In his account, seduction is not that which opposes but that
which seduces production; not the opposition between 'masculine' and 'feminine' (for this very opposition is 'masculine'),
but that which is outside such categorization; not a superficiality
which opposes profundity, but the indistinction between the
surface and the depth; not artificiality as opposed to authenticity, but the indifference between the two. Cosmetics, for
example, are not 'false', since, in being falser than false, they
attain instead a kind of innocence and transparency (*Seduction*,
94)—indeed, Baudrillard quotes from Joan Rivière's work
on 'Femininity in the Masquerade' that it is 'immaterial'
whether femininity is genuine or assumed (p. 10). Thus his
definition of seduction has links with Austin's theory of the
performative in which speech is neither true nor false but
(in)felicitous and with those Don Juans (including Byron's
text) who play with the illusion of truth which they claim
to express. Baudrillard's seduction is non-dialectical. Its challenge is not subversive but reversible. It is outside of the laws

---

[16] Molière, *Dom Juan*, Act I, scene 2, p. 32: 'la beauté me ravit partout où je la
trouve, et je cède facilement à cette douce violence dont elle nous entraîne'.

of exchange or equivalence, an outbidding which cannot end ('une surenchère où les jeux ne sont jamais faits', *De la séduction*, 39). Seduction is therefore outside of the laws which would determine responsibility, since the line which would separate seducer from seduced, 'active' perpetrator from 'passive' victim, is indecipherable.[17]

The ideal of mutual and interchangeable relations is illustrated within Byron's *Don Juan*, and especially in the representation of Haidée: to her, Don Juan seems both 'a creature meant | To be her happiness, and whom she deemed | To render happy' (II, 172). Moreover, the poem implies that this reciprocity of desire involves not only mutual but also necessarily simultaneous domination and submission: 'Haidée was made to love, to feel that she was his | Who was her chosen' (II, 202). It is the reversibility of seduction which might explain such seemingly oxymoronic descriptions as that of Don Juan's 'proud humility': he 'showed such deference to what females say, | As if each charming word were a decree' (XV, 82). These lines recall the argument that the heroines' unusual dominance in the relationships disguises the special circumstances which allow it to occur, that it is Don Juan who determines their behaviour rather than vice versa. But they also speak of the irresistible challenge intrinsic in the act of seduction, so that each charming word *is* a decree. Byron's attempt to argue that his heroines are the true seducers of the narrative, like Baudrillard's definition of seduction, is in this way a literalization of a concept which is integral to traditional treatments of the legend: if Don Juan is overwhelmed by the beauty of the woman then, effectively, *he* is seduced by *her*. However, the inevitable reversibility of Baudrillard's definition of seduction undermines criticism's attempts to label Don Juan as either the seducer (as in previous more 'traditional' treatments of the legend) or the seduced (as in Byron's *Don Juan*). His seduction makes any distinction between seducer and seduced not only inappropriate but impossible.

[17] See e.g. *L'Autre par lui-même*, 63: 'Coupable ou innocent, c'est son statut de sujet—séduit et séducteur, c'est son destin d'objet.' ('Guilty or innocent, it is its status as a subject—seduced and seducing—which is the destiny of the object.') And *Seduction*, 45: 'No more dominant and dominated, no more victims and executioners (but "exploiters" and "exploited", they certainly exist, though quite separately, for there is no reversibility in production . . .)'.

Baudrillard's writing on seduction is evidently opposed to
the kinds of social and cultural history applied in the consideration of Byron's Don Juan in Chapter 5. His utopian
consideration of seduction would be impossible in the sphere
of 'production'. However, although Baudrillard dismisses the
importance of the sphere of the 'real', he does write of women's
material history, of how women were expected to be modest
and sexually restrained. Far from such behaviour being that of
an oppressed sex, he claims that women all along have been
able to exploit this as a secret weapon.[18] Whether or not women
themselves were always aware of such 'powers' (we have seen
how Wollstonecraft recognized but refused such influence in
her opposition to Rousseau), they were certainly urged by
the authors of the conduct books to behave with decorum *in
order to* attract men. In *The Unsex'd Females* (1798), a prescriptive
guide to the conduct proper to women, the Reverend Richard
Polwhele suggested that a conspicuously modest demeanour
would win male approval: 'the crimsoning blush of modesty will
be always more attractive than the sparkle of confident intel-
ligence'.[19] It is hardly surprising, therefore, that within the
considerably more libertine context of *Don Juan*, the depiction
of blushing heroines creates erotic rather than strictly modest
demeanours. The only exception to these blushing (or flushed)
heroines is the pregnant serving girl, who is described as too
poor for the lady-like accomplishment, an obvious inference
that the trait is cultivated (XVI, 64).[20]

In Canto VI, stanzas 15–16, the narrator elaborates his own
advice on attractive female demeanour:

> A slight blush, a soft tremor, a calm kind
> Of gentle feminine delight and shown
> More in the eyelids than the eyes, resigned

---

[18] See *Seduction*, 86: 'Love and the carnal act are only so much seductive finery,
the most refined and subtle invented by women to seduce men. But modesty and
rejection can play the same role.' See also p. 19 where Baudrillard suggests that
women's resistance to the pill is a consequence of their reluctance to relinquish the
right to sexual reticence.

[19] Richard Polwhele, *The Unsex'd Females: A Poem* (1798; repr. New York:
Garland, 1978), 16.

[20] See *Don Juan*, V, 108 (Gulbeyaz); VI, 85 (Dudù); although Aurora is reproved
for her failure to blush, she is described within the same stanza, and despite her
usual paleness, as 'sometimes faintly flushed' (XVI, 94).

> Rather to hide what pleases most unknown,
> Are the best tokens (to a modest mind)
> Of love, when seated on his loveliest throne,
> A sincere woman's breast, for over warm
> Or over cold annihilates the charm.
>
> (VI, 15)

To achieve such equipoise was evidently a delicate task and therefore paradoxically required a consciousness at all times. By pretending to a reluctance which she may not have felt, the woman successfully attracted all the more (XII, 34–6). And since the 'efficacy' of modesty was directly proportionate to its conspicuousness, a correct deployment of modesty would ensure the success of activating desire which it ostensibly sought to deny. In addition, a modest demeanour appeared to demonstrate not only that female sexuality was under control, but also that it required such control.[21] This logic is evident in the narrator's claim that innocence does not need '[n]or use those palisades by dames erected, | Whose virtue lies in never being detected' (XIV, 61). The arguable duplicity of the virgin is parodied in Don Juan's mimicry of a Pamela-like woman, whose play of abashed modesty and conscious morality is ridiculed as ploy and whose insistence upon marriage becomes sexual innuendo, or at least knowingness (V, 84). From this perspective, the deployment of modesty can be interpreted as sexual allure:

> Then there were sighs, the deeper for suppression,
> And stolen glances, sweeter for the theft,
> And burning blushes, though for no transgression.
>
> (I, 74)

And in the following stanza, the narrator's libertinism associatively links attractiveness with the 'chaste' and the 'goodly', and with the force which may be required to obtain it:

> Much I respect, and much I have adored,
> In my young days that chaste and goodly veil,
> Which holds a treasure like a miser's hoard
> And more attracts by all it doth conceal,
> A golden scabbard on a damask sword,
> A loving letter with a mystic seal,

[21] See Mary Poovey, *The Proper Lady and the Woman Writer* (Chicago: University of Chicago Press, 1984), 21.

> A cure for grief—for what can ever rankle
> Before a petticoat and peeping ankle?
>   (XIV, 27)

These apparent contradictions were compounded by the rake's enjoyment of seduction as a sport, a game in which the more challenging the prospect, the greater the satisfaction in winning. Literary seducers traditionally proclaimed their preference for and delight in resistance. An 'easy' conquest was unflattering to the seducer's self-esteem. In *Les Liaisons dangereuses*, with its detailed instructions in the designs and strategies of seduction, Valmont epigrammatically expresses this libertine thinking: 'Let her be too weak to prevail, but strong enough to resist'.[22] The proximity between seduction and actual assault was narrowed because of the professional seducer's determination to conquer and because he frequently used the language of conquest and capitulation while relying on the exoneration of his conduct which expressions of consent and acquiescence alone could effect. Jane Austen recognized the easy slide between the two when she mockingly gave her most conscientious of seducers, Sir Edward of *Sanditon*, a concerted strategy to 'seduce' Clara: 'If she could not be won by affection, he must carry her off. He knew his business.'[23] It is also implicit within *Don Juan* in Donna Julia's assertion that she has spurned all potential suitors, including Count Strongstroganoff (I, 149).

In addition, the difficulty of understanding a lady's expression of refusal was compounded by the cultural taboo of her replying 'yes'. It is this imagery which underlies Donna Julia's attempts to suppress her illicit desire for Don Juan: 'And whispering "I will ne'er consent"—consented' (I, 117). This equivocation is also represented in the vacillations of the coquette (XII, 34 and 63) and in the moral complexities of the relationship between Donna Julia and Don Juan, in which

---

[22] Choderlos de Laclos, *Les Liaisons dangereuses*, tr. P. W. K. Stone (Harmondsworth: Penguin, 1981), 63, letter 23, Vicomte de Valmont to the Marquise de Merteuil.

[23] Jane Austen, *Lady Susan/The Watsons/Sanditon* (Harmondsworth: Penguin, 1963), 192. For the exoneration of the rapist which the period's elevation of 'nature' enabled, see Anna Clark, *Women's Silence, Men's Violence* (London: Pandora Press, 1987), 34.

innocence and hypocrisy are indistinguishable (I, 72–3). Reversibilities of responsibility are easily made when the distinguishing of modesty from allure in a blush and of consent from refusal in a 'no' is blurred. This explains how the context of Regency mores enabled *Don Juan*'s Baudrillard-like definition of reversible seduction and why feminists should be aware of the moral complexity which makes it possible.

The Ismail episode of female rape fantasy also reveals the contextual denial of female sexuality, since the rape fantasy allows the woman to be blameless. 'She didn't want it, so cannot be guilty of any illicit desires', might be the psychological motivation in an ironic parody of the defence's argument in the rape trial:

> But on the whole their continence was great,
> So that some disappointment there ensued
> To those who had felt the inconvenient state
> Of 'single blessedness' and thought it good
> (*Since it was not their fault, but only fate,*
> *To bear these crosses*) for each waning prude
> To make a Roman sort of Sabine wedding
> Without the expense and the suspense of bedding.
>
>   (VIII, 131, my italics)

The Ismail widows therefore fantasize about seduction rather than rape, since the distinction between the two relies upon the woman's consent, and its operation as a kind of activity. The issue of consent is crucial in that it not only decides the apportioning of blame in the rape trial but also raises the difficulties of doing so. The issue of rape polarizes the attributions of responsibility which are implicit within many considerations of seduction (excluding Baudrillard's) and foregrounds what is at stake for a feminist politics.[24] Psychoanalysis speaks always of seduction rather than of rape because in Freudian terms there is no zero degree of desire, there is always some desire even if it

---

[24] See e.g. John Forrester's comment, in *The Seductions of Psychoanalysis* (Cambridge: Cambridge University Press, 1990), 42, that the seducer's aim of transforming a refusal into consent entails that 'the seducer will always be prey to doubt as to the status of the other's consent, so that a seduction that is viewed from the standpoint of a questioning of the status of the consent will always be confused with rape, just as rape in which any ignorance as to the nature of the victim's desire is admitted will in retrospect be deemed to have been seduction'.

manifests itself as horror. There can be no initial innocence because the very involvement within the act represents some form of desire, just as the act of reading *Don Juan* presumes, as it effects, the contamination of interpretation (see Chapter 4).

Baudrillard's consideration of seduction is similar to that of psychoanalysis, even though he denies the validity of 'desire' as that which is 'pro-duced'. In his theory, it is seduction which always already exists and this is especially so in the case of the 'seductrice'. His division of seduction into two, apparently gendered, categories of strategy and animality is the most problematic development of his theory for feminism. Seduction itself in his writing is consistently non-gendered, although this has not been maintained in translations of his work into English. Brian Singer's translation—*Seduction* (Macmillan, 1990)— for example, consistently mistranslates *féminin* as 'female', even though Baudrillard states that the feminine is outside of any masculine/feminine opposition, that '[t]he irony is lost when the feminine is instituted as a sex' (*Seduction*, 17) and that '[t]he feminine considered not as a sex, but as the form transversal to every sex, as well as to every power, as the secret, virulent form of in-sexuality' (p. 16).[25] Yet, although Baudrillard denies that seduction is (biologically) female, there is a privileged relationship between seduction and woman, and this is especially so in his consideration of seduction as animality.

Two central sections of *De la séduction*—'The Effigy of the Seductress' ('L'effigie de la séductrice') and 'The Ironic Strategy of the Seducer' ('La stratégie ironique du séducteur')— structurally reinforce this gendered polarization, despite the claims within each section that they are not 'essentially' divided, not 'essential'. 'The Effigy of the Seductress' considers animal attraction, primitive ritual gestures, make-up, and film stars, so that even the masculine film star is 'feminine' according to this definition. The effeminate Don Juan of Byron's poem, as an illustration of Baudrillard's theory of seduction, might support the avoidance of essentialism: it is *his* beauty which seduces the heroines, *he* literalizes the pleasures and powers of being

---

[25] Singer translates 'Pour ce qui est du féminin, le piège de la révolution sexuelle est de l'enfermer dans cette seule structure où il est condamné' (*De la séduction*, 17) as 'The danger of the sexual revolution for the female is that she will be enclosed within a structure that condemns her' (p. 6).

a sexual object. However, Baudrillard's concentration upon Kierkegaard's 'The Seducer's Diary' in 'The Ironic Strategy of the Seducer', and especially its opening lines which connect this section with 'The Effigy of the Seductress', fall back on an implicit causality which is consistently gendered—that of the woman's always already present seduction: 'Now if a woman's finery is also strategic, a calculated display, is not the seducer's strategy a display of calculation with which to defend himself from some opposing force?' (*Seduction*, 98). Thus in describing 'The Seducer's Diary', Cordelia possesses a matchless advantage for she is naturally endowed with all seduction (p. 99). The seducer's vocation is the 'extermination of the girl's natural power by an artificial power of his own' (*Seduction*, 99; translation of *De la séduction*, 136, my italics: 'exterminer cette puissance naturelle *de la femme* ou de la jeune fille par une enterprise délibérée'). Baudrillard here seems to relapse into the kinds of essentialism to which he is opposed since the natural power of 'woman' is evoked even though it is surplus to Kierkegaard's narrative of Johannes and the young girl, Cordelia. (It is interesting that Brian Singer omits 'de la femme' in his translation.) The female seduction which Baudrillard most admires is unintentional, involuntary, 'natural', and automatic. Indeed these characteristics are why he so admires it. And this in turn leads him into the brutal logic that anything which is attractive provokes, with the hint of justification, its own destruction.[26] Despite Baudrillard's disavowal of apportioning responsibility, female beauty always seems to pre-originate any other form of seduction.

Despite Byron's portrayal of Don Juan as the sexual object of women, the 'overpowering' beauty of *Don Juan*'s heroines implies the same kind of disavowal of (Don Juan's) responsibility. When the narrator of *Don Juan* describes Haidée's look as like 'the snake late coiled, who pours his length | And hurls at once his venom and his strength' (II, 117), her sexual attractiveness makes her inherently, rather than incipiently, treacherous. Haidée's 'overpowering' presence, the narrator claims, 'made you feel | It would not be idolatry to kneel' (III, 74), a dynamic in which both positions, her dominance and his submission, are

[26] See Mike Gane's discussion of Baudrillard's tale of the sacrifice of the Dutch girl in *Baudrillard: Critical and Fatal Theory* (London: Routledge, 1991), 57–65.

involuntary and reversible. Gulbeyaz's beauty is also described as 'of that overpowering kind', as, implicitly, are all the heroines of the poem (with the exception of the ageing Catherine). Their beauty is thus of the same kind as that of the Romagnole singer, whose ('active') wish to please and ('passive') power to please are simultaneous:

> And through her clear brunette complexion shone a
> Great wish to please, a most attractive dower,
> Especially when added to the power.
>
> (IV, 94)

And this perspective exacerbates the context in which modesty becomes sexual allure. Woman is never truly 'virgin', but sexually knowing before the event: 'Even innocence itself has many a wile' (I, 72).

Chapter 5 considered Wollstonecraft's *Vindication* as a response to the libertine discourse of Rousseau—as to Byron's *Don Juan*. The texts of *Emile*, *Don Juan*, and *De la séduction* demonstrate significant affiliations despite their obviously different historicities. Rousseau's prescriptions for womanhood as embodied in Sophie (see Chapter 5 above) anticipate Baudrillard: 'We seduce with our weakness, never with strong signs or powers' (*Seduction*, 83). Baudrillard's claim that women have been able to deploy their sexual 'repression' as seductive strategy was already evident in Rousseau. And Rousseau's advice to women: 'The more women are like men, the less influence they will have over men, and then men will be masters indeed', parallels Baudrillard's claim that feminism's aim of power in the realm of production is foolish since women already possess a mastery of a greater realm—that of the symbolic.[27] Because social codes in both mid-eighteenth-century France and Regency England dictated that woman's desire should be reciprocal and never initiatory, she had to manipulate appearances in order to return to the man his prerogative of leading the courtship—even if that prerogative was more apparent than real. Thus, although some of *Don Juan*'s heroines initiate their relationships with Don Juan, their actions have to disguise this.

---

[27] This connection has been made by several commentators. See Mike Gane, *Harmless Lovers?* (London: Routledge, 1993), 61 and 207 n. 5; and *Baudrillard: Critical and Fatal Theory*, 225.

Donna Julia, for example, gives Don Juan the illusion of control: the squeeze of her hand is described euphemistically as only the slight *return* of pressure: 'The hand which still held Juan's, by degrees | Gently but palpably confirmed its grasp'. Her tentative approach therefore seems to say 'Detain me, if *you* please' (I, 111, my italics). Their necessary mastery of signs links such heroines to the postmodern age of total signification portrayed by Baudrillard.

If such 'strategies' were inadmissible to the puritan discourse of Wollstonecraft, modern feminists can be no less suspicious. Feminist psychoanalytical approaches and responses to Lacan have advised women to adopt the role of seducers—Jane Gallop's valorization of 'infidelity' as 'a feminist practice of undermining the Name-of-the-Father' or Irigaray's claim that she is having 'a fling with the philosophers' are both examples of this. But such flirtatious or seductive positions are advocated as conscious strategies—the ironic strategy which Baudrillard tropes as masculine in his gendered division of methods.[28]

The radical nature of the consideration of seduction in both *Don Juan* and *De la séduction* is thus undermined by their use of sexual-political conventions. Byron was attempting to rewrite the Don Juan legend by depicting the poem's heroines as frankly libidinous, a manifesto of libertarianism for both sexes. However this gesture was implicated within, and contaminated by, the frame of the Don Juan legend itself. The reversal of responsibility within such a polemical context becomes an inflammatory revision, a provocation. In a similar way, Baudrillard attempted to counter the essentialism which he perceived as pervasive in contemporary discourse, and not least in feminist theories. But in choosing Kierkegaard's 'The Seducer's Diary' as exemplary of his argument, Baudrillard selected a text whose causal dynamic only compounds the reader's uneasiness with the already loaded and thoroughly conventionalized terms of 'masculine' and 'feminine'. *Her* beauty invites and thus indirectly justifies a defilement in which there is no reversibility. Cordelia is not permitted to counterattack. A second story which recurs in Baudrillard's writing is that of the woman 'S'

[28] See Jane Gallop, *Feminism and Psychoanalysis* (London: Macmillan, 1992), 48, and Luce Irigaray, *This Sex Which Is Not One* (Ithaca NY: Cornell University Press, 1985), 150.

who shadows a man wherever he goes. Yet Baudrillard repeatedly quotes her as saying 'Please follow me', even though it is
she who follows. Baudrillard also fails to identify the story of 'S'
as an ironic parody of the man who menacingly trails women, a
common form of contemporary persecution and one, moreover, which is evident in Johannes's tracking of Cordelia in 'The
Seducer's Diary'. Both Byron and Baudrillard therefore attempt
to reverse traditional roles—Don Juan is seduced by women, the
woman 'S' sinisterly trails a man. Yet Don Juan is as much
the seducer as seduced while his female 'seducers' conventionally pine for him, and 'S', far from enjoying the power
which this pursuit appears to give (male) prowlers, dreams
pathetically and hopelessly of the man.[29] The subversive potential of both *Don Juan* and *De la séduction* collapses under, as
indeed it returns to, the conventional asymmetry of the sexes.

In Kierkegaard's 'The Seducer's Diary', Johannes claimed: 'It
would certainly be interesting if some literary drudge could be
found to count up in fairy tales, legends, folk ballads, and myths
whether a girl is more often faithless or a man.'[30] This epilogue
does not claim to have settled such a question—nor indeed
does it wish to. Instead it suggests that reading Byron against
Baudrillard—and Baudrillard against Byron—is a way in which
feminists might see played out both the contemporary implications of Byron's poem and of Baudrillard's theory.

---

[29] The story of 'S' appears in *Please Follow Me* (Paris: Éditions de l'Étoile, 1983),
and in *La Transparence du Mal* (Paris: Galilée, 1990), 162–6. See Mike Gane,
Baudrillard: Critical and Fatal Theory, 217 n. 4 and 227 n. 2: after 'S' is discovered 'she
is at a loss, dreaming, pathetically, of "taking his room, sleeping in his bed"'. Gane
quotes from the translation of *Please Follow Me* (Seattle: Bay Press, 1988), 68.
[30] Kierkegaard, *Either/Or: I*, 'The Seducer's Diary', 301–445, 380.

Bibliography

PUBLISHED WORKS

Abert, Hermann, *Mozart's* Don Giovanni, tr. Peter Gelhorn (London: Eulenberg, 1976).

Adolphus, John, *Biographical Memoirs of the French Revolution* (London: J. Cadell, Jn. & W. Davies, 1799).

Almeida, Hermione de, *Byron and Joyce through Homer* (London: Macmillan, 1981).

Armesta, Víctor Said, *La leyenda de Don Juan* (1946; repr. Madrid: Colección Austral, Espasa-Calpe, 1968).

Auden, Wystan Hugh, *The Dyer's Hand* (London: Faber & Faber, 1948).

Austen, Jane, *Sense and Sensibility* (1811; repr. Harmondsworth: Penguin, 1969).

—— *Lady Susan/The Watsons/Sanditon* (Harmondsworth: Penguin, 1963).

Jane Austen's Letters to her Sister Cassandra and Others, ed. R. W. Chapman (1932; repr. London: Oxford University Press, 1952).

Austen, John, *The Story of Don Juan: A Study of the Legend and of the Hero* (London: Martin Secker, 1939).

Bage, Robert, *Hermsprong* (1796; repr. Oxford and New York: Oxford University Press, 1985).

Barthes, Roland, *Mythologies*, tr. Annette Lavers (London: Paladin, 1973).

Barton, Anne, *Byron:* Don Juan (Cambridge: Cambridge University Press, 1992).

Baudrillard, Jean, *De la séduction* (Paris: Denoël, 1979); tr. by Brian Singer as *Seduction* (London: Macmillan, 1990).

—— *L'Autre par lui-même* (Paris: Éditions Galilée, 1987).

Beatty, Bernard, *Byron's Don Juan* (Beckenham, Kent: Croom Helm, 1985).

—— 'Fiction's Limit and Eden's Door', in Bernard Beatty and Vincent Newey (eds.), *Byron and the Limits of Fiction* (Liverpool: Liverpool University Press, 1988), 1–38.

—— 'Byron and the Paradoxes of Nationalism', in Vincent Newby and Ann Thompson (eds.), *Literature and Nationalism* (Liverpool: Liverpool University Press, 1991), 152–62.

Beaty, Frederick L., 'Harlequin Don Juan', *Journal of English and Germanic Philology*, 67/3 (1968), 395–405.

Beaumarchais, *The Marriage of Figaro* (1784), tr. John Wood (Harmondsworth: Penguin, 1964).

Bergerolle, Claude, 'Révolte sexuelle et liberté individuelle dans le "Don Juan"', *Romantisme: Revue de la Société des Études romantiques*, 7 (1974), 44–59.

Bertati, *Don Giovanni*, tr. Lionel Salter, booklet for Orfeo Recording (C214 902 H).

Bévotte, Georges Gendarme de, *La Légende de Don Juan: Son évolution dans la littérature, des origines au romantisme*, 2 vols. (1906; repr. Paris: Hachette, 1929).

Blanco y Quiñones, José Luis, *Lord Byron* (Madrid: EPESA, 1971).

Blau, Robinson, *Throwing the Scabbard Away: Byron's Battle Against the Censors of* Don Juan (American University Studies Series, 4/126; New York: Peter Lang, 1991).

Boyd, Elizabeth, *Byron's* Don Juan*: A Critical Study* (New Brunswick, NJ: Rutgers University Press, 1945).

Bryant, Arthur, *The Age of Elegance, 1812–1822* (1950; repr. Glasgow: William Collins, 1975).

Burke, Edmund, *Reflections on the Revolution in France* (1790; repr. Harmondsworth: Penguin, 1968).

Burton, Robert, *The Anatomy of Melancholy*, ed. Thomas C. Faulkner, Nicholas K. Kiesling, Rhonda L. Blair, 2 vols. (1621; repr. Oxford: Clarendon Press, 1989).

Bushee, A. S., *Three Centuries of Tirso de Molina* (Philadelphia: University of Pennsylvania Press, 1939).

Butler, Marilyn, 'Myth and Mythmaking in the Shelley Circle', *ELH* 49 (1982), 50–72.

Byron, Lord, *The Complete Poetical Works of Lord Byron*, ed. Jerome J. McGann, 7 vols. (Oxford: Clarendon Press, 1980–93).

——*Don Juan*, ed. T. G. Steffan, E. Steffan, and W. W. Pratt (Harmondsworth: Penguin, 1973).

——*Don Juan, o El hijo de Doña Inés* (Madrid, 1843–4), translator unknown.

——*Don Juan: El hijo de Doña Inés*, 2 vols. (Madrid, 1876), translator unknown.

——*Don Juan*, traducción de A. Espina (Madrid: Editorial Meditterraneo, 1966).

—— *Byron's Letters and Journals*, ed. Leslie A. Marchand, 12 vols. (London: John Murray, 1973–82).

——*Miscellaneous Prose*, ed. Andrew Nicholson (Oxford: Clarendon Press, 1991).

Chew, Samuel C., *Byron in England: His Fame and After-Fame* (London: John Murray, 1924).

Christensen, Jerome, *Lord Byron's Strength: Romantic Writing and Commercial Society* (London and Baltimore: Johns Hopkins University Press, 1993).

Clairmont, Claire, *The Journals of Claire Clairmont*, ed. Marion Kington Stocking (Cambridge, Mass.: Harvard University Press, 1968).

Clark, Anna, *Women's Silence, Men's Violence: Sexual Assault in England, 1770–1845* (London: Pandora Press, 1987).

Clément, Catherine, *Opera, or The Undoing of Women* (London: Virago Press, 1989).

Coleridge, Samuel Taylor, *The Collected Works of Samuel Taylor Coleridge*, ed. Walter Engell and W. Jackson Bate, 16 vols. (Princeton: Princeton University Press, 1983), vii. *Biographia Literaria: II.*

Colley, Linda, *Britons: Forging the Nation, 1707–1837* (New Haven and London: Yale University Press, 1992).

Conrad, Peter, *Shandyism: The Character of Romantic Irony* (Oxford: Basil Blackwell, 1978).

Crompton, Louis, *Byron and Greek Love: Homophobia in Nineteenth-Century England* (Berkeley: University of California Press, 1985).

Davidoff, Leonore, and Hall, Catherine, *Family Fortunes: Men and Women of the English Middle Class, 1780–1850* (London: Century Hutchinson, 1987).

Dent, Edward J., *Mozart's Operas* (1913; repr. Oxford: Oxford University Press, 1973).

—— 'Italian Opera in London', *Proceedings of the Royal Musical Association*, 71 (1944–5), 19–42.

Deutsch, O. E., *Mozart: A Documentary Biography*, tr. E. Blom, P. Brascombe, and J. Noble (London: Simon & Schuster, 1961).

Dibdin, Thomas, *Don Giovanni; or, A Spectre on Horseback!: A comic, heroic, operatic, tragic, burletta, Spectacular Extravaganza, in Two Acts; Adapted to Hodgson's Theatrical Characters and Scenes in the Same* (London: Hodgson, 1817).

—— *The Reminiscences of Thomas Dibdin*, 2 vols. (London: Henry Colburn, 1827).

Didier, Beatrice, 'Des Lumières au Romantisme: A-t-on guillotiné le commandeur?' in *Don Juan* (Paris: Bibliothèque Nationale, 1991), 153–8.

Disher, M. Willson, *Clowns and Pantomimes* (New York: Benjamin Blom, 1968).

Il Don Giovanni (London: W. Winchester, 15 Apr. 1817).

Don Giovanni: A Poem in Two Cantos (Edinburgh: Edward West, 1825).

'Don John' or 'Don Juan' Unmasked; Being a Key to the Mystery, Attending that Remarkable Publication; with A Descriptive Review of the Poem and Extracts (London: William Hone, 1819).

Don Juan: Canto the Third (London: William Hone, 1819).

Don Juan; or the Libertine destroyed, The History of (London: J. Roe, c.1815).

Don Juan; or, The Battle of Tolosa: A Poem in Three Cantos (London: James Harper, 1816).

Donohue, Joseph, *Theatre in the Age of Kean* (Oxford: Basil Blackwell, 1975).

Edgeworth, Maria, *Patronage* (1814; repr. London: Pandora Press, 1986).

Engels, Frederick, *Engels: Selected Writings*, ed. W. O. Henderson (Harmondsworth: Penguin, 1967), 'The Condition of the English Working-Class Movement in 1844', pp. 26–93.

Erdman, David V., 'Byron and Revolt in England', *Science and Society*, 11 (1947), 234–48.

Felman, Shoshana, *Le Scandale du corps parlant* (Paris: Seuil, 1980); tr. Catherine Porter as *The Literary Speech Act: Don Juan with J. L. Austin or Seduction in Two Languages* (Ithaca, NY: Cornell University Press, 1983).

Fielding, Henry, *The Complete Works of Henry Fielding, Comprising his Novels, Plays, and Miscellaneous Writings* (London: George Bell, 1889).

——*Joseph Andrews* (1742; repr. Harmondsworth: Penguin, 1977).

Finck, Henry T., *Richard Strauss: The Man and his Works* (Boston, Mass.: Little Brown, 1917).

Findlater, Richard, *Grimaldi, King of Clowns* (London: Macgibbon & Kee, 1955).

Foot, Michael, *The Politics of Paradise: A Vindication of Byron* (London: William Collins, 1988).

Ford, Charles, *Così?: Sexual Politics in Mozart's Operas* (Manchester: Manchester University Press, 1991).

Forrester, John, *The Seductions of Psychoanalysis* (Cambridge: Cambridge University Press, 1990).

Franklin, Caroline, *Byron's Heroines* (Oxford: Clarendon Press, 1992).

——'Juan's Sea Changes: Class, Race and Gender in Byron's *Don Juan*', in Nigel Wood (ed.), Don Juan (Buckingham: Open University Press, 1993), 56–89.

——' "Quiet cruising o'er the ocean woman" ': Byron's *Don Juan* and the Woman Question', *Studies in Romanticism*, 29 (Winter 1990), 603–31.

Frye, Northrop, *The Anatomy of Criticism* (Princeton, NJ: Princeton University Press, 1957).

Furst, Lilian, *Fictions of Romantic Irony in European Narrative, 1760–1857* (London: Macmillan, 1984).

Gallop, Jane, *Feminism and Psychoanalysis: The Daughter's Seduction* (London: Macmillan, 1982).

—— 'French Theory and the Seduction of Feminism', in Alice Jardine and Paul Smith (eds.), *Men in Feminism* (New York, London: Methuen, 1987), 111–15.

Gane, Mike, *Baudrillard: Critical and Fatal Theory* (London: Routledge, 1991).

—— (ed.), *Baudrillard Live: Selected Interviews* (London: Routledge, 1993).

—— *Harmless Lovers?: Gender, Theory and Personal Relationships* (London: Routledge, 1993).

Ganzel, Dewey, 'Drama and the Law in the Early Nineteenth Century', *PMLA* 76 (1961), 384–96.

Gaskell, Elizabeth, *The Life of Charlotte Brontë* (1857; repr. Harmondsworth: Penguin, 1975).

Gasset, Ortega y, *Meditaciones sobre la literatura y el arte* (1921; repr. Madrid: Clásicos Castalia, 1987), 'Introducción a un "Don Juan"', 369–89.

The Poetical Works of John Gay, ed. G. C. Faber (London: Oxford University Press, 1926), *The Beggar's Opera* (1728), 483–532.

Godwin, William, *Enquiry Concerning Political Justice* (1798; repr. Harmondsworth: Pelican, 1976).

Goldoni, Carlo, *Memoirs* (1787), tr. John Black, 2 vols. (London: Henry Colburn, 1814).

Graham, Peter W. (ed.), *Byron's Bulldog: The Letters of John Cam Hobhouse to Lord Byron* (Columbus, Ohio: Ohio State University Press, 1984).

—— *Don Juan and Regency England* (Charlottesville, Va.: University Press of Virginia, 1990).

Grebanier, Bernard, *The Uninhibited Byron: An Account of his Sexual Confusion* (London: Peter Owen, 1971).

Grimaldi, Joseph, *Memoirs of Joseph Grimaldi*, ed. 'Boz' (Charles Dickens) and Revd. Charles Whitehead, 2 vols. (2nd edn.; London: Richard Bentley, 1846).

Guiccioli, Teresa, *Lord Byron jugé par les témoins de sa vie*, 2 vols. (London: Richard Bentley, 1869).

Gunn, Peter, *My Dearest Augusta* (London: Bodley Head, 1968).

Hays, Mary, *Memoirs of Emma Courtney* (1796; repr. London and New York: Pandora Press, 1987).

Hazlitt, William, *The Complete Works of William Hazlitt*, ed. P. P. Howe, 21 vols. (London: J. M. Dent, 1930–4).

An Historical Account of the Tragi-Comic Pantomime Intituled Don Juan, or The Libertine Destroyed, As it is Performed at Drury-Lane Theatre (London: G. Bigg, 1782).

Hoffmann, E. T. A., *Six German Romantic Tales*, tr. Ronald Taylor (London: Angel Books, 1985), 'Don Giovanni: A Strange Episode in the Life of a Music Fanatic' (1813), 104–17.

Holland, Lord Henry Richard, *Some Account of the Lives and Writings of Lope Felix de Vega Carpio and Guillen de Castro* (London, 1817).

Hone, William, and George Cruikshank, *Radical Squibs and Loyal Ripostes* (Bath: Adams & Dart, 1971).

Horace, *Satires, Epistles, and Ars Poetica*, tr. H. R. Fairclough (Cambridge, Mass.: Harvard University Press, 1926).

Horney, Karen, 'The Problem of the Monogamous Ideal' (1928), *Feminine Psychology*, ed. Harold Kelman (New York: W. W. Norton, 1967), 84–98.

Hunt, Leigh, *Autobiography of Leigh Hunt*, ed. J. E. Morpurgo (London: The Cresset Press, 1949).

——*Leigh Hunt's Dramatic Criticism, 1808–1831*, ed. Lawrence Huston Houtchens and Carolyn Washburn Houtchens (New York: Columbia University Press, 1949).

——*Leigh Hunt's Literary Criticism*, ed. Lawrence Huston Houtchens and Carolyn Washburn Houtchens (New York: Columbia University Press, 1956).

Huray, P. Le, and Day, James (eds.), *Music and Aesthetics in Eighteenth and Early Nineteenth Centuries* (Cambridge: Cambridge University Press, 1981).

Hyde, H. Montgomery, *A Tangled Web: Sex Scandals in British Politics and Society* (London: Constable, 1986).

Irigaray, Luce, *This Sex Which Is Not One* (Ithaca, NY: Cornell University Press, 1985).

Jack the Giant Queller; or Prince Juan (W. Horncastle, 1819). Printed in *Political Satires 1810–1819*.

Jacobus, Mary, *Reading Woman: Essays in Feminist Criticism* (London: Methuen, 1986), 'Dora and the Pregnant Madonna', 137–93.

Jones, Regina M., 'On the Reception of Mary Wollstonecraft's *A Vindication of the Rights of Woman*', *Journal of the History of Ideas*, 39 (1978), 293–302.

Joseph, M. K., *Byron the Poet* (London: Victor Gollancz, 1964).

Juan Secundus (London: John Miller, 1825).

Jung, C. G., *Collected Works of C. G. Jung* (2nd edn.; Princeton: Princeton University Press, 1969), ix/1. 'Psychological Aspects of the Mother Archetype'.

Kaplan, Cora, *Sea Changes: Culture and Feminism* (London: Verso, 1986).

Keats, John, *Letters of John Keats*, ed. Robert Gittings (Oxford: Oxford University Press, 1970).

—— *The Poetical Works and Other Writings of John Keats*, ed. Harry Buxton Forman, revised with additions by Maurice Buxton Forman, 5 vols. (New York: C. Scribner's Sons, 1938–9), v. 252–6, review of *Don Giovanni*, first published in *The Champion* (4 Jan. 1818).

Kelsall, Malcolm, *Byron's Politics* (Brighton: The Harvester Press, 1987).

Kennedy, Ruth Lee, *Studies in Tirso*, i. *The Dramatist and his Competitors, 1620–26* (Chapel Hill, NC: North Carolina Studies in the Romance Studies in the Romance Languages and Literatures, 1974).

Kernberger, Katherine, 'Power and Sex: The Implications of Rôle Reversal in Catherine's Russia', *The Byron Journal*, 8 (1980), 42–9.

Kierkegaard, Søren, *Either/Or: Part I* (1843), ed. and tr. Howard V. Hong and Edna H. Hong (Princeton: Princeton University Press, 1987).

Klancher, Jon P., *The Making of English Reading Audiences, 1790–1832* (Madison, Wis.: University of Wisconsin Press, 1987).

Knapp, Oswald G. (ed.), *The Intimate Letters of Hester Piozzi and Penelope Pennington, 1788–1821* (London: John Lane, 1914).

Kristeva, Julia, 'The Adolescent Novel', in John Fletcher and Andrew Benjamin (eds.), *Abjection, Melancholia and Love: The Work of Julia Kristeva* (London: Routledge, 1990), 8–23.

—— *Étrangers à nous-mêmes* (Paris: Fayard, 1988).

—— *Histoires d'amour* (Paris: Éditions Denoël, 1983), 'Don Juan ou aimer pouvoir', 243–63.

Laclos, Choderlos de, *Les Liaisons dangereuses* (1782), tr. P. W. K. Stone (Harmondsworth: Penguin, 1981).

Lacqueur, Thomas W., 'The Queen Caroline Affair: Politics as Art in the Reign of George IV', *Journal of Modern History*, 54 (1982), 417–44.

Laffay, Albert, 'Le Donjuanisme de "Don Juan"', *Romantisme: Revue de la Société des Études romantiques*, 7 (1974), 32–43.

Lamb, Lady Caroline, *Glenarvon* (1816), *Revolution and Romanticism, 1789–1834: A Series of Facsimile Reprints Chosen and Introduced by Jonathan Wordsworth* (Oxford and New York: Woodstock Books, 1993).

—— *Gordon: A Tale* (London: T. & J. Allman, 1821).

—— *A New Canto* (London: William Wright, 1819).

Lamb, Charles and Mary, *The Works of Charles and Mary Lamb*, ed. E. V. Lucas, 7 vols. (London: Methuen, 1903–5).

Lansdown, Richard, *Byron's Historical Dramas* (Oxford: Clarendon Press, 1992).

Lévi-Strauss, Claude, *Journal of American Folklore*, 68/270 (Oct.–Dec. 1955), 'The Structural Study of Myth', 428–44.

—— *The Raw and the Cooked: Introduction to the Science of Mythology, I*, (1964), tr. John and Doreen Weightman (Harmondsworth: Penguin, 1986).

—— *Structural Anthropology*, tr. Claire Jacobson, Brooke Grundfest Schoepf, and Monique Layton, 2 vols. (New York: Basic Books, 1963).

Loewenberg, Alfred, '*Don Giovanni* in London', *Music and Letters* (July 1943), 164–8.

—— 'Lorenzo da Ponte in London', *Music Review*, 4 (1943), 171–89.

Lonsdale, Roger (ed.), *Eighteenth-Century Women Poets* (Oxford and New York: Oxford University Press, 1990).

Lovell, Ernest J. (ed.), *His Very Self and Voice: Collected Conversations of Lord Byron* (New York: Macmillan, 1954).

—— (ed.), *Lady Blessington's Conversations of Lord Byron* (Princeton: Princeton University Press, 1969).

—— (ed.), *Medwin's Conversations with Lord Byron: Noted during a Residence with His Lordship at Pisa in the Years, 1821–1822* (Princeton: Princeton University Press, 1969).

Luke, Hugh J., Jr., 'The Publishing of Byron's *Don Juan*', *PMLA* 80/2 (June 1965), 199–209.

McClary, Susan, 'Structures of Identity and Difference in *Carmen*', *Women: a cultural review*, 3/1 (Summer 1992), 1–15.

McDonald, Sheila J., 'The Impact of Libertinism on Byron's *Don Juan*', *Bulletin of Research in the Humanities*, 86/3 (1983–5), 291–317.

McDowell, Robert E., 'Tirso, Byron and the Don Juan Tradition', *The Arlington Quarterly*, 1/1 (Autumn 1967), 57–68.

McGann, Jerome, *Don Juan in Context* (Chicago: University of Chicago Press, 1976).

—— 'Byron and "The Truth in Masquerade"', in Robert Brinkley and Keith Hanley (eds.), *Romantic Revisions* (Cambridge: Cambridge University Press, 1992), 191–209.

Maeztu, Ramiro de, *Don Quijote, Don Juan y la Celestina* (Madrid: Colección Austral, Espasa-Calpe, 1938).

Mandel, Oscar (ed.), *The Theatre of Don Juan: A Collection of Plays and Views, 1630–1963* (Lincoln, Nebr.: University of Nebraska Press, 1963).

Mandrell, James Bennet, *Don Juan and the Point of Honour: Seduction, Patriarchal Society, and Literary Tradition* (Philadelphia: Pennsylvania State University Press, 1992).

Mann, William, *The Operas of Mozart* (London: Cassell Opera Guides, 1977).

Manning, Peter J., *Reading Romantics* (New York and Oxford: Oxford University Press, 1990), '*Don Juan* and Byron's Imperceptiveness to the Spoken Word', 115–44; 'The Hone-ing of Byron's *Corsair*', 216–37.

Marañón, Gregorio, *Don Juan: Ensayos sobre el origen de su leyenda* (1940; repr. Madrid: Colección Austral, Espasa-Calpe, 1967).

Marchand, Leslie A., *Byron: A Biography*, 3 vols. (London: John Murray, 1958).

Martin, Philip W., *Byron: A Poet Before his Public* (Cambridge: Cambridge University Press, 1982).

Massin, Jean, *Don Juan: Mythe littéraire et musical* (Paris: Éditions Stock, 1979).

Maturin, Revd. Charles, *Bertram; or the Castle of Maldobrand* (London: John Murray, 1816).

Maurois, André, *Byron: Don Juan, ou la vie de Byron*, 2 vols. (Paris: Bernard Grasset, 1930).

Mayer, David, *Harlequin in his Element: The English Pantomime, 1806–1836* (Cambridge, Mass.: Harvard University Press, 1969).

Mayne, Ethel Colburn, *The Life and Letters of Anne Isabella, Lady Noel Byron* (London: Constable, 1929).

Mérimée, Prosper, *Colomba et dix autres nouvelles* (Paris: Gallimard, 1964), 'Les Ames du Purgatoire', 209–78.

Miller, Jane, *Seductions: Studies in Reading and Culture* (London: Virago Press, 1990).

Miller, Jonathan (ed.), *The* Don Giovanni *Book: Myths of Seduction and Betrayal* (London: Faber & Faber, 1990).

Minguet, Charles, *Don Juan* (Paris: Éditions Hispaniques, 1977).

Mitford, Mary Russell, *The Life of Mary Russell Mitford*, ed. Revd. A. G. l'Estrange, 3 vols. (London: Richard Bentley, 1870).

Molière, *Dom Juan* (1682; repr. Paris: Librairie Larousse, 1965).

——— *The Miser and Other Plays*, tr. John Wood (Harmondsworth: Penguin, 1953).

Molina, Tirso de, *El burlador de Sevilla* (1630; repr. Madrid: Colección Austral, Espasa-Calpe, 1989).

Montesquieu, *Lettres persanes* (1721; repr. Paris: Garnier Frères, 1960).

Montherlant, Henry de, *La Mort qui fait le trottoir* (1959; repr. Folio: Éditions Gallimard, 1972).

Montoto, Santiago, *El teatro, el baile y la danza en Sevilla* (Archivo Hispalense, 103–4; Seville: Imprenta Provincial, 1960).

Moore, Doris Langley, *Lord Byron: Accounts Rendered* (London: John Murray, 1974).

Moore, Thomas, *The Letters of Thomas Moore*, ed. Wilfred S. Dowden, 2 vols. (Oxford: Clarendon Press, 1964).

—— *Memoirs, Journal and Correspondence of Thomas Moore* (2nd edn.; London: Longman, Green, Longman & Roberts, 1860).

—— *The Poetical Works of Thomas Moore*, ed. A. D. Godley (Oxford: Oxford University Press, 1915).

Morgan, Lady Sydney, *Lady Morgan's Memoirs: Autobiography, Diaries and Correspondence*, 2 vols. (London: Wm. H. Allen, 1912).

—— *Passages from my Autobiography* (London: Richard Bentley, 1859).

Musset, Alfred de, *Premières Poésies, Poésies nouvelles* (Paris: Gallimard, 1976), 'Namouna' (1832), 156–99.

Myers, Mitzi, 'Reform or Ruin: "A Revolution in Female Manners"', *Studies in the Eighteenth-Century*, 2 (1982), 199–216.

Newlyn, Lucy, *Paradise Lost and the Romantic Reader* (Oxford: Oxford University Press, 1993).

Nicoll, Allardyce, *A History of English Drama, 1600–1900*, 6 vols. (London: Cambridge University Press, 1952–9).

—— 'The Theatre', in G. M. Young (ed.), *Early Victorian England* (London: Oxford University Press, 1934), ii.

Noske, Frits, *The Signifier and the Signified: Studies in the Operas of Mozart and Verdi* (The Hague: Martinus Nijhoff, 1977).

Oulton, W. C., *A History of the Theatres of London: Containing an Annual Register of New Pieces, Revivals, Pantomimes etc., 1795–1817*, 3 vols. (London: C. Chapple, 1818).

Paglia, Camille, *Sexual Personae* (London: Penguin, 1991).

Paine, Thomas, *The Rights of Man* (1791–2; repr. Harmondsworth: Pelican, 1969).

Parakilas, James, 'The Afterlife of *Don Giovanni*: Turning Production History into Criticism', *The Journal of Musicology*, 8/2 (Spring 1990), 251–65.

Parke, W. T., *Musical Memoirs: Comprising an Account of the General State of Music in England, 1784–1830*, 2 vols. (London: Henry Colburn & Richard Bentley, 1830).

La Passion selon Don Juan, Exposition Ville d'Aix-en-Provence (12 July–30 Sept., 1991).

Paston, George, and Quennell, Peter, '*To Lord Byron': Feminine Profiles Based Upon Unpublished Letters, 1807–1824* (London: John Murray, 1939).

Peacock, Thomas Love, *Memoirs of Shelley and Other Essays and Reviews*, ed. Howard Mills (London: Rupert Hart-Davis, 1970).

—— *Peacock's Memoirs of Shelley*, ed. H. F. B. Brett-Smith (1858; repr. London: Henry Frowde, 1909).

Petty, Frederick C., *Italian Opera in London, 1760–1800* (Ann Arbor, Mich.: UMI Research Press, 1980).

Piñal, Francisco Aguilar, 'Cartelera Prerromantica Sevillaña Años 1800–1836', *Cuadernos Bibliograficos XXII* (Madrid: Artes Gráficas Clavileño, 1968).

—— *Sevilla y el teatro en el siglo XVIII* (Oviedo: Universidad de Oviedo, 1974).

Pirotta, Nino, 'The Tradition of Don Juan Plays and Comic Operas', *Proceedings of the Musical Association*, 107 (1981), 60–70.

Plato, *Symposium*, tr. Robin Waterfield (Oxford and New York: Oxford University Press, 1994).

Poe, Edgar Allan, *Selected Writings* (Harmondsworth: Penguin, 1967), 'The Purloined Letter', 330–49.

Polwhele, Richard, *The Unsex'd Females: A Poem* (1798; repr. New York: Garland, 1978).

Ponte, Lorenzo da, *Don Giovanni*, tr. William Mann (Hayes, Middlesex: EMI Ltd., 1987), booklet for EMI recording (CDS 7472608).

—— *Le nozze di Figaro*, tr. Lionel Salter (1968), booklet for Deutsche Gramophon recording (429869-2).

Poovey, Mary, *The Proper Lady and the Woman Writer: Ideology as Style in the Works of Mary Wollstonecraft, Mary Shelley, and Jane Austen* (Chicago: University of Chicago Press, 1984).

Porter, Roy, 'Libertinism and Promiscuity', in Jonathan Miller (ed.), *The Don Giovanni Book* (London: Faber & Faber, 1990), 1–19.

Pujals, Esteban, *Lord Byron en España y otros temas Byronianos* (Madrid: Editorial Alhambra, 1982).

Punter, David, '*Don Juan*, or, the Deferral of Decapitation: Some Psychological Approaches' in Nigel Wood (ed.), Don Juan: *Theory in Practice* (Buckingham: Open University Press, 1993), 122–53.

Raeburn, Christopher, 'Mozart's Operas in England', *Musical Times*, 97 (Jan. 1956), 15–17.

Raitt, A. W., *Prosper Mérimée* (London: Eyre & Spottiswoode, 1970).

Rank, Otto D., *The Legend of Don Juan*, tr. David G. Winter (1924; Princeton: Princeton University Press, 1975).

Reiman, Donald (ed.), *The Romantics Reviewed, part B*, 5 vols. (New York: Garland Press, 1972).

Remarks Critical and Moral on the Talents of Lord Byron and the Tendencies of Don Juan: By the Author of Hypocrisy, A Satire, With Notes and Anecdotes Political and Historical (London: G. Woodfall, 1819).

Richardson, Joanna (ed.), *Lord Byron and Some of his Contemporaries* (London: The Folio Society, 1988).

Richardson, Samuel, *Clarissa* (1747–8; repr. Harmondsworth: Penguin, 1985).

Richardson, Samuel, *Pamela* (1740; Harmondsworth: Penguin, 1985).

Robertson, Michael, 'The Byron of *Don Juan* as Whig Aristocrat', *Texas Studies in Literature and Language*, 17/4 (Winter 1976), 709–23.

Robinson, Henry Crabb, *The London Theatre, 1811–1866: Selections from the Diary of Henry Crabb Robinson*, ed. Eluned Brown (London: The Society for Theatre Research, 1966).

Roose-Evans, James, *The London Theatre* (Oxford: Phaidon, 1977).

Ross, Marlon B., 'Feminine Quest and Conquest: Troping Masculine Power in the Crisis of Poetic Identity', in Anne Mellor (ed.), *Romanticism and Feminism* (Bloomington, Ill.: Indianapolis University Press, 1988), 26–51.

Rousseau, Jean-Jacques, *The Confessions* (1771), tr. J. M. Cohen (Harmondsworth: Penguin Classics, 1981).

——*Emile* (1762), tr. Barbara Foxley (London: J. M. Dent, 1950).

Ruiz, Alan, 'Un regard sur le jacobinisme allemand', in *The French Revolution and the Creation of Modern Political Culture* (Oxford: Pergamon Press, 1989), iii. *The Transformation of Political Culture, 1789–1848*.

Rushton, Julian, *W. A. Mozart:* Don Giovanni (Cambridge: Cambridge University Press, 1981).

Russell, Charles C., 'The Libertine Reformed: "Don Juan" by Gluck and Angiolini', *Music and Letters*, 65 (Jan. 1984), 17–27.

Rutherford, Andrew (ed.), *Byron: Augustan and Romantic* (London: Macmillan, 1990).

——(ed.), *Byron: The Critical Heritage* (London: Routledge and Kegan Paul, 1970).

St Clair, William, *The Godwins and the Shelleys* (London: Faber & Faber, 1989).

——'The Impact of Byron's Writings: An Evaluative Approach', in Andrew Rutherford (ed.), *Byron: Augustan and Romantic* (London: Macmillan, 1990), 1–25.

Sand, George, *Lélia*, ed. Pierre Reboul (Paris: Éditions Garnier Frères, 1960).

Sedgwick, Eve Kosofsky, *The Epistemology of the Closet* (Hemel Hempstead: Harvester Wheatsheaf, 1991).

Serres, Michel, 'The Apparition of Hermes: *Dom Juan*', in Josue V. Harari and David F. Bell (eds.), *Hermes: Literature, Science, Philosophy* (Baltimore: Johns Hopkins University Press, 1982), 3–14.

Seymour, Lady, *The Pope of Holland House* (London: Fisher & Unwin, 1906).

Shadwell, Thomas, *The Complete Works of Thomas Shadwell*, ed. Montague Summers, 3 vols. (London: Benjamin Blom, 1968).

Shaw, George Bernard, 'Don Giovanni Explains' (1887), in *Short Stories, Scraps and Shavings* (London: Constable, 1932), 95–116.
—— *The Great Composers* (London: University of California Press, 1978).
—— *Man and Superman* (1903; repr. Harmondsworth: Penguin, 1973).
Shelley, Mary, *The Letters of Mary Shelley*, ed. Frederick L. Jones, 2 vols. (Oklahoma: University of Oklahoma Press, 1944).
Letters of Mary W. Shelley (Mostly Unpublished), with Introduction and Notes by Henry H. Harpur (Boston: Bibliophile Society, 1918).
The Letters of Mary Wollstonecraft Shelley, 2 vols. (Baltimore and London: Johns Hopkins University Press, 1980).
—— *Mary Shelley's Journal*, ed. Frederick L. Jones (Oklahoma: University of Oklahoma Press, 1947).
Shelley, Percy Bysshe, *The Letters of Percy Bysshe Shelley*, ed. Frederick L. Jones, 2 vols. (Oxford: Clarendon Press, 1964).
Shelley and his Circle: 1773–1822, ed. Kenneth Neill Cameron (Cambridge, Mass.: Harvard University Press, 1970), iv.
Shelley and his Circle: 1773–1822, ed. Donald Reiman (Cambridge, Mass.: Harvard University Press, 1986), vii.
Smeed, J. W., *Don Juan: Variations on a Theme* (London: Routledge, 1990).
Smiles, Samuel, *A Publisher and his Friends: Memoirs and Correspondence of the late John Murray*, 2 vols. (London: John Murray, 1891).
Smith, William C., *The Italian Opera and Contemporary Ballet in London, 1789–1820* (London: Society for Theatre Research, 1955).
Solís, Ramon, *El Cádiz de las Cortes: La vida en la ciudad en los años, 1810 a 1813* (Madrid: Instituto de Estudios Politicos, 1958).
Southey, Robert, *Letters from England: by Don Manuel Alvarez Espriella, Translated from the Spanish* (1807; repr. London: The Cresset Press, 1951).
Spacks, Patricia Meyer, 'Ev'ry Woman is at Heart a Rake', *Eighteenth-Century Studies*, 8/1 (Fall 1974), 38.
Stearns, William, and Chaloupka, William (eds.), *Jean Baudrillard: The Disappearance of Art and Politics* (London: Macmillan, 1992).
Steffan, Truman Guy, and Pratt, W. W. (eds.), *Byron's Don Juan: A Variorum Edition*, 4 vols. (Austin, Tex.: University of Texas Press, 1957), i. *The Making of a Masterpiece*.
Steiger, August, *Thomas Shadwell's 'Libertine'* (1904; repr. Hildesheim: Verlag Dr. H. A. Gerstenberg, 1975).
Stendhal, *Love (De l'amour, 1822)*, tr. Gilbert and Suzanne Sale (Harmondsworth: Penguin, 1975).

Steptoe, Andrew, *The Mozart-da Ponte Operas* (Oxford: Clarendon Press, 1988).

Sterne, Laurence, *A Sentimental Journey* (1768; repr. Harmondsworth: Penguin, 1972).

Stone, Lawrence, *The Family, Sex, and Marriage in England, 1500–1800* (London: Weidenfeld & Nicolson, 1977).

Taylor, Barbara, *Eve and the New Jerusalem: Socialism and Feminism in the Nineteenth Century* (London: Virago Press, 1983).

Thomas, Keith, 'The Double Standard', *Journal of the History of Ideas*, 20 (Apr. 1959), 195–215.

Thompson, E. P., *The Making of the English Working Class* (Harmondsworth: Pelican, 1963).

Thompson, Flora, *Lark Rise to Candleford* (Harmondsworth: Penguin, 1973), *Candleford Green* (1943).

Thornbury, Walter, *London Theatres and London Actors* (London, 1869).

Thorslev, Peter L., *The Byronic Hero: Types and Prototypes* (Minneapolis: Minnesota University Press, 1962).

Torrance, Robert M., *The Comic Hero* (Cambridge, Mass.: Harvard University Press, 1978).

Trueblood, Paul Graham (ed.), *Byron's Political and Cultural Influence in Nineteenth-Century Europe* (London: Macmillan, 1981).

Unamuno, Miguel de, *El otro, El hermano Juan* (1934; repr. Madrid: Colección Austral, Espasa-Calpe, 1981).

—— *Tres novelas ejemplares y un prólogo* (1939; repr. Madrid: Colección Austral, Espasa-Calpe, 1990), 'Dos madres', 63–103.

Vestris, Madame, *Memoirs of the Life, Public and Private Adventures of Madame Vestris* (London, 1939).

Vitale, Marina, 'The Domesticated Heroine in Byron's *Corsair* and William Hone's Prose Adaptation', *Literature and History*, 10 (1984), 72–94.

Waitzkin, Leo, *The Witch of Wych Street: A Study of the Theatrical Reforms of Madame Vestris* (Cambridge, Mass.: Harvard University Press, 1933).

Warner, Marina, *Managing Monsters: Six Myths of Our Time, the 1994 Reith Lectures* (London: Vintage, 1994).

—— 'Valmont—or the Marquise Unmasked', in Jonathan Miller (ed.), *The* Don Giovanni *Book: Myths of Seduction and Betrayal* (London: Faber & Faber, 1990), 93–107.

Warner, Sylvia Townsend, *After the Death of Don Juan* (1938; repr. London: Virago, 1989).

Weeks, Jeffrey, *Sex, Politics and Society* (1981; repr. London: Longman, 1989).

Weinstein, Leo, *The Metamorphoses of Don Juan* (Stanford Studies in Language and Literature, 18; Stanford, Calif.: Stanford University Press, 1959).

White, Eric Walter, *A History of English Opera* (London: Faber & Faber, 1983).

Williams, Clifford John, *Madam Vestris: A Theatrical Biography* (London: Sidgwick & Jackson, 1973).

Williams, Simon, ' "No Meat for the Teeth of my Viennese": *Don Giovanni* and the Theatre of its Time', *Theatre Research International*, 14/1 (Spring 1989), 23–40.

Wilson, Harriette, *Memoirs of Harriette Wilson*, 4 vols. (2nd edn.; London: J. J. Stockdale, 1825).

Wilson, James D., 'Tirso, Molière and Byron: The Emergence of Don Juan as Romantic Hero', *The South Central Bulletin*, 32/4 (Winter 1972), 246–8.

Winter, David G., *The Power Motive* (New York: The Free Press, 1973).

Wolfson, Susan J., ' "A Problem Few Dare Imitate": *Sardanapalus* and "Effeminate Character" ', *ELH* 58 (1991), 867–902.

——' "Their She Condition": Cross-Dressing and the Politics of Gender in *Don Juan*', *ELH* 54 (1987), 585–617.

Wollstonecraft, Mary, *Mary and The Wrongs of Woman* (1976; repr. Oxford: Oxford University Press, 1991).

——*A Vindication of the Rights of Woman* (1792; repr. Harmondsworth: Penguin, 1992).

Woodring, Carl, *Politics in English Romantic Poetry* (Cambridge, Mass.: Harvard University Press, 1970).

Wycherley, *The Plain Dealer* (1676; repr. London: Methuen, Swan Theatre Plays Series, 1988).

Zizek, Slavoj, *For They Know Not What They Do: Enjoyment as a Political Factor* (London: Verso, 1991).

THEATRE PLAYBILLS AND CUTTINGS FROM THE BRITISH LIBRARY COLLECTION

Astley's Royal Amphitheatre: *A Collection of Playbills for Astley's Royal Amphitheatre for the years 1821–1845* (London, 1821–45).

Covent-Garden: *An Incomplete Series of Playbills of Covent-Garden Theatre, 1753–1822*, 16 vols. (London, 1753–1811).

Drury Lane: *A Collection of Playbills of Drury Lane Theatre from October 1780 to March 1885, including the Playbills of the performances at the*

Lyceum Theatre by members of the Drury Lane Company between the destruction of their theatre by fire, February 24th 1809, and its reopening October 10th 1812, 45 vols. (London, 1780–1885).

—— *A Collection of Playbills of Drury Lane Theatre, from 19 February 1754 to 31 December 1845* (London, 1754–1845).

—— *A Collection of Playbills of Drury Lane Theatre from 20 September 1814– 8 June 1819 and from 20 October 1820–25 June 1821*, 3 vols. (London, 1805–33).

—— *A Collection of Newspaper Cuttings etc., relating to Drury Lane Theatre from 1777 to 1834* (London, 1777–1834).

—— *A Collection of Newspaper Cuttings, dating from 1805 to 1833, referring to Drury Lane Theatre* (London, 1805–33).

King's and Haymarket: *A Collection of Cuttings from newspapers relating to the King's and Haymarket Theatres, 1813–29* (London, 1813–29).

Lyceum: *A Collection of Cuttings from newspapers, playbills, letters and other manuscripts etc., relating to the Lyceum Theatre from 1781 to 1840*, 3 vols. (London, 1781–1840).

—— *A Series of Playbills of the Lyceum Theatre from 1809 to 1858, incomplete* (London, 1809–58).

Olympic: *A Collection of Playbills for the Olympic Theatre for the years 1822– 1845* (London, 1822–45).

Sadler's Wells: *A Collection of Playbills for Sadler's Wells, for the years 1821– 26, 1828–36, 1838–45* (London, 1821–45).

Surrey: *A Collection of Playbills of the Surrey Theatre, 19 November 1810–18 October 1858; 23 October 1882* (London, 1810–82).

The Theatrical Repertory: Containing Criticisms on the Performances which were represented at Drury-Lane and Covent-Garden Theatres during the season 1801-2 with Occasional Observations on other Places of Public Entertainment (London, 1802).

Index

Coláiste na hOllscoile Gaillimh

3 1111 30108 7985